HOW TO WRITE SPECIAL FEATURE ARTICLES

A HANDBOOK FOR REPORTERS, CORRESPONDENTS
AND FREE-LANCE WRITERS WHO DESIRE TO
CONTRIBUTE TO POPULAR MAGAZINES AND
MAGAZINE SECTIONS OF NEWSPAPERS

BY

WILLARD GROSVENOR BLEYER, PH.D.

_Author of "Newspaper Writing and Editing," and "Types of News Writing";
Director of the Course in Journalism in the University of Wisconsin_

BOSTON, NEW YORK, CHICAGO, SAN FRANCISCO

HOUGHTON MIFFLIN COMPANY

The Riverside Press Cambridge

The Riverside Press
CAMBRIDGE, MASSACHUSETTS
PRINTED IN THE U.S.A.

PREFACE

This book is the result of twelve years' experience in teaching
university students to write special feature articles for newspapers and
popular magazines. By applying the methods outlined in the following
pages, young men and women have been able to prepare articles that have
been accepted by many newspaper and magazine editors. The success that
these students have achieved leads the author to believe that others who
desire to write special articles may be aided by the suggestions given
in this book.

Although innumerable books on short-story writing have been published,
no attempt has hitherto been made to discuss in detail the writing of
special feature articles. In the absence of any generally accepted
method of approach to the subject, it has been necessary to work out a
systematic classification of the various types of articles and of the
different kinds of titles, beginnings, and similar details, as well as
to supply names by which to identify them.

A careful analysis of current practice in the writing of special feature
stories and popular magazine articles is the basis of the methods
presented. In this analysis an effort has been made to show the
application of the principles of composition to the writing of articles.
Examples taken from representative newspapers and magazines are freely
used to illustrate the methods discussed. To encourage students to
analyze typical articles, the second part of the book is devoted to a
collection of newspaper and magazine articles of various types, with an

outline for the analysis of them.

Particular emphasis is placed on methods of popularizing such knowledge as is not available to the general reader. This has been done in the belief that it is important for the average person to know of the progress that is being made in every field of human endeavor, in order that he may, if possible, apply the results to his own affairs. The problem, therefore, is to show aspiring writers how to present discoveries, inventions, new methods, and every significant advance in knowledge, in an accurate and attractive form.

To train students to write articles for newspapers and popular magazines may, perhaps, be regarded by some college instructors in composition as an undertaking scarcely worth their while. They would doubtless prefer to encourage their students to write what is commonly called "literature." The fact remains, nevertheless, that the average undergraduate cannot write anything that approximates literature, whereas experience has shown that many students can write acceptable popular articles. Moreover, since the overwhelming majority of Americans read only newspapers and magazines, it is by no means an unimportant task for our universities to train writers to supply the steady demand for well-written articles. The late Walter Hines Page, founder of the _World's Work_ and former editor of the _Atlantic Monthly_, presented the whole situation effectively in an article on "The Writer and the University," when he wrote:

> The journeymen writers write almost all that almost all Americans read. This is a fact that we love to fool ourselves about. We talk about "literature" and we talk about "hack writers," implying that the reading that we do is of literature. The truth all the while is, we read little else than the writing of the hacks--living hacks, that is, men and women who write for pay. We may hug the notion that our life and thought are not really affected by current literature, that we read the living writers only for utilitarian reasons, and that our real intellectual life is fed by the great dead writers. But hugging this delusion does not change the fact that the intellectual life even of most educated persons, and certainly of the mass of the population, is fed chiefly by the writers of our own time....
>
> Every editor of a magazine, every editor of an earnest and worthy newspaper, every publisher of books, has dozens or hundreds of important tasks for which he cannot find capable men; tasks that require scholarship, knowledge of science, or of politics, or of industry, or of literature, along with experience in writing accurately in the language of the people.

Special feature stories and popular magazine articles constitute a type of writing particularly adapted to the ability of the novice, who has developed some facility in writing, but who may not have sufficient maturity or talent to undertake successful short-story writing or other distinctly literary work. Most special articles cannot be regarded as literature. Nevertheless, they afford the young writer an opportunity to develop whatever ability he possesses. Such writing teaches him four things that are invaluable to any one who aspires to do literary work. It trains him to observe what is going on about him, to select what will interest the average reader, to organize material effectively, and to present it attractively. If this book helps the inexperienced writer, whether he is in or out of college, to acquire these four essential qualifications for success, it will have accomplished its purpose.

For permission to reprint complete articles, the author is indebted to the editors of the Boston Herald_, the _Christian Science Monitor_, the _Boston Evening Transcript_, the _New York Evening Post_, the _Detroit News_, the _Milwaukee Journal_, the _Kansas City Star_, the _New York Sun_, the _Providence Journal_, the _Ohio State Journal_, the _New York World_, the _Saturday Evening Post_, the _Independent_, the _Country Gentleman_, the _Outlook_, _McClure's Magazine_, _Everybody's Magazine_, the _Delineator_, the _Pictorial Review_, _Munsey's Magazine_, the _American Magazine_, _System_, _Farm and Fireside_, the _Woman's Home Companion_, the _Designer_, and the Newspaper Enterprise Association. The author is also under obligation to the many newspapers and magazines from which excerpts, titles, and other material have been quoted.

At every stage in the preparation of this book the author has had the advantage of the coöperation and assistance of his wife, Alice Haskell Bleyer.

_University of Wisconsin
Madison, August, 1919_

CONTENTS

PART I

      I. THE FIELD FOR SPECIAL ARTICLES   3

     II. PREPARATION FOR SPECIAL FEATURE WRITING   14

    III. FINDING SUBJECTS AND MATERIAL   25

     IV. APPEAL AND PURPOSE   39

      V. TYPES OF ARTICLES   52

     VI. WRITING THE ARTICLE   99

    VII. HOW TO BEGIN   131

   VIII. STYLE   160

     IX. TITLES AND HEADLINES   170

      X. PREPARING AND SELLING THE MANUSCRIPT   182

     XI. PHOTOGRAPHS AND OTHER ILLUSTRATIONS   193

PART II

AN OUTLINE FOR THE ANALYSIS OF SPECIAL FEATURE ARTICLES   201

TEACH CHILDREN LOVE OF ART THROUGH STORY-TELLING   204
   (_Boston Herald_)

WHERE GIRLS LEARN TO WIELD SPADE AND HOE   206
   (_Christian Science Monitor_)

BOYS IN SEARCH OF JOBS (_Boston Transcript_)   209

GIRLS AND A CAMP (_New York Evening Post_)   213

YOUR PORTER (_Saturday Evening Post_)   218

THE GENTLE ART OF BLOWING BOTTLES (_Independent_)   233

THE NEIGHBORHOOD PLAYHOUSE (_New York World_)   240

THE SINGULAR STORY OF THE MOSQUITO MAN   242
   (_New York Evening Post_)

A COUNTY SERVICE STATION (_Country Gentleman_)   248

GUARDING A CITY'S WATER SUPPLY (_Detroit News_)   260

THE OCCUPATION AND EXERCISE CURE (_Outlook_)   264

THE BRENNAN MONO-RAIL CAR (_McClure's Magazine_)   274

A NEW POLITICAL WEDGE (_Everybody's Magazine_)   281

THE JOB LADY (_Delineator_)   293

MARK TWAIN'S FIRST SWEETHEART (_Kansas City Star_)   299

FOUR MEN OF HUMBLE BIRTH HOLD WORLD DESTINY IN   305
   THEIR HANDS (_Milwaukee Journal_)

THE CONFESSIONS OF A COLLEGE PROFESSOR'S WIFE   307
   (_Saturday Evening Post_)

A PARADISE FOR A PENNY (_Boston Transcript_)   326

WANTED: A HOME ASSISTANT (_Pictorial Review_)   331

SIX YEARS OF TEA ROOMS (_New York Sun_)   336

BY PARCEL POST (_Country Gentleman_)   341

SALES WITHOUT SALESMANSHIP (_Saturday Evening Post_)   349

THE ACCIDENT THAT GAVE US WOOD-PULP PAPER   356
   (_Munsey's Magazine_)

CENTENNIAL OF THE FIRST STEAMSHIP TO CROSS THE ATLANTIC   360
   (_Providence Journal_)

SEARCHING FOR THE LOST ATLANTIS   364
   (_Syndicate Sunday Magazine Section_)

INDEX   369

HOW TO WRITE SPECIAL FEATURE ARTICLES

PART I

CHAPTER I

THE FIELD FOR SPECIAL ARTICLES

ORIGIN OF SPECIAL ARTICLES. The rise of popular magazines and of
magazine sections of daily newspapers during the last thirty years has
resulted in a type of writing known as the "special feature article."
Such articles, presenting interesting and timely subjects in popular
form, are designed to attract a class of readers that were not reached
by the older literary periodicals. Editors of newspapers and magazines a
generation ago began to realize that there was no lack of interest on
the part of the general public in scientific discoveries and inventions,
in significant political and social movements, in important persons and
events. Magazine articles on these themes, however, had usually been
written by specialists who, as a rule, did not attempt to appeal to the
"man in the street," but were satisfied to reach a limited circle of
well-educated readers.

To create a larger magazine-reading public, editors undertook to develop
a popular form and style that would furnish information as attractively
as possible. The perennial appeal of fiction gave them a suggestion for
the popularization of facts. The methods of the short story, of the
drama, and even of the melodrama, applied to the presentation of general
information, provided a means for catching the attention of the casual
reader.

Daily newspapers had already discovered the advantage of giving the
day's news in a form that could be read rapidly with the maximum degree
of interest by the average man and woman. Certain so-called sensational
papers had gone a step further in these attempts to give added
attractiveness to news and had emphasized its melodramatic aspects.
Other papers had seen the value of the "human interest" phases of the
day's happenings. It was not surprising, therefore, that Sunday editors
of newspapers should undertake to apply to special articles the same
methods that had proved successful in the treatment of news.

The product of these efforts at popularization was the special feature
article, with its story-like form, its touches of description, its
"human interest," its dramatic situations, its character portrayal--all

effectively used to furnish information and entertainment for that rapid reader, the "average American."

DEFINITION OF A SPECIAL ARTICLE. A special feature article may be defined as a detailed presentation of facts in an interesting form adapted to rapid reading, for the purpose of entertaining or informing the average person. It usually deals with (1) recent news that is of sufficient importance to warrant elaboration; (2) timely or seasonal topics not directly connected with news; or (3) subjects of general interest that have no immediate connection with current events.

Although frequently concerned with news, the special feature article is more than a mere news story. It aims to supplement the bare facts of the news report by giving more detailed information regarding the persons, places, and circumstances that appear in the news columns. News must be published as fast as it develops, with only enough explanatory material to make it intelligible. The special article, written with the perspective afforded by an interval of a few days or weeks, fills in the bare outlines of the hurried news sketch with the life and color that make the picture complete.

The special feature article must not be confused with the type of news story called the "feature," or "human interest," story. The latter undertakes to present minor incidents of the day's news in an entertaining form. Like the important news story, it is published immediately after the incident occurs. Its purpose is to appeal to newspaper readers by bringing out the humorous and pathetic phases of events that have little real news value. It exemplifies, therefore, merely one distinctive form of news report.

The special feature article differs from the older type of magazine article, not so much in subject as in form and style. The most marked difference lies in the fact that it supplements the recognized methods of literary and scientific exposition with the more striking devices of narrative, descriptive, and dramatic writing.

SCOPE OF FEATURE ARTICLES. The range of subjects for special articles is as wide as human knowledge and experience. Any theme is suitable that can be made interesting to a considerable number of persons. A given topic may make either a local or a general appeal. If interest in it is likely to be limited to persons in the immediate vicinity of the place with which the subject is connected, the article is best adapted to publication in a local newspaper. If the theme is one that appeals to a larger public, the article is adapted to a periodical of general circulation. Often local material has interest for persons in many other communities, and hence is suitable either for newspapers or for magazines.

Some subjects have a peculiar appeal to persons engaged in a particular occupation or devoted to a particular avocation or amusement. Special articles on these subjects of limited appeal are adapted to agricultural, trade, or other class publications, particularly to such of these periodicals as present their material in a popular rather than a technical manner.

THE NEWSPAPER FIELD. Because of their number and their local character, daily newspapers afford a ready medium for the publication of

special articles, or "special feature stories," as they are generally
called in newspaper offices. Some newspapers publish these articles from
day to day on the editorial page or in other parts of the paper. Many
more papers have magazine sections on Saturday or Sunday made up
largely of such "stories." Some of these special sections closely
resemble regular magazines in form, cover, and general make-up.

The articles published in newspapers come from three sources: (1)
syndicates that furnish a number of newspapers in different cities with
special articles, illustrations, and other matter, for simultaneous
publication; (2) members of the newspaper's staff; that is, reporters,
correspondents, editors, or special writers employed for the purpose;
(3) so-called "free-lance" writers, professional or amateur, who submit
their "stories" to the editor of the magazine section.

Reporters, correspondents, and other regular members of the staff may be
assigned to write special feature stories, or may prepare such stories
on their own initiative for submission to the editor of the magazine
section. In many offices regular members of the staff are paid for
special feature stories in addition to their salaries, especially when
the subjects are not assigned to them and when the stories are prepared
in the writer's own leisure time. Other papers expect their regular
staff members to furnish the paper with whatever articles they may
write, as a part of the work covered by their salary. If a paper has one
or more special feature writers on its staff, it may pay them a fixed
salary or may employ them "on space"; that is, pay them at a fixed
"space rate" for the number of columns that an article fills when
printed.

Newspaper correspondents, who are usually paid at space rates for news
stories, may add to their monthly "string," or amount of space, by
submitting special feature articles in addition to news. They may also
submit articles to other papers that do not compete with their own
paper. Ordinarily a newspaper expects a correspondent to give it the
opportunity of printing any special feature stories that he may write.

Free-lance writers, who are not regularly employed by newspapers or
magazines as staff members, submit articles for the editor's
consideration and are paid at space rates. Sometimes a free lance will
outline an article in a letter or in personal conference with an editor
in order to get his approval before writing it, but, unless the editor
knows the writer's work, he is not likely to promise to accept the
completed article. To the writer there is an obvious advantage in
knowing that the subject as he outlines it is or is not an acceptable
one. If an editor likes the work of a free lance, he may suggest
subjects for articles, or may even ask him to prepare an article on a
given subject. Freelance writers, by selling their work at space rates,
can often make more money than they would receive as regular members of
a newspaper staff.

For the amateur the newspaper offers an excellent field. First, in every
city of any size there is at least one daily newspaper, and almost all
these papers publish special feature stories. Second, feature articles
on local topics, the material for which is right at the amateur's hand,
are sought by most newspapers. Third, newspaper editors are generally
less critical of form and style than are magazine editors. With some
practice an inexperienced writer may acquire sufficient skill to prepare

an acceptable special feature story for publication in a local paper, and even if he is paid little or nothing for it, he will gain experience from seeing his work in print.

The space rate paid for feature articles is usually proportionate to the size of the city in which the newspaper is published. In small cities papers seldom pay more than $1 a column; in larger places the rate is about $3 a column; in still larger ones, $5; and in the largest, from $8 to $10. In general the column rate for special feature stories is the same as that paid for news stories.

WHAT NEWSPAPERS WANT. Since timeliness is the keynote of the newspaper, current topics, either growing out of the news of the week or anticipating coming events, furnish the subjects for most special feature stories. The news columns from day to day provide room for only concise announcements of such news as a scientific discovery, an invention, the death of an interesting person, a report on social or industrial conditions, proposed legislation, the razing of a landmark, or the dedication of a new building. Such news often arouses the reader's curiosity to know more of the persons, places, and circumstances mentioned. In an effort to satisfy this curiosity, editors of magazine sections print special feature stories based on news.

By anticipating approaching events, an editor is able to supply articles that are timely for a particular issue of his paper. Two classes of subjects that he usually looks forward to in this way are: first, those concerned with local, state, and national anniversaries; and second, those growing out of seasonal occasions, such as holidays, vacations, the opening of schools and colleges, moving days, commencements, the opening of hunting and fishing seasons.

The general policy of a newspaper with regard to special feature stories is the same as its policy concerning news. Both are determined by the character of its circulation. A paper that is read largely by business and professional men provides news and special articles that satisfy such readers. A paper that aims to reach the so-called masses naturally selects news and features that will appeal to them. If a newspaper has a considerable circulation outside the city where it is published, the editors, in framing their policy, cannot afford to overlook their suburban and rural readers. The character of its readers, in a word, determines the character of a paper's special feature stories.

The newspaper is primarily local in character. A city, a state, or at most a comparatively small section of the whole country, is its particular field. Besides the news of its locality, it must, of course, give significant news of the world at large. So, too, in addition to local feature articles, it should furnish special feature stories of a broader scope. This distinctively local character of newspapers differentiates them from magazines of national circulation in the matter of acceptable subjects for special articles.

The frequency of publication of newspapers, as well as their ephemeral character, leads, in many instances, to the choice of comparatively trivial topics for some articles. Merely to give readers entertaining matter with which to occupy their leisure at the end of a day's work or on Sunday, some papers print special feature stories on topics of little or no importance, often written in a light vein. Articles with no more serious purpose than that of helping readers to while away a few spare moments are obviously better adapted to newspapers, which are read rapidly and immediately cast aside, than to periodicals.

The sensationalism that characterizes the policy of some newspapers affects alike their news columns and their magazine sections. Gossip, scandal, and crime lend themselves to melodramatic treatment as readily in special feature articles as in news stories. On the other hand, the relatively few magazines that undertake to attract readers by sensationalism, usually do so by means of short stories and serials rather than by special articles.

All newspapers, in short, use special feature stories on local topics, some papers print trivial ones, and others "play up" sensational material; whereas practically no magazine publishes articles of these types.

SUNDAY MAGAZINE SECTIONS. The character and scope of special articles for the Sunday magazine section of newspapers have been well summarized by two well-known editors of such sections. Mr. John O'Hara Cosgrove, editor of the _New York Sunday World Magazine_, and formerly editor of _Everybody's Magazine_, gives this as his conception of the ideal Sunday magazine section:

> The real function of the Sunday Magazine, to my thinking, is to present the color and romance of the news, the most authoritative opinions on the issues and events of the day, and to chronicle promptly the developments of science as applied to daily life. In the grind of human intercourse all manner of curious, heroic, delightful things turn up, and for the most part, are dismissed in a passing note. Behind every such episode are human beings and a story, and these, if fairly and artfully explained, are the very stuff of romance. Into every great city men are drifting daily from the strange and remote places of the world where they have survived perilous hazards and seen rare spectacles. Such adventures are the treasure troves of the skilful reporter. The cross currents and reactions that lead up to any explosion of greed or passion that we call crime are often worth following, not only for their plots, but as proofs of the pain and terror of transgression. Brave deeds or heroic resistances are all too seldom presented in full length in the news, and generously portrayed prove the nobility inherent in every-day life.

> The broad domain of the Sunday magazine editor covers all that may be rare and curious or novel in the arts and sciences, in music and verse, in religion and the occult, on the stage and in sport. Achievements and controversies are ever culminating in these diverse fields, and the men and women actors therein make admirable subjects for his pages. Provided the editor has at his disposal skilled writers who have the fine arts of vivid and simple exposition and of the brief personal sketch, there is nothing of human interest that may not be presented.

The ideal Sunday magazine, as Mr. Frederick Boyd Stevenson, Sunday editor of the _Brooklyn Eagle_, sees it, he describes thus:

> The new Sunday magazine of the newspaper bids fair to be a crisp,

sensible review and critique of the live world. It has developed a special line of writers who have learned that a character sketch and interview of a man makes you "see" the man face to face and talk with him yourself. If he has done anything that gives him a place in the news of to-day, he is presented to you. You know the man.

It seems to me that the leading feature of the Sunday magazine should be the biggest topic that will be before the public on the Sunday that the newspaper is printed. It should be written by one who thoroughly knows his subject, who is forceful in style and fluent in words, who can make a picture that his readers can see, and seeing, realize. So every other feature of the Sunday magazine should have points of human interest, either by contact with the news of the day or with men and women who are doing something besides getting divorces and creating scandals.

I firmly believe that the coming Sunday magazine will contain articles of information without being dull or encyclopædic, articles of adventure that are real and timely, articles of scientific discoveries that are authentic, interviews with men and women who have messages, and interpretations of news and analyses of every-day themes, together with sketches, poems, and essays that are not tedious, but have a reason for being printed.

THE MAGAZINE FIELD. The great majority of magazines differ from all newspapers in one important respect--extent of circulation. Popular magazines have a nation-wide distribution. It is only among agricultural and trade journals that we find a distinctly sectional circulation. Some of these publications serve subscribers in only one state or section, and others issue separate state or sectional editions. The best basis of differentiation among magazines, then, is not the extent of circulation but the class of readers appealed to, regardless of the part of the country in which the readers live. The popular general magazine, monthly or weekly, aims to attract readers of all classes in all parts of the United States.

HOW MAGAZINES GET MATERIAL. Magazine articles come from (1) regular members of the magazine's staff, (2) professional or amateur free-lance writers, (3) specialists who write as an avocation, and (4) readers of the periodical who send in material based on their own experience.

The so-called "staff system" of magazine editing, in accordance with which practically all the articles are prepared by writers regularly employed by the publication, has been adopted by a few general magazines and by a number of class periodicals. The staff is recruited from writers and editors on newspapers and other magazines. Its members often perform various editorial duties in addition to writing articles. Publications edited in this way buy few if any articles from outsiders.

Magazines that do not follow the staff system depend largely or entirely on contributors. Every editor daily receives many manuscripts submitted by writers on their own initiative. From these he selects the material best adapted to his publication. Experienced writers often submit an outline of an article to a magazine editor for his approval before preparing the material for publication. Free-lance writers of reputation may be asked by magazine editors to prepare articles on given subjects.

In addition to material obtained in these ways, articles may be secured from specialists who write as an avocation. An editor generally decides on the subject that he thinks will interest his readers at a given time and then selects the authority best fitted to treat it in a popular way. To induce well-known men to prepare such articles, an editor generally offers them more than he normally pays.

A periodical may encourage its readers to send in short articles giving their own experiences and explaining how to do something in which they have become skilled. These personal experience articles have a reality and "human interest" that make them eminently readable. To obtain them magazines sometimes offer prizes for the best, reserving the privilege of publishing acceptable articles that do not win an award. Aspiring writers should take advantage of these prize contests as a possible means of getting both publication and money for their work.

OPPORTUNITIES FOR UNKNOWN WRITERS. The belief is common among novices that because they are unknown their work is likely to receive little or no consideration from editors. As a matter of fact, in the majority of newspaper and magazine offices all unsolicited manuscripts are considered strictly on their merits. The unknown writer has as good a chance as anybody of having his manuscript accepted, provided that his work has merit comparable with that of more experienced writers.

With the exception of certain newspapers that depend entirely on syndicates for their special features, and of a few popular magazines that have the staff system or that desire only the work of well-known writers, every publication welcomes special articles and short stories by novices. Moreover, editors take pride in the fact that from time to time they "discover" writers whose work later proves popular. They not infrequently tell how they accepted a short story, an article, or some verse by an author of whom they had never before heard, because they were impressed with the quality of it, and how the verdict of their readers confirmed their own judgment.

The relatively small number of amateurs who undertake special articles, compared with the hundreds of thousands who try their hand at short stories, makes the opportunities for special feature writers all the greater. Then, too, the number of professional writers of special articles is comparatively small. This is particularly true of writers who are able effectively to popularize scientific and technical material, as well as of those who can present in popular form the results of social and economic investigations.

It is not too much to say, therefore, that any writer who is willing (1) to study the interests and the needs of newspaper and magazine readers, (2) to gather carefully the material for his articles, and (3) to present it accurately and attractively, may be sure that his work will receive the fullest consideration in almost every newspaper and magazine office in the country, and will be accepted whenever it is found to merit publication.

WOMEN AS FEATURE WRITERS. Since the essential qualifications just enumerated are not limited to men, women are quite as well fitted to write special feature and magazine articles as are their brothers in the craft. In fact, woman's quicker sympathies and readier emotional response to many phases of life give her a distinct advantage. Her insight into the lives of others, and her intuitive understanding of them, especially fit her to write good "human interest" articles. Both the delicacy of touch and the chatty, personal tone that characterize the work of many young women, are well suited to numerous topics.

In some fields, such as cooking, sewing, teaching, the care of children, and household management, woman's greater knowledge and understanding of conditions furnish her with topics that are vital to other women and often not uninteresting to men. The entry of women into occupations hitherto open only to men is bringing new experiences to many women, and is furnishing women writers with additional fields from which to draw subjects and material. Ever since the beginning of popular magazines and of special feature writing for newspapers, women writers have proved their ability, but at no time have the opportunities for them been greater than at present.

CHAPTER II

PREPARATION FOR SPECIAL FEATURE WRITING

QUALIFICATIONS FOR FEATURE WRITING. To attain success as a writer of special feature articles a person must possess at least four qualifications: (1) ability to find subjects that will interest the average man and woman, and to see the picturesque, romantic, and significant phases of these subjects; (2) a sympathetic understanding of the lives and interests of the persons about whom and for whom he writes; (3) thoroughness and accuracy in gathering material; (4) skill to portray and to explain clearly, accurately, and attractively.

The much vaunted sense of news values commonly called a "nose for news," whether innate or acquired, is a prime requisite. Like the newspaper reporter, the writer of special articles must be able to recognize what at a given moment will interest the average reader. Like the reporter, also, he must know how much it will interest him. An alert, responsive attitude of mind toward everything that is going on in the world, and especially in that part of the world immediately around him, will reveal a host of subjects. By reading newspapers, magazines, and books, as well as by intercourse with persons of various classes, a writer keeps in contact with what people are thinking and talking about, in the world at large and in his own community. In this way he finds subjects and also learns how to connect his subjects with events and movements of interest the country over.

Not only should he be quick to recognize a good subject; he must be able to see the attractive and significant aspects of it. He must understand which of its phases touch most closely the life and the interests of the average person for whom he is writing. He must look at things from "the other fellow's" point of view. A sympathetic insight into the lives of his readers is necessary for every writer who hopes to quicken his subject with vital interest.

The alert mental attitude that constantly focuses the writer's attention on the men and women around him has been called "human curiosity," which

Arnold Bennett says "counts among the highest social virtues (as indifference counts among the basest defects), because it leads to the disclosure of the causes of character and temperament and thereby to a better understanding of the springs of human conduct." The importance of curiosity and of a keen sense of wonder has been emphasized as follows by Mr. John M. Siddall, editor of the _American Magazine_, who directed his advice to college students interested in the opportunities afforded by writing as a profession:

> A journalist or writer must have consuming curiosity about other human beings--the most intense interest in their doings and motives and thoughts. It comes pretty near being the truth to say that a great journalist is a super-gossip--not about trivial things but about important things. Unless a man has a ceaseless desire to learn what is going on in the heads of others, he won't be much of a journalist--for how can you write about others unless you know about others?
>
> In journalism men are needed who have a natural sense of wonder.... You must wonder at man's achievements, at man's stupidity, at his honesty, crookedness, courage, cowardice--at everything that is remarkable about him wherever and whenever it appears. If you haven't this sense of wonder, you will never write a novel or become a great reporter, because you simply won't see anything to write about. Men will be doing amazing things under your very eyes--and you won't even know it.

Ability to investigate a subject thoroughly, and to gather material accurately, is absolutely necessary for any writer who aims to do acceptable work. Careless, inaccurate writers are the bane of the magazine editor's life. Whenever mistakes appear in an article, readers are sure to write to the editor calling his attention to them. Moreover, the discovery of incorrect statements impairs the confidence of readers in the magazine. If there is reason to doubt the correctness of any data in an article, the editor takes pains to check over the facts carefully before publication. He is not inclined to accept work a second time from a writer who has once proved unreliable.

To interpret correctly the essential significance of data is as important as to record them accurately. Readers want to know the meaning of facts and figures, and it is the writer's mission to bring out this meaning. A sympathetic understanding of the persons who figure in his article is essential, not only to portray them accurately, but to give his story the necessary "human interest." To observe accurately, to feel keenly, and to interpret sympathetically and correctly whatever he undertakes to write about, should be a writer's constant aim.

Ability to write well enough to make the average person see as clearly, feel as keenly, and understand as well as he does himself the persons and things that he is portraying and explaining, is obviously the _sine qua non_ of success. Ease, fluency, and originality of diction, either natural or acquired, the writer must possess if his work is to have distinction.

TRAINING FOR FEATURE WRITING. The ideal preparation for a writer of special articles would include a four-year college course, at least a year's work as a newspaper reporter, and practical experience in some other occupation or profession in which the writer intends to specialize in his writing. Although not all persons who desire to do special feature work will be able to prepare themselves in this way, most of them can obtain some part of this preliminary training.

A college course, although not absolutely essential for success, is generally recognized to be of great value as a preparation for writing. College training aims to develop the student's ability to observe accurately, to think logically, and to express his ideas clearly and effectively--all of which is vital to good special feature writing. In addition, such a course gives a student a knowledge of many subjects that he will find useful for his articles. A liberal education furnishes a background that is invaluable for all kinds of literary work. Universities also offer excellent opportunities for specialization. Intensive study in some one field of knowledge, such as agriculture, banking and finance, home economics, public health, social service, government and politics, or one of the physical sciences, makes it possible for a writer to specialize in his articles. In choosing a department in which to do special work in college, a student may be guided by his own tastes and interests, or he may select some field in which there is considerable demand for well trained writers. The man or woman with a specialty has a superior equipment for writing.

With the development of courses in journalism in many colleges and universities has come the opportunity to obtain instruction and practice, not only in the writing of special feature and magazine articles, but also in newspaper reporting, editing, and short story writing. To write constantly under guidance and criticism, such as it is impossible to secure in newspaper and magazine offices, will develop whatever ability a student possesses.

Experience as a newspaper reporter supplements college training in journalism and is the best substitute for college work generally available to persons who cannot go to college. For any one who aspires to write, reporting has several distinct advantages and some dangers.

The requirement that news be printed at the earliest possible moment teaches newspaper workers to collect facts and opinions quickly and to write them up rapidly under pressure. Newspaper work also develops a writer's appreciation of what constitutes news and what determines news values; that is, it helps him to recognize at once, not only what interests the average reader, but how much it interests him. Then, too, in the course of his round of news gathering a reporter sees more of human life under a variety of circumstances than do workers in any other occupation. Such experience not only supplies him with an abundance of material, but gives him a better understanding and a more sympathetic appreciation of the life of all classes.

To get the most out of his reporting, a writer must guard against two dangers. One is the temptation to be satisfied with superficial work hastily done. The necessity of writing rapidly under pressure and of constantly handling similar material, encourages neglect of the niceties of structure and of style. In the rush of rapid writing, the importance of care in the choice of words and in the arrangement of phrases and clauses is easily forgotten. Even though well-edited newspapers insist on the highest possible degree of accuracy in presenting news, the exigencies of newspaper publishing often make it impossible to verify facts or to attain absolute accuracy. Consequently a reporter may drop into the habit of being satisfied with less thorough methods of collecting and presenting his material than are demanded by the higher standards of magazine writing.

The second danger is that he may unconsciously permit a more or less cynical attitude to replace the healthy, optimistic outlook with which he began his work. With the seamy side of life constantly before him, he may find that his faith in human nature is being undermined. If, however, he loses his idealism, he cannot hope to give his articles that sincerity, hopefulness, and constructive spirit demanded by the average reader, who, on the whole, retains his belief that truth and righteousness prevail.

Of the relation of newspaper reporting to the writing of magazine articles and to magazine editing, Mr. Howard Wheeler, editor of Everybody's Magazine, has said:

> It is the trained newspaper men that the big periodical publishers are reaching out for. The man who has been through the newspaper mill seems to have a distinct edge on the man who enters the field without any newspaper training.
>
> The nose for news, the ability to select and play up leads, the feel of what is of immediate public interest is just as important in magazine work as in newspaper work.
>
> Fundamentally the purpose of a magazine article is the same as the purpose of a newspaper story--to tell a tale, to tell it directly, convincingly, and interestingly.

Practical experience in the field of his specialty is of advantage in familiarizing a writer with the actual conditions about which he is preparing himself to write. To engage for some time in farming, railroading, household management, or any other occupation, equips a person to write more intelligently about it. Such practical experience either supplements college training in a special field, or serves as the best substitute for such specialized education.

WHAT EDITORS WANT. All the requirements for success in special feature writing may be reduced to the trite dictum that editors want what they believe their readers want. Although a commonplace, it expresses a point of view that aspiring writers are apt to forget. From a purely commercial standpoint, editors are middlemen who buy from producers what they believe they can sell to their customers. Unless an editor satisfies his readers with his articles, they will cease to buy his publication. If his literary wares are not what his readers want, he finds on the newsstands unsold piles of his publication, just as a grocer finds on his shelves faded packages of an unpopular breakfast food. Both editor and grocer undertake to buy from the producers what will have a ready sale and will satisfy their customers.

The writer, then, as the producer, must furnish wares that will attract and satisfy the readers of the periodical to which he desires to sell his product. It is the ultimate consumer, not merely the editor, that he must keep in mind in selecting his material and in writing his article. "Will the reader like this?" is the question that he must ask himself at every stage of his work. Unless he can convince himself that the average person who reads the periodical to which he proposes to submit his article will like what he is writing, he cannot hope to sell it to the editor.

UNDERSTANDING THE READER. Instead of thinking of readers as a more or less indefinite mass, the writer will find it advantageous to picture to himself real persons who may be taken as typical readers. It is very easy for an author to think that what interests him and his immediate circle will appeal equally to people in general. To write successfully, however, for the Sunday magazine of a newspaper, it is necessary to keep in mind the butcher, the baker, and--if not the candlestick-maker, at least the stenographer and the department store clerk--as well as the doctor, lawyer, merchant, and chief. What is true of the Sunday newspaper is true of the popular magazine.

The most successful publisher in this country attributes the success of his periodical to the fact that he kept before his mind's eye, as a type, a family of his acquaintance in a Middle-Western town of fifteen hundred inhabitants, and shaped the policy of his publication to meet the needs and interests of all its members. An editor who desired to reach such a family would be immeasurably helped in selecting his material by trying constantly to judge from their point of view whatever passed through his hands. It is equally true that a writer desiring to gain admittance to that magazine, or to others making the same appeal, would greatly profit by visualizing as vividly as possible a similar family. Every successful writer, consciously or unconsciously, thus pictures his readers to himself.

If, for example, an author is preparing an article for an agricultural journal, he must have in his mind's eye an average farmer and this farmer's family. Not only must he see them in their surroundings; he must try to see life from their point of view. The attitude of the typical city man toward the farm and country life is very different from that of the countryman. Lack of sympathy and insight is a fatal defect in many an article intended by the writer for farm readers.

Whatever the publication to which an author desires to contribute, he should consider first, last, and all the time, its readers--their surroundings, their education, their income, their ambitions, their amusements, their prejudices--in short, he must see them as they really are.

The necessity of understanding the reader and his point of view has been well brought out by Mr. John M. Siddall, editor of the _American Magazine_, in the following excerpt from an editorial in that periodical:

   The man who refuses to use his imagination to enable him to look at
   things from the other fellow's point of view simply cannot exercise
   wide influence. He cannot reach people.

   Underneath it, somehow, lies a great law, the law of service. You
   can't expect to attract people unless you do something for them. The
   business man who has something to sell must have something useful to
   sell, and he must talk about it from the point of view of the people
   to whom he wants to sell his goods. In the same way, the journalist,

the preacher, and the politician must look at things from the point of view of those they would reach. They must feel the needs of others and then reach out and meet those needs. They can never have a large following unless they give something. The same law runs into the human relation. How we abhor the man who talks only about himself--the man who never inquires about _our_ troubles, _our_ problems; the man who never puts himself in _our_ place, but unimaginatively and unsympathetically goes on and on, egotistically hammering away on the only subject that interests him--namely _himself_.

STUDYING NEWSPAPERS AND MAGAZINES. Since every successful publication may be assumed to be satisfying its readers to a considerable degree, the best way to determine what kind of readers it has, and what they are interested in, is to study the contents carefully. No writer should send an article to a publication before he has examined critically several of its latest issues. In fact, no writer should prepare an article before deciding to just what periodical he wishes to submit it. The more familiar he is with the periodical the better are his chances of having his contribution accepted.

In analyzing a newspaper or magazine in order to determine the type of reader to which it appeals, the writer should consider the character of the subjects in its recent issues, and the point of view from which these subjects are presented. Every successful periodical has a distinct individuality, which may be regarded as an expression of the editor's idea of what his readers expect of his publication. To become a successful contributor to a periodical, a writer must catch the spirit that pervades its fiction and its editorials, as well as its special articles.

In his effort to determine the kind of topics preferred by a given publication, a writer may at first glance decide that timeliness is the one element that dominates their choice, but a closer examination of the articles in one or more issues will reveal a more specific basis of selection. Thus, one Sunday paper will be found to contain articles on the latest political, sociological, and literary topics, while another deals almost exclusively with society leaders, actors and actresses, and other men and women whose recent experiences or adventures have brought them into prominence.

It is of even greater value to find out by careful reading of the entire contents of several numbers of a periodical, the exact point of view from which the material is treated. Every editor aims to present the contents of his publication in the way that will make the strongest appeal to his readers. This point of view it is the writer's business to discover and adopt.

ANALYSIS OF SPECIAL ARTICLES. An inexperienced writer who desires to submit special feature stories to newspapers should begin by analyzing thoroughly the stories of this type in the daily papers published in his own section of the country. Usually in the Saturday or Sunday issues he will find typical articles on topics connected with the city and with the state or states in which the paper circulates. The advantage of beginning his study of newspaper stories with those published in papers near his home lies in the fact that he is familiar with the interests of the readers of these papers and can readily understand their point of view. By noting the subjects, the point of view, the form, the style, the length, and the illustrations, he will soon discover what these papers want, or rather, what the readers of these papers want. The "Outline for the Analysis of Special Articles" in Part II will indicate the points to keep in mind in studying these articles.

In order to get a broader knowledge of the scope and character of special feature stories, a writer may well extend his studies to the magazine sections of the leading papers of the country. From the work of the most experienced and original of the feature writers, which is generally to be found in these metropolitan papers, the novice will derive no little inspiration as well as a valuable knowledge of technique.

The methods suggested for analyzing special feature stories in newspapers are applicable also to the study of magazine articles. Magazines afford a better opportunity than do newspapers for an analysis of the different types of articles discussed in Chapter V. Since magazine articles are usually signed, it is possible to seek out and study the work of various successful authors in order to determine wherein lies the effectiveness of their writing. Beginning with the popular weekly and monthly magazines, a writer may well extend his study to those periodicals that appeal to particular classes, such as women's magazines, agricultural journals, and trade publications.

IDEALS IN FEATURE WRITING. After thoughtful analysis of special articles in all kinds of newspapers and magazines, the young writer with a critical sense developed by reading English literature may come to feel that much of the writing in periodicals falls far short of the standards of excellence established by the best authors. Because he finds that the average uncritical reader not only accepts commonplace work but is apparently attracted by meretricious devices in writing, he may conclude that high literary standards are not essential to popular success. The temptation undoubtedly is great both for editors and writers to supply articles that are no better than the average reader demands, especially in such ephemeral publications as newspapers and popular magazines. Nevertheless, the writer who yields to this temptation is sure to produce only mediocre work. If he is satisfied to write articles that will be characterized merely as "acceptable," he will never attain distinction.

The special feature writer owes it both to himself and to his readers to do the best work of which he is capable. It is his privilege not only to inform and to entertain the public, but to create better taste and a keener appreciation of good writing. That readers do not demand better writing in their newspapers and magazines does not mean that they are unappreciative of good work. Nor do originality and precision in style necessarily "go over the heads" of the average person. Whenever writers and editors give the public something no better than it is willing to accept, they neglect a great opportunity to aid in the development of better literary taste, particularly on the part of the public whose reading is largely confined to newspapers and periodicals.

Because of the commercial value of satisfying his readers, an editor occasionally assumes that he must give all of them whatever some of them crave. "We are only giving the public what it wants," is his excuse for printing fiction and articles that are obviously demoralizing in their effect. A heterogeneous public inevitably includes a considerable number of individuals who are attracted by a suggestive treatment of morbid phases of life. To cater to the low desires of some readers, on the ground of "giving the public what it wants," will always be regarded by self-respecting editors and authors as indefensible.

The writer's opportunity to influence the mental, moral, and æsthetic ideals of hundreds of thousands of readers is much greater than he often realizes. When he considers the extent to which most men and women are unconsciously guided in their ideas and aspirations by what they read in newspapers and magazines, he cannot fail to appreciate his responsibility. Grasping the full significance of his special feature writing, he will no longer be content to write just well enough to sell his product, but will determine to devote his effort to producing articles that are the best of which he is capable.

CHAPTER III

FINDING SUBJECTS AND MATERIAL

SOURCES OF SUBJECTS. "What shall I write about?" is the first question that inexperienced writers ask their literary advisers. "If you haven't anything to write about, why write at all?" might be an easy answer. Most persons, as a matter of fact, have plenty to write about but do not realize it. Not lack of subjects, but inability to recognize the possibilities of what lies at hand, is their real difficulty.

The best method of finding subjects is to look at every person, every event, every experience--in short, at everything--with a view to seeing whether or not it has possibilities for a special feature article. Even in the apparently prosaic round of everyday life will be found a variety of themes. A circular letter from a business firm announcing a new policy, a classified advertisement in a newspaper, the complaint of a scrub-woman, a new variety of fruit in the grocer's window, an increase in the price of laundry work, a hurried luncheon at a cafeteria--any of the hundred and one daily experiences may suggest a "live" topic for an article.

"Every foot of ground is five feet deep with subjects; all you have to do is to scratch the surface for one," declared the editor of a popular magazine who is also a successful writer of special articles. This statement may be taken as literally true. Within the narrow confines of one's house and yard, for instance, are many topics. A year's experience with the family budget, a home-made device, an attempt to solve the servant problem, a method of making pin-money, a practical means of economizing in household management, are forms of personal experience that may be made interesting to newspaper and magazine readers. A garden on a city lot, a poultry house in a back yard, a novel form of garage, a new use for a gasoline engine, a labor-saving device on the farm, may afford equally good topics. One's own experience, always a rich field, may be supplemented by experiences of neighbors and friends.

A second source of subjects is the daily newspaper. Local news will give the writer clues that he can follow up by visiting the places mentioned, interviewing the persons concerned, and gathering other relevant material. When news comes from a distance, he can write to the persons most likely to have the desired information. In neither case can he be sure, until he has investigated, that an item of news will prove to contain sufficient available material for an article. Many pieces of news, however, are worth running down carefully, for the day's events are rich in possibilities.

Pieces of news as diverse as the following may suggest excellent subjects for special articles: the death of an interesting person, the sale of a building that has historic associations, the meeting of an uncommon group or organization, the approach of the anniversary of an event, the election or appointment of a person to a position, an unusual occupation, an odd accident, an auction, a proposed municipal improvement, the arrival of a well-known person, an official report, a legal decision, an epidemic, the arrest of a noted criminal, the passing of an old custom, the publication of the city directory, a railroad accident, a marked change in fashion in dress.

A third source of both subjects and material is the report of special studies in some field, the form of the report ranging from a paper read at a meeting to a treatise in several volumes. These reports of experiments, surveys, investigations, and other forms of research, are to be found in printed bulletins, monographs, proceedings of organizations, scientific periodicals, and new books. Government publications--federal, state, and local--giving results of investigative work done by bureaus, commissions, and committees, are public documents that may usually be had free of charge. Technical and scientific periodicals and printed proceedings of important organizations are generally available at public libraries.

As Mr. Waldemar Kaempffert, editor of _Popular Science Monthly,_ has said:

> There is hardly a paper read before the Royal Institution or the French Academy or our American engineering and chemical societies that cannot be made dramatically interesting from a human standpoint and that does not chronicle real news.

"If you want to publish something where it will never be read," a wit has observed, "print it in an official document." Government reports are filled with valuable information that remains quite unknown to the average reader unless newspapers and magazines unearth it and present it in popular form. The popularization of the contents of all kinds of scientific and technical publications affords great opportunities for the writer who can present such subjects effectively.

In addressing students of journalism on "Science and Journalism," Dr. Edwin E. Slosson, literary editor of the _Independent_, who was formerly a professor of chemistry, has said:

> The most radical ideas of our day are not apt to be found in the popular newspaper or in queer little insurrectionary, heretical and propaganda sheets that we occasionally see, but in the technical journals and proceedings of learned societies. The real revolutions are hatched in the laboratory and study. The papers read before the

annual meetings of the scientific societies, and for the most part unnoticed by the press, contain more dynamite than was ever discovered in any anarchist's shop. Political revolutions merely change the form of government or the name of the party in power. Scientific revolutions really turn the world over, and it never settles back into its former position.

    *   *   *   *   *

The beauty and meaning of scientific discoveries can be revealed to the general reader if there is an intermediary who can understand equally the language of the laboratory and of the street. The modern journalist knows that anything can be made interesting to anybody, if he takes pains enough with the writing of it. It is not necessary, either, to pervert scientific truths in the process of translation into the vernacular. The facts are sensational enough without any picturesque exaggeration.

    *   *   *   *   *

The field is not an unprofitable one even in the mercenary sense. To higher motives the task of popularizing science makes a still stronger appeal. Ignorance is the source of most of our ills. Ignorant we must always be of much that we need to know, but there is no excuse for remaining ignorant of what somebody on earth knows or has known. Rich treasure lies hidden in what President Gilman called "the bibliothecal cairn" of scientific monographs which piles up about a university. The journalist might well exchange the muckrake for the pick and dig it out.

Nothing could accelerate human progress more than to reduce the time between the discovery of a new truth and its application to the needs of mankind.... It is regarded as a great journalistic achievement when the time of transmission of a cablegram is shortened. But how much more important it is to gain a few years in learning what the men who are in advance of their age are doing than to gain a few seconds in learning what the people of Europe are doing? This lag in intellectual progress ... is something which it is the especial duty of the journalist to remove. He likes to score a beat of a few hours. Very well, if he will turn his attention to science, he can often score a beat of ten years.

The three main sources, therefore, of subjects and material for special feature and magazine articles are (1) personal observation and experience, (2) newspapers, (3) scientific and technical publications and official reports.

PERSONAL OBSERVATION. How a writer may discover subjects for newspaper feature articles in the course of his daily routine by being alive to the possibilities around him can best be shown by concrete examples.

A "community sing" in a public park gave a woman writer a good subject for a special article published in the _Philadelphia North American_.

In the publication of a city directory was found a timely subject for an article on the task of getting out the annual directory in a large city; the story was printed in a Sunday issue of the _Boston Herald_.

A glimpse of some children dressed like Arctic explorers in an outdoor school in Kansas City was evidently the origin of a special feature story on that institution, which was published in the _Kansas City Star_.

A woman standing guard one evening over a partially completed school building in Seattle suggested a special feature in the _Seattle Post Intelligencer_ on the unusual occupation of night "watchman" for a woman.

While making a purchase in a drug store, a writer overheard a clerk make a request for a deposit from a woman who desired to have a prescription filled, an incident which led him to write a special feature for the _New York Times_ on this method of discouraging persons from adding to the drug store's "morgue" of unclaimed prescriptions.

From a visit to the Children's Museum in Brooklyn was developed a feature article for the _New York Herald_, and from a story-telling hour at the Boston Museum of Fine Arts was evolved a feature story for the _Boston Herald_ on the telling of stories as a means of interesting children in pictures.

Magazine articles also may originate in the writer's observation of what is going on about him. The specific instances given below, like those already mentioned, will indicate to the inexperienced writer where to look for inspiration.

A newspaper reporter who covered the criminal courts compiled the various methods of burglars and sneak thieves in gaining entrance to houses and apartments, as he heard them related in trials, and wrote a helpful article for _Good Housekeeping_ on how to protect one's house against robbery.

The exhibition of a novel type of rack for curing seed corn gave a writer a subject for an article on this "corn tree," which was published in the _Illustrated World_.

During a short stop at a farm while on an automobile trip, a woman writer noticed a concrete storage cellar for vegetables, and from an interview with the farmer obtained enough material for an article, which she sold to a farm journal.

While a woman writer was making a purchase in a plumber's shop, the plumber was called to the telephone. On returning to his customer, he remarked that the call was from a woman on a farm five miles from town, who could easily have made the slight repairs herself if she had known a little about the water-supply system on her farm. From the material which the writer obtained from the plumber, she wrote an article for an agricultural paper on how plumber's bills can be avoided.

A display of canned goods in a grocer's window, with special prices for dozen and case lots, suggested an article, afterwards published in the _Merchants Trade Journal_, on this grocer's method of fighting mail-order competition.

PERSONAL EXPERIENCE. What we actually do ourselves, as well as what we see others do, may be turned to good use in writing articles. Personal experiences not only afford good subjects and plenty of material but are more easily handled than most other subjects, because, being very real and vital to the writer, they can the more readily be made real and vital to the reader. Many inexperienced writers overlook the possibilities of what they themselves have done and are doing.

To gain experience and impressions for their articles, special writers on newspapers even assume temporarily the roles of persons whose lives and experiences they desire to portray. One Chicago paper featured every Sunday for many weeks articles by a reporter who, in order to get material, did a variety of things just for one day, from playing in a strolling street band to impersonating a convict in the state penitentiary. Thirty years ago, when women first entered the newspaper field as special feature writers, they were sometimes sent out on "freak" assignments for special features, such as feigning injury or insanity in order to gain entrance to hospitals in the guise of patients. Recently one woman writer posed as an applicant for a position as moving-picture actress; another applied for a place as housemaid; a third donned overalls and sorted scrap-iron all day in the yard of a factory; and still another accompanied a store detective on his rounds in order to discover the methods of shop-lifting with which department stores have to contend.

It is not necessary, however, to go so far afield to obtain personal experiences, as is shown by the following newspaper and magazine articles based on what the writers found in the course of their everyday pursuits.

The results obtained from cultivating a quarter-acre lot in the residence district of a city of 100,000 population were told by a writer in the _Country Gentleman_.

A woman's experience with bees was related in _Good Housekeeping_ under the title, "What I Did with Bees."

Experience in screening a large porch on his house furnished a writer with the necessary information for a practical story in _Popular Mechanics_.

Some tests that he made on the power of automobiles gave a young engineer the suggestion for an article on the term "horse power" as applied to motor-cars; the article was published in the _Illustrated World_.

"Building a Business on Confidence" was the title of a personal experience article published in _System_.

The evils of tenant farming, as illustrated by the experiences of a farmer's wife in moving during the very early spring, were vividly depicted in an article in _Farm and Fireside_.

The diary of an automobile trip from Chicago to Buffalo was embodied in an article by a woman writer, which she sold to the _Woman's Home Companion_.

Both usual and unusual means employed to earn their college expenses have served as subjects for many special articles written by undergraduates and graduates.

Innumerable articles of the "how-to-do-something" type are accepted every year from inexperienced writers by publications that print such useful information. Results of experiments in solving various problems of household management are so constantly in demand by women's magazines and women's departments in newspapers, that housewives who like to write find a ready market for articles based on their own experience.

CONFESSION ARTICLES. One particular type of personal experience article that enjoys great popularity is the so-called "confession story." Told in the first person, often anonymously, a well-written confession article is one of the most effective forms in which to present facts and experiences.

Personal experiences of others, as well as the writer's own, may be given in confession form if the writer is able to secure sufficiently detailed information from some one else to make the story probable.

A few examples will illustrate the kind of subjects that have been presented successfully in the confession form.

Some criticisms of a typical college and of college life were given anonymously in the _Outlook_ under the title, "The Confessions of an Undergraduate."

"The Story of a Summer Hotel Waitress," published in the _Independent_, and characterized by the editor as "a frank exposure of real life below stairs in the average summer hotel," told how a student in a normal school tried to earn her school expenses by serving as a waitress during the summer vacation.

In _Farm and Fireside_ was published "The Confession of a Timber Buyer," an article exposing the methods employed by some unscrupulous lumber companies in buying timber from farmers.

"How I Cured Myself of Being Too Sensitive," with the sub-title, "The Autobiography of a Young Business Man Who Nearly Went to Smash through Jealousy," was the subject of a confession article in the _American Magazine_.

An exposure of the impositions practiced by an itinerant quack was made in a series of three confession articles, in Sunday issues of the _Kansas City Star_, written by a young man whom the doctor had employed to drive him through the country districts.

To secure confession features from readers, magazines have offered prizes for the best short articles on such topics as, "The Best Thing Experience has Taught Me," "How I Overcame My Greatest Fault," "The Day of My Great Temptation," "What Will Power Did for Me."

SUBJECTS FROM THE DAY'S NEWS. In his search for subjects a writer will find numberless clues in newspapers. Since the first information concerning all new things is usually given to the world through the columns of the daily press, these columns are scanned carefully by writers in search of suggestions. Any part of the paper, from the "want ads" to the death notices or the real estate transfers, may be the starting point of a special article. The diversity of topics suggested by newspapers is shown by the following examples.

The death of a well-known clown in New York was followed by a special feature story about him in the Sunday magazine section of a Chicago paper.

A newspaper report of the discovery in Wisconsin of a method of eliminating printing ink from pulp made from old newspapers, so that white print paper might be produced from it, led a young writer to send for information to the discoverer of the process, and with these additional details he wrote an article that was published in the _Boston Transcript._

A news story about a clever swindler in Boston, who obtained possession of negotiable securities by means of a forged certified check, was made the basis of a special feature story in the _Providence Journal_ on the precautions to be taken against losses from forged checks.

News of the energetic manner in which a New Jersey sheriff handled a strike suggested a personality sketch of him that appeared in the _American Magazine_.

The publication, in a newspaper, of some results of a survey of rural school conditions in a Middle Western state, led to two articles on why the little red schoolhouse fails, one of which was published in the _Country Gentleman_, and the other in the _Independent_.

From a brief news item about the success of a farmer's widow and her daughter, in taking summer boarders in their old farmhouse, was developed a practical article telling how to secure and provide for these boarders on the ordinary farm. The article appeared in _Farm and Fireside_.

OFFICIAL DOCUMENTS. Bulletins and reports of government officials are a mine for both subjects and material. For new developments in agriculture one may consult the bulletins of the United States Department of Agriculture and those of state agricultural experiment stations. Reports on new and better methods of preparing food, and other phases of home economics, are also printed in these bulletins. State industrial commissions publish reports that furnish valuable material on industrial accidents, working-men's insurance, sanitary conditions in factories, and the health of workers. Child welfare is treated in reports of federal, state, and city child-welfare boards. The reports of the Interstate Commerce Commission, like those of state railroad commissions, contain interesting material on various phases of transportation. State and federal census reports often furnish good subjects and material. In short, nearly every official report of any kind may be a fruitful source of ideas for special articles.

The few examples given below suggest various possibilities for the use of these sources.

Investigations made by a commission of American medical experts constituting the Committee on Resuscitation from Mine Gases, under the direction of the U.S. Bureau of Mines, supplied a writer in the _Boston

Transcript_ with material for a special feature story on the dangers involved in the use of the pulmotor.

A practical bulletin, prepared by the home economics department of a state university, on the best arrangement of a kitchen to save needless steps, was used for articles in a number of farm journals.

From a bulletin of the U.S. Department of Agriculture a writer prepared an article on "the most successful farmer in the United States" and what he did with twenty acres, for the department of "Interesting People" in the _American Magazine_.

The results of a municipal survey of Springfield, Illinois, as set forth in official reports, were the basis of an article in the _Outlook_ on "What is a Survey?" Reports of a similar survey at Lawrence, Kansas, were used for a special feature story in the _Kansas City Star_.

"Are You a Good or a Poor Penman?" was the title of an article in _Popular Science Monthly_ based on a chart prepared by the Russell Sage Foundation in connection with some of its educational investigations.

The _New York Evening Post_ published an interesting special article on the "life tables" that had been prepared by the division of vital statistics of the Bureau of the Census, to show the expectation of life at all ages in the six states from which vital statistics were obtained.

A special feature story on how Panama hats are woven, as printed in the _Ohio State Journal_, was based entirely on a report of the United States consul general at Guayaquil, Ecuador.

SCIENTIFIC AND TECHNICAL PUBLICATIONS. Almost every science and every art has its own special periodicals, from which can be gleaned a large number of subjects and much valuable material that needs only to be popularized to be made attractive to the average reader. The printed proceedings of scientific and technical societies, including the papers read at their meetings, as well as monographs and books, are also valuable. How such publications may be utilized is illustrated by the articles given below.

The report of a special committee of an association of electrical engineers, given at its convention in Philadelphia, furnished a writer with material for an article on "Farming by Electricity," that was published in the Sunday edition of the _Springfield Republican_.

Studies of the cause of hunger, made by Prof. A.J. Carlson of the University of Chicago and published in a volume entitled "The Control of Hunger in Health and Disease," furnished the subject for an article in the _Illustrated World._ Earlier results of the same investigation were given in the Sunday magazine of one of the Chicago papers.

From the _Journal of Heredity_ was gleaned material for an article entitled "What Chance Has the Poor Child?" It was printed in _Every Week_.

"Golfer's Foot, One of Our Newest Diseases," was the subject of a special feature in the _New York Times_, that was based on an article in the _Medical Record_.

That the canals on Mars may be only an optical illusion was demonstrated
in an article in the Sunday magazine of the _New York Times_, by means
of material obtained from a report of the section for the Observation of
Mars, a division of the British Astronomical Association.

ANTICIPATING TIMELY SUBJECTS. By looking forward for weeks or even
months, as editors of Sunday newspapers and of magazines are constantly
doing, a writer can select subjects and gather material for articles
that will be particularly appropriate at a given time. Holidays,
seasonal events, and anniversaries may thus be anticipated, and special
articles may be sent to editors some time in advance of the occasion
that makes them timely. Not infrequently it is desirable to begin
collecting material a year before the intended time of publication.

An article on fire prevention, for instance, is appropriate for the
month of October just before the day set aside for calling attention to
fires caused by carelessness. Months in advance, a writer might begin
collecting news stories of dangerous fires resulting from carelessness;
and from the annual report of the state fire marshal issued in July, he
could secure statistics on the causes of fires and the extent of the
losses.

To secure material for an article on the Christmas presents that
children might make at a cost of twenty-five cents or less, a woman
writer jotted down after one Christmas all the information that she
could get from her friends; and from these notes she wrote the article
early in the following summer. It was published in the November number
of a magazine, at a time when children were beginning to think about
making Christmas presents.

Articles on ways and means of earning college expenses are particularly
appropriate for publication in the summer or early fall, when young men
and women are preparing to go to college, but if in such an article a
student writer intends to describe experiences other than his own, he
may well begin gathering material from his fellow students some months
before.

Anniversaries of various events, such as important discoveries and
inventions, the death or birth of a personage, and significant
historical occasions, may also be anticipated. The fiftieth anniversary
of the arrival of the first railroad train in Kansas City was
commemorated in a special feature story in the _Kansas City Star_,
published the day before the anniversary. The day following the
fifty-sixth anniversary of the discovery of petroleum in Pennsylvania,
the _New York Times_ printed in its Sunday magazine section a special
article on the man who first found oil there. The centenary of the
launching of the first steam-propelled ship to cross the Atlantic, was
commemorated by an article in the Sunday edition of the _Providence
Journal_. _Munsey's Magazine_ printed an article on the semi-centennial
of the discovery of the process of making paper from wood pulp.

By looking over tables giving dates of significant events, writers will
find what anniversaries are approaching; or they may glean such
information from news stories describing preparations made for
celebrating these anniversaries.

KEEPING LISTS OF SUBJECTS. Every writer who is on the lookout for subjects and sources of material should keep a notebook constantly at hand. Subjects suggested by everyday experiences, by newspaper and magazine reading, and by a careful study of special articles in all kinds of publications, are likely to be forgotten unless they are recorded at once. A small notebook that can be carried in the pocket or in a woman's hand-bag is most convenient. Besides topics for articles, the titles of books, reports, bulletins, and other publications mentioned in conversation or in newspapers, should be jotted down as possible sources of material. Facts and figures from publications may be copied for future use. Good titles and interesting methods of treatment that a writer observes in the work of others may prove helpful in suggesting titles and methods for his own articles. Separate sections of even a small notebook may conveniently be set aside for all of these various points.

FILING MATERIAL. The writer who makes methodical preparation for his work generally has some system of filing good material so that it will be at hand when he wants it. One excellent filing device that is both inexpensive and capable of indefinite expansion consists of a number of stout manilla envelopes, large enough to hold newspaper clippings, printed reports, magazine articles, and photographs. In each envelope is kept the material pertaining to one subject in which the writer is interested, the character of the subject-matter being indicated on one side of the envelope, so that, as the envelopes stand on end, their contents can readily be determined. If a writer has many of these envelopes, a one-drawer filing case will serve to keep them in good order. By constantly gathering material from newspapers, magazines, and printed reports, he will soon find that he has collected a considerable amount of information on which to base his articles.

CHAPTER IV

APPEAL AND PURPOSE

ANALYZING THE SUBJECT. When from many available subjects a writer is about to choose one, he should pause to consider its possibilities before beginning to write. It is not enough to say, "This is a good subject; I believe that I can write an article on it." He needs to look at the topic from every angle. He ought to ask himself, "How widespread is the interest in my subject? How much will it appeal to the average individual? What phases of it are likely to have the greatest interest for the greatest number of persons?" To answer these questions he must review the basic sources of pleasure and satisfaction.

WHAT INTERESTS READERS. To interest readers is obviously the prime object in all popular writing. The basis of interest in the news story, the special feature article, and the short story is essentially the same. Whatever the average person likes to hear and see, whatever gives him pleasure and satisfaction, is what he wants to read about. In order to test all phases of a given subject from this point of view, a writer needs to keep in mind the fundamental sources of satisfaction.

Subjects and phases of subjects that attract readers may, for convenience, be divided into the following classes, which, however, are not mutually exclusive: (1) timely topics, (2) unique, novel, and extraordinary persons, things, and events, (3) mysteries, (4) romance, (5) adventure, (6) contests for supremacy, (7) children, (8) animals, (9) hobbies and amusements, (10) familiar persons, places, and objects, (11) prominent persons, places, and objects, (12) matters involving the life, property, and welfare of others, (13) matters that affect the reader's own success and well-being.

Timeliness. Though not absolutely essential, timeliness is a valuable attribute of any subject. Readers like to feel that they are getting the latest facts and the newest ideas, in special feature articles as well as in the news. A subject need not be discarded, however, because it does not make a timely appeal. It may have interest in other respects sufficiently great to compensate for its lack of timeliness.

Many topics that at first glance seem quite unrelated to current activities are found on closer examination to have some aspects that may be brought into connection with timely interests. To a writer keenly alive to everything that is going on in the world, most subjects will be found to have some bearing on what is uppermost in men's minds. Emphasis on that point of contact with current ideas will give to the article the desired timeliness.

NOVELTY. When a person, object, or circumstance is unique, it arouses an unusual degree of interest. The first person to accomplish something out of the ordinary, the first event of its kind, the first of anything, arrests attention.

Closely associated with the unique is the extraordinary, the curious. If not absolutely the only one of its kind, a thing may still be sufficiently unusual to excite an uncommon degree of interest. Novelty has a perennial charm. Careful study of a subject is often necessary to reveal the novel and extraordinary phase of it that can best be emphasized.

MYSTERIES. The fascination for the human mind of whatever baffles it is so well known that it scarcely needs elaboration. Mysteries, whether real or fictitious, pique curiosity. Even the scholar and the practical man of affairs find relaxation in the mystery of the detective story. Real life often furnishes events sufficiently mysterious to make a special feature story that rivals fiction. Unexplained crimes and accidents; strange psychical phenomena, such as ghosts, presentiments, spiritism, and telepathy; baffling problems of the scientist and the inventor--all have elements of mystery that fascinate the average reader.

ROMANCE. The romance of real life is quite as interesting as that of fiction. As all the world loves a lover, almost all the world loves a love story. The course of true love may run smooth or it may not; in either case there is the romantic appeal. To find the romantic element in a topic is to discover a perennial source of attraction for all classes of readers.

ADVENTURE. Few in number are the persons who will not gladly escape from humdrum routine by losing themselves in an exciting tale of adventure. The thrilling exploits in real life of the engineer, the explorer, the soldier of fortune, the pioneer in any field, hold us spellbound. Even more commonplace experiences are not without an element of the adventurous, for life itself is a great adventure. Many special feature stories in narrative form have much the same interest that is created by the fictitious tale of adventure.

CONTESTS FOR SUPREMACY. Man has never lost his primitive love of a good fight. Civilization may change the form of the contest, but fighting to win, whether in love or politics, business or sport, still has a strong hold on all of us. Strikes, attempted monopolies, political revolutions, elections, championship games, diplomacy, poverty, are but a few of the struggles that give zest to life. To portray dramatically in a special article the clash and conflict in everyday affairs is to make a well-nigh universal appeal.

CHILDREN. Because we live in and for our children, everything that concerns them comes close to our hearts. A child in a photo-drama or in a news story is sure to win sympathy and admiration. The special feature writer cannot afford to neglect so vital a source of interest. Practical articles on the care and the education of children also have especial value for women readers.

ANIMALS. Wild or tame, at large or in captivity, animals attract us either for their almost human intelligence or for their distinctively animal traits. There are few persons who do not like horses, dogs, cats, and other pets, and fewer still who can pass by the animal cages at the circus or the "zoo." Hunting, trapping, and fishing are vocations for some men, and sport for many more. The business of breeding horses and cattle, and the care of live stock and poultry on the farm, must not be overlooked in the search for subjects. The technical aspects of these topics will interest readers of farm journals; the more popular phases of them make a wide general appeal.

HOBBIES AND AMUSEMENTS. Pastimes and avocations may be counted good subjects. Moving pictures, theaters, music, baseball, golf, automobiles, amateur photography, and a host of hobbies and recreations have enough enthusiastic devotees to insure wide reading for special feature stories about them.

THE FAMILIAR. Persons whom we know, places that we constantly see, experiences that we have had again and again, often seem commonplace enough, even when familiarity has not bred contempt; but when they appear unexpectedly on the stage or in print, we greet them with the cordiality bestowed on the proverbial long-lost friend. Local news interests readers because it concerns people and places immediately around them. Every newspaper man understands the desirability of increasing the attractiveness of a news event that happens elsewhere by rinding "local ends," or by giving it "a local turn." For special feature stories in newspapers, local phases are no less important. But whether the article is to be published in a newspaper or a magazine, familiar persons and things should be "played up" prominently.

THE PROMINENT. Many persons, places, and objects that we have never seen are frequently as real to us as are those that we see daily. This is because their names and their pictures have greeted us again and again in print. It is thus that prominent men and women become familiar to us.

Because of their importance we like to read about them. If a special feature article in any of its phases concerns what is prominent, greater attractiveness can be given to it by "playing up" this point, be it the President of the United States or a well-known circus clown, Fifth Avenue or the Bowery, the Capitol at Washington or Coney Island, the Twentieth Century Limited or a Ford.

LIFE AND WELFARE OF OTHERS. Sympathy with our fellow beings and an instinctive recognition of our common humanity are inherent in most men and women. Nowhere is this more strikingly shown than in the quick and generous response that comes in answer to every call for aid for those in distress. So, too, we like to know how others feel and think. We like to get behind the veil with which every one attempts to conceal his innermost thoughts and feelings. Our interest in the lives and the welfare of others finds expression in various ways, ranging from social service and self-sacrificing devotion to gossip and secret confidences. These extremes and all that lies between them abound in that "human interest" upon which all editors insist.

This widespread interest in others affords to the writer of special articles one of his greatest opportunities, not only for preparing interesting stories, but for arousing readers to support many a good cause. To create sympathy for the unfortunate, to encourage active social service, to point the way to political reform, to show the advantages of better industrial conditions, to explain better business methods--all these are but a few of the helpful, constructive appeals that he may make effectively.

He may create this interest and stir his readers to action by either one of two methods: by exposing existing evils, or by showing what has been done to improve bad conditions. The exposure of evils in politics, business, and society constituted the "muck-raking" to which several of the popular monthly magazines owe their rise. This crusading, "searchlight" type of journalism has been largely superseded by the constructive, "sunlight" type. To explain how reforms have been accomplished, or are being brought about, is construed by the best of the present-day journals to be their special mission.

PERSONAL SUCCESS AND HAPPINESS. Every one is vitally concerned about his own prosperity and happiness. To make a success of life, no matter by what criterion we may measure that success, is our one all-powerful motive. Happiness, as the goal that we hope to reach by our success, and health, as a prime requisite for its attainment, are also of great importance to every one of us. How to make or save more money, how to do our work more easily, how to maintain our physical well-being, how to improve ourselves mentally and morally, how to enjoy life more fully--that is what we all want to know. To the writer who will show us how to be "healthy, wealthy, and wise," we will give our undivided attention.

Business and professional interests naturally occupy the larger part of men's thoughts, while home-making is the chief work of most women. Although women are entering many fields hitherto monopolized by men, the home remains woman's peculiar sphere. The purchase and preparation of food, the buying and making of clothing, the management of servants, the care of children--these are the vital concerns of most women. They realize, however, that conditions outside the home have a direct bearing on home-making; and each year they are taking a more active part in civic affairs. Matters of public health, pure food legislation, the milk and the water supply, the garbage collection, the character of places of amusement, the public schools, determine, in no small degree, the success and happiness of the home-maker.

Since the dominant interests of men and women alike are their business and their home, the special writer should undertake to connect his subject as closely as possible with these interests. To show, for example, how the tariff, taxes, public utility rates, price-fixing, legislation, and similar matters affect the business and home affairs of the average reader, is to give to these political and economic problems an interest for both men and women far in excess of that resulting from a more general treatment of them. The surest way to get the reader's attention is to bring the subject home to him personally.

Of the importance of presenting a subject in such a manner that the reader is led to see its application to himself and his own affairs, Mr. John M. Siddall, editor of the _American Magazine_, has said:

> Every human being likes to see himself in reading matter--just as he likes to see himself in a mirror.
>
> The reason so much reading matter is unpopular and never attracts a wide reading public lies in the fact that the reader sees nothing in it for himself. Take an article, we'll say, entitled "The Financial System of Canada." It looks dull, doesn't it? It looks dull because you can't quite see where it affects you. Now take an article entitled "Why it is easier to get rich in Canada than in the United States." That's different! Your interest is aroused. You wonder wherein the Canadian has an advantage over you. You look into the article to find out whether you can't get an idea from it. Yet the two articles may be basically alike, differing only in treatment. One bores you and the other interests you. One bores you because it seems remote. The other interests you because the writer has had the skill to translate his facts and ideas into terms that are personal to you. The minute you become personal in this world you become interesting.

COMBINING APPEALS. When the analysis of a topic shows that it possesses more than one of these appeals, the writer may heighten the attractiveness of his story by developing several of the possibilities, simultaneously or successively. The chance discovery by a prominent physician of a simple preventive of infantile paralysis, for instance, would combine at least four of the elements of interest enumerated above. If such a combination of appeals can be made at the very beginning of the article, it is sure to command attention.

DEFINITENESS OF PURPOSE. In view of the multiplicity of possible appeals, a writer may be misled into undertaking to do too many diverse things in a single article. A subject often has so many different aspects of great interest that it is difficult to resist the temptation to use all of them. If a writer yields to this temptation, the result may be a diffuse, aimless article that, however interesting in many details, fails to make a definite impression.

To avoid this danger, the writer must decide just what his purpose is to be. He must ask himself, "What is my aim in writing this article?" and, "What do I expect to accomplish?" Only in this way will he clarify in his mind his reason for writing on the proposed topic and the object to be attained.

With a definitely formulated aim before him, he can decide just what material he needs. An objective point to be reached will give his article direction and will help him to stick to his subject. Furthermore, by getting his aim clearly in mind, he will have the means of determining, when the story is completed, whether or not he has accomplished what he set out to do.

In selecting material, in developing the article, and in testing the completed product, therefore, it is important to have a definitely formulated purpose.

THREE GENERAL AIMS. Every special article should accomplish one of three general aims: it should (1) entertain, or (2) inform, or (3) give practical guidance.

The same subject and the same material may sometimes be so treated as to accomplish any one of these three purposes. If the writer's aim is merely to help readers pass a leisure hour pleasantly, he will "play up" those aspects of a topic that will afford entertainment and little or nothing else. If he desires to supply information that will add to the reader's stock of knowledge, he will present his facts in a manner calculated to make his readers remember what he has told them. If he proposes to give information that can be applied by readers to their own activities, he must include those details that are necessary to any one who desires to make practical use of the information.

When, for example, a writer is about to prepare an article, based on experience, about keeping bees on a small suburban place, he will find that he may write his story in any one of three ways. The difficulties experienced by the amateur bee-keeper in trying to handle bees in a small garden could be treated humorously with no other purpose than to amuse. Or the keeping of bees under such circumstances might be described as an interesting example of enterprise on the part of a city man living in the suburbs. Or, in order to show other men and women similarly situated just how to keep bees, the writer might explain exactly what any person would need to know to attain success in such a venture. Just as the purpose of these articles would vary, so the material and the point of view would differ.

ENTERTAINING ARTICLES. To furnish wholesome entertainment is a perfectly legitimate end in special feature writing. There is no reason why the humor, the pathos, the romance, the adventure, and mystery in life should not be presented in special feature stories for our entertainment and amusement, just as they are presented for the same purpose in the short story, the drama, and the photo-play. Many readers find special feature stories with real persons, real places, and real circumstances, more entertaining than fiction. A writer with the ability to see the comedies and the tragedies in the events constantly happening about him, or frequently reported in the press, will never lack for subjects and material.

WHOLESOME ENTERTAINMENT. The effect of entertaining stories on the ideas and ideals of readers ought not to be overlooked. According to the best journalistic standards, nothing should be printed that will exert a demoralizing or unwholesome influence. Constructive journalism goes a step further when it insists that everything shall tend to be helpful and constructive. This practice applies alike to news stories and to special articles.

These standards do not necessarily exclude news and special feature stories that deal with crime, scandal, and similar topics; but they do demand that the treatment of such subjects shall not be suggestive or offensive. To portray violators of the criminal or moral codes as heroes worthy of emulation; to gratify some readers' taste for the morbid; to satisfy other readers by exploiting sex--all are alike foreign to the purpose of respectable journalism. No self-respecting writer will lend the aid of his pen to such work, and no self-respecting editor will publish it.

To deter persons from committing similar crimes and follies should be the only purpose in writing on such topics. The thoughtful writer, therefore, must guard against the temptation to surround wrong-doers with the glamour of heroic or romantic adventure, and, by sentimental treatment, to create sympathy for the undeserving culprit. Violations of law and of the conventions of society ought to be shown to be wrong, even when the wrong-doer is deserving of some sympathy. This need not be done by moralizing and editorializing. A much better way is to emphasize, as the results of wrong-doing, not only legal punishment and social ostracism, but the pangs of a guilty conscience, and the disgrace to the culprit and his family.

A cynical or flippant treatment of serious subjects gives many readers a false and distorted view of life. Humor does not depend on ridicule or satire. The fads and foibles of humanity can be good-naturedly exposed in humorous articles that have no sting. Although many topics may very properly be treated lightly, others demand a serious, dignified style.

The men and women whom a writer puts into his articles are not puppets, but real persons, with feelings not unlike his own. To drag them and their personal affairs from the privacy to which they are entitled, and to give them undesired and needless publicity, for the sake of affording entertainment to others, often subjects them to great humiliation and suffering. The fact that a man, woman, or child has figured in the day's news does not necessarily mean that a writer is entitled to exploit such a person's private affairs. He must discriminate between what the public is entitled to know and what an individual has a right to keep private. Innocent wives, sweethearts, or children are not necessarily legitimate material for his article because their husband, lover, or father has appeared in the news. The golden rule is the best guide for a writer in such cases. Lack of consideration for the rights of others is the mark neither of a good writer nor of a true gentleman. Clean, wholesome special feature stories that present interesting phases of life accurately, and that show due consideration for the rights of the persons portrayed, are quite as entertaining as are any others.

INFORMATIVE ARTICLES. Since many persons confine their reading largely to newspapers and magazines, they derive most of their information and ideas from these sources. Even persons who read new books rely to some extent on special articles for the latest information about current topics. Although most readers look to periodicals primarily for new, timely facts, they are also interested to find there biographical and historical material that is not directly connected with current events. Every special feature writer has a great opportunity to furnish a large circle of readers with interesting and significant information.

In analyzing subjects it is necessary to discriminate between significant and trivial facts. Some topics when studied will be found to contain little of real consequence, even though a readable article might be developed from the material. Other themes will reveal aspects that are both trivial and significant. When a writer undertakes to choose between the two, he should ask himself, "Are the facts worth remembering?" and, "Will they furnish food for thought?" In clarifying his purpose by such tests, he will decide not only what kind of information he desires to impart, but what material he must select, and from what point of view he should present it.

ARTICLES OF PRACTICAL GUIDANCE. The third general purpose that a writer may have is to give his readers sufficiently explicit information to enable them to do for themselves what has been done by others. Because all persons want to know how to be more successful, they read these "how-to-do-something" articles with avidity. All of us welcome practical suggestions, tactfully given, that can be applied to our own activities. Whatever any one has done successfully may be so presented that others can learn how to do it with equal success. Special feature articles furnish the best means of giving this practical guidance.

In preparing a "how-to-do-something" article, a writer needs to consider the class of readers for which it is intended. A special feature story, for example, on how to reduce the cost of milk might be presented from any one of three points of view: that of the producer, that of the distributor, or that of the consumer. To be practical for dairy farmers, as producers of milk, the article would have to point out possible economies in keeping cows and handling milk on the farm. To be helpful to milk-dealers, as distributors, it would concern itself with methods of lowering the cost of selling and delivering milk in the city. To assist housewives, as consumers, the article would have to show how to economize in using milk in the home. An informative article for the general reader might take up all these phases of the subject, but an article intended to give practical guidance should consider the needs of only one of these three classes of persons.

In many constructive articles of practical guidance, the writer's purpose is so successfully concealed that it may at first escape the notice of the average reader. By relating in detail, for example, how an actual enterprise was carried out, a writer may be able to give his readers, without their realizing it, all the information they need to accomplish a similar undertaking. When he analyzes such articles, the student should not be misled into thinking that the writer did not have the definite purpose of imparting practical information. If the same material can be developed into an article of interesting information or into one of practical guidance, it is desirable to do the latter and, if necessary, to disguise the purpose.

STATEMENT OF PURPOSE. In order to define his purpose clearly and to keep it constantly before him, a writer will do well to put down on paper his exact aim in a single sentence. If, for example, he desired to write a

constructive article about an Americanization pageant held in his home
city on the Fourth of July, he might write out the statement of his aim
thus: "I desire to show how the Americanization of aliens may be
encouraged in small industrial centers of from 3000 to 20,000
inhabitants, by describing how the last Fourth of July Americanization
pageant was organized and carried out in a typical Pennsylvania
industrial town of 5000."

Such a statement will assist a writer in selecting his material, in
sticking to his subject, and in keeping to one point of view. Without
this clearly formulated aim before him, it is easy for him to dwell too
long on some phase of the subject in which he is particularly interested
or on which he has the most material, to the neglect of other phases
that are essential to the accomplishment of his purpose. Or, failing to
get his aim clearly in mind, he may jump from one aspect of the subject
to another, without accomplishing anything in particular. Many a
newspaper and magazine article leaves a confused, hazy impression on the
minds of readers because the writer failed to have a definite objective.

CHAPTER V

TYPES OF ARTICLES

METHODS OF TREATMENT. After choosing a subject and formulating his
purpose, a writer is ready to consider methods of treatment. Again it is
desirable to survey all the possibilities in order to choose the one
method best adapted to his subject and his purpose. His chief
consideration should be the class of readers that he desires to reach.
Some topics, he will find, may be treated with about equal success in
any one of several ways, while others lend themselves to only one or two
forms of presentation. By thinking through the various possible ways of
working out his subject, he will be able to decide which meets his needs
most satisfactorily.

EXPOSITION BY NARRATION AND DESCRIPTION. The commonest method of
developing a special feature article is that which combines narration
and description with exposition. The reason for this combination is not
far to seek. The average person is not attracted by pure exposition. He
is attracted by fiction. Hence the narrative and descriptive devices of
fiction are employed advantageously to supplement expository methods.
Narratives and descriptions also have the advantage of being concrete
and vivid. The rapid reader can grasp a concrete story or a word
picture. He cannot so readily comprehend a more general explanation
unaccompanied by specific examples and graphic pictures of persons,
places, and objects.

Narration and description are used effectively for the concrete examples
and the specific instances by which we illustrate general ideas. The
best way, for example, to make clear the operation of a state system of
health insurance is to relate how it has operated in the case of one or
more persons affected. In explaining a new piece of machinery the writer
may well describe it in operation, to enable readers to visualize it
and follow its motions. Since the reader's interest will be roused the

more quickly if he is given tangible, concrete details that he can grasp, the examples are usually put first, to be followed by the more general explanation. Sometimes several examples are given before the explanatory matter is offered. Whole articles are often made up of specific examples and generalizations presented alternately.

To explain the effects of a new anæsthetic, for example, Mr. Burton J. Hendrick in an article in _McClure's Magazine_, pictured the scene in the operating-room of a hospital where it was being given to a patient, showed just how it was administered, and presented the results as a spectator saw them. The beginning of the article on stovaine, the new anæsthetic, illustrating this method of exposition, follows:

A few months ago, a small six-year-old boy was wheeled into the operating theater at the Hospital for Ruptured and Crippled Children, in New York City. He was one of the several thousand children of the tenements who annually find their way into this great philanthropic institution, suffering from what, to the lay mind, seems a hopelessly incurable injury or malformation. This particular patient had a crippled and paralyzed leg, and to restore its usefulness, it was necessary to cut deeply into the heel, stretch the "Achilles tendon," and make other changes which, without the usual anesthetic, would involve excruciating suffering. According to the attendant nurses, the child belonged to the "noisy" class; that is, he was extremely sensitive to pain, screamed at the approach of the surgeon, and could be examined only when forcibly held down.

As the child came into the operating-room he presented an extremely pathetic figure--small, naked, thin, with a closely cropped head of black hair, and a face pinched and blanched with fear. Surrounded by a fair-sized army of big, muscular surgeons and white-clothed nurses, and a gallery filled with a hundred or more of the leading medical men of the metropolis, he certainly seemed a helpless speck of humanity with all the unknown forces of science and modern life arrayed against him. Under ordinary conditions he would have been etherized in an adjoining chamber and brought into the operating-room entirely unconscious. This cripple, however, had been selected as a favorable subject for an interesting experiment in modern surgery, for he was to undergo an extremely torturous operation in a state of full consciousness.

Among the assembled surgeons was a large-framed, black moustached and black-haired, quick-moving, gypsy-like Rumanian--Professor Thomas Jonnesco, dean of the Medical Department of the University of Bucharest, and one of the leading men of his profession in Europe. Dr. Jonnesco, who had landed in New York only two days before, had come to the United States with a definite scientific purpose. This was to show American surgeons that the most difficult operations could be performed without pain, without loss of consciousness, and without the use of the familiar anesthetics, ether or chloroform. Dr. Jonnesco's reputation in itself assured him the fullest opportunity of demonstrating his method in New York, and this six-year-old boy had been selected as an excellent test subject.

Under the gentle assurances of the nurses that "no one was going to hurt" him, the boy assumed a sitting posture on the operating-table, with his feet dangling over the edge. Then, at the request of Dr. Jonnesco, he bent his head forward until it almost touched his breast. This threw the child's back into the desired position--that of the typical bicycle "scorcher,"--making each particular vertebra stand out sharply under the tight drawn skin. Dr. Jonnesco quickly ran his finger along the protuberances, and finally selected the space between the twelfth dorsal and the first lumbar vertebræ--in other words, the space just above the small of the back. He then took an ordinary hypodermic needle, and slowly pushed it through the skin and tissues until it entered the small opening between the lower and upper vertebræ, not stopping until it reached the open space just this side of the spinal cord.

As the needle pierced the flesh, the little patient gave a sharp cry--the only sign of discomfiture displayed during the entire operation. When the hollow needle reached its destination, a few drops of a colorless liquid spurted out--the famous cerebro-spinal fluid, the substance which, like a water-jacket, envelops the brain and the spinal cord. Into this same place Dr. Jonnesco now introduced an ordinary surgical syringe, which he had previously filled with a pale yellowish liquid--the much-famed stovaine,--and slowly emptied its contents into the region that immediately surrounds the spinal cord.

For a few minutes the child retained his sitting posture as if nothing extraordinary had happened. Dr. Jonnesco patted him on the back and said a few pleasant words in French, while the nurses and assistants chatted amiably in English.

"How do you feel now?" the attending surgeon asked, after the lapse of three or four minutes.

"All right," replied the boy animatedly, "'cept that my legs feel like they was going to sleep."

The nurses now laid the patient down upon his back, throwing a handkerchief over his eyes, so that he could not himself witness the subsequent proceedings. There was, naturally, much holding of breath as Dr. Virgil P. Gibney, the operating surgeon, raised his knife and quickly made a deep incision in the heel of this perfectly conscious patient. From the child, however, there was not the slightest evidence of sensation.

"Didn't you feel anything, my boy?" asked Dr. Gibney, pausing.

"No, I don't feel nothin'," came the response from under the handkerchief.

An operation lasting nearly half an hour ensued. The deepest tissues were cut, the tendons were stretched, the incision was sewed up, all apparently without the patient's knowledge.

Some types of articles, although expository in purpose, are entirely narrative and descriptive in form. By relating his own experiences in a confession story, for example, a writer may be able to show very clearly and interestingly the dangers of speculations in stocks with but small capital. Personality sketches are almost always narrative and descriptive.

Many of the devices of the short story will be found useful in articles. Not only is truth stranger than fiction, but facts may be so presented as to be even more interesting than fiction. Conversation, character-drawing, suspense, and other methods familiar to the writer of short stories may be used effectively in special articles. Their application to particular types of articles is shown in the following pages.

SPECIAL TYPES OF ARTICLES. Although there is no generally recognized classification of special feature articles, several distinct types may be noted, such as (1) the interview, (2) the personal experience story, (3) the confession article, (4) the "how-to-do-something" article, (5) the personality sketch, (6) the narrative in the third person. These classes, it is evident, are not mutually exclusive, but may for convenience be treated separately.

THE INTERVIEW. Since the material for many articles is obtained by means of an interview, it is often convenient to put the major part, if not the whole, of the story in interview form. Such an article may consist entirely of direct quotation with a limited amount of explanatory material concerning the person interviewed; or it may be made up partly of direct quotation and partly of indirect quotation, combined with the necessary explanation. For greater variety it is advisable to alternate direct and indirect quotations. A description of the person interviewed and of his surroundings, by way of introduction, gives the reader a distinct impression of the individual under characteristic conditions. Or some striking utterance of his may be "played up" at the beginning, to be followed by a picture of him and his surroundings. Interviews on the same topic with two or more persons may be combined in a single article.

The interview has several obvious advantages. First, the spoken word, quoted _verbatim_, gives life to the story. The person interviewed seems to be talking to each reader individually. The description of him in his surroundings helps the reader to see him as he talks. Second, events, explanations, and opinions given in the words of one who speaks with authority, have greater weight than do the assertions of an unknown writer. Third, the interview is equally effective whether the writer's purpose is to inform, to entertain, or to furnish practical guidance. Romance and adventure, humor and pathos, may well be handled in interview form. Discoveries, inventions, new processes, unusual methods, new projects, and marked success of any kind may be explained to advantage in the words of those responsible for these undertakings.

In obtaining material for an interview story, a writer should bear in mind a number of points regarding interviewing in general. First, in advance of meeting the person to be interviewed, he should plan the series of questions by which he hopes to elicit the desired information. "What would my readers ask this person if they had a chance to talk to him about this subject?" he must ask himself. That is, his questions should be those that readers would like to have answered. Since it is the answers, however, and not the questions, that will interest readers, the questions in the completed article should be subordinated as much as possible. Sometimes they may be skillfully embodied in the replies; again they may be implied merely, or entirely omitted. In studying an interview article, one can generally infer what questions the interviewer used. Second, he must cultivate his memory so that he can recall a person's exact words without taking notes. Most men talk more freely and easily when they are not reminded of the fact that what they are saying is to be printed. In interviewing, therefore, it is desirable to keep pencil and paper out of sight. Third, immediately after leaving the person whom he has interviewed, the writer should jot down facts, figures, striking statements, and anything else that he might forget.

EXAMPLES OF THE INTERVIEW ARTICLE. As a timely special feature story for Arbor Day, a Washington correspondent used the following interview with an expert as a means of giving readers practical advice on tree-planting:

ARBOR DAY ADVICE

WASHINGTON, April 1.--Three spadefuls of rich, pulverized earth will do more to make a young tree grow than a 30-minute Arbor day address by the president of the school board and a patriotic anthem by the senior class, according to Dr. Furman L. Mulford, tree expert for the department of agriculture.

Not that Dr. Mulford would abbreviate the ceremonies attendant upon Arbor day planting, but he thinks that they do not mean much unless the roots planted receive proper and constant care. For what the Fourth of July is to the war and navy departments, and what Labor day is to the department of labor, Arbor day is to the department of agriculture.

While the forestry bureau has concerned itself primarily with trees from the standpoint of the timber supply, Dr. Mulford has been making a study of trees best adapted for streets and cities generally. And nobody is more interested than he in what Arbor day signifies or how trees should be chosen and reared.

"We need trees most where our population is the thickest, and some trees, like some people, are not adapted to such a life," said Dr. Mulford. "For street or school yard planting one of the first considerations is a hardy tree, that can find nourishment under brick pavements or granite sidewalks. It must be one that branches high from the ground and ought to be native to the country and climate. America has the prettiest native trees and shrubs in the world and it is true patriotism to recognize them.

"For Southern states one of the prettiest and best of shade trees is the laurel oak, and there will be thousands of them planted this spring. It is almost an evergreen and is a quick growing tree. The willow oak is another.

"A little farther north the red oak is one of the most desirable, and in many places the swamp maple grows well, though this latter tree does not thrive well in crowded cities.

"Nothing, however, is prettier than the American elm when it reaches the majesty of its maturity and I do not believe it will ever cease to be a favorite. One thing against it, though, is the 'elm beetle,' a pest which is spreading and which will kill some of our most beautiful trees unless spraying is consistently practised. China berry trees, abundant in the South, and box elders, native to a score of states, are quick growing, but they reach maturity too soon and begin to go to pieces."

"What is the reason that so many Arbor day trees die?" Dr. Mulford was asked.

"Usually lack of protection, and often lack of care in planting," was the answer. "When the new tree begins to put out tender rootlets a child brushing against it or 'inspecting' it too closely will break them off and it dies. Or stock will nip off the new leaves and shoots and the result is the same. A frame around the tree would prevent this.

"Then, often wild trees are too big when transplanted. Such trees have usually only a few long roots and so much of these are lost in transplanting that the large trunk cannot be nourished by the remainder. With nursery trees the larger they are the better it is, for they have a lot of small roots that do not have to be cut off.

"Fruit trees are seldom so successful as shade trees, either along a street or road or in a yard. In the first place their branches are too low and unless carefully pruned their shape is irregular. Then they are subject to so many pests that unless constant care is given them they will not bear a hatful of fruit a season.

"On the other hand, nut trees are usually hardy and add much to the landscape. Pecan, chestnut, walnut and shaggy bark hickory are some of the more popular varieties."

The first Arbor day was observed in Nebraska, which has fewer natural trees than any other state. This was in 1872, and Kansas was the second to observe the day, falling into line in 1875. Incidentally Kansas ranks next to Nebraska in dearth of trees.

The Arbor day idea originated with J. Sterling Morton, a Nebraskan who was appointed secretary of agriculture by Cleveland. Now every state in the Union recognizes the day and New York, Pennsylvania, New Jersey, Minnesota, Iowa, Illinois, Wisconsin and others have gotten out extensive Arbor day booklets giving information concerning trees and birds; most of them even contain appropriate songs and poems for Arbor day programs.

How an interview combined with a description of a person may serve to create sympathy for her and for the cause that she represents is shown in the following article, which was published anonymously in the Sunday magazine section of the _Ohio State Journal_. It was illustrated with two half-tone portraits, one of the young woman in Indian costume, the other showing her in street dress.

JUST LIKE POCAHONTAS OF 300 YEARS AGO

"_Oh, East is East and West is West,
And never the two shall meet_."

BUT they may send messengers. Hark to the words of
"One-who-does-things-well."

"I carry a message from my people to the Government at Washington,"
says Princess Galilolie, youngest daughter of John Ross, hereditary
King of the "Forest Indians," the Cherokees of Oklahoma. "We have
been a nation without hope. The land that was promised us by solemn
treaty, 'so long as the grass should grow and the waters run,' has
been taken from us. It was barren and wild when we received it
seventy years ago. Now it is rich with oil and cultivation, and the
whites coveted our possessions. Since it was thrown open to settlers
no Cherokee holds sovereign rights as before, when it was his
nation. We are outnumbered. I have come as a voice from my people to
speak to the people of the Eastern States and to those at
Washington--most of all, if I am permitted to do so, to lay our
wrongs before the President's wife, in whose veins glows the blood
of the Indian."

Only nineteen is this Indian princess--this twentieth century
Pocahontas--who travels far to the seats of the mighty for her race.

She is a tall, slim, stately girl from the foothills of the Ozarks,
from Tahlequah, former capital of the Cherokee Nation. She says she
is proud of every drop of Indian blood that flows in her veins. But
her skin is fair as old ivory and she is a college girl--a girl of
the times to her finger-tips.

"When an Indian goes through college and returns to his or her
people," she says with a smile, "they say, 'Back to the blanket!' We
have few blankets among the Cherokees in Tahlequah. I am the
youngest of nine children, and we are all of us college graduates,
as my father was before us."

He is John Ross 3d, Chief of the Cherokee Nation, of mingled Scotch
and Indian blood, in descent from "Cooweeskowee," John Ross I., the
rugged old Indian King who held out against Andrew Jackson back in
1838 for the ancient rights of the Five Nations to their lands along
the Southern Atlantic States.

She sat back on the broad window seat in the sunlight. Beyond the
window lay a bird's-eye view of New York housetops, the white man's
permanent tepee. Some spring birds alighted on a nearby telephone
wire, sending out twittering mating cries to each other.

"They make me want to go home," she said with a swift, expressive
gesture. "But I will stay until the answer comes to us. Do you know
what they have called me, the old men and women who are wise--the
full-bloods? Galilolie--'One-who-does-things-well.' With us, when a
name is given it is one with a meaning, something the child must
grow to in fulfillment. So I feel I must not fail them now."

"You see," she went on, lifting her chin, "it is we young
half-bloods who must carry the strength and honor of our people to
the world so it may understand us. All our lives we have been told
tales by the old men--how our people were driven from their homes by
the Government, how Gen. Winfield Scott's soldiers came down into
our quiet villages and ordered the Indians to go forth leaving

everything behind them. My great-grandfather, the old King Cooweeskowee, with his wife and children, paused at the first hilltop to look back at his home, and already the whites were moving into it. The house is still standing at Rossville, Ga. Do you know what the old people tell us children when we wish we could go back there?" Her eyes are half closed, her lips compressed as she says slowly, thrillingly: "They tell us it is easy to find the way over that 'Trail of Tears,' that through the wilderness it is blazed with the gravestones of those who were too weak to march.

"That was seventy years ago, in 1838. The Government promised to pay amply for all it took from us, our homes and lands, cattle--even furniture. A treaty was made solemnly between the Indians and the United States that Oklahoma should be theirs 'as long as the grass should grow and the waters run.'

"That meant perpetuity to us, don't you see?" She makes her points with a directness and simplicity that should disarm even the diplomatic suavity of Uncle Sam when he meets her in Washington. "Year after year the Cherokees waited for the Government to pay. And at last, three years ago, it came to us--$133.19 to each Indian, seventy-eight years after the removal from Georgia had taken place.

"Oil was discovered after the Indians had taken the wilderness lands in Oklahoma and reclaimed them. It was as if God, in reparation for the wrongs inflicted by whites, had given us the riches of the earth. My people grew rich from their wells, but a way was found to bind their wealth so they could not use it. It was said the Indians were not fit to handle their own money."

She lifts eyebrows and shoulders, her hands clasped before her tightly, as if in silent resentment of their impotence to help.

"These are the things I want to tell; first our wrongs and then our colonization plan, for which we hope so much if the Government will grant it. We are outnumbered since the land was opened up and a mass of 'sooners,' as we call them--squatters, claimers, settlers--swarmed in over our borders. The Government again offered to pay us for the land they took back--the land that was to be ours in perpetuity 'while the grass grew and the waters ran.' We were told to file our claims with the whites. Some of us did, but eight hundred of the full-bloods went back forty miles into the foothills under the leadership of Red Bird Smith. They refuse to sell or to accept the Government money for their valuable oil lands. To appease justice, the Government allotted them lands anyway, in their absence, and paid the money for their old property into the banks, where it lies untouched. Red Bird and his 'Night Hawks' refuse to barter over a broken treaty.

"Ah, but I have gone up alone to the old men there." Her voice softens. "They will talk to me because I am my father's daughter. My Indian name means 'One-who-does-things-well.' So if I go to them they tell me their heart longings, what they ask for the Cherokee.

"And I shall put the message, if I can, before our President's wife. Perhaps she will help."

THE PERSONAL EXPERIENCE ARTICLE. A writer's own experiences, given under his name, under a pseudonym, or in anonymous form, can easily be made interesting to others. Told in the first person, such stories are realistic and convincing. The pronoun "I" liberally sprinkled through the story, as it must be, gives to it a personal, intimate character that most readers like. Conversation and description of persons, places, and objects may be included to advantage in these personal narratives.

The possibilities of the personal experience story are as great as are those of the interview. Besides serving as a vehicle for the writer's own experiences, it may be employed to give experiences of others. If, for example, a person interviewed objects to having his name used, it is possible to present the material obtained by the interview in the form of a personal experience story. In that case the article would have to be published without the writer's name, since the personal experiences that it records are not his own. Permission to present material in a personal experience story should always be obtained from the individual whose experiences the writer intends to use.

Articles designed to give practical guidance, to show readers how to do something, are particularly effective when written in the first person. If these "how-to-do-something" articles are to be most useful to readers, the conditions under which the personal experience was obtained must be fairly typical. Personal experience articles of this type are very popular in women's magazines, agricultural journals, and publications that appeal to business men.

EXAMPLES OF THE PERSONAL EXPERIENCE STORY. The opportunities for service offered to women by small daily newspapers are set forth in the story below, by means of the personal experiences of one woman. The article was published in the _Woman's Home Companion_, and was illustrated by a half-tone reproduction of a wash drawing of a young woman seated at her desk in a newspaper office.

    "THEY CALL ME THE 'HEN EDITOR'"

    THE STORY OF A SMALL-TOWN NEWSPAPER WOMAN

    By SADIE L. MOSSLER

    "What do you stay buried in this burg for? Why, look how you drudge! and what do you get out of it? New York or some other big city is the place for you. There's where you can become famous instead of being a newspaper woman in a one-horse town."

    A big city newspaper man was talking. He was in our town on an assignment, and he was idling away spare time in our office. Before I could answer, the door opened and a small girl came to my desk.

    "Say," she said, "Mama told me to come in here and thank you for that piece you put in the paper about us. You ought to see the eatin's folks has brought us! Heaps an' heaps! And Ma's got a job scrubbin' three stores."

    The story to which she referred was one that I had written about a family left fatherless, a mother and three small children in real poverty. I had written a plain appeal to the home people, with the usual results.

"That," I said, "is one reason that I am staying here. Maybe it isn't fame in big letters signed to an article, but it's another kind."

His face wore a queer expression; but before he could retort another caller appeared, a well-dressed woman.

"What do you mean," she declared, "by putting it in the paper that I served light refreshments at my party?"

"Wasn't it so?" I meekly inquired.

"No!" she thundered. "I served ice cream, cake and coffee, and that makes two courses. See that it is right next time, or we'll stop the paper."

Here my visitor laughed. "I suppose that's another reason for your staying here. When we write anything about a person we don't have to see them again and hear about it."

"But," I replied, "that's the very reason I cling to the small town. I want to see the people about whom I am writing, and live with them. That's what brings the rewards in our business. It's the personal side that makes it worth while, the real living of a newspaper instead of merely writing to fill its columns."

In many small towns women have not heretofore been overly welcome on the staff of the local paper, for the small town is essentially conservative and suspicious of change. This war, however, is changing all that, and many a woman with newspaper ambitions will now have her chance at home.

For ten years I have been what may be classified as a small town newspaper woman, serving in every capacity from society reporter to city and managing editor. During this time I have been tempted many times to go to fields where national fame and a larger salary awaited those who won. But it was that latter part that held me back, that and one other factor: "Those who won," and "What do they get out of it more than I?"

It is generally conceded that for one woman who succeeds in the metropolitan newspaper field about ten fail before the vicissitudes of city life, the orders of managing editors, and the merciless grind of the big city's working world. And with those who succeed, what have they more than I? They sign their names to articles; they receive big salaries; they are famous--as such fame goes. Why is a signed name to an article necessary, when everyone knows when the paper comes out that I wrote the article? What does national fame mean compared with the fact that the local laws of the "Society for the Prevention of Cruelty to Animals" were not being enforced and that I wrote stories that remedied this condition?

I began newspaper life as society reporter of a daily paper in a Middle-Western town of ten thousand inhabitants. That is, I supposed

I was going to be society reporter, but before very long I found myself doing police assignments, sport, editing telegraph, and whatever the occasion demanded.

I suppose that the beginnings of everyone's business life always remain vivid memories. The first morning I reported for work at seven o'clock. Naturally, no one was in the front office, as the news department of a small-town newspaper office is sometimes called. I was embarrassed and nervous, and sat anxiously awaiting the arrival of the city editor. In five minutes he gave me sufficient instructions to last a year, but the only one I remember was, "Ask all the questions you can think of, and don't let anyone bluff you out of a story."

My first duty, and one that I performed every morning for several years, was to "make" an early morning train connecting with a large city, forty miles away. It was no easy task to approach strangers and ask their names and destination; but it was all good experience, and it taught me how to approach people and to ask personal questions without being rude.

During my service as society reporter I learned much, so much that I am convinced there is no work in the smaller towns better suited to women. Any girl who is bright and quick, who knows the ethics of being a lady, can hold this position and make better money at it than by teaching or clerking.

Each trade, they say, has its tricks, and being a society reporter is no exception. In towns of from one thousand to two thousand inhabitants, the news that Mrs. X. is going to give a party spreads rapidly by that system of wireless telegraphy that excels the Marconi--neighborhood gossip. But in the larger towns it is not so easy. In "our town," whenever there is a party the ice cream is ordered from a certain confectioner. Daily he permitted us to see his order book. If Mrs. Jones ordered a quart of ice cream we knew that she was only having a treat for the family. If it were two quarts or more, it was a party, and if it was ice cream in molds, we knew a big formal function was on foot.

Society reporting is a fertile field, and for a long time I had been thinking that society columns were too dull. My ideal of a newspaper is that every department should be edited so that everyone would read all the paper. I knew that men rarely read the social column. One day a man said to me that he always called his wife his better judgment instead of his better half. That appealed to me as printable, but where to put it in the paper? Why not in my own department? I did so. That night when the paper came out everyone clamored to know who the man was, for I had merely written, "A man in town calls his wife his better judgment instead of his better half."

Then I decided to make the society department a reflection of our daily life and sayings. In order to get these in I used the initials of my title, "S.R." I never used names, but I always managed to identify my persons.

As one might expect, I brought down a storm about my head. Many

persons took the hints for themselves when they were not so
intended, and there were some amusing results. For instance, when I
said in the paper that "a certain man in a down-town store has
perfect manners," the next day twelve men thanked me, and I received
four boxes of candy as expressions of gratitude.

There were no complaints about the society column being dull after
this; everyone read it and laughed at it, and it was quoted in many
exchanges. Of course, I was careful to hurt no one's feelings, but I
did occasionally have a little good-natured fun at the expense of
people who wouldn't mind it. Little personal paragraphs of this
sort must never be malicious or mean--if the paper is to keep its
friends.

Of all my newspaper experience I like best to dwell on the society
reporting; but if I were to advance I knew that I must take on more
responsibility, so I became city editor of another paper. I was
virtually managing editor, for the editor and owner was a politician
and was away much of the time. It was then that I began to realize
the responsibility of my position, to grapple with the problem of
dealing fairly both with my employer and the public. The daily life
with its varying incidents, the big civic issues, the stories to be
handled, the rights of the advertisers to be considered, the
adjusting of the news to the business department--all these were
brought before me with a powerful clarity.

When a woman starts on a city paper she knows that there are
linotypes, presses and other machinery. Often she has seen them
work; but her knowledge of "how" they work is generally vague. It
was on my third day as city editor that I realized my woeful
ignorance of the newspaper business from the mechanical viewpoint. I
had just arrived at the office when the foreman came to my desk.

"Say," he said, "we didn't get any stuff set last night. Power was
off. Better come out and pick out the plate you want to fill with."

What he meant by the power being off I could understand, and
perforce I went out to select the plate. He handed me long slabs of
plate matter to read. Later I learned that printed copies of the
plate are sent for selection, but in my ignorance I took up the
slabs and tried to read the type. To my astonishment it was all
backward, and I found myself wondering if it were a Chinese feature
story. Finally I threw myself on his mercy and told him to select
what he chose. As I left the composing-room I heard him say to one
of the printers: "That's what comes of the boss hiring a hen
editor."

Shortly after noon a linotype operator came to me with his hands
full of copy.

"If you want any of this dope in the paper," he said, "you'll have
to grab off a paragraph here and there. My machine's got a bad
squirt, and it'll take an hour or more to fix it."

Greek, all Greek! A squirt! I was too busy "grabbing off" paragraphs
to investigate; but then and there I resolved to penetrate all these
mysteries. I found the linotype operator eager to show me how his

machine works, and the foreman was glad to take me around and
instruct me in his department and also in the pressroom. I have had
trouble with printers since; but in the end they had to admit that
the "hen editor" knew what she was talking about.

There is a great cry now for woman's advancement. If the women are
hunting equality as their goal let them not seek out the crowded,
hostile cities, but remain in the smaller places where their work
can stand out distinctly. A trite phrase expresses it that a
newspaper is the "voice of the people." What better than that a
woman should set the tune for that voice?

Equality with men! I sit at my desk looking out over the familiar
home scene. A smell of fresh ink comes to me, and a paper just off
the press is slapped down on my desk.

"Look!" says the foreman. "We got out some paper today, didn't we?"

"_We_!" How's that for equality? He has been twenty years at his
trade and I only ten, yet he includes me.

When I am tempted to feel that my field is limited, my tools crude,
and my work unhonored and unsung, I recall a quotation I read many
years ago, and I will place it here at the end of the "hen editor's"
uneventful story.

Back before my mind floats that phrase, "Buried in this burg." If a
person has ability, will not the world learn it?

"If a man can write a better book, preach a better sermon, or sing a
more glorious song than his neighbor, though he build his house in
the woods, the world will make a beaten path to his door."

That a personal experience story may be utilized to show readers how to
do something is demonstrated in the following article taken from _The
Designer_. It was illustrated by a half-tone made from a wash drawing of
one corner of the burlap room.

A BEDROOM IN BURLAP

THE MOST SATISFACTORY ROOM IN OUR BUNGALOW

BY KATHERINE VAN DORN

Our burlap room is the show room of our bungalow. Visitors are
guided through the living-room, the bedroom, the sleeping-porch and
kitchen, and allowed to express their delight and satisfaction while
we wait with bated breath for the grand surprise to be given them.
Then, when they have concluded, we say:

   "But you should see our burlap room!" Then we lead the way up the
   stairs to the attic and again stand and wait. We know what is
   coming, and, as we revel in the expressions of admiration evoked,

we

   again declaim with enormous pride: "We made it all ourselves!"

There is a solid satisfaction in making a room, especially for an amateur who hardly expects to undertake room-making as a profession. We regard our room as an original creation produced by our own genius, not likely to be duplicated in our personal experience. It grew in this wise:

When we came to the bungalow last spring the family numbered three instead of the two of the year before. Now number three, a healthy and bouncing young woman, necessitated a "sleeping-in" maid if her parents were ever to be able to detach themselves from her person. We had never had a sleeping-in maid at the bungalow before and the problem of where to put her was a serious one. We well knew that no self-respecting servant would condescend to sleep in an attic, although the attic was cool, airy and comfortable. We rather thought, too, that the maid might despise us if we gave her the bedroom and took up our quarters under the rafters. It would be an easy enough matter for carpenters and plasterers to put a room in the attic, but we lacked the money necessary for such a venture. And

so we puzzled. At first we thought of curtains, but the high winds which visit us made curtains impracticable. Then we thought of tacking the curtains top and bottom, and from this the idea evolved. The carpenter whom we consulted proved to be amenable to suggestion and agreed to put us up a framework in a day. We helped. We outlined the room on the floor. This took two strips of wood about one and a half by two inches. The other two sides of the room were formed by the wall of the attic and by the meeting place of the

roof and floor--that is, there was in reality no fourth wall; the room simply ended where floor and roof met. Two strips were nailed to the rafters in positions similar to those on the floor, and then an upright strip was inserted and nailed fast at intervals of every three feet. This distance was decided by the fact that curtain materials usually come a yard wide. For a door we used a discarded screen-door, which, having been denuded of the bits of wire clinging

to it, answered the purpose very well. The door completed the skeleton.

We used a beautiful soft blue burlap. Tacking on proved a more difficult matter than we had anticipated, owing to the fact that our

carpenter had used cypress for the framework. We stretched the material taut and then tacked it fast with sharp-pointed, large-headed brass tacks, and while inserting these we measured carefully the distances between the tacks in order to keep this trimming uniform. The two walls supplied by the framework were quickly covered, but the rough wall of the attic necessitated some cutting, as we had to tack the burlap to the uprights and these had not been placed with yard-wide material in view. Above the screen-door frame was a hiatus of space running up into the peak. The carpenter had thoughtfully run two strips up to the roof and this enabled us to fill in by cutting and turning in the cloth. A corresponding space above the window received similar treatment. Then we covered the inner surface of the screen door and we had a room.

But we were far from satisfied. The room looked bare and crude. We

bought a can of dark-oak stain and gave the floor a coat and this
improved matters so much that we stained the wood visible on the
door frame and about the window. Having finished this, we saw the
need of doing something for the ceiling. The ceiling was merely the
inner surface of the roof. The builders had made it of boards of
varying sizes, the rafters were rough and splintery and there were
myriads of nails sticking through everywhere. It looked a hopeless
task. But we bought more stain and went to work. Before beginning
we
covered our precious blue walls with newspapers, donned our oldest
clothes and spread papers well over the floor. It was well that we
did. The staining was not difficult work but the nails made it
splashy and we were pretty well spotted when we finished.

But when we did finish we felt compensated. The nails had become
invisible. The dull blue walls with their bright brass trimming,
the
soft brown floor and the stained, raftered roof made the room the
most attractive in the house. We could not rest, although the hour
was late and we were both tired, until we had furnished it. We put
in a couple of small rugs, a brass bed, and a white bureau. We hung
two pictures securely upon the uprights of the skeleton. We added a
couple of chairs and a rack for clothing, put up a white madras
curtain at the window, and regarded the effect with the utmost
satisfaction. The room answered the purpose exactly. The burlap was
thick enough to act as a screen. It was possible to see movement
through it, but not form. It insured privacy and still permitted
the
air to pass through for ventilation. As a finishing touch we
screwed
a knob on the outside of the door, put a brass hook on the inside
and went downstairs to count the cost.

As a quick and inexpensive method of adding to the number of rooms
in one's house, the making of a burlap room is without an equal.
The
idea is not patented, and we who deem ourselves its creators, are
only too happy to send it on, in the hope that it may be of service
to some other puzzled householder who is wondering where to put an
added family member.

THE CONFESSION STORY. Closely akin to the personal experience article is
the so-called "confession story." Usually published anonymously,
confession stories may reveal more personal and intimate experiences
than a writer would ordinarily care to give in a signed article.
Needless to say, most readers are keenly interested in such revelations,
even though they are made anonymously. Like personal experience stories,
they are told in the first person with a liberal use of the pronoun "I."

A writer need not confine himself to his own experiences for confession
stories; he may obtain valuable material for them from others. Not
infrequently his name is attached to these articles accompanied by the
statement that the confession was "transcribed," "taken down," or
"recorded" by the writer.

Conditions of life in classes of society with which the reader is not
familiar may be brought home to him through the medium of the confession

story. It may be made the means of arousing interest in questions about which the average reader cares little. The average man or woman, for example, is probably little concerned with the problem of the poorly paid college professor, but hundreds of thousands doubtless read with interest the leading article in an issue of the _Saturday Evening Post_ entitled, "The Pressure on the Professor." This was a confession story, which did not give the author's own experiences but appeared as "Transcribed by Walter E. Weyl." This article was obviously written with the purpose, skillfully concealed, of calling attention to the hard lot of the underpaid professor.

Constructive criticism of existing conditions may be successfully embodied in the form of a confession article that describes the evils as they have been experienced by one individual. If the article is to be entirely effective and just, the experience of the one person described must be fairly typical of that of others in the same situation. In order to show that these experiences are characteristic, the writer may find it advantageous to introduce facts and figures tending to prove that his own case is not an isolated example. In the confession article mentioned above, "The Pressure on the Professor," the assistant professor who makes the confession, in order to demonstrate that his own case is typical, cites statistics collected by a colleague at Stanford University giving the financial status of 112 assistant professors in various American universities.

Confessions that show how faults and personal difficulties have been overcome prove helpful to readers laboring under similar troubles. Here again, what is related should be typical rather than exceptional.

EXAMPLES OF THE CONFESSION STORY. That an intimate account of the financial difficulties of a young couple as told by the wife, may not only make an interesting story but may serve as a warning to others, is shown in the confession story below. Signed "F.B.," and illustrated with a pen and ink sketch of the couple at work over their accounts, it was printed in _Every Week_, a popular illustrated periodical formerly published by the Crowell Publishing Company, New York.

THE THINGS WE LEARNED TO DO WITHOUT

We were married within a month of our commencement, after three years of courtship at a big Middle West university. Looking back, it seems to me that rich, tumultuous college life of ours was wholly pagan. All about us was the free-handed atmosphere of "easy money," and in our "crowd" a tacit implication that a good time was one of the primary necessities of life. Such were our ideas when we married on a salary of one hundred dollars a month. We took letters of introduction to some of the "smart" people in a suburb near Chicago, and they proved so delightfully cordial that we settled down among them without stopping to consider the discrepancies between their ways and our income. We were put up at a small country club--a simple affair enough, comparatively speaking--that demanded six weeks' salary in initial dues and much more in actual subsequent expense. "Everybody" went out for Saturday golf and stayed for dinner and dancing.

By fall there was in working operation a dinner club of the "younger married set," as our local column in the city papers called us; an afternoon bridge club; and a small theater club that went into town every fortnight for dinner and a show. Costly little amusements, but hardly more than were due charming young people of our opportunities and tastes. I think that was our attitude, although we did not admit it. In September we rented a "smart" little apartment. We had planned to furnish it by means of several generous checks which were family contributions to our array of wedding gifts. What we did was to buy the furniture on the instalment plan, agreeing to pay twenty dollars a month till the bill was settled, and we put the furniture money into running expenses.

It was the beginning of a custom. They gave most generously, that older generation. Visiting us, Max's mother would slip a bill into my always empty purse when we went shopping; or mine would drop a gold piece into my top bureau drawer for me to find after she had gone. And there were always checks for birthdays.

Everything went into running expenses; yet, in spite of it, our expenses ran quite away. Max said I was "too valuable a woman to put into the kitchen," so we hired a maid, good-humoredly giving her _carte blanche_ on the grocery and meat market. Our bills, for all our dining out, were enormous. There were clothes, too. Max delighted in silk socks and tailored shirts, and he ordered his monogramed cigarettes by the thousand. My own taste ran to expensive little hats.

It is hardly necessary to recount the details. We had our first tremendous quarrel at the end of six months, when, in spite of our furniture money and our birthday checks, we found ourselves two hundred and fifty dollars in debt. But as we cooled we decided that there was nothing we could do without; we could only be "more careful."

Every month we reached that same conclusion. There was nothing we could do without. At the end of the year on a $1200 salary we were $700 behind; eight months later, after our first baby came, we were over a thousand--and by that time, it seemed, permanently estranged. I actually was carrying out a threat of separation and stripping the apartment, one morning, when Max came back from town and sat down to discuss matters with me.

A curious labyrinthine discussion it was, winding from recriminations and flat admissions that our marriage was a failure and our love was dead, to the most poignant memories of our engagement days. But its central point was Max's detached insistence that we make marriage over into a purely utilitarian affair.

"Man needs the decencies of a home," he said over and over. "It doesn't do a fellow any good with a firm like mine to have them know he can't manage his affairs. And my firm is the kind of firm I want to work for. This next year is important; and if I spend it dragging through a nasty divorce business, knowing that everybody knows, I'll be about thirty per cent efficient. I'm willing to admit that marriage--even a frost like ours--is useful. Will you?"

I had to. My choice rested between going home, where there were two younger sisters, or leaving the baby somewhere and striking out for myself.

"It seems to me," said Max, taking out his pencil, "that if two reasonably clever people can put their best brain power and eight hours a day into a home, it might amount to something sometime. The thing resolves itself into a choice between the things we can do without and the things we can't. We'll list them. We can't do without three meals and a roof; but there must be something."

"You can certainly give up silk socks and cigarettes," I said; and, surprisingly, on this old sore point between us Max agreed.

"You can give up silk stockings, then," he said, and put them down. Silk socks and silk stockings! Out of all possible economies, they were the only things that we could think of. Finally--

"We could make baby an excuse," I said, "and never get out to the club till very late--after dinner--and stay just for the dancing. And we could get out of the dinner club and the theater bunch. Only, we ought to have some fun."

"You can go to matinées, and tell me about them, so we can talk intelligently. We'll say we can't leave the kid nights--"

"We can buy magazines and read up on plays. We'll talk well enough if we do that, and people won't know we haven't been. Put down: 'Magazines for plays.'"

He did it quite seriously. Do we seem very amusing to you? So anxious lest we should betray our economies--so impressed with our social "position" and what people might think! It is funny enough to me, looking back; but it was bitter business then.

I set myself to playing the devoted and absorbed young mother. But it was a long, long time before it became the sweetest of realities. I cried the first time I refused a bridge game to "stay with baby"; and I carried a sore heart those long spring afternoons when I pushed his carriage conspicuously up and down the avenue while the other women motored past me out for tea at the club. Yet those long walks were the best thing that ever happened to me. I had time to think, for one thing; and I gained splendid health, losing the superfluous flesh I was beginning to carry, and the headaches that usually came after days of lunching and bridge and dining.

I fell into the habit, too, of going around by the market, merely to have an objective, and buying the day's supplies. The first month of that habit my bills showed a decrease of $16.47. I shall always remember that sum, because it is certainly the biggest I have ever seen. I began to ask the prices of things; and I made my first faint effort at applying our game of substitution to the food problem, a thing which to me is still one of the most fascinating factors in housekeeping.

One afternoon in late summer, I found a delightful little bungalow in process of building, on a side street not so _very_ far from the proper avenue. I investigated idly, and found that the rent was thirty dollars less than we were paying. Yet even then I hesitated.

It was Max who had the courage to decide.

"The only thing we are doing without is the address," he said, "And that isn't a loss that looks like $360 to me."

All that fall and winter we kept doggedly at our game of substitution. Max bought a ready-made Tuxedo, and I ripped out the label and sewed in one from a good tailor. I carried half a dozen dresses from the dyer's to a woman who evolved three very decent gowns; and then I toted them home in a box with a marking calculated to impress any chance acquaintance. We were so ashamed of our attempts at thrift that they came hard.

Often enough we quarreled after we had been caught in some sudden temptation that set us back a pretty penny, and we were inevitably bored and cross when we refused some gayety for economy's sake. We resolutely decided to read aloud the evenings the others went to the theater club; and as resolutely we substituted a stiff game of chess for the bridge that we could not afford. But we had to learn to like them both.

Occasionally we entertained at very small, very informal dinners, "on account of the baby"; and definitely discarded the wines that added the "smartness" demanded at formal affairs. People came to those dinners in their second or third best: but they stayed late, and laughed hilariously to the last second of their stay.

In the spring we celebrated Max's second respectable rise in salary by dropping out of the country club. We could do without it by that time. At first we thought it necessary to substitute a determined tramp for the Sunday morning golf game; but we presently gave that up. We were becoming garden enthusiasts. And as a substitution for most of the pleasure cravings of life, gardening is to be highly recommended. Discontent has a curious little trick of flowing out of the earthy end of a hoe.

Later that summer I found that a maid was one of the things I could do without, making the discovery in an interregnum not of my original choosing. A charwoman came in for the heavier work, and I took over the cooking. Almost immediately, in spite of my inexperience, the bills dropped. I could not cook rich pastries and fancy desserts, and fell back on simple salads and fruit instead. I dipped into the household magazines, followed on into technical articles on efficiency, substituted labor-savers wherever I could, and started my first muddled set of accounts.

At the beginning of the new year I tried my prentice hand on a budget; and that was the year that we emerged from debt and began to save.

That was six very short years ago. When, with three babies, the bungalow became a trifle small, we built a little country house and moved farther out. Several people whom we liked best among that first "exclusive younger set" have moved out too, and formed the nucleus of a neighborhood group that has wonderful times on incomes no one of which touches $4000 a year.

Ours is not as much as that yet; but it is enough to leave a wide and comfortable margin all around our wants. Max has given up his pipe for cigarettes (unmonogramed), and patronizes a good tailor for business reasons. But in everything else our substitutions stand: gardening for golf; picnics for roadhouse dinners; simple food, simple clothing, simple hospitality, books, a fire, and a game of chess on winter nights.

We don't even talk about economies any more. We like them. But--every Christmas there comes to me via the Christmas tree a box of stockings, and for Max a box of socks--heavy silk. There never is any card in either box; but I think we'll probably get them till we die.

The following short confession, signed "Mrs. M.F.E.," was awarded the first prize by the _American Magazine_ in a contest for articles on "The Best Thing Experience Has Taught Me":

Forty Years Bartered for What?

A tiny bit of wisdom, but as vital as protoplasm. I know, for I bartered forty precious years of wifehood and motherhood to learn it.

During the years of my childhood and girlhood, our family passed from wealth to poverty. My father and only brother were killed in battle during the Civil War; our slaves were freed; our plantations melted from my mother's white hands during the Reconstruction days; our big town house was sold for taxes.

When I married, my only dowry was a fierce pride and an overwhelming ambition to get back our material prosperity. My husband was making a "good living." He was kind, easy-going, with a rare capacity for enjoying life and he loved his wife with that chivalrous, unquestioning, "the queen-can-do-no-wrong" type of love.

But even in our days of courting I answered his ardent love-making with, "And we will work and save and buy back the big house; then we will--" etc., etc.

And he? Ah, alone at sixty, I can still hear echoing down the years his big tender laugh, as he'd say, "Oh, what a de-ah, ambitious little sweetheart I have!"

He owned a home, a little cottage with a rose garden at one side of it--surely, with love, enough for any bride. But I--I saw only the ancestral mansion up the street, the big old house that had passed out of the hands of our family.

I would have no honeymoon trip; I wanted the money instead. John kissed each of my palms before he put the money into them. My fingers closed greedily over the bills; it was the nest egg, the beginning.

Next I had him dismiss his bookkeeper and give me the place. I didn't go to his store--Southern ladies didn't do that in those

days--but I kept the books at home, and I wrote all the business
letters. So it happened when John came home at night, tired from his
day's work at the store, I had no time for diversions, for
love-making, no hours to walk in the rose garden by his side--no, we
must talk business.

I can see John now on many a hot night--and summer _is_ hot in the
Gulf States--dripping with perspiration as he dictated his letters
to me, while I, my aching head near the big hot lamp, wrote on and
on with hurried, nervous fingers. Outside there would be the evening
breeze from the Gulf, the moonlight, the breath of the roses, all
the romance of the southern night--but not for us!

The children came--four, in quick succession. But so fixed were my
eyes on the goal of Success, I scarcely realized the mystery of
motherhood. Oh, I loved them! I loved John, too. I would willingly
have laid down my life for him or for any one of the children. And I
intended _sometime_ to stop and enjoy John and the children. Oh,
yes, I was going really to _live_ after we had bought back the big
house, and had done so and so! In the meanwhile, I held my breath
and worked.

"I'll be so glad," I remember saying one day to a friend, "when all
my children are old enough to be off at school all day!" Think of
that! Glad when the best years of our lives together were passed!
The day came when the last little fellow trudged off to school and I
no longer had a baby to hamper me. We were living now in the big
old home. We had bought it back and paid for it. I no longer did
John's bookkeeping for him--he paid a man a hundred dollars a month
to do that--but I still kept my hand on the business.

Then suddenly one day--John died. _Died_ in what should have been
the prime and vigor of his life.

I worked harder than ever then, not from necessity, but because in
the first few years after John left I was _afraid_ to stop and
think. So the years hurried by! One by one the children grew up and
entered more or less successful careers of their own.... I don't
feel that I know them so very well.

And now that the time of life has come when I must stop and think, I
ask myself: "What did you do with the wonderful gifts Life laid in
your lap--the love of a good man, domestic happiness, the chance to
know intimately four little souls?"

And being honest I have to answer: "I bartered Life's great gifts
for Life's pitiful extras--for pride, for show!"

If my experience were unique it would not be worth publishing, but
it is only too common. Think of the wives who exchange the best
years of their lives, their husband's comfort, his peace of mind, if
not to buy back the family mansion, then for a higher social
position; sometimes it is merely for--clothes!

It is to you women who still have the opportunity to "walk with John
in the garden" that I give my dearly bought bit of experience. Stop
holding your breath until you get this or that; stop reaching out

blindly for to-morrow's prize; _live_ to-day!

THE "HOW-TO-DO-SOMETHING" ARTICLE. Articles the primary purpose of which
is to give directions for doing something in a particular way, are
always in demand. The simplest type is the recipe or formula containing
a few directions for combining ingredients. More elaborate processes
naturally demand more complex directions and require longer articles. In
the simpler types the directions are given in the imperative form; that
is, the reader is told to "take" this thing and that, and to "mix" it
with something else. Although such recipe directions are clear, they are
not particularly interesting. Many readers, especially those of
agricultural journals, are tired of being told to do this and that in
order to get better results. They are inclined to suspect the writer of
giving directions on the basis of untried theory rather than on that of
successful practice. There is an advantage, therefore, in getting away
from formal advice and directions and in describing actual processes as
they have been carried on successfully.

Articles intended to give practical guidance are most interesting when
cast in the form of an interview, a personal experience, or a narrative.
In an interview article, a person may indirectly give directions to
others by describing in his own words the methods that he has used to
accomplish the desired results. Or the writer, by telling his own
experiences in doing something, may give readers directions in an
interesting form.

Whatever method he adopts, the writer must keep in mind the questions
that his readers would be likely to ask if he were explaining the method
or process to them in person. To one who is thoroughly familiar with a
method the whole process is so clear that he forgets how necessary it is
to describe every step to readers unfamiliar with it. The omission of a
single point may make it impossible for the reader to understand or to
follow the directions. Although a writer need not insult the
intelligence of his readers by telling them what they already know, he
may well assume that they need to be reminded tactfully of many things
that they may have known but have possibly forgotten.

TWO PRACTICAL GUIDANCE ARTICLES. A method of filing office records, as
explained apparently by the man who devised it, is well set forth in the
following combination of the personal experience and the
"how-to-do-something" types of articles. It appeared in _System_ with a
half-tone reproduction of a photograph showing a man looking over
records in a drawer of the desk at which he is seated.

    WHO'LL DO JOHN'S WORK?

    BY M. C. HOBART

    "It's a quarter after 8 and Schuyler hasn't showed up," telephoned
    Beggs, one of our foremen, last Tuesday morning. "I've put Fanning
    on his machine, but that won't help much unless I can get somebody
    to work at Fanning's bench. Got anybody you can let me have for
    to-day?"

    I didn't know offhand. But I told Beggs I'd call him back.

    Ten minutes later a young lathe operator reported to Beggs. He was

able to run Fanning's machine while the latter temporarily filled
the shoes of the absent Schuyler.

Scarcely a week passes that does not bring a similar call to our
employment office. While our plant, as plants go, is not large, we
always have a number of men working with us who are fitted by
experience and adaptability to do other work than that which they
are hired to do. Such men are invaluable to know about, especially
when an operator stays away for a day or perhaps a week and the shop
is full of orders. Once it was a problem to find the right man
immediately. A few additions to our employment records made it
possible to keep track of each man's complete qualifications.

The employment records I keep in my desk in the deep drawer. They
are filed alphabetically by name. When we hire a man we write his
name and the job he is to fill on the outside of a 9 by 12 manila
envelope. Into this envelope we put his application, his references,
and other papers. His application tells us what kinds of work he can
do and has done in other shops.

There are 29 different kinds of work to be done in our shops, from
gear cutting to running errands. I have listed these operations,
alphabetically, on a cardboard the exact length of the employment
record envelope, 12 inches. When a man tells me in his application
that he not only can operate a drill press, for which he is hired,
but has also worked at grinding, I fit my cardboard list to the top
of the employment record envelope and punch two notches along the
top directly opposite the words "drill press" and "grinding" on my
list. Then I file away the envelope.

I rest secure now in my knowledge that I have not buried a potential
grinder in a drill press operator, or that I do not have to carry
his double qualifications in my mind. I know that if Beggs should
suddenly telephone me some morning that his grinder is absent--sick,
or fishing, perhaps--I need only take my cardboard list and,
starting at A, run it down my file until I come to the envelope of
the drill press operator. I am stopped there automatically by the
second notch on the envelope which corresponds in position to the
word "grinder" on my list.

And there is every likelihood that, with the necessary explanation
to the man's own foreman, Beggs will get his grinder for the day.

From the following article, printed in _Farm and Fireside_ city and
country readers alike may glean much practical information concerning
ways and means of making a comfortable living from a small farm. It was
illustrated by four half-tone reproductions of photographs showing (1)
the house, (2) the woman at her desk with a typewriter before her, (3)
the woman in her dining-room about to serve a meal from a labor-saving
service wagon, and (4) the woman in the poultry yard with a basket of
eggs.

TEN ACRES AND A LIVING

SHE WAS YOUNG, POPULAR, AND HAD BEEN REARED IN THE CITY. EVERYBODY
LAUGHED WHEN SHE DECIDED TO FARM--BUT THAT WAS FOUR YEARS AGO

BY ALICE MARY KIMBALL

When she decided to be a farmer everybody laughed. She was young,
popular, unusually fond of frocks and fun. She had been reared in
the city. She didn't know a Jersey from a Hereford, or a Wyandotte
from a Plymouth Rock.

"You'll be back in six months," her friends said.

Four years have passed. Mrs. Charles S. Tupper still is "buried" in
the country. Moreover, she is supplying eggs, chickens, honey, and
home-canned goods to those of her former associates who are willing
to pay for quality.

"Farming," said Mrs. Tupper, "is the ideal vocation for the woman
who feels the modern desire for a job and the need of marriage and a
home.

"I never wanted a job so keenly as when I found myself in a small
city apartment without enough to do to keep me busy. After I'd swept
and dusted and prepared meals for two, I had hours of time on my
hands. The corner bakeshop, the laundry, and modern conveniences had
thrust upon me more leisure than I could use. Mr. Tupper is a young
engineer whose work takes him to various parts of the Southwest. In
his absence I felt strongly the need of filling up my idle hours in
some interesting, useful way.

"I didn't quite like the idea of spending all my spare time on
cards, calling, women's clubs, and social pleasures. I longed to be
a real partner to my husband and to share in making the family
income as well as spending it.

"We had a few thousand saved for a home, and were trying to decide
where to build. One day it flashed upon me: 'Why invest in city
property? Why not a little farm? Then we'll have a home; I'll have a
job, and can make our living.'"

The idea materialized into a modern bungalow on a 10-acre farm in
Westdale, Missouri, an hour's drive from Kansas City. Mr. Tupper's
salary furnished working capital for the enterprise and Mrs. Tupper
has found congenial work as farmer-in-chief.

Poultry, bees, and a vegetable garden are Mrs. Tupper's
specialities. Her side lines are a pig and a registered Jersey cow.
She looks after the poultry, works in garden and apiary, and milks
the cow herself. She employs very little help.

"It wasn't difficult to get a start in learning to farm," Mrs.
Tupper explained. "I visited farms and studied the methods of
farmers and their wives. I asked lots of questions.

"I didn't have any old fogyisms to unlearn, and I didn't acquire
any. I went straight to the agricultural college and the state
poultry experiment station for instructions. While I was living in
the country supervising the building of the bungalow, I read and
digested every bulletin I could get. I'm still studying bulletins. I
subscribe for several farm papers and a bee journal.

"Of course, I learned a great deal from the practical experience of the people about me, but I checked up everything to the rules and directions of government and state agricultural experts, which may be had for the price of a postage stamp. I tried to take orders intelligently. I ignored old rules for poultry and bee-keeping."

Mrs. Tupper's chickens are hatched in incubators, hovered in a coal-heated brooder house, fed according to experiment-station directions, and reared in poultry houses built from experiment-station designs. From the first they have been practically free from lice and disease. She gets winter eggs. Even in zero weather and at times when feed is most costly, her spring pullets more than pay their way.

"Bees responded as readily to proper treatment," she said. "My second season I harvested $265 worth of comb honey from twenty working swarms. And I was stung not a half-dozen times at that."

Some of Mrs. Tupper's neighbors were inclined to joke at first at her appetite for bulletins, her belief in experts, and her rigid insistence on pure-bred stock and poultry. They admit now that her faith has been justified.

If Mrs. Tupper had trod in the well-worn neighborhood ruts, she would have marketed her produce by the country-store-commission-man-retailer-consumer route; but again she did not. From the first she planned to plug the leakage of farm profits in middlemen's commissions. When she had anything to sell, she put on a good-looking tailored suit, a becoming hat, smart shoes and gloves, and went to the city to talk to ultimate consumers.

The consciousness of being dressed appropriately--not expensively or ornately--is a valuable aid to the farm saleswoman, Mrs. Tupper thinks.

"If a salesman comes to me shabbily dressed or flashily dressed, I can't give him a fair hearing," she said. "I may let him talk on, but I decide against him the instant I look at him. So I reasoned that a trim, pleasing appearance would be as valuable an asset to me as to the men who sell pickles, insurance, or gilt-edged bonds. It would mean a favorable first impression and open the way to show samples and make a sales talk.

"If I tried to interview a prospective customer handicapped by the consciousness that my skirt hung badly or that my shoes were shabby, not only would I be timid and ill at ease, but my appearance would suggest to the city buyer the very slipshodness and lack of reliability he fears in buying direct from the farm.

"I go strong on attractive samples. It would be useless to try for fancy prices if I brought honey to town in mean-looking cases or rusty cans. A slight drip down the side of a package might not be proof positive of poor quality, but it would frighten away a careful buyer. Likewise, I do not illustrate my egg sales talks with a sample dozen of odd sizes and shapes. It is needless to add that goods delivered to customers must be of the same quality and appearance as the samples, and that one must keep one's promises to the dot. A little well-directed enterprise will land a customer, but only good service can hold him."

When the current wholesale price of honey was $3 a case, Mrs. Tupper's comb honey has been in demand at from 20 to 30 cents a pound. She disposes of every pound to private customers and to one grocery store which caters to "fancy" trade. She sells eggs from her 400 Anconas at from 4 to 6 cents more a dozen than the country store is paying its patrons who bring in eggs and "take them out in trade."

Mrs. Tupper figured that if a trademark has advertising pull for a manufacturing concern, it would help the farm business. She christened her 10 acres "Graceland Farm," and this name is stamped on everything that leaves her place. She had cards printed bearing the name of the farm, its telephone number, and its products. Graceland Farm is also emphasized on letter heads.

"Prompt attention to correspondence is an easy method of advertising a farm business," she suggested. "A typewritten letter on letterhead stationery, mailed promptly, creates a pleasant impression on the man who has written to inquire the price of a setting of eggs or a trio of chickens.

"Suppose I delayed a week and wrote the reply with pen and ink, or, worse, with a pencil on ruled tablet paper. I'd stand a good chance of losing a customer, wouldn't I? If I didn't miss an order outright, I should certainly leave a suggestion of inefficiency and carelessness which could only be charged to the debit side of the business."

She has found that a $50 typewriter and a letter file have helped greatly to create the good-will which is as essential to the farmer business woman as to the woman who runs a millinery shop or an insurance office.

Mrs. Tupper has encouraged automobile trade. Her apiary is within sight of the road, and a "Honey for Sale" sign brings many a customer. Many of her city patrons have the habit of driving to the farm and returning with a hamper laden with eggs, honey, butter, or canned stuff from the vegetable garden. The garden last summer supplied material for more than 900 cans of vegetables.

The neighbors smile at her zeal for fairs and poultry shows.

"It isn't fun altogether; it's business," she tells them.

It was cold, disagreeable work, for instance, to prepare an exhibit for the Heart of America Poultry Show at Kansas City last fall; but Mrs. Tupper felt repaid. She won first prize on hen, first and second on pullet, and fourth on cockerel. Then she exhibited at the St. Joseph, Missouri, Poultry Show with even better success.

"These prizes will add to the value of every chicken I have, and to all my poultry products. They give me another advertising point," she said.

"The shows gave me a fine opportunity to meet possible customers and to make friends for my business. I was on the job for days. I met scores of people and distributed hundreds of cards. I learned a lot, too, in talks with judges and experienced breeders."

The Tupper bungalow is neat and attractive. In spite of her duties in the poultry house and apiary, Mrs. Tupper serves appetizing meals. She finds time for church work and neighborhood calls, and gives every Thursday to the Red Cross.

The housework is speeded up with such conveniences as hot and cold water in kitchen and bathroom, and steam heat. The kitchen is an efficient little workshop lined by cupboards and shelves. Mrs. Tupper can sit before her kitchen cabinet and prepare a meal without moving about for ingredients and utensils. A service wagon saves steps between kitchen and dining-room.

The floors of the bungalow are of hard wood. They are waxed a few times each year, and a little work each morning with dust mop and carpet sweeper keeps them in good order. The washing is sent out.

"I couldn't earn an income from the farm if I had a farmhouse without modern improvements," Mrs. Tupper declared. "Reducing drudgery to a minimum is only plain business sense. Laundry work, scrubbing, and dishwashing have a low economic value. Such unskilled labor eats up the time and strength one needs for the more profitable and interesting tasks of farm management, accounting and correspondence, advertising and marketing."

THE PERSONALITY SKETCH. We all like to read about prominent and successful people. We want to know more about the men and women who figure in the day's news, and even about interesting persons whose success has not been great enough to be heralded in the press. What appeals to us most about these individuals is, not mere biographical facts such as appear in _Who's Who_, but the more intimate details of character and personality that give us the key to their success. We want to see them as living men and women. It is the writer's problem to present them so vividly that we shall feel as if we had actually met them face to face.

The purpose of the personality sketch may be (1) to give interesting information concerning either prominent or little known persons, (2) to furnish readers inspiration that may bear fruit in their own lives, (3) to give practical guidance by showing how one individual has accomplished a certain thing. Whether the aim is to afford food for thought, inspiration to action, or guidance in practical matters, the treatment is essentially the same.

The recognized methods of describing characters in fiction may be used to advantage in portraying real persons. These are (1) using general descriptive terms, (2) describing personal appearance, (3) telling of characteristic actions, (4) quoting their words, (5) giving biographical facts, (6) citing opinions of others about them, (7) showing how others react to them. By a judicious combination of several of these methods, a writer can make his readers visualize the person, hear him speak, watch him in characteristic actions, and understand his past life, as well as realize what others think of him and how they act toward him.

Material for a personality sketch may be obtained in one of three ways: (1) from a more or less intimate acquaintance with the person to be described; (2) from an interview with the person, supplemented by conversation with others about him; (3) from printed sketches of him combined with information secured from others. It is easier to write personality sketches about men and women whom we know well than it is about those whom we have never met, or with whom we have had only a short interview. Inexperienced writers should not attempt to prepare sketches of persons whom they know but slightly. In a single interview a writer who is observant, and who is a keen judge of human nature, may be able to get an impression sufficiently strong to serve as the basis of a satisfactory article, especially if the material obtained in the interview is supplemented by printed sketches and by conversations with others. Personality sketches sometimes include long interviews giving the person's opinions on the subject on which he is an authority. In such articles the sketch usually precedes the interview.

EXAMPLES OF THE PERSONALITY SKETCH. The first of the following sketches appeared, with a half-tone portrait, in the department of "Interesting People" in the _American Magazine_; the second was sent out by the Newspaper Enterprise Association, Cleveland, Ohio, which supplies several hundred daily newspapers with special features.

(1)

"TOMMY"--WHO ENJOYS STRAIGHTENING OUT THINGS

BY SAMPSON RAPHAELSON

Six years ago a young Bulgarian immigrant, dreamy-eyed and shabby, came to the University of Illinois seeking an education. He inquired his way of a group of underclassmen and they pointed out to him a large red building on the campus.

"Go there," they said gayly, "and ask for Tommy."

He did, and when he was admitted to the presence of Thomas Arkle Clark, Dean of Men, and addressed him in his broken English as "Mis-terr Tommy," the dean did not smile. Although Mr. Clark had just finished persuading an irascible father to allow his reprobate sophomore son to stay at college, and although he was facing the problem of advising an impetuous senior how to break an engagement with a girl he no longer loved, he adapted himself to the needs and the temperament of the foreigner instantly, sympathetically, and efficiently.

In five minutes the Bulgarian had a job, knew what courses in English he ought to take, and was filled with a glow of hope, inspiration, and security which only a genius in the art of graciousness and understanding like "Tommy Arkle," as he is amiably called by every student and alumnus of Illinois, can bestow.

This is a typical incident in the extremely busy, richly human daily routine of the man who created the office of Dean of Men in American universities. Slender, short, well-dressed, his gray hair smartly parted, with kindly, clever, humorous blue eyes and a smile that is an ecstasy of friendliness, "Tommy" sits behind his big desk in the Administration Building from eight to five every day and handles all of the very real troubles and problems of the four thousand-odd men students at the University of Illinois.

He averages one hundred callers a day, in addition to answering a heavy mail and attendance upon various committee, board, and council meetings. He is known all over the country as an authority on fraternities and their influence, and a power for making that influence constantly better and finer. In business, farmer, and school circles in the Middle West Mr. Clark is famous for his whimsical, inspiring speeches. His quick, shaft-like humor, his keen, devastating sarcasm, and his rare, resilient sympathy have made him a personality beloved particularly by young persons.

They still tell the story on the campus of an ingenuous youngster who walked into the dean's office one fall, set his suitcase on the floor, and drawing two one-dollar bills and a fifty-cent piece from his pocket, laid the money on the big desk, saying:

"That's all the money I have. I've come to work my way through. Will you help me to get a job?"

In a flash "Tommy" noted the boy's eager, imaginative brown eyes, his wide, compact lips and strong jaw. Reaching over, he took the two bills and pocketed them, leaving the half-dollar.

"The traditional great men," said the dean, "started their university careers with only fifty cents. I don't want you to be handicapped, so I'll keep this two dollars. You can get work at ---- Green Street waiting on table for your meals, and the landlady at ---- Chalmers Street wants a student to fire her furnace in exchange for room rent."

The boy earned his way successfully for several months. Then suddenly he was taken sick. An operation was necessary. Mr. Clark wired for a Chicago specialist and paid all expenses out of his own pocket. The student recovered, and two years after he was graduated sent "Tommy" a letter enclosing a check for five hundred dollars. "To redeem my two dollars which you have in trust," the letter said, "and please use the money as a medical fund for sick students who need, but cannot afford, Chicago specialists."

The dean has an abnormal memory for names and faces. Every year he makes a "rogues' gallery"--the photographs of all incoming freshmen are taken and filed away. And many an humble, unknown freshman has been exalted by the "Hello, Darby," or "Good morning, Boschenstein"--or whatever his name happened to be--with which the dean greeted him.

Mr. Clark once revealed to me the secret of his life. Fifteen years ago he was professor of English and had strong literary ambitions, with no little promise. There came the offer of the office of Dean of Men. He had to choose between writing about peoples lives or living those lives with people. And he chose, with the result that at all times of the day and night it's "Tommy this, and Tommy that";

an accident case may need him at two A.M. in the hospital, or a
crowd of roystering students may necessitate his missing a night's
sleep in order to argue an irate sheriff into the conviction that
they are not robbers and murderers. He has been known to spend many
evenings in the rooms of lonesome students who "need a friend."

"Tommy Arkle" is one of the Middle West's finest contributions to
the modern ideal of human service.

(2)

TWO NEW MACHINE GUNS ARE INVENTED FOR THE U.S. ARMY BY THE "EDISON
OF FIREARMS"

BY HARRY B. HUNT

HARTFORD, CONN., NOV. 12.--"Well, Old J.M. has done it again."

That is the chief topic of conversation these days in the big shops
of Hartford, New Haven and Bridgeport, where the bulk of the rifles,
pistols and machine guns for Uncle Sam's army is being turned out.

For in these towns to say that "Old J.M. has done it again" is the
simplest and most direct way of stating that John M. Browning has
invented a new kind of firearm.

This time, however, "Old J.M." has done it twice. He has invented
not one, but two new guns. Both have been accepted by the United
States government, contracts for immense numbers of each have been
signed, and work of production is being pushed night and day. The
new weapons will be put into the field against Germany at the
earliest possible day.

Who is John Browning? You never heard of him?

Well, Browning is the father of rapid-fire and automatic firearms.
His is the brain behind practically every basic small firearm
invention in the past 40 years. He has been to the development of
firearms what Edison has been to electricity.

"Unquestionably the greatest inventor of firearms in the world," is
the unanimous verdict of the gun experts of the Colt, Remington and
Winchester plants, whose business it is to study and criticise every
development in firearms.

But if Browning is our greatest gun inventor, he is the most
"gun-shy" genius in the country when it comes to publicity. He
would rather face a machine gun than a reporter.

A few years ago a paper in his home state--Utah--published a little
story about his success as an inventor, and the story was copied by
the Hartford Courant.

"I'd rather have paid $1,000 cash than have had that stuff printed,"
Browning says.

Friends, however, who believe that the world should know something about this firearms wizard, furnish the following sidelights on his career:

Browning comes from an old-stock Mormon family of Ogden, Utah. As a young man he was a great hunter, going off into the woods for a month or six weeks at a time, with only his gun for company. He was only 24 when he worked out his ideas for a gun carrying a magazine full of cartridges, which could be fired rapidly in succession. He pounded out the parts for his first rapid-fire gun with hammer and cold chisel.

Since that time, pump and "trombone" shotguns, automatic pistols, rapid-fire rifles produced by the biggest firearms manufacturers in the country have been Browning's products.

The United States army pistol is a Browning invention.

A Browning pistol manufactured by the Fabrique Nationale of Belgium was made the standard equipment for the armies of Belgium, Russia, Spain, Italy and Serbia.

On completion of the one-millionth pistol by the Fabrique Nationale, King Albert of Belgium knighted the modest inventor, so he is now, officially, "Sir" John Browning.

Browning is tall, slender, slightly stooped, 62, bald except for a rim of gray hair, and wears a closely clipped gray moustache. His face is marked by a network of fine lines.

Although Browning will not talk of himself or of his career as an inventor, he can't help talking when the conversation is turned on guns.

"I always think of a gun as something that is made primarily to shoot," he says. "The best gun is the simplest gun. When you begin loading a gun up with a lot of fancy contraptions and 'safety devices,' you are only inviting trouble. You complicate the mechanism and make that many more places for dirt and grit to clog the action.

"You can make a gun so 'safe' that it won't shoot."

Of Browning's new guns it is not, of course, permissible to give any details. One, however, is a light rapid-fire gun, weighing only 15 pounds, which can be fired from the shoulder like the ordinary rifle. Each magazine carries 20 rounds and the empty magazine can be detached and another substituted by pressing a button.

The heavier gun is a belt-fed machine, capable of firing 600 shots a minute. Although it is water-cooled, it weighs, water jacket and all, only 28 pounds. For airplane work, where the firing is in bursts and the speed of the machine helps cool the gun, the jacket is discarded and the gun weighs only 20 pounds.

Both guns are counted upon as valuable additions to the equipment of our overseas forces.

THE NARRATIVE IN THE THIRD PERSON. Although the interview, the personal experience article, and the confession story are largely narrative, they are always told in the first person, whereas the term "narrative article" as used in this classification is applied only to a narrative in the third person. In this respect it is more like the short story. As in the short story so in the narrative article, description of persons, places, and objects involved serves to heighten the effect.

Narrative methods may be employed to present any group of facts that can be arranged in chronological order. A process, for example, may be explained by showing a man or a number of men engaged in the work involved, and by giving each step in the process as though it were an incident in a story. The story of an invention or a discovery may be told from the inception of the idea to its realization. A political situation may be explained by relating the events that led up to it. The workings of some institution, such as an employment office or a juvenile court, may be made clear by telling just what takes place in it on a typical occasion. Historical and biographical material can best be presented in narrative form.

Suspense, rapid action, exciting adventure, vivid description, conversation, and all the other devices of the short story may be introduced into narrative articles to increase the interest and strengthen the impression. Whenever, therefore, material can be given a narrative form it is very desirable to do so. A writer, however, must guard against exaggeration and the use of fictitious details.

EXAMPLES OF THE NARRATIVE ARTICLE. How narration with descriptive touches and conversation may be effectively used to explain a new institution like the community kitchen, or the methods of recruiting employed in the army, is shown in the two articles below. The first was taken from the _New York World_, and the second from the _Outlook_.

(1)

NOW THE PUBLIC KITCHEN

BY MARIE COOLIDGE RASK

The Community Kitchen Menu

+--+
| Vegetable soup   pint, 3¢ |
| Beef stew   half pint, 4¢ |
| Baked beans   half pint, 3¢ |
| Two frankfurters, one potato and cup full of |
| boiled cabbage   all for 7¢ |
| Rice pudding, 3¢ Stewed peaches   3¢ |
| Coffee or cocoa with milk   half pint,3¢ |
+--+

"My mother wants three cents' worth of vegetable soup."

"And mine wants enough beef stew for three of us."

Two battered tin pails were handed up by small, grimy fingers. Two eager little faces were upturned toward the top of the bright green counter which loomed before them. Two pairs of roguish eyes smiled back at the woman who reached over the counter and took the pails.

"The beef stew will be twelve cents," she said. "It is four cents for each half pint, you know."

"I know," answered the youth. "My mother says when she has to buy the meat and all and cook it and put a quarter in the gas meter, it's cheaper to get it here. My father got his breakfast here, too, and it only cost him five cents."

"And was he pleased?" asked the woman, carefully lowering the filled pail to the outstretched little hand.

"You bet," chuckled the lad, as he turned and followed the little procession down the length of the room and out through the door on the opposite side.

The woman was Mrs. William K. Vanderbilt, jr.

The boy was the son of a 'longshoreman living on "Death Avenue," in close proximity to the newly established People's Kitchen, situated on the southeast corner of Tenth Avenue and West Twenty-seventh Street, New York.

So it is here at last--the much talked of, long hoped for, community kitchen.

Within three days after its doors had been opened to the public more than 1,100 persons had availed themselves of its benefits. Within three years, it is promised, the community kitchen will have become national in character. Its possibilities for development are limitless.

Way was blazed for the pioneer kitchen by Edward F. Brown, executive secretary of the New York school lunch committee.

The active power behind the cauldrons of soup, cabbage and frankfurters, beans and rice pudding is vested in Mrs. James A. Burden, jr., and Mrs. William K. Vanderbilt, jr.

The evolution of the community kitchen is going to be of interest to every housewife and to every wage earner in all classes of society.

First of all, let it be distinctly understood that the kitchen as inaugurated is not a charity. It is social and philanthropic in character, and it will ultimately reduce the cost of living by almost 50 per cent. This much has been demonstrated already to the extent that the Tenth Avenue kitchen has not only paid expenses, but has so overrun its confines that plans are in preparation for the establishment of other and larger kitchens in rapid succession.

The object is to give to the purchaser the maximum quantity of highest grade food, properly cooked, at minimum cost. This cost includes rent, light, heat, power, interest on investment, depreciation, cost of food materials, labor and supervision. The principle is that of barter and sale on an equitable business basis.

The project as now formulated is to establish for immediate use a small group of public kitchens having one central depot. This depot will be in constant operation throughout the twenty-four hours. Here the food will be prepared and distributed to the smaller kitchens where, by means of steam tables, it can be kept hot and dispensed. The character of the food to be supplied each district will be chosen with regard to what the population is accustomed to, that which is simple and wholesome, which contains bulk, can be prepared at minimum cost, can be conveniently dispensed and easily carried away.

Opposite a large school building, in a small room that had been at one time a saloon, the kitchen of the century was fitted up and formally opened to the public.

Three long green tables with green painted benches beside them encircle the room on two sides. Their use was manifest the second day after the kitchen was opened.

At 4 o'clock in the morning, from various tenement homes near by, sturdy 'longshoremen and laborers might have been seen plodding silently from their respective homes, careful not to disturb their wives and families, and heading straight for the new kitchen on the corner. From trains running along "Death Avenue" came blackened trainmen after their night's work. They, too, stopped at the corner kitchen. By the time the attendant arrived to unlock the doors forty men were in line waiting for breakfast.

Ten minutes later the three tables were fully occupied.

"Bread, cereal and coffee for five cents!" exclaimed one of the men, pushing the empty tray from him, after draining the last drop of coffee in his mug. "This kitchen's all right."

Noon came. The children from the school building trooped in.

"My mamma works in a factory," said one. "I used to get some cakes at a bakery at noontime. Gee! There's raisins in this rice puddin', ain't there?" He carried the saucerful of pudding over to the table. "Only three cents," he whispered to the little girl beside him. "You better get some, too. That'll leave you two cents for a cup of cocoa."

"Ain't it a cinch!" exclaimed the little girl.

Behind the counter the women who had made these things possible smiled happily and dished out pudding, beans and soup with generous impartiality. The daughter of Mrs. Vanderbilt appeared.

"I'm hungry, mother," she cried. "I'll pay for my lunch."

"You'll have to serve yourself," was the rejoinder of the busy woman with the tin pail in her hand. "There's a tray at the end of the counter--but don't get in the way."

So rich and poor lunched together.

"Oh, but I'm tired!" exclaimed a woman, who, satchel in hand, entered, late in the afternoon, "It's hard to go home and cook after canvassing all day. Will you mind if I eat supper here?"

Then the women and children poured in with pails and dishes and pans.

"We're getting used to it now," said one. "It's just like a store, you know, and it saves us a lot of work--"

"And expense! My land!" cried another. "Why, my man has only been working half time, and the pennies count when you've got children to feed and clothe. When I go to work by the day it's little that's cooked at home. Now--" She presented a dish as the line moved along. "Beef stew for four," she ordered, "and coffee in this pitcher, here."

(2)

GATHERING IN THE RAW RECRUIT

BY KINGSLEY MOSES

MEN WANTED FOR THE UNITED STATES ARMY

A tall, gaunt farmer boy with a very dirty face and huge gnarled hands stood open-mouthed before the brilliant poster displayed before the small-town recruiting office. In his rather dull mind he pictured himself as he would look, straight and dignified, in the khaki uniform, perhaps even with the three stripes of the sergeant on his arm.

"Fifteen dollars a month," he thought to himself, "and board and clothes and lodgings and doctor's bills. Why, that's more than I'm gettin' now on the farm! I'd see the world; I might even get to learn a regular trade." He scratched his chin thoughtfully. "Well, I ain't gettin' nowhere now, that's sure," he concluded, and slowly climbed the stairs.

This boy had not come to his decision in a moment. His untrained but thoroughly honest mind worked slowly. He had been pondering the opportunities of army life for many weeks. The idea had come to him by chance, he thought.

Over a month ago he had been plowing the lower forty of Old Man Huggins's farm. The road to the mountains lay along one side of the field, and as the boy turned and started to plow his furrow toward the road he noticed that a motor cycle had stopped just beyond the

fence. "Broke down," the boy commented to himself, as he saw the
tan-clad rider dismounting. Over the mule's huge back he watched as
he drew nearer. "Why, the rider was in uniform; he must be a
soldier!"

Sure enough, when the fence was reached the boy saw that the
stranger was dressed in the regulation khaki of Uncle Sam, with the
U.S. in block letters at the vent of the collar and two stripes on
the left sleeve.

"Broke down?" the boy queried, dropping his plow-handles.

The corporal grunted and continued to potter with the machine.

"You in the army?" the boy continued, leaning on the fence.

"You bet!" assented the soldier. Then, looking up and taking in the
big, raw-boned physique of the youngster, "Ever think of joinin'?"

"Can't say's I did."

"Got any friends in the army?"

"Nope."

"Fine life." The motor cycle was attracting little of the recruiting
officer's attention now, for he was a recruiting officer, and
engaged in one of the most practical phases of his work.

"Them soldiers have a pretty easy life, don't they?" Evidently the
boy was becoming interested.

The recruiting officer laid down his tools, pulled out a pipe, and
sat down comfortably under a small sycamore tree at the roadside.

"Not so very easy," he replied, "but interesting and exciting." He
paused for a minute to scrutinize the prospective recruit more
closely. To his experienced eye the boy appeared desirable. Slouchy,
dirty, and lazy-looking, perhaps; but there were nevertheless good
muscles and a strong body under those ragged overalls. The corporal
launched into his story.

For twenty minutes the boy listened open-mouthed to the stories of
post life, where baseball, football, and boxing divided the time
with drilling; of mess-halls where a fellow could eat all he wanted
to, free; of good-fellowship and fraternal pride in the
organization; of the pleasant evenings in the amusement rooms in
quarters. And then of the life of the big world, of which the boy
had only dreamed; of the Western plains, of Texas, the snowy ridges
of the great Rockies, New York, Chicago, San Francisco, the
Philippines, Hawaii, the strange glamour of the tropics, the great
wildernesses of the frozen North.

"It seems 'most like as I'd like to join," was the timid venture.

"What's your name?"

"Steve Bishop."

"All right, Steve, come in and see me the next time you're in town," said the corporal, rising. "We'll talk it over."

And, mounting his motor cycle, he was gone down the road in a whirl of red dust. Nor did the farmer boy think to wonder at the sudden recovery of the apparently stalled machine.

"Missionary work," explains the corporal. "We never beg 'em to join; but we do sort of give 'em the idea. Like joinin' the Masons, you know," he winked, giving me the grip.

So it happened that Steve Bishop mounted the stairs that day, resolved to join the army if they would take him.

In the small, bare, but immaculately clean room at the head of the stairs he found his friend the corporal banging away at a typewriter. "How are you, Steve? Glad to see you," was the welcome. "Sit down a minute, and we'll talk."

The soldier finished his page, lit his pipe again, and leisurely swung round in his chair.

"Think you'll like to soldier with us?" he said.

Unconsciously the boy appreciated the compliment; it was flattering to be considered on a basis of equality with this clean-cut, rugged man of the wide world.

"I reckon so," he replied, almost timidly.

"Well, how old are you, Steve?"

"Twenty-one." The corporal nodded approval. That was all right, then; no tedious formality of securing signed permission from parent or guardian was necessary.

Then began a string of personal questions as to previous employment, education, details of physical condition, moral record (for the army will have no ex-jailbirds), etc., and finally the question, "Why do you want to join?"

"They don't know why I ask that," says the corporal, "but I have a mighty good reason. From the way a boy answers I can decide which branch of the service he ought to be connected with. If he wants to be a soldier just for travel and adventure, I advise the infantry or the cavalry; but if he seriously wants to learn and study, I recommend him to the coast artillery or the engineers."

Then comes the physical examination, a vigorous but not exacting course of sprouts designed to find out if the applicant is capable of violent exertion and to discover any minor weaknesses; an examination of eyes, ears, teeth, and nose; and, finally, a cursory scrutiny for functional disorders.

"I'll take you, Steve," the corporal finally says. "In about a week we'll send you to the barracks."

"But what am I goin' to do till then? I ain't got a cent."

"Don't worry about that. You'll eat and sleep at Mrs.
Barrows's,"--naming a good, clean boarding-house in the town, the
owner of which has a yearly contract with the Government to take
care of just such embryo recruits; "in the daytime you can hang
around town, and the police won't bother you if you behave yourself.
If they call you for loafin' tell them you're waitin' to get into
the army."

In a week the district recruiting officer, a young lieutenant, drops
in on his regular circuit. The men who have been accepted by the
non-commissioned officer are put through their paces again, and so
expert is the corporal in judging good material that none of Steve's
group of eight are rejected.

"All right," says the corporal when the lieutenant has gone; "here's
your tickets to the training station at Columbus, Ohio, and
twenty-eight cents apiece for coffee on the way. In these boxes
you'll find four big, healthy lunches for each one of you. That'll
keep you until you get to Columbus."

One of the new recruits is given charge of the form ticket issued by
the railway expressly for the Government; is told that when
meal-time comes he can get off the train with the others and for
fifty cents buy a big pail of hot coffee for the bunch at the
station lunch-room. Then the corporal takes them all down to the
train, tells them briefly but plainly what is expected in the way of
conduct from a soldier, and winds up with the admonition: "And,
boys, remember this first of all; the first duty of a soldier is
this: do what you're told to do, do it without question, and _do it
quick_. Good-bye."

In twenty-four hours Steve and his companions are at the training
station, have taken the oath of allegiance, and are safely and well
on their way to full membership in the family of Uncle Sam.

CHAPTER VI

WRITING THE ARTICLE

VALUE OF A PLAN. Just as a builder would hesitate to erect a house
without a carefully worked-out plan, so a writer should be loath to
begin an article before he has outlined it fully. In planning a
building, an architect considers how large a house his client desires,
how many rooms he must provide, how the space available may best be
apportioned among the rooms, and what relation the rooms are to bear to
one another. In outlining an article, likewise, a writer needs to
determine how long it must be, what material it should include, how much
space should be devoted to each part, and how the parts should be
arranged. Time spent in thus planning an article is time well spent.

Outlining the subject fully involves thinking out the article from beginning to end. The value of each item of the material gathered must be carefully weighed; its relation to the whole subject and to every part must be considered. The arrangement of the parts is of even greater importance, because much of the effectiveness of the presentation will depend upon a logical development of the thought. In the last analysis, good writing means clear thinking, and at no stage in the preparation of an article is clear thinking more necessary than in the planning of it.

Amateurs sometimes insist that it is easier to write without an outline than with one. It undoubtedly does take less time to dash off a special feature story than it does to think out all of the details and then write it. In nine cases out of ten, however, when a writer attempts to work out an article as he goes along, trusting that his ideas will arrange themselves, the result is far from a clear, logical, well-organized presentation of his subject. The common disinclination to make an outline is usually based on the difficulty that most persons experience in deliberately thinking about a subject in all its various aspects, and in getting down in logical order the results of such thought. Unwillingness to outline a subject generally means unwillingness to think.

THE LENGTH OF AN ARTICLE. The length of an article is determined by two considerations: the scope of the subject, and the policy of the publication for which it is intended. A large subject cannot be adequately treated in a brief space, nor can an important theme be disposed of satisfactorily in a few hundred words. The length of an article, in general, should be proportionate to the size and the importance of the subject.

The deciding factor, however, in fixing the length of an article is the policy of the periodical for which it is designed. One popular publication may print articles from 4000 to 6000 words, while another fixes the limit at 1000 words. It would be quite as bad judgment to prepare a 1000-word article for the former, as it would be to send one of 5000 words to the latter. Periodicals also fix certain limits for articles to be printed in particular departments. One monthly magazine, for instance, has a department of personality sketches which range from 800 to 1200 words in length, while the other articles in this periodical contain from 2000 to 4000 words.

The practice of printing a column or two of reading matter on most of the advertising pages influences the length of articles in many magazines. To obtain an attractive make-up, the editors allow only a page or two of each special article, short story, or serial to appear in the first part of the magazine, relegating the remainder to the advertising pages. Articles must, therefore, be long enough to fill a page or two in the first part of the periodical and several columns on the pages of advertising. Some magazines use short articles, or "fillers," to furnish the necessary reading matter on these advertising pages.

Newspapers of the usual size, with from 1000 to 1200 words in a column, have greater flexibility than magazines in the matter of make-up, and can, therefore, use special feature stories of various lengths. The arrangement of advertisements, even in the magazine sections, does not affect the length of articles. The only way to determine exactly the requirements of different newspapers and magazines is to count the words in typical articles in various departments.

SELECTION AND PROPORTION. After deciding on the length of his article, the writer should consider what main points he will be able to develop in the allotted space. His choice will be guided by his purpose in writing the article. "Is this point essential to the accomplishment of my aim?" is the test he should apply. Whatever is non-essential must be abandoned, no matter how attractive it may be. Having determined upon the essential topics, he next proceeds to estimate their relative value for the development of his theme, so that he may give to each one the space and the prominence that are proportionate to its importance.

ARRANGEMENT OF MATERIAL. The order in which to present the main topics requires thoughtful study. A logical development of a subject by which the reader is led, step by step, from the first sentence to the last in the easiest and most natural way, is the ideal arrangement. An article should march right along from beginning to end, without digressing or marking time. The straight line, in writing as in drawing, is the shortest distance between two points.

In narration the natural order is chronological. To arouse immediate interest, however, a writer may at times deviate from this order by beginning with a striking incident and then going back to relate the events that led up to it. This method of beginning _in medias res_ is a device well recognized in fiction. In exposition the normal order is to proceed from the known to the unknown, to dovetail the new facts into those already familiar to the reader.

When a writer desires by his article to create certain convictions in the minds of his readers, he should consider the arrangement best calculated to lead them to form such conclusions. The most telling effects are produced, not by stating his own conclusions as strongly as possible, but rather by skillfully inducing his readers to reach those conclusions by what they regard as their own mental processes. That is, if readers think that the convictions which they have reached are their own, and were not forced upon them, their interest in these ideas is likely to be much deeper and more lasting. It is best, therefore, to understate conclusions or to omit them entirely. In all such cases the writer's aim in arranging his material should be to direct his readers' train of thought so that, after they have finished the last sentence, they will inevitably form the desired conclusion.

With the main topics arranged in the best possible order, the writer selects from his available material such details as he needs to amplify each point. Examples, incidents, statistics, and other particulars he jots down under each of the chief heads. The arrangement of these details, in relation both to the central purpose and to each other, requires some consideration, for each detail must have its logical place in the series. Having thus ordered his material according to a systematic plan, he has before him a good working outline to guide him in writing.

PLANNING A TYPICAL ARTICLE. The process of gathering, evaluating, and organizing material may best be shown by a concrete example. The publication in a New York paper of a news story to the effect that the

first commencement exercises were about to be held in the only factory
school ever conducted in the city, suggested to a special feature writer
the possibility of preparing an article on the work of the school. To
obtain the necessary material, he decided to attend the exercises and to
interview both the principal of the school and the head of the factory.
In thinking over the subject beforehand, he jotted down these points
upon which to secure data: (1) the origin and the purpose of the school;
(2) its relation to the work of the factory; (3) the methods of
instruction; (4) the kind of pupils and the results accomplished for
them; (5) the cost of the school; (6) its relation to the public school
system. At the close of the graduation exercises, he secured the
desired interviews with the teacher in charge and with the head of the
firm, copied typical examples from the exhibition of the pupils' written
work, and jotted down notes on the decoration and furnishing of the
schoolroom. Since the commencement exercises had been reported in the
newspapers, he decided to refer to them only incidentally in his story.

After considering the significance of the work of the school and what
there was about it that would appeal to different classes of readers, he
decided to write his story for the magazine section of the New York
newspaper that he believed was most generally read by business men who
operated factories similar to the one described. His purpose he
formulated thus: "I intend to show how illiterate immigrant girls can be
transformed quickly into intelligent, efficient American citizens by
means of instruction in a factory school; this I wish to do by
explaining what has been accomplished in this direction by one New York
factory." He hoped that his article would lead readers to encourage the
establishment of similar schools as a means of Americanizing alien
girls. The expository type of article containing concrete examples,
description, and interviews he concluded to adopt as the form best
suited to his subject.

The average length of the special feature stories, in the magazine
section of the paper to which he intended to submit the article, proved
to be about 2000 words. In order to accomplish his purpose in an article
of this length, he selected five main topics to develop: (1) the reasons
that led the firm to establish the school; (2) the results obtained; (3)
the methods of instruction; (4) the cost of the school; (5) the
schoolroom and its equipment.

"What part of my material will make the strongest appeal to the readers
of this newspaper?" was the question he asked himself, in order to
select the best point with which to begin his article. The feature that
would attract the most attention, he believed, was the striking results
obtained by the school in a comparatively short time.

In reviewing the several types of beginnings to determine which would
best suit the presentation of these remarkable results, he found two
possibilities: first, the summary lead with a striking statement for the
first sentence; and second, a concrete example of the results as shown
by one of the pupils. He found, however, that he did not have sufficient
data concerning any one girl to enable him to tell the story of her
transformation as an effective concrete case. He determined, therefore,
to use a striking statement as the feature of a summary lead.

From his interview with the head of the firm, and from a formal
statement of the purpose of the school printed on the commencement

program, he obtained the reasons why the school had been established. These he decided to give _verbatim_ in direct quotation form.

To show most interestingly the results of the teaching, he picked out four of the six written exercises that he had copied from those exhibited on the walls of the schoolroom. The first of these dealt with American history, the second with thrift and business methods, and the third with personal hygiene. For the fourth he selected the work of a woman of forty whose struggles to get into the school and to learn to write the teacher had described to him.

Figures on the cost of the school he had secured from the head of the firm according to his preliminary plan. These covered the expense both to the employers and to the city.

His description of the schoolroom he could base on his own observation, supplemented by the teacher's explanations.

For his conclusion he determined to summarize the results of this experiment in education as the firm stated them on the commencement program, and to give his own impression of the success of the school. Thus he sought to give final reinforcement to the favorable impression of the school that he wished his article to create, with the aim of leading readers to reach the conclusion that such schools should be encouraged as invaluable aids to the Americanization of alien girls.

OUTLINING THE ARTICLE. Having selected the main topics and having decided in a general way how he intended to develop each one, he then fixed upon the best order in which to present them.

After his introduction giving the striking results of the school in a summary lead, it seemed logical to explain the firm's purpose in undertaking this unusual enterprise. He accordingly jotted down for his second topic, "Purpose in establishing the school," with the two sub-topics, "Firm's statement on program" and "Head of firm's statement in interview."

The methods of-instruction by which the remarkable success was attained, impressed him as the next important point. His readers, having learned the results and the purpose of the school, would naturally want to know by what methods these girls had been transformed in so short a time. As his third topic, therefore, he put down, "Methods of instruction."

For his fourth division he had to choose between (1) the results as shown by the pupils' written work, (2) the cost of the school, and (3) the schoolroom and its equipment. From the point of view of logical order either the results or the schoolroom might have been taken up next, but, as all the explanations of the methods of instruction were quoted directly in the words of the teacher, and as the pupils' exercises were to be given _verbatim_, he thought it best to place his own description of the schoolroom between these two quoted parts. Greater variety, he foresaw, would result from such an arrangement. "The schoolroom," then, became the fourth topic.

Since the pupils' work which he planned to reproduce had been exhibited on the walls of the schoolroom, the transition from the description of the room to the exhibits on the walls was an easy and logical one.

By this process of elimination, the cost of the school became the sixth
division, to be followed by the summary conclusion.

He then proceeded to fill in the details needed to develop each of
these main topics, always keeping his general purpose in mind. The
result of this organization of material was the following outline:

    I. Summary lead
        1. Striking results--time required
        2. Commencement--when and where held
        3. Graduates--number, nationality, certificates
        4. School--when and where established
        5. Example to other firms

    II. Purpose of school
        1. Firm's statement on commencement program
        2. Head of firm's statement in interview

    III. Methods of instruction
        1. Practical education
        2. Letter writing--geography, postal regulations, correspondence
        3. Arithmetic--money, expense accounts, reports of work
        4. Civics--history, biography, holidays, citizenship, patriotism
        5. Personal hygiene--cleanliness, physical culture, first aid,
            food
        6. Cotton goods--growing cotton, spinning, shipping
        7. Means of communication--telephone, directory, map of city,
            routes of travel, telephone book
        8. Study outside of classroom

    IV. The schoolroom
        1. Location--floor space, windows
        2. Decorations--flowers, motto, photograph of Miss Jessie Wilson
        3. Furnishings--piano, phonograph
        4. Library--reading to the girls, _The Promised Land_, Mary
Antin,
            library cards

    V. Results shown by pupils' work
        1. Italian's theme and her remarkable progress
        2. Russian's essay on saving
        3. Polish girl's exercise about picture
        4. Woman of forty and her work

    VI. Cost of school
        1. Expense to firm
        2. Cost to Board of Education--salaries and supplies
        3. Entire cost per pupil
        4. Returns to firm outweigh cost, says employer

    VII. Summary conclusion
        1. Results quoted from program
        2. Impression made by girls receiving diplomas

THE COMPLETED ARTICLE. Since the establishment of a school in a factory
was the novel feature of the enterprise, he worked out a title based on

this idea, with a sub-title presenting the striking results accomplished by the school. The completed article follows, with a brief analysis of the methods used in developing the outline.

TAKING THE SCHOOL TO THE FACTORY

HOW ALIEN GIRLS ARE BEING CHANGED INTO INTELLIGENT AMERICAN WORKERS BY INSTRUCTION DURING WORKING HOURS

In from twenty to thirty-five weeks an illiterate immigrant girl can be transformed into an intelligent, efficient American citizen, in this city, without interfering with the daily work sentence. by which she earns her living. Only forty-five minutes a day in a factory schoolroom is required to accomplish such striking results.

I. SUMMARY LEAD
1. Striking results
   Striking statement
   in two sentence to
   avoid unwieldy

This has just been demonstrated at the first commencement of the only school conducted in a New York factory. The classes have been held on one of the upper floors of the white goods factory of D. E. Sicher & Co., 49 West 21st Street, where the graduation exercises were held last Thursday evening.

2. Commencement
   Timeliness brought
   out immediately after
   striking statement

   Address has local
   interest

Forty girls--Italians, Poles, Russians, Hungarians, Austrians among the number--received the first "certificates of literacy" ever issued by the Board of Education. Twenty weeks ago many of these young women could not speak English; many of them had never been to school a day in their lives. Every one present on Thursday night felt that this was indeed a commencement for these girls.

3. Graduates
   Note concrete details

   Striking results
   emphasized by device
   of contrast

   Impression on audience
   of remarkable
   results

It is due to the instruction of Miss Florence Meyers, formerly a public school teacher, that the girls can now speak English, write good letters, make out money-orders, cash checks, and send telegrams. They have also been taught the principles of our government, the importance of personal hygiene, and the processes by which cotton goods used in their work are manufactured.

   Teacher's name has
   local interest

   Additional concrete
   details of striking
   results

The school was organized this year at the suggestion of Dudley E. Sicher, head of the firm, in coöperation with

4. School

the Board of Education, and has been
under the supervision of Miss Lizzie E.
Rector, Public School No. 4, Manhattan.

What has been accomplished in this
factory, which is the largest white
goods muslin underwear plant in the
world, will doubtless serve as an example
to be followed by other firms.

Its purpose the firm expresses in
these words: "To hasten assimilation
necessary to national unity, to promote
industrial betterment, by reducing
the friction caused by failure to comprehend
directions, and to decrease the
waste and loss of wage incidental to the
illiterate worker."

"When a girl understands English
and has been taught American business
and factory methods," says Mr.
Sicher, "she doesn't hesitate and
blunder; she understands what she is
told and she does it.

"Intelligent employees do much better
work than illiterate ones, and since
we can afford to pay them better wages,
they are much more contented. From
a business point of view, the school is a
good investment."

The instruction that has accomplished
such remarkable results has
been eminently practical. "There
was no time to spend in teaching the
girls anything but the most necessary
things," explains Miss Meyers, "for I
could have each one of them for only
forty-five minutes a day, and there was
much to be done in that time.

"Here was a girl, for example, who
could hardly say 'good morning.'
Here was another who had never written
a word in her life, either in English
or in any other language. The problem
was how to give each of them what
she most needed in the short time allotted
every day. This essentially
practical training I organized under
several subjects, each of which was
broadly inclusive.

"When I undertook to teach letter

Principal and school
have local interest.

5. Example to other
   firms
   Veiled suggestion to
   readers

II. PURPOSE OF SCHOOL
   1. Firm's statement

   Statement in general
   terms

   2. Head of firm's
      statement

   Statement in concrete
   terms

III. METHODS OF INSTRUCTION

   1. Practical education

   Teacher's statement
   of her problem

   Problem concretely
   shown

   Statement of general
   plan

   2. Letter writing

writing, it meant teaching the English
language, as well as writing and spelling.
It meant teaching the geography
of the country, the postal regulations,
and the forms of business and personal
correspondence.

"In teaching arithmetic, I use money   3. Arithmetic
and show them how to make change by
means of addition, subtraction, and
division. I also ask them to keep personal
expense accounts and to make
out reports of the work that they do.

"Civics included American history,   4. Civics
the lives of our statesmen--for these
girls are so eager to be true Americans
that they want to know about our great
men--the origin of legal holidays, the
merits of our system of government,
the meaning of citizenship, and the essence
of patriotism.

"Hygiene is another important   5. Personal hygiene
subject. American standards of living,
personal cleanliness, and sanitary regulations
have to be emphasized. To
aid in counteracting the effects of long
hours at the sewing machines, we have
physical culture exercises. Instruction
in first aid measures is also given so
that they will know what to do in case
of an accident. The nutritive value of
different foods in relation to their cost
is discussed to enable them to maintain
their health by a proper diet.

"As these young women are engaged   6. Cotton goods
in making muslin underwear, it seemed
desirable for them to know where cotton
grows, how it is spun, where the
mills are and how it is shipped to New
York. After they understand the various
processes through which the material
goes before it reaches them, they
take much more interest in their work,
as a part of the manufacture of cotton
goods into clothing."

The use of the telephone, the telegraph,   7. Means of communication
the subway, surface lines, and
railways is another subject of instruction.
A dummy 'phone, telegraph   Method of presentation
blanks, the city directory, maps with   in this paragraph
routes of rapid transit lines, and the   changed for
telephone book, are some of the practical   variety
laboratory apparatus and textbooks

that are employed.

"We encourage them to learn for
themselves outside of school hours
many of the necessary things that we
have not time for in the classroom,"
says the teacher.

    8. Study outside of
       classroom

To reach the schoolroom in which
this work has been carried on, you take
the elevator to the last floor but one of
the factory building. There you find
only a portion of the floor space cleared
for tables and chairs. It is a clean,
airy room with big windows opening
on the street, made gay with boxes of
flowers.

IV. THE SCHOOLROOM
  1. Location
    Note effect of using
    "you"

Flags of many nations about the
room appropriately represent the many
nationalities among the pupils. On
one wall hangs a card with the legend:

  2. Decorations

    Note character of
    decorations selected

    Four things come not back:
      The spoken word
      The sped arrow
      The past life
      The neglected opportunity.

A photograph of Miss Jessie Wilson,
now Mrs. Francis B. Sayre, occupies
the space between the two windows.
The picture was presented to the girls
by Miss Wilson herself, just before she
enterprising
was married, when a party of them with
Miss Meyers went to Washington to
girls,
give her a white petticoat they had
made themselves, as a wedding present.
After Miss Wilson had shown them
through the White House and they had
seen her wedding presents, she gave
them this signed photograph.

    This shows

    spirit on the
    part of teacher,

    and firm

A piano and a phonograph at one
end of the room make it possible for
the girls to enjoy dancing during the
noon hours on three days of the week,
and to have musicals on other occasions.

  3. Furnishings

Shelves filled with books line the
walls of a smaller office room opening
off the schoolroom. On two days of
the week during the noon hour, the
teacher read aloud to the girls until
they were able to read for themselves.

  4. Library

Then they were permitted to take
books home with them. Besides this,
they have been encouraged to use the
public libraries, after being shown how
to make out applications for library
cards.

"One girl is reading 'The Promised
Land,' by Mary Antin," Miss Meyers
tells you, "and thinks it is a wonderful
book. She was so much interested in
it that I asked her to tell the others
about it. Although a little shy at
first, she soon forgot herself in her eagerness
to relate Miss Antin's experiences.
She told the story with such
dramatic effect that she quite carried
away her classmates. If we had done
no more than to teach this girl to read a
book that meant so much to her, I believe
our school would have justified
its existence."

Mary Antin herself accepted the
girls' invitation to attend the graduation
exercises, and made a short address.

The pupils' written work was exhibited
on the walls of the room on the occasion
of the exercises, and showed conclusively
the proficiency that they have
attained.

The greatest progress made by any
of the pupils was probably that of an
Italian girl. Before coming to this
country, she had attended school and
besides this she had been teaching her
father at night whatever she had
learned during the day. Her short
essay on her adopted country read:

> This country is the United States
> of America. It is the land of freedom
> and liberty, because the people
> govern themselves. All citizens love
> their country, because they know
> that this freedom was earned by men
> who gave their lives for it. The
> United States is in North America.
> North America is one of the greatest
> divisions of the earth. North America
> was discovered on October 12,
> 1492, by Christopher Columbus.

The fact that Columbus, one of her
countrymen, had discovered the country

Concrete example
has "human interest,"
as related in
the teacher's own
words

Is this paragraph
out of logical order?

V. RESULTS SHOWN BY
   PUPILS' WORK

1. Italian's theme and
   progress

   Example of greatest
   progress is put
   first

   Note use of narrow
   measure without
   quotation marks for
   examples quoted

Is this comment by
the writer effective?

in which she and her father had
found a new life, doubtless appealed to
her keen imagination.

That a Russian girl appreciated the
lessons she had received in the value of
opening a dime-savings account, is indicated
by this composition:

I must save money out of my earnings
to put in the bank. I know that
money is safe in the bank.

To deposit means to put money in
the bank.

Cashing a cheque means changing
a cheque for money.

How practical lessons in personal hygiene
may be emphasized in connection
with the teaching of composition was
illustrated in an essay of a Polish girl
written under a picture of a woman
combing her hair:

   She wished to comb her hair.
   She takes the comb in her hand.
   She combs her hair.
   She wishes to brush her hair.
   She takes the brush in her hand.
   She brushes her hair.
   She combs and brushes her hair
     every morning.
   She washes her hair often with
     soap and water.

The pathetic eagerness of one woman
of forty to learn to read and write was
told by Miss Meyers in connection with
one of the pieces of work exhibited.

"She was an old woman; at least she
seems to me to be over fifty, although
she gave her age as only forty," explained
the teacher. "She couldn't
read or even write her name. Despite
her age, she begged for a long time to
be permitted to enter the school, but
there were so many young girls who desired
to learn that they were given the
preference. She pleaded so hard that
finally I asked to have her admitted on
trial."

"It was hard work to teach her,"
continued Miss Meyers as she pointed

2. Russian's essay on
saving

3. Polish girl's essay

4. Woman of forty
and her work

"Human interest"
appeal heightened
by quoting teacher
verbatim

Progress in penmanship
could not be

to some of the woman's writing. The
first attempts were large, irregular
letters that sprawled over the sheet
like the work of a child when it begins
to write. After twenty weeks of struggle,
her work took on a form that, although
still crude, was creditable for
one who had never written until she
was over forty. "Her joy at her success
was great enough to repay me
many times over for my efforts to teach
her," remarked Miss Meyers.

The exact cost to the firm of conducting
the school, including the wages
paid for the time spent by the girls in
the classroom, has been itemized by
Mr. Sicher for the year just closed, as
follows:

Floor space	$175.00
Rent, light, and heat	105.00
Janitor	357.00
Wages at 17¢ an hr., 40 girls	375.00

Total cost, 40 girls	$672.00
Total cost per girl	16.80

The Board of Education, for its part
of the school, paid out $560 for the
teacher's salary and for supplies. This
was an expense of $14.80 for each pupil.

The entire cost for educating each
one of the forty girl workers, therefore,
was only $31.60.

That this money has been well spent
is the opinion of the employer, for the
school work increases the efficiency in
the factory sufficiently to make up for
the time taken out of working hours.

"I would rather have these girls in
statement
my employ whom I can afford to pay
from ten to twenty dollars a week,"
declares Mr. Sicher, "than many more
whom I have to pay low wages simply
because they aren't worth higher ones.
From a business point of view, it saves
space and space is money."

That the result has been what the
firm had anticipated in establishing
the school is shown by the following

shown by quoting
exercise

VI. COST OF SCHOOL
   1. Expense to firm

      Short table of figures
      is comprehensible
      and not uninteresting

   2. Cost to Board of
      Education

   3. Entire cost per pupil

   4. Returns outweigh
      cost

      Head of firm's

      given to convince
      readers

VII. SUMMARY CONCLUSION

   1. Results quoted from

statement which was made on the commencement
program: "It is the present
belief of the firm that the workers
who have been thus trained have
gained from 20 to 70 per cent in efficiency."

How much the girls themselves have
gained more vital to them even than
efficiency was very evident to everyone
who looked into their faces as they received
the certificates that recognize
them as "Literate American Citizens."

program

Note appeal of
"efficiency" to
practical readers

2. Impression given
by girls
Note patriotic appeal
in closing
phrase, which was
a happy choice.

ANOTHER ARTICLE ON THE SAME SUBJECT. This commencement at the factory
school furnished another writer, Nixola Greeley Smith, with material for
a special feature story which was sent out by a syndicate, the Newspaper
Enterprise Association, for publication in several hundred newspapers.
Her story contains only 375 words and is thus less than one fifth the
length of the other article. The author centers the interest in one of
the pupils, and shows the value of the school in terms of this girl's
experience. The girl's own account of what the school has meant to her
makes a strong "human interest" appeal. By thus developing one concrete
example effectively, the author is able to arouse more interest in the
results of the school than she would have done if in the same space she
had attempted to give a greater number of facts about it. Unlike the
longer article, her story probably would not suggest to the reader the
possibility of undertaking a similar enterprise, because it does not
give enough details about the organization and methods of the school to
show how the idea could be applied elsewhere.

The beginning of the shorter story was doubtless suggested by the
presence at the exercises of Mary Antin, the author of "The Promised
Land," who addressed the girls. The first sentence of it piques our
curiosity to know how "the promised land" has kept its promise, and the
story proceeds to tell us. The article, with an analysis of its main
points, follows:

WONDERFUL AMERICA! THINKS LITTLE AUSTRIAN
WHO GRADUATES FROM FACTORY SCHOOL

"The promised land" has kept its
promise to Rebecca Meyer!

Eight months ago an illiterate Austrian
immigrant girl, unable to speak or
write English, went to work in a New
York garment factory.

To-day, speaking and writing fluently
the language of her adopted country,
proficient in other studies, she
proudly cherishes the first "certificate
of literacy" issued by a factory--a
factory which has paid her for going to
school during working hours!

It was Rebecca Meyer who received

I. STORY OF REBECCA
MEYER

1. Striking statement
beginning
Note effective use of
device of contrast

Second and third
paragraphs show
striking results in
one concrete case.

2. Commencement

this first certificate, at the graduation
exercises held on the top floor of the
big women's wear factory of D.E.
Sicher & Co. It was Rebecca Meyer
who delivered the address of welcome
to the members of the board of education,
the members of the firm, her fellow
employees, and all the others gathered
at these exercises--the first of
their kind ever held in any commercial
establishment, anywhere!

Note that Rebecca
is the central figure

Dash used to set off
unique element

"Isn't it wonderful!" she said.
"When I came from Austria, I hoped
to find work. That was all. How I
should learn to speak the English language,
I did not know. It might take
me years, I thought. That I should go
to school every day, while I worked--who
could dream of such a thing? It
could not be in any other country except
America."

3. Rebecca's statement
   Slightly unidiomatic
   English is suggestive

Dudley E. Sicher, head of the firm,
in whose workrooms a regularly organized
class of the New York public
schools has held its sessions all winter,
firm
stood smiling in the background. Mr.
Sicher is president of the Cotton Goods
Manufacturers' Association. It was
he who conceived the idea, about a
year ago, of increasing the efficiency
of his women employees by giving them
an education free of cost, during working
hours.

II. STORY OF THE SCHOOL
   1. Origin of school
      Note method of
      introducing head of

"One of the first and most noticeable
results of the factory school has
been a marked decrease in the friction
and the waste of time caused by the
inability of employees to comprehend
directions. A girl who understands
English, and has been enabled thereby
to school herself in factory methods
and conditions, doesn't hesitate and
blunder; she understands, and does.
And what then? Why, higher pay."

2. Results of school
   Statement of head
   of firm

No wonder Rebecca Meyer is grateful
for the 45 minutes a day in which
button-sewing has given place to study--no
wonder she thinks America must
be the wonderland of all the world!

III. CONCLUSION
   Rebecca again made
   the central figure
   Appeal to reader's
   pride in his country.

ARTICLES COMPOSED OF UNITS. The study of the two special feature stories
on the factory school shows how articles of this type are built up out

of a number of units, such as examples, incidents, and statistics. A
similar study of the other types of articles exemplified in Chapter V
will show that they also are made up of various kinds of units. Again,
if we turn to the types of beginnings illustrated in Chapter VII, we
shall find that they, too, are units, which in some cases might have
been used in the body of the article instead of as an introduction.
Since, then, every division of a subject may be regarded as a unit that
is complete in itself whatever its position in the article, each of the
several kinds of units may be studied separately. For this purpose we
may discuss five common types of units: (1) examples, (2) incidents, (3)
statistics, (4) scientific and technical processes, and (5) recipes and
directions.

METHODS OF DEVELOPING UNITS. In order to present these units most
effectively, and to vary the form of presentation when occasion demands,
a writer needs to be familiar with the different methods of developing
each one of these types. Four common methods of handling material
within these units are: (1) exposition, narration, or description in
the writer's own words; (2) dialogue; (3) the interview; (4) direct or
indirect quotation. Statistics and recipes may also be given in tabular
form.

When a unit may be developed with equal effectiveness by any one of
several methods, a writer should choose the one that gives variety to
his article. If, for example, the units just before and after the one
under consideration are to be in direct quotation, he should avoid any
form that involves quoted matter.

   EXAMPLES. In all types of articles the concrete example is the
   commonest and most natural means of explaining a general idea. To
   most readers, for instance, the legal provisions of an old age
   pension law would be neither comprehensible nor interesting, but a
   story showing how a particular old man had been benefited by the law
   would appeal to practically every one. That is, to explain the
   operation and advantages of such a law, we give, as one unit, the
   concrete example of this old man. Actual examples are preferable to
   hypothetical ones, but the latter may occasionally be used when real
   cases are not available. Imaginary instances may be introduced by
   such phrases as, "If, for example," or "Suppose, for instance,
   that."

   To explain why companies that insure persons against loss of their
   jewelry are compelled to investigate carefully every claim filed
   with them, a writer in the _Buffalo News_ gave several cases in
   which individuals supposed that they were entitled to payment for
   losses although subsequent investigation showed that they had not
   actually sustained any loss. One of these cases, that given below,
   he decided to relate in his own words, without conversation or
   quotation, although he might have quoted part of the affidavit, or
   might have given the dialogue between the detective and the woman
   who had lost the pin. No doubt he regarded the facts themselves,
   together with the suspense as to the outcome of the search, as
   sufficiently interesting to render unnecessary any other device for
   creating interest.

   Another woman of equal wealth and equally undoubted honesty lost a
   horseshoe diamond pin. She and her maid looked everywhere, as they

thought, but failed to find it. So she made her "proof of loss" in affidavit form and asked the surety company with which she carried the policy on all her jewelry to replace the article.

She said in her affidavit that she had worn the pin in a restaurant a few nights before and had lost it that night, either in the restaurant or on her way there or back. The restaurant management had searched for it, the restaurant help had been questioned closely, the automobile used that night had been gone over carefully, and the woman's home had been ransacked. Particular attention had been given to the gown worn by the woman on that occasion; every inch of it had been examined with the idea that the pin, falling from its proper place, had caught in the folds.

The surety company assigned one of its detectives to look for the pin. From surface indications the loss had the appearance of a theft--an "inside job." The company, however, asked that its detective be allowed to search the woman's house itself. The request was granted readily. The detective then inquired for the various gowns which the woman had worn for dress occasions within the preceding several weeks.

This line of investigation the owner of the pin considered a waste of time, since she remembered distinctly wearing the pin to the restaurant on that particular night, and her husband also remembered seeing it that night and put his memory in affidavit form. But the detective persisted and with the help of a maid examined carefully those other gowns.

In the ruffle at the bottom of one of them, worn for the last time at least a week before the visit to the restaurant, she found the pin. The woman and her husband simply had been mistaken--honestly mistaken. She hadn't worn the pin to the restaurant, and her husband hadn't seen it that night. The error was unintentional, but it came very near costing the surety company a large sum of money.

The benefits of a newly established clinic for animals were demonstrated in a special feature article in the _New York Times_ by the selection of several animal patients as typical cases. Probably the one given below did not seem to the writer to be sufficiently striking if only the bare facts were given, and so he undertook to create sympathy by describing the poor, whimpering little dog and the distress of the two young women. By arousing the sympathies of the readers, he was better able to impress them with the benefits of the clinic.

The other day Daisy, a little fox terrier, was one of the patients. She was a pretty little thing, three months old, with a silky coat and big, pathetic eyes. She was escorted to the clinic by two hatless young women, in shawls, and three children. The children waited outside in the reception room, standing in a line, grinning self-consciously, while the women followed Daisy into the examination room. There she was gently muzzled with a piece of bandage, and the doctor examined her. There was something the matter with one hind leg, and the poor little animal whimpered pitifully, as dogs do, while the doctor searched for a broken bone. It was too

much for one of the women. She left the room, and, standing outside
the door, put her fingers in her ears, while the tears rolled down
her cheeks.

"Well, I wouldn't cry for a dog," said a workman, putting in some
S.P.C.A. receiving boxes, with a grin, while the three children--and
children are always more or less little savages--grinned
sympathetically. But it was a very real sorrow for Daisy's mistress.

There was no reason for alarm; it was only a sprain, caused by her
mistress' catching the animal by the leg when she was giving her a
bath. Her friends were told to take her home, bathe the leg with
warm water, and keep her as quiet as possible. Her mistress, still
with a troubled face, wrapped her carefully in the black shawl she
was wearing, so that only the puppy's little white head and big,
soft eyes peeped out, and the small procession moved away.

In a special feature story designed to show how much more intelligently
the first woman judge in this country could deal with cases of
delinquent girls in the juvenile court than could the ordinary police
court judge, a writer selected several cases that she had disposed of in
her characteristic way. The first case, which follows, he decided could
best be reported _verbatim_, as by that method he could show most
clearly the kindly attitude of the judge in dealing with even the least
appreciative of girls.

The first case brought in the other day was that of a girl of 16,
who hated her home and persisted in running away, sometimes to a
married sister, and sometimes to a friend. She was accompanied by
her mother and older sister, both with determined lower jaws and
faces as hard as flint. She swaggered into the room in an impudent
way to conceal the fact that her bravado was leaving her.

"Ella," said Miss Bartelme, looking up from her desk, "why didn't
you tell me the truth when you came in here the other day? You did
not tell me where you had been. Don't you understand that it is much
easier for me to help you if you speak the truth right away?"

Ella hung her head and said nothing. The older sister scowled at the
girl and muttered something to the mother.

"No," refused the mother, on being questioned. "We don't want
nothing more to do with her."

"Humph," snorted Ella, "you needn't think I want to come back. I
don't want nothing more to do with you, either."

Miss Bartelme often lets the family fight things out among
themselves; for in this way, far more than by definite questioning,
she learns the attitude of the girl and the family toward each
other, and indirectly arrives at most of the actual facts of the
case.

"How would you like to go into a good home where some one would love
you and care for you?" asked the judge.

"I don't want nobody to love me."

"Why, Ella, wouldn't you like to have a kind friend, somebody you could confide in and go walking with and who would be interested in you?"

"I don't want no friends. I just want to be left alone."

"Well, Ella," said the judge, patiently, ignoring her sullenness, "I think we shall send you back to Park Ridge for a while. But if you ever change your mind about wanting friends let us know, because we'll be here and shall feel the same way as we do now about it."

To explain to readers of the _Kansas City Star_ how a bloodhound runs down a criminal, a special feature writer asked them to imagine that a crime had been committed at a particular corner in that city and that a bloodhound had been brought to track the criminal; then he told them what would happen if the crime were committed, first, when the streets were deserted, or second, when they were crowded. In other words, he gave two imaginary instances to illustrate the manner in which bloodhounds are able to follow a trail. Obviously these two hypothetical cases are sufficiently plausible and typical to explain the idea.

If a bloodhound is brought to the scene of the crime within a reasonable length of time after it has been committed, and the dog has been properly trained, he will unfailingly run down the criminal, provided, of course, that thousands of feet have not tramped over the ground.

If, for instance, a crime were committed at Twelfth and Walnut streets at 3 o'clock in the morning, when few persons are on the street, a well-trained bloodhound would take the trail of the criminal at daybreak and stick to it with a grim determination that appears to be uncanny, and he would follow the trail as swiftly as if the hunted man had left his shadow all along the route.

But let the crime be committed at noon when the section is alive with humanity and remain undiscovered until after dark, then the bloodhound is put at a disadvantage and his wonderful powers would fail him, no doubt.

INCIDENTS. Narrative articles, such as personal experience stories, confessions, and narratives in the third person, consist almost entirely of incidents. Dialogue and description are very frequently employed in relating incidents, even when the greater part of the incident is told in the writer's own words. The incidents given as examples of narrative beginnings on pages 135-37 are sufficient to illustrate the various methods of developing incidents as units.

STATISTICS. To make statistical facts comprehensible and interesting is usually a difficult problem for the inexperienced writer. Masses of figures generally mean very little to the average reader. Unless the significance of statistics can be quickly grasped, they are almost valueless as a means of explanation. One method of simplifying them is to translate them into terms with which the average reader is familiar. This may often be done by reducing large figures to smaller ones. Instead of saying, for example, that a press prints 36,000 newspapers an hour, we may say that it prints 10 papers a second, or 600 a minute. To most persons 36,000 papers an hour means little more than a large number, but 10 papers and one second are figures sufficiently small to be understood at a glance. Statistics sometimes appear less formidable if they are incorporated in an interview or in a conversation.

In undertaking to explain the advantages of a coöperative community store, a writer was confronted with the problem of handling a considerable number of figures. The first excerpt below shows how he managed to distribute them through several paragraphs, thus avoiding any awkward massing of figures. In order to present a number of comparative prices, he used the concrete case, given below, of an investigator making a series of purchases at the store.

(1)

Here's the way the manager of the community store started. He demonstrated to his neighbors by actual figures that they were paying anywhere from $2 to $8 a week more for their groceries and supplies than they needed to. This represented the middlemen's profits.

He then proposed that if a hundred families would pay him regularly 50 cents a week, he would undertake to supply them with garden truck, provisions and meats at wholesale prices. To clinch the demonstration he showed that an average family would save this 50-cent weekly fee in a few days' purchases.

*   *   *   *   *

There is no difference in appearance between the community store and any other provision store. There is no difference in the way you buy your food. The only difference is that you pay 50 cents a week on a certain day each week and buy food anywhere from 15 to 40 per cent less than at the commercial, non-coöperative retail stores.

(2)

The other day an investigator from the department of agriculture went to the Washington community store to make an experiment. He paid his 50-cent weekly membership fee and made some purchases. He bought a 10-cent carton of oatmeal for 8 cents; a 10-cent loaf of bread for 8 cents; one-half peck of string beans for 20 cents, instead of for 30 cents, the price in the non-coöperative stores; three pounds of veal for 58 cents instead of 80 cents; a half dozen oranges for 13 cents instead of the usual price of from 20 to 25 cents. His total purchases amounted to $1.32, and the estimated saving was 49 cents--within 1 cent of the entire weekly fee.

Since to the average newspaper reader it would not mean much to say that the cost of the public schools amounted to several hundred thousand dollars a year, a special feature writer calculated the relation of the school appropriation to the total municipal expenditure and then presented the results as fractions of a dollar, thus:

Of every dollar that each taxpayer in this city paid to the city treasurer last year, 45 cents was spent on the public schools. This means that nearly one-half of all the taxes were expended on giving boys and girls an education.

Of that same dollar only 8 cents went to maintain the police
department, 12 cents to keep up the fire department, and 13 cents
for general expenses of the city offices.

Out of the 45 cents used for school purposes, over one-half, or 24
cents, was paid as salaries to teachers and principals. Only 8 cents
went for operation, maintenance, and similar expenses.

How statistics may be effectively embodied in an interview is
demonstrated by the following excerpt from a special feature story on a
workmen's compensation law administered by a state industrial board:

Judge J.B. Vaughn, who is at the head of the board, estimates that
the system of settling compensation by means of a commission instead
of by the regular courts has saved the state $1,000,000 a year since
its inception in 1913. "Under the usual court proceedings," he says,
"each case of an injured workman versus his employer costs from $250
to $300. Under the workings of the industrial board the average cost
is no more than $20.

"In three and one-half years 8,000 cases have come before us. Nine
out of every ten have been adjusted by our eight picked
arbitrators, who tour the state, visiting promptly each scene of an
accident and adjusting the compensation as quickly as possible. The
tenth case, which requires a lengthier or more painstaking hearing,
is brought to the board.

"Seven million dollars has been in this time ordered to be paid to
injured men and their families. Of this no charge of any sort has
been entered against the workers or their beneficiaries. The costs
are taken care of by the state. Fully 90 per cent of all the cases
are settled within the board, which means that only 10 per cent are
carried further into the higher courts for settlement."

PROCESSES. To make scientific and technical processes sufficiently
simple to appeal to the layman, is another problem for the writer of
popular articles. A narrative-descriptive presentation that enables the
reader to visualize and follow the process, step by step, as though it
were taking place before his eyes, is usually the best means of making
it both understandable and interesting.

In a special feature story on methods of exterminating mosquitoes, a
writer in the _Detroit News_ undertook to trace the life history of a
mosquito. In order to popularize these scientific details, he describes
a "baby mosquito" in a concrete, informal manner, and, as he tells the
story of its life, suggests or points out specifically its likeness to a
human being.

The baby mosquito is a regular little water bug. You call him a
"wiggler" when you see him swimming about in a puddle. His head is
wide and flat and his eyes are set well out at the sides, while in
front of them he has a pair of cute little horns or feelers. While
the baby mosquito is brought up in the water, he is an air-breather
and comes to the top to breathe as do frogs and musk-rats and many
other water creatures of a higher order.

Like most babies the mosquito larva believes that his mission is to eat as much as he can and grow up very fast. This he does, and if the weather is warm and the food abundant, he soon outgrows his skin. He proceeds to grow a new skin underneath the old one, and when he finds himself protected, he bursts out of his old clothes and comes out in a spring suit. This molting process occurs several times within a week or two, but the last time he takes on another form. He is then called a pupa, and is in a strange transition period during which he does not eat. He now slowly takes on the form of a true mosquito within his pupal skin or shell.

After two or three days, or perhaps five or six, if conditions are not altogether favorable, he feels a great longing within him to rise to something higher. His tiny shell is floating upon the water with his now winged body closely packed within. The skin begins to split along the back and the true baby mosquito starts to work himself out. It is a strenuous task for him and consumes many minutes.

At last he appears and sits dazed and exhausted, floating on his old skin as on a little boat, and slowly working his new wings in the sunlight, as if to try them out before essaying flight. It is a moment of great peril. A passing ripple may swamp his tiny craft and shipwreck him to become the prey of any passing fish or vagrant frog. A swallow sweeping close to the water's surface may gobble him down. Some ruthless city employe may have flooded the surface of the pond with kerosene, the merest touch of which means death to a mosquito. Escaping all of the thousand and one accidents that may befall, he soon rises and hums away seeking whom he may devour.

A mechanical process, that of handling milk at a model dairy farm, was effectively presented by Constance D. Leupp in an article entitled, "The Fight for Clean Milk," printed in the _Outlook_. By leading "you," the reader, to the spot, as it were, by picturing in detail what "you" would see there, and then by following in story form the course of the milk from one place to another, she succeeded in making the process clear and interesting.

Here at five in the afternoon you may see long lines of sleek, well-groomed cows standing in their cement-floored, perfectly drained sheds. The walls and ceilings are spotless from constant applications of whitewash, ventilation is scientifically arranged, doors and windows are screened against the flies. Here the white-clad, smooth-shaven milkers do their work with scrubbed and manicured hands. You will note that all these men are studiously low-voiced and gentle in movement; for a cow, notwithstanding her outward placidity, is the most sensitive creature on earth, and there is an old superstition that if you speak roughly to your cow she will earn no money for you that day.

As each pail is filled it is carried directly into the milk-house; not into the bottling-room, for in that sterilized sanctum nobody except the bottler is admitted, but into the room above, where the pails are emptied into the strainer of a huge receptacle. From the base of this receptacle it flows over the radiator in the bottling-room, which reduces it at once to the required temperature,

thence into the mechanical bottler. The white-clad attendant places
a tray containing several dozen empty bottles underneath, presses a
lever, and, presto! they are full and not a drop spilled. He caps
the bottles with another twist of the lever, sprays the whole with a
hose, picks up the load and pushes it through the horizontal
dumb-waiter, where another attendant receives it in the
packing-room. The second man clamps a metal cover over the
pasteboard caps and packs the bottles in ice. Less than half an hour
is consumed in the milking of each cow, the straining, chilling,
bottling, and storing of her product.

PRACTICAL GUIDANCE UNITS. To give in an attractive form complete and
accurate directions for doing something in a certain way, is another
difficult problem for the inexperienced writer. For interest and
variety, conversation, interviews and other forms of direct quotation,
as well as informal narrative, may be employed.

Various practical methods of saving fuel in cooking were given by a
writer in _Successful Farming_, in what purported to be an account of a
meeting of a farm woman's club at which the problem was discussed. By
the device of allowing the members of the club to relate their
experiences, she was able to offer a large number of suggestions. Two
units selected from different portions of the article illustrate this
method:

"I save dollars by cooking in my furnace," added a practical worker.
"Potatoes bake nicely when laid on the ledge, and beans, stews,
roasts, bread--in fact the whole food list--may be cooked there. But
one must be careful not to have too hot a fire. I burned several
things before I learned that even a few red coals in the fire-pot
will be sufficient for practically everything. And then it does
blacken the pans! But I've solved that difficulty by bending a piece
of tin and setting it between the fire and the cooking vessel. This
prevents burning, too, if the fire should be hot. Another plan is
to set the vessel in an old preserving kettle. If this outer kettle
does not leak, it may be filled with water, which not only aids in
the cooking process but also prevents burning. For broiling or
toasting, a large corn popper is just the thing."

     *   *   *   *   *

"My chief saving," confided the member who believes in preparedness,
"consists in cooking things in quantities, especially the things
that require long cooking, like baked beans or soup. I never think
of cooking less than two days' supply of beans, and as for soup,
that is made up in quantity sufficient to last a week. If I have no
ice, reheating it each day during warm weather prevents spoiling.
Most vegetables are not harmed by a second cooking, and, besides the
saving in fuel it entails, it's mighty comforting to know that you
have your dinner already prepared for the next day, or several days
before for that matter. In cold weather, or if you have ice, it will
not be necessary to introduce monotony into your meals in order to
save fuel, for one can wait a day or two before serving the extra
quantity. Sauces, either for vegetables, meats or puddings, may just
as well be made for more than one occasion, altho if milk is used in
their preparation, care must be taken that they are kept perfectly
cold, as ptomaines develop rapidly in such foods. Other things that

it pays to cook in large portions are chocolate syrup for making cocoa, caramel for flavoring, and apple sauce."

By using a conversation between a hostess and her guest, another writer in the same farm journal succeeded in giving in a novel way some directions for preparing celery.

"Your escalloped corn is delicious. Where did you get your recipe?"

Mrs. Field smiled across the dining table at her guest. "Out of my head, I suppose, for I never saw it in print. I just followed the regulation method of a layer of corn, then seasoning, and repeat, only I cut into small pieces a stalk or two of celery with each layer of corn."

"Celery and corn--a new combination, but it's a good one. I'm so glad to learn of it; but isn't it tedious to cut the celery into such small bits?"

"Not at all, with my kitchen scissors. I just slash the stalk into several lengthwise strips, then cut them crosswise all at once into very small pieces."

"You always have such helpful ideas about new and easy ways to do your work. And economical, too. Why, celery for a dish like this could be the outer stalks or pieces too small to be used fresh on the table."

"That's the idea, exactly. I use such celery in soups and stews of all kinds; it adds such a delicious flavor. It is especially good in poultry stuffings and meat loaf. Then there is creamed celery, of course, to which I sometimes add a half cup of almonds for variety. And I use it in salads, too. Not a bit of celery is wasted around here. Even the leaves may be dried out in the oven, and crumbled up to flavor soups or other dishes."

"That's fine! Celery is so high this season, and much of it is not quite nice enough for the table, unless cooked."

A number of new uses for adhesive plaster were suggested by a writer in the _New York Tribune_, who, in the excerpt below, employs effectively the device of the direct appeal to the reader.

Aside from surgical "First Aid" and the countless uses to which this useful material may be put, there are a great number of household uses for adhesive plaster.

If your pumps are too large and slip at the heel, just put a strip across the back and they will stay in place nicely. When your rubbers begin to break repair them on the inside with plaster cut to fit. If the children lose their rubbers at school, write their names with black ink on strips of the clinging material and put these strips inside the top of the rubber at the back.

In the same way labels can be made for bottles and cans. They are easy to put on and to take off. If the garden hose, the rubber tube of your bath spray, or your hot water bag shows a crack or a small break, mend it with adhesive.

A cracked handle of a broom, carpet sweeper, or umbrella can be repaired with this first aid to the injured. In the same way the handles of golf sticks, baseball bats, flagstaffs and whips may be given a new lease on life.

If your sheet music is torn or the window shade needs repairing, or there is a cracked pane of glass in the barn or in a rear window, apply a strip or patch of suitable size.

In an article in the _Philadelphia Ledger_ on "What Can I Do to Earn Money?" Mary Hamilton Talbot gave several examples of methods of earning money, in one of which she incorporated practical directions, thus:

A resourceful girl who loved to be out-of-doors found her opportunity in a bed of mint and aromatic herbs. She sends bunches of the mint neatly prepared to various hotels and cafés several times a week by parcel post, but it is in the over-supply that she works out best her original ideas. Among the novelties she makes is a candied mint that sells quickly. Here is her formula: Cut bits of mint, leaving three or four small leaves on the branch; wash well; dry and lay in rows on a broad, level surface. Thoroughly dissolve one pound of loaf sugar, boil until it threads and set from the fire. While it is still at the boiling point plunge in the bits of mint singly with great care. Remove them from the fondant with a fork and straighten the leaves neatly with a hatpin or like instrument. If a second plunging is necessary, allow the first coating to become thoroughly crystalized before dipping them again. Lay the sweets on oiled paper until thoroughly dry. With careful handling these mints will preserve their natural aroma, taste, and shape, and will keep for any length of time if sealed from the air. They show to best advantage in glass. The sweet-smelling herbs of this girl's garden she dries and sells to the fancy goods trade, and they are used for filling cushions, pillows, and perfume bags. The seasoning herbs she dries, pulverizes, and puts in small glasses, nicely labeled, which sell for 10 cents each, and reliable grocers are glad to have them for their fastidious customers.

CHAPTER VII

HOW TO BEGIN

IMPORTANCE OF THE BEGINNING. The value of a good beginning for a news story, a special feature article, or a short story results from the way in which most persons read newspapers and magazines. In glancing through current publications, the average reader is attracted chiefly by headlines or titles, illustrations, and authors' names. If any one of these interests him, he pauses a moment or two over the beginning "to see what it is all about." The first paragraphs usually determine whether or not he goes any further. A single copy of a newspaper or magazine offers so much reading matter that the casual reader, if disappointed in the introduction to one article or short story, has plenty of others to choose from. But if the opening sentences hold his attention, he reads on. "Well begun is half done" is a saying that applies with peculiar fitness to special feature articles.

STRUCTURE OF THE BEGINNING. To accomplish its purpose an introduction must be both a unit in itself and an integral part of the article. The beginning, whether a single paragraph in form, or a single paragraph in essence, although actually broken up into two or more short paragraphs, should produce on the mind of the reader a unified impression. The conversation, the incident, the example, or the summary of which it consists, should be complete in itself. Unless, on the other hand, the introduction is an organic part of the article, it fails of its purpose. The beginning must present some vital phase of the subject; it should not be merely something attractive attached to the article to catch the reader's notice. In his effort to make the beginning attractive, an inexperienced writer is inclined to linger over it until it becomes disproportionately long. Its length, however, should be proportionate to the importance of that phase of the subject which it presents. As a vital part of the article, the introduction must be so skillfully connected with what follows that a reader is not conscious of the transition. Close coherence between the beginning and the body of the article is essential.

The four faults, therefore, to be guarded against in writing the beginning are: (1) the inclusion of diverse details not carefully coordinated to produce a single unified impression; (2) the development of the introduction to a disproportionate length; (3) failure to make the beginning a vital part of the article itself; (4) lack of close connection or of skillful transition between the introduction and the body of the article.

TYPES OF BEGINNINGS. Because of the importance of the introduction, the writer should familiarize himself with the different kinds of beginnings, and should study them from the point of view of their suitability for various types of articles. The seven distinct types of beginnings are: (1) summary; (2) narrative; (3) description; (4) striking statement; (5) quotation; (6) question; (7) direct address. Combinations of two or more of these methods are not infrequent.

Summary Beginnings. The general adoption by newspapers of the summary beginning, or "lead," for news stories has accustomed the average reader to finding most of the essential facts of a piece of news grouped together in the first paragraph. The lead, by telling the reader the nature of the event, the persons and things concerned, the time, the place, the cause, and the result, answers his questions, What? Who? When? Where? Why? How? Not only are the important facts summarized in such a beginning, but the most striking detail is usually "played up" in the first group of words of the initial sentence where it catches the eye at once. Thus the reader is given both the main facts and the most significant feature of the subject. Unquestionably this news story lead, when skillfully worked out, has distinct advantages alike for the news report and for the special article.

SUMMARY BEGINNINGS

(1)

(_Kansas City Star_)

A FRESH AIR PALACE READY

A palace of sunshine, a glass house of fresh air, will be the
Christmas offering of Kansas City to the fight against tuberculosis,
the "Great White Plague." Ten miles from the business district of
the city, overlooking a horizon miles away over valley and hill,
stands the finest tuberculosis hospital in the United States. The
newly completed institution, although not the largest hospital of
the kind, is the best equipped and finest appointed. It is symbolic
of sunshine and pure air, the cure for the disease.

(2)

(_New York World_)

STOPPING THE COST OF LIVING LEAKS

BY MARIE COOLIDGE RASK

After ten weeks' instruction in domestic economy at a New York high
school, a girl of thirteen has been the means of reducing the
expenditure in a family of seven to the extent of five dollars a
week.

The girl is Anna Scheiring, American born, of Austrian ancestry,
living with her parents and brothers and sisters in a five-room
apartment at No. 769 East One Hundred and Fifty-eighth Street, where
her father, Joseph Scheiring is superintendent of the building.

The same economic practices applied by little Anna Scheiring are at
the present time being worked out in two thousand other New York
homes whose daughters are pupils in the Washington Irving High
School.

(3)

(_The Outlook_)

THE FIGHT FOR CLEAN MILK

BY CONSTANCE D. LEUPP

Two million quarts of milk are shipped into New York every day. One
hundred thousand of those who drink it are babies. The milk comes
from forty-four thousand dairy farms scattered through New York, New
Jersey, Connecticut, Massachusetts, Pennsylvania, Vermont, and even
Ohio.

A large proportion of the two million quarts travels thirty-six
hours before it lands on the front doorstep of the consumer. The

situation in New York is duplicated in a less acute degree in every city in the United States.

NARRATIVE BEGINNINGS. To begin a special feature article in the narrative form is to give it a story-like character that at once arouses interest. It is impossible in many instances to know from the introduction whether what follows is to be a short story or a special article. An element of suspense may even be injected into the narrative introduction to stimulate the reader's curiosity, and descriptive touches may be added to heighten the vividness.

If the whole article is in narrative form, as is the case in a personal experience or confession story, the introduction is only the first part of a continuous story, and as such gives the necessary information about the person involved.

Narrative beginnings that consist of concrete examples and specific instances are popular for expository articles. Sometimes several instances are related in the introduction before the writer proceeds to generalize from them. The advantage of this inductive method of explanation grows out of the fact that, after a general idea has been illustrated by an example or two, most persons can grasp it with much less effort and with much greater interest than when such exemplification follows the generalization.

Other narrative introductions consist of an anecdote, an incident, or an important event connected with the subject of the article.

Since conversation is an excellent means of enlivening a narrative, dialogue is often used in the introduction to special articles, whether for relating an incident, giving a specific instance, or beginning a personal experience story.

Narrative Beginnings

(1)

(_The Outlook_)

BOOKER T. WASHINGTON

BY EMMETT J. SCOTT AND LYMAN BEECHER STOWE

It came about that in the year 1880, in Macon County, Alabama, a certain ex-Confederate colonel conceived the idea that if he could secure the Negro vote he could beat his rival and win the seat he coveted in the State Legislature. Accordingly the colonel went to the leading Negro in the town of Tuskegee and asked him what he could do to secure the Negro vote, for Negroes then voted in Alabama without restriction. This man, Lewis Adams by name, himself an ex-slave, promptly replied that what his race most wanted was education, and what they most needed was industrial education, and that if he (the colonel) would agree to work for the passage of a bill appropriating money for the maintenance of an industrial school for Negroes, he, Adams, would help to get for him the Negro vote and the election. This bargain between an ex-slaveholder and an ex-slave was made and faithfully observed on both sides, with the result that the following year the Legislature of Alabama appropriated $2,000 a year for the establishment of a normal and industrial school for Negroes in the town of Tuskegee. On the recommendation of General Armstrong, of Hampton Institute, a young colored man, Booker T. Washington, a recent graduate of and teacher at the Institute, was called from there to take charge of this landless, buildingless, teacherless, and studentless institution of learning.

(2)

(_Leslie's Weekly_)

MILLIONAIRES MADE BY WAR

BY HOMER CROY

A tall, gaunt, barefooted Missouri hill-billy stood beside his rattly, dish-wheeled wagon waiting to see the mighty proprietor of the saw mill who guessed only too well that the hill-billy had something he wanted to swap for lumber.

"What can I do for you?"

The hillman shifted his weight uneasily. "I 'low I got somethun of powerful lot of interest to yuh." Reaching over the side of the wagon he placed his rough hand tenderly on a black lump. "I guess yuh know what it is."

The saw mill proprietor glanced at it depreciatingly and turned toward the mill.

"It's lead, pardner, pure lead, and I know where it come from. I could take you right to the spot--ef I wanted to."

The mill proprietor hooked a row of fingers under the rough stone and tried to lift it. But he could not budge it. "It does seem to have lead in it. What was you calc'lating askin' for showin' me where you found it?"

The farmer from the foothills cut his eyes down to crafty slits. "I was 'lowing just tother day as how a house pattern would come in handy. Ef you'll saw me out one I'll take you to the spot." And so the deal was consummated, the hill-billy gleefully driving away, joyous over having got a fine house pattern worth $40 for merely showing a fellow where you could pick up a few hunks of lead.

That was forty-five years ago and it was thus that the great Joplin lead and zinc district was made known to the world.

(3)

(_Munsey's Magazine_)

FRANK A. SCOTT, CHAIRMAN OF THE WAR INDUSTRIES BOARD

BY THEODORE TILLER

One day in the year 1885 a twelve-year-old boy, who had to leave
school and make his own way in the world on account of his father's
death, applied for a job in a railroad freight-office in Cleveland,
Ohio.

"I'm afraid you won't do," said the chief. "We need a boy, but
you're not tall enough to reach the letter-press."

"Well, couldn't I stand on a box?" suggested the young seeker of
employment.

That day a box was added to the equipment of the freight-office and
the name of Frank A. Scott to the payroll.

(4)

(_New York Times_)

NEW YORKER INVENTS NEW EXPLOSIVE AND GIVES IT TO THE UNITED STATES

Nine young men recently rowed to the middle of the Hudson River with
a wooden box to which wires were attached, lying in the bottom of
the boat. They sank the box in deep water very cautiously, and then
rowed slowly back to land, holding one end of the wire. Presently a
column of water 40 feet through and 300 feet high shot into the air,
followed by a deafening detonation, which tore dead branches from
trees.

The nine young men were congratulating one man of the group on the
explosion when an irate farmer ran up, yelling that every window in
his farmhouse, nearly a mile away, had been shattered. The party of
young men didn't apologize then; they gathered about the one who was
being congratulated and recongratulated him.

The farmer did not know until later that the force which broke his
windows and sent the huge column of water into the air was the War
Department's newest, safest, and most powerful explosive; that the
young men composed the dynamite squad of the Engineer Corps of the
New York National Guard; and that the man they were congratulating
was Lieut. Harold Chase Woodward, the inventor of the explosive.

(5)

(_System_)

WHY THE EMPLOYEES RUN OUR BUSINESS

A BUSINESS OF THE WORKERS, BY THE WORKERS, AND FOR THE WORKERS--HOW
IT SUCCEEDS.

BY EDWARD A. FILENE

"I know I am right. Leave it to any fair-minded person to decide."

"Good enough," I replied; "you name one, I will name another, and let them select a third."

She agreed; we selected the umpires and they decided against the store!

It had come about in this way. The store rule had been that cashiers paid for shortages in their accounts as--in our view--a penalty for carelessness; we did not care about the money. This girl had been short in an account; the amount had been deducted from her pay, and, not being afraid to speak out, she complained:

"If I am over in my accounts, it is a mistake; but if I am short, am I a thief? Why should I pay back the money? Why can't a mistake be made in either direction?"

This arbitration--although it had caused a decision against us--seemed such a satisfactory way of ending disputes that we continued the practice in an informal way. Out of it grew the present arbitration board, which is the corner-stone of the relation between our store and the employees, because it affords the machinery for getting what employees are above all else interested in--a square deal.

DESCRIPTIVE BEGINNINGS. Just as description of characters or of scene and setting is one method of beginning short stories and novels, so also it constitutes a form of introduction for an article. In both cases the aim is to create immediate interest by vivid portrayal of definite persons and places. The concrete word picture, like the concrete instance in a narrative beginning, makes a quick and strong appeal. An element of suspense or mystery may be introduced into the description, if a person, a place, or an object is described without being identified by name until the end of the portrayal.

The possibilities of description are not limited to sights alone; sounds, odors and other sense impressions, as well as emotions, may be described. Frequently several different impressions are combined. To stir the reader's feelings by a strong emotional description is obviously a good method of beginning.

A descriptive beginning, to be clear to the rapid reader, should be suggestive rather than detailed. The average person can easily visualize a picture that is sketched in a few suggestive words, whereas he is likely to be confused by a mass of details. Picture-making words and those imitative of sounds, as well as figures of speech, may be used to advantage in descriptive beginnings. For the description of feelings, words with a rich emotional connotation are important.

DESCRIPTIVE BEGINNINGS

(1)

(_Munsey's Magazine_)

OUR HIGHEST COURT

BY HORACE TOWNER

"The Honorable the Supreme Court of the United States!"

Nearly every week-day during the winter months, exactly at noon,
these warning words, intoned in a resonant and solemn voice, may be
heard by the visitor who chances to pass the doors of the Supreme
Court Chamber in the Capitol of the United States. The visitor sees
that others are entering those august portals, and so he, too, makes
bold to step softly inside.

If he has not waited too long, he finds himself within the chamber
in time to see nine justices of our highest court, clad in long,
black robes, file slowly into the room from an antechamber at the
left.

Every one within the room has arisen, and all stand respectfully at
attention while the justices take their places. Then the voice of
the court crier is heard again:

"_Oyez, oyez, oyez_! All persons having business with the Supreme
Court of the United States are admonished to draw near and give
their attention, for the court is now sitting."

Then, after a slight pause:

"God save the United States and this honorable court!"

The justices seat themselves; the attorneys at the bar and visitors
do likewise. The Supreme Court of the United States, generally held
to be the most powerful tribunal on earth, is in session.

(2)

(_Collier's Weekly_)

JAMES WHITCOMB BROUGHER, A PREACHER TO THE PROCESSION

BY PETER CLARK MACFARLANE

Imagine the Hippodrome--the largest playhouse of New York and of the
New World! Imagine it filled with people from foot-lights to the
last row in the topmost gallery--orchestra, dress circle, and
balconies--a huge uprising, semicircular bowl, lined with human
beings. Imagine it thus, and then strip the stage; take away the
Indians and the soldiers, the elephants and the camels; take away
the careening stage coaches and the thundering hoofs of horses, and
all the strange conglomeration of dramatic activities with which
these inventive stage managers are accustomed to panoply their
productions. Instead of all this, people the stage with a chorus

choir in white smocks, and in front of the choir put a lean,
upstanding, shock-headed preacher; but leave the audience--a regular
Hippodrome audience on the biggest Saturday night. Imagine all of
this, I say, and what you have is not the Hippodrome, not the
greatest play in the New World, nor any playhouse at all, but the
Temple Baptist Church of Los Angeles, California, with James
Whitcomb Brougher, D.D., in the pulpit.

(3)

(_The Independent_)

THE LITTLE RED SCHOOLHOUSE A "FAKE"

What the Country Schoolhouse Really Is, and Why

BY EDNA M. HILL

The schoolhouse squats dour and silent in its acre of weeds. A
little to the rear stand two wretched outbuildings. Upon its gray
clapboarded sides, window blinds hang loose and window sashes sag
away from their frames. Groaning upon one hinge the vestibule door
turns away from lopsided steps, while a broken drain pipe sways
perilously from the east corner of the roof.

Within and beyond the vestibule is the schoolroom, a monotony of
grimy walls and smoky ceiling. Cross lights from the six windows
shine upon rows of desks of varying sizes and in varying stages of
destruction. A kitchen table faces the door. Squarely in the middle
of the rough pine floor stands a jacketed stove. A much torn
dictionary and a dented water pail stand side by side on the shelf
below the one blackboard.

And this is the "little red schoolhouse" to which I looked forward
so eagerly during the summer--nothing but a tumbledown shack set in
the heart of a prosperous farming district.

(4)

(_New York Tribune_)

THE ONE WOMAN OFFICIAL AT PLATTSBURG

BY ELENE FOSTER

The tramp, tramp of feet on a hard road; long lines of khaki figures
moving over the browning grass of the parade ground; rows of faces,
keen and alert, with that look in the eyes that one sees in LePage's
Jeanne d'Arc; the click, click of bullets from the distant rifle
range blended with a chorus of deep voices near at hand singing
"Over There"; a clear, blue sky, crisp autumn air and the sparkling
waters of Lake Champlain--that's Plattsburg.

(5)

(_Good Housekeeping_)

NEW ENGLAND MILL SLAVES

BY MARY ALDEN HOPKINS

In the pale light of an early winter morning, while a flat, white
moon awaited the dawn and wind-driven clouds flung faint scudding
shadows across the snow, two little girls, cloaked, shawled, hooded
out of all recognition, plodded heavily along a Vermont mountain
road. Each carried a dangling dinner pail.

The road was lonely. Once they passed a farmhouse, asleep save for a
yellow light in a chamber. Somewhere a cock crowed. A dog barked in
the faint distance.

Where the road ascended the mountain--a narrow cut between dark,
pointed firs and swaying white-limbed birches--the way was slushy
with melting snow. The littler girl, half dozing along the
accustomed way, slipped and slid into puddles.

At the top of the mountain the two children shrank back into their
mufflers, before the sweep of the wet, chill wind; but the mill was
in sight--beyond the slope of bleak pastures outlined with stone
walls--sunk deep in the valley beside a rapid mountain stream, a dim
bulk already glimmering with points of light. Toward this the two
little workwomen slopped along on squashy feet.

They were spinners. One was fifteen. She had worked three years.
The other was fourteen. She had worked two years. The terse record
of the National Child Labor Committee lies before me, unsentimental,
bare of comment:

"They both get up at four fifteen A.M. and after breakfast start for
the mill, arriving there in time not to be late, at six. Their home
is two and one-half miles from the mill. Each earns three dollars a
week--So they cannot afford to ride. The road is rough, and it is
over the mountains."

(6)

(_Providence Journal_)

HOW TO SING THE NATIONAL SONGS

To Interpret the Text Successfully the Singer Must Memorize,
Visualize, Rhythmize, and Emphasize

BY JOHN G. ARCHER

The weary eye of the toastmaster looks apologetically down long rows of tables as he says with a sorry-but-it-must-be-done air, "We will now sing 'The Star Spangled Banner'"; the orchestra starts, the diners reach frantically for their menus and each, according to his musical inheritance and patriotic fervor, plunges into the unknown with a resolute determination to be in on the death of the sad rite.

Some are wrecked among the dizzy altitudes, others persevere through uncharted shoals, all make some kind of a noisy noise, and lo, it is accomplished; and intense relief sits enthroned on every dewy brow.

In the crowded church, the minister announces the "Battle Hymn of the Republic," and the organist, armed with plenary powers, crashes into the giddy old tune, dragging the congregation resistingly along at a hurdy gurdy pace till all semblance of text or meaning is irretrievably lost.

Happy are they when the refrain, "Glory, Glory, Hallelujah," provides a temporary respite from the shredded syllables and scrambled periods, and one may light, as it were, and catch up with himself and the organist.

At the close of an outdoor public meeting the chairman, with fatuous ineptitude, shouts that everybody will sing three verses of "America." Granting that the tune is pitched comfortably, the first verse marches with vigor and certitude, but not for long; dismay soon smites the crowd in sections as the individual consciousness backs and fills amid half learned lines.

The trick of catching hopefully at a neighbor's phrase usually serves to defeat itself, as it unmasks the ignorance of said neighbor, and the tune ends in a sort of polyglot mouthing which is not at all flattering to the denizens of an enlightened community.

These glimpses are not a whit over-drawn, and it is safe to say that they mirror practically every corner of our land to-day. Why is it, then, that the people make such a sorry exhibition of themselves when they attempt to sing the patriotic songs of our country? Is it the tunes or the words or we ourselves?

BEGINNING WITH A STRIKING STATEMENT. When the thought expressed in the first sentence of an article is sufficiently unusual, or is presented in a sufficiently striking form, it at once commands attention. By stimulating interest and curiosity, it leads the average person to read on until he is satisfied.

A striking statement of this sort may serve as the first sentence of one of the other types of beginning, such as the narrative or the descriptive introduction, the quotation, the question, or the direct address. But it may also be used entirely alone.

Since great size is impressive, a statement of the magnitude of something is usually striking. Numerical figures are often used in the opening sentences to produce the impression of enormous size. If these figures are so large that the mind cannot grasp them, it is well, by means of comparisons, to translate them into terms of the reader's own experience. There is always danger of overwhelming and confusing a person with statistics that in the mass mean little or nothing to him.

To declare in the first sentence that something is the first or the only one of its kind immediately arrests attention, because of the universal interest in the unique.

An unusual prediction is another form of striking statement. To be told at the beginning of an article of some remarkable thing that the future holds in store for him or for his descendants, fascinates the average person as much as does the fortune-teller's prophecy. There is danger of exaggeration, however, in making predictions. When writers magnify the importance of their subject by assuring us that what they are explaining will "revolutionize" our ideas and practices, we are inclined to discount these exaggerated and trite forms of prophecy.

A striking figure of speech--an unusual metaphor, for example--may often be used in the beginning of an article to arouse curiosity. As the comparison in a metaphor is implied rather than expressed, the points of likeness may not immediately be evident to the reader and thus the figurative statement piques his curiosity. A comparison in the form of a simile, or in that of a parable or allegory, may serve as a striking introduction.

A paradox, as a self-contradictory statement, arrests the attention in the initial sentence of an article. Although not always easy to frame, and hence not so often employed as it might be, a paradoxical expression is an excellent device for a writer to keep in mind when some phase of his theme lends itself to such a striking beginning.

Besides these readily classified forms of unusual statements, any novel, extraordinary expression that is not too bizarre may be employed. The chief danger to guard against is that of making sensational, exaggerated, or false statements, merely to catch the reader's notice.

STRIKING STATEMENT BEGINNINGS

(1)

(_Illustrated World_)

FIRE WRITES A HEART'S RECORD

BY H.G. HUNTING

A human heart, writing its own record with an actual finger of flame, is the startling spectacle that has recently been witnessed by scientists. It sounds fanciful, doesn't it? But it is literally a fact that the automatic recording of the heart's action by means of tracings from the point of a tiny blaze appears to have been made a practicable method of determining the condition of the heart, more reliable than any other test that can be applied.

(2)

(_Boston Transcript_)

TAKING HOSPITALS TO THE EMERGENCY By F.W. COBURN

Taking the hospital to the emergency instead of the emergency to the hospital is the underlying idea of the Bay State's newest medical unit--one which was installed in three hours on the top of Corey Hill, and which in much less than half that time may tomorrow or the next day be en route post haste for Peru, Plymouth, or Pawtucketville.

(3)

(_Kansas City Star_)

MUST YOUR HOME BURN?

Autumn is the season of burning homes.

Furnaces and stoves will soon be lighted. They have been unused all summer and rubbish may have been piled near them or the flues may have rusted and slipped out of place unobserved in the long period of disuse. Persons start their fires in a sudden cold snap. They don't take time to investigate. Then the fire department has work to do.

(4)

(_New York Times_)

ONLY PUBLIC SCHOOL FOR CHILDREN WITH POOR EYES

There was opened down Hester Street way last week the only public school in the world for children with defective eyes. Bad eyesight has been urged for years as a cause of backwardness and incorrigibility in school children. Now the public school authorities plan, for the first time, not only to teach children whose eyes are defective, but to cure them as well.

(5) (_The Outlook_)

DISEASED TEETH AND BAD HEALTH BY MATTHIAS NICOLL, JR.

The complete disappearance of teeth from the human mouth is the condition towards which the most highly cultivated classes of humanity are drifting. We have already gone far on a course that leads to the coming of a toothless age in future generations. Only by immediate adoption of the most active and widespread measures of prevention can the human tooth be saved from the fate that has befallen the leg of the whale.

(6)

(_Harper's Weekly_)

THE SPAN OF LIFE

BY WALTER E. WEYL

You who begin this sentence may not live to read its close. There is
a chance, one in three or four billions, that you will die in a
second, by the tick of the watch. The chair upon which you sit may
collapse, the car in which you ride may collide, your heart may
suddenly cease. Or you may survive the sentence and the article, and
live twenty, fifty, eighty years longer.

No one knows the span of your life, and yet the insurance man is
willing to bet upon it. What is life insurance but the bet of an
unknown number of yearly premiums against the payment of the
policy? * * * * The length of your individual life is a guess, but
the
insurance company bets on a sure thing, on the average death rate.

(7)

(_The Outlook_)

"AMERICANS FIRST"

BY GREGORY MASON

Every third man you meet in Detroit was born in a foreign country.
And three out of every four persons there were either born abroad or
born here of foreign-born parents. In short, in Detroit, only every
fourth person you meet was born in this country of American parents.
Such is the make-up of the town which has been called "the most
American city in the United States."

(8)

(_Kansas City Star_)

A KANSAS TOWN FEELS ITS OWN PULSE

Lawrence, Kas., was not ill. Most of its citizens did not even think
it was ailing, but there were some anxious souls who wondered if the
rosy exterior were not the mockery of an internal fever. They called
in physicians, and after seven months spent in making their
diagnosis, they have prescribed for Lawrence, and the town is
alarmed to the point of taking their medicine.

That is the medical way of saying that Lawrence has just completed
the most thorough municipal survey ever undertaken by a town of its

size, and in so doing has found out that it is afflicted with a lot of ills that all cities are heir to. Lawrence, however, with Kansas progressiveness, proposes to cure these ills.

Prof. F.W. Blackmar, head of the department of sociology at the University of Kansas, and incidentally a sort of city doctor, was the first "physician" consulted. He called his assistant, Prof. B.W. Burgess, and Rev. William A. Powell in consultation, and about one hundred and fifty club women were taken into the case. Then they got busy. That was April 1. This month they completed the examination, set up an exhibit to illustrate what they had to report, and read the prescription.

(9)

(_Popular Science Monthly_)

BREAKING THE CHAIN THAT BINDS US TO EARTH

BY CHARLES NEVERS HOLMES

Man is chained to this Earth, his planet home. His chain is invisible, but the ball is always to be seen--the Earth itself. The chain itself is apparently without weight, while the chain's ball weighs about 7,000,000,000,000,000,000,000 tons!

(10)

(_Associated Sunday Magazine_)

IN TUNE WHEN OUT OF TUNE

BY JOHN WARREN

How many persons who own pianos and play them can explain why a piano cannot be said to be in tune unless it is actually out of tune?

(11)

(_Railroad Man's Magazine_)

MAKING STEEL RAILS

BY CHARLES FREDERICK CARTER

To make steel rails, take 2 pounds of iron ore, 1 pound of coke, ½ pound of limestone, and 4½ pounds of air for each pound of iron to be produced. Mix and melt, cast in molds, and roll to shape while hot. Serve cold.

Rail-making certainly does seem to be easy when stated in its simplest terms; it also seems attractive from a business standpoint.

(12)

(_Leslie's Weekly_)

WHAT ELECTRICITY MEANS TO YOU

ONE CENT'S WORTH OF ELECTRICITY AT TEN CENTS PER KILOWATT-HOUR WILL
OPERATE:

    Sixteen candle-power Mazda lamp for five hours
    Six pound flatiron 15 minutes
    Radiant toaster long enough to produce ten slices of toast
    Sewing machine for two hours
    Fan 12 inches in diameter for two hours
    Percolator long enough to make five cups of coffee
    Heating pad from two to four hours
    Domestic buffer for 1¼ hours
    Chafing dish 12 minutes
    Radiant grill for 10 minutes
    Curling iron once a day for two weeks
    Luminous 500 watt radiator for 12 minutes

Hardly as old as a grown man, the electrical industry--including
railways, telephones and telegraphs--has already invested
$8,125,000,000 in the business of America. Its utility companies
alone pay Uncle Sam $200,000,000 every year for taxes--seven out of
every ten use it in some form every day. It is unmistakably the most
vital factor to-day in America's prosperity. Its resources are
boundless. As Secretary of the Interior Lane expresses it, there is
enough hydro-electric energy running to waste to equal the daily
labor of 1,800,000,000 men or 30 times our adult population.

BEGINNING WITH A QUOTATION. Words enclosed in quotation marks or set
off in some distinctive form such as verse, an advertisement, a letter,
a menu, or a sign, immediately catch the eye at the beginning of an
article. Every conceivable source may be drawn on for quotations,
provided, of course, that what is quoted has close connection with the
subject. If the quotation expresses an extraordinary idea, it possesses
an additional source of interest.

Verse quotations may be taken from a well-known poem, a popular song, a
nursery rhyme, or even doggerel verse. Sometimes a whole poem or song
prefaces an article. When the verse is printed in smaller type than the
article, it need not be enclosed in quotation marks. In his typewritten
manuscript a writer may indicate this difference in size of type by
single-spacing the lines of the quotation.

Prose quotations may be taken from a speech or an interview, or from
printed material such as a book, report, or bulletin. The more
significant the quoted statement, the more effective will be the
introduction. When the quotation consists of several sentences or of one
long sentence, it may comprise the first paragraph, to be followed in
the second paragraph by the necessary explanation.

Popular sayings, slogans, or current phrases are not always enclosed in quotation marks, but are often set off in a separate paragraph as a striking form of beginning.

The most conspicuous quotation beginnings are reproductions of newspaper clippings, advertisements, price lists, menus, telegrams, invitations, or parts of legal documents. These are not infrequently reproduced as nearly as possible in the original form and may be enclosed in a frame, or "box."

QUOTATION BEGINNINGS

(1)

(_New York Evening Post_)

"DIGNIFIED AND STATELY"

BEING AN ACCOUNT OF SOME HIGH AND LOW JINKS PRACTICED ABOUT THIS TIME ON COLLEGE CLASS DAYS

BY EVA ELISE VOM BAUR

  _Our sorrows are forgotten,
  And our cares are flown away,
  While we go marching through Princeton_.

Singing these words, 'round and 'round the campus they marched, drums beating time which no one observed, band clashing with band, in tune with nothing but the dominant note--the joy of reunion. A motley lot of men they are--sailors and traction engineers, Pierrots, soldiers, and even vestal virgins--for the June Commencement is college carnival time.

Then hundreds upon thousands of men, East, West, North and South, drop their work and their worries, and leaving families and creditors at home, slip away to their respective alma maters, "just to be boys again" for a day and a night or two.

(2)

(_Harper's Monthly_)

THE PARTY OF THE THIRD PART

BY WALTER E. WEYL

"The quarrel," opined Sir Lucius O'Trigger, "is a very pretty quarrel as it stands; we should only spoil it by trying to explain it."

Something like this was once the attitude of the swaggering youth of Britain and Ireland, who quarreled "genteelly" and fought out their bloody duels "in peace and quietness." Something like this, also, after the jump of a century, was the attitude of employers and

trade-unions all over the world toward industrial disputes. Words
were wasted breath; the time to strike or to lock out your employees
was when you were ready and your opponent was not. If you won, so
much the better; if you lost--at any rate, it was your own business.
Outsiders were not presumed to interfere. "Faith!" exclaimed Sir
Lucius, "that same interruption in affairs of this nature shows very
great ill-breeding."

(3)

(_McClure's Magazine_)

RIDING ON BUBBLES

BY WALDEMAR KAEMPFFERT

"And the Prince sped away with his princess in a magic chariot, the
wheels of which were four bubbles of air."

Suppose you had read that in an Andersen or a Grimm fairy tale in
the days when you firmly believed that Cinderella went to a ball in
a state coach which had once been a pumpkin; you would have accepted
the magic chariot and its four bubbles of air without question.

What a pity it is that we have lost the credulity and the wonder of
childhood! We have our automobiles--over two and a half million of
them--but they have ceased to be magic chariots to us. And as for
their tires, they are mere "shoes" and "tubes"--anything but the
bubbles of air that they are.

In the whole mechanism of modern transportation there is nothing so
paradoxical, nothing so daring in conception as these same bubbles
of air which we call tires.

(4)

(_Good Housekeeping_)

GERALDINE FARRAR'S ADVICE TO ASPIRING SINGERS

INTERVIEW BY JOHN CORBIN

"When did I first decide to be an opera singer?" Miss Farrar smiled.
"Let me see. At least as early as the age of eight. This is how I
remember. At school I used to get good marks in most of my studies,
but in arithmetic my mark was about sixty. That made me unhappy. But
once when I was eight, I distinctly remember, I reflected that it
didn't really matter because I was going to be an opera singer. How
long before that I had decided on my career I can't say."

(5)

(_The Delineator_)

HOW TO START A CAFETERIA

BY AGNES ATHOL

"If John could only get a satisfactory lunch for a reasonable amount
of money!" sighs the wife of John in every sizable city in the
United States, where work and home are far apart.

"He hates sandwiches, anyway, and has no suitable place to eat them;
and somehow he doesn't feel that he does good work on a cold box
lunch. But those clattery quick-lunch places which are all he has
time for, or can afford, don't have appetizing cooking or
surroundings, and all my forethought and planning over our good home
meals may be counteracted by his miserable lunch. I believe half the
explanation of the 'tired business man' lies in the kind of lunches
he eats."

Twenty-five cents a day is probably the outside limit of what the
great majority of men spend on their luncheons. Some cannot spend
over fifteen. What a man needs and so seldom gets for that sum is
good, wholesome, appetizing food, quickly served. He wants to eat in
a place which is quiet and not too bare and ugly. He wants to buy
real food and not table decorations. He is willing to dispense with
elaborate service and its accompanying tip, if he can get more food
of better quality.

The cafeteria lunch-room provides a solution for the mid-day lunch
problem and, when wisely located and well run, the answer to many a
competent woman or girl who is asking: "What shall I do to earn a
living?"

(6)

(_Newspaper Enterprise Association_)

AMERICANIZATION OF AMERICA IS PLANNED

BY E.C. RODGERS

Washington, D.C.--America Americanized!

That's the goal of the naturalization bureau of the United States
department of labor, as expressed by Raymond P. Crist, deputy
commissioner, in charge of the Americanization program.

(7)

(_Tractor and Gas Engine Review_)

FIRE INSURANCE THAT DOESN'T INSURE

BY A.B. BROWN

"This entire policy, unless otherwise provided by agreement endorsed
hereon, or added hereto, shall be void if the interest of the

insured be other than unconditional and sole ownership."

If any farmer anywhere in the United States will look up the fire insurance policy on his farm building, and will read it carefully, in nine cases out of ten, he will find tucked away somewhere therein a clause exactly like the one quoted above, or practically in the same words.

BEGINNING WITH A QUESTION. Every question is like a riddle; we are never satisfied until we know the answer. So a question put to us at the beginning of an article piques our curiosity, and we are not content until we find out how the writer answers it.

Instead of a single question, several may be asked in succession. These questions may deal with different phases of the subject or may repeat the first question in other words. It is frequently desirable to break up a long question into a number of short ones to enable the rapid reader to grasp the idea more easily. Greater prominence may be gained for each question by giving it a separate paragraph.

Rhetorical questions, although the equivalent of affirmative or negative statements, nevertheless retain enough of their interrogative effect to be used advantageously for the beginning of an article.

That the appeal may be brought home to each reader personally, the pronoun "you," or "yours," is often embodied in the question, and sometimes readers are addressed by some designation such as "Mr. Average Reader," "Mrs. Voter," "you, high school boys and girls."

The indirect question naturally lacks the force of the direct one, but it may be employed when a less striking form of beginning is desired. The direct question, "Do you know why the sky is blue?" loses much of its force when changed into the indirect form, "Few people know why the sky is blue"; still it possesses enough of the riddle element to stimulate thought. Several indirect questions may be included in the initial sentence of an article.

QUESTION BEGINNINGS

(1)

(_Kansas City Star_)

TRACING THE DROUTH TO ITS LAIR

What becomes of the rainfall in the plains states? This region is the veritable bread basket of our country; but in spite of the fact that we have an average rainfall of about thirty-six inches, lack of moisture, more frequently than any other condition, becomes a limiting factor in crop production. Measured in terms of wheat production, a 36-inch rainfall, if properly distributed through the growing season and utilized only by the crop growing land, is sufficient for the production of ninety bushels of wheat an acre. The question as to what becomes of the rainfall, therefore, is of considerable interest in this great agricultural center of North America, where we do well if we average twenty-five bushels to the acre.

(2)

(_New York Evening Sun_)

WE WASTE ONE-QUARTER OF OUR FOOD

If a family of five using twenty-five bushels of potatoes a year at
$2 a bushel, lose 20 per cent on a bushel by paring, how much has
the family thrown into the garbage can during the year? Answer, $10.
Applying this conservative estimate of dietitians to other foods,
the average family might save at least $100 a year on its table.

(3)

(_New York Times)_

FARM WIZARD ACHIEVES AGRICULTURAL WONDERS

BY ROBERT G. SKERRETT

Can a farm be operated like a factory? Can fickle nature be offset
and crops be brought to maturity upon schedule time?

These are questions that a farmer near Bridgeton, N.J., has answered
in the most practical manner imaginable.

(4)

(_San Francisco Call_)

DOES IT PAY THE STATE TO EDUCATE PRETTY GIRLS FOR TEACHERS?

BY KATHERINE ATKINSON

Does it pay the state to educate its teachers?

Do normal school and university graduates continue teaching long
enough to make adequate return for the money invested in their
training?

(5)

(_Newspaper Feature Service_)

HOW HUNGER IS NOW MEASURED AND PHOTOGRAPHED

Just what hunger is, why all living creatures suffer this feeling
and what the difference is between hunger and appetite have always
been three questions that puzzled scientists. Not until Dr. A.J.
Carlson devised a method of ascertaining exactly the nature of

hunger by measuring and comparing the degrees of this sensation, have investigators along this line of scientific research been able to reach any definite conclusion.

(6)

(_The Outlook_)

GROW OLD ALONG WITH ME

BY CHARLES HENRY LERRIGO

Are you interested in adding fifteen years to your life?

Perhaps you are one of those sound strong persons absolutely assured of perfect health.

Very well. Two thousand young persons, mostly men, average age thirty, employees of commercial houses and banks in New York City, were given a medical examination in a recent period of six months; 1,898 of them were positive of getting a perfect bill of health.

Here are the findings:

Sixty-three were absolutely sound.

The remaining 1,937 all suffered from some defect, great or small, which was capable of improvement.

(7)

(_Country Gentleman_)

SIMPLE ACCOUNTS FOR FARM BUSINESS

BY MORTON O. COOPER

Is your farm making money or losing it? What department is showing a profit? What one is piling up a loss? Do you know? Not one farmer in ten does know and it is all because not one in ten has any accounts apart from his bankbook so he can tell at the end of the year whether he has kept the farm or the farm has kept him.

(8)

(_The Outlook_)

AN ENFORCED VACATION

BY A CITY DWELLER

Have you, my amiable male reader, felt secretly annoyed when your friends--probably your wife and certainly your physician--have suggested that you cut your daily diet of Havanas in two, feeling

that your intimate acquaintance with yourself constituted you a
better judge of such matters than they? Have you felt that your
physician's advice to spend at least three-quarters of an hour at
lunch was good advice for somebody else, but that you had neither
time nor inclination for it? Have you felt that you would _like_ to
take a month's vacation, but with so many "irons in the fire" things
would go to smash if you did? Do you know what it is to lie awake at
night and plan your campaign for the following day? Then _you_ are
getting ready for an enforced vacation.

(9)

(_Leslie's Weekly_)

TAKING THE STARCH OUT OF THE MARCH

BY GERALD MYGATT

Don't most of us--that is, those of us who are unfamiliar with army
life and with things military in general--don't most of us picture
marching troops as swinging down a road in perfect step, left arms
moving in unison, rifles held smartly at the right shoulder, head
and eyes straight to the front (with never so much as a forehead
wrinkled to dislodge a mosquito or a fly), and with the band of the
fife-and-drum corps playing gaily at the head of the column? Of
course we do. Because that's the way we see them on parade.

A march is a far different thing. A march is simply the means of
getting so many men from one place to another in the quickest time
and in the best possible condition. And it may astonish one to be
told that marching is the principal occupation of troops in the
field--that it is one of the hardest things for troops to learn to
do properly, and that it is one of the chief causes of loss.

ADDRESSING THE READER DIRECTLY. A direct personal appeal makes a good
opening for an article. The writer seems to be talking to each reader
individually instead of merely writing for thousands. This form of
address may seem to hark back to the days of the "gentle reader," but
its appeal is perennial. To the pronoun "you" may be added the
designation of the particular class of readers addressed, such as "You,
mothers," or "You, Mr. Salaried Man." The imperative verb is perhaps the
strongest form of direct address. There is danger of overdoing the
"do-this-and-don't-do-that" style, particularly in articles of practical
guidance, but that need not deter a writer from using the imperative
beginning occasionally.

DIRECT ADDRESS BEGINNINGS

(1)

(_New York Times_)

SMALL CHANCE FOR DRAFT DODGERS IF DOCTORS KNOW THEIR BUSINESS

A word with you, Mr. Would-Be-Slacker. If you 're thinking of trying
to dodge the selective draft by pretending physical disability when

you get before the local exemption board, here's a bit of advice:
Don't. Since you are Mr. Would-Be-Slacker there is no use preaching
patriotism to you. But here is something that will influence you: If
you try to dodge the draft and are caught, there is a heavy penalty,
both fine and imprisonment; and you're almost sure to get caught.

(2)

(_American Magazine_)

THE GENERAL MANAGER OF COWBELL "HOLLER"

BY BRUCE BARTON

You would never in the world find Cowbell "Holler" alone, so I will
tell you how to get there. You come over the Big Hill pike until you
reach West Pinnacle. It was from the peak of West Pinnacle that
Daniel Boone first looked out over the blue grass region of
Kentucky. You follow the pike around the base of the Pinnacle, and
there you are, right in the heart of Cowbell "Holler," and only two
pastures and a creek away from Miss Adelia Fox's rural social
settlement--the first of its kind, so far as I know, in America.

(3)

(_Chicago Tribune_)

THE ROAD TO RETAIL SUCCESS

BY BENJAMIN H. JEFFERSON

You all know the retail druggist who has worked fifteen or sixteen
hours a day all his life, and now, as an old man, is forced to
discharge his only clerk. You all know the grocer who has changed
from one store to another and another, and who finally turns up as a
collector for your milkman. You all know the hard working milliner
and, perhaps, have followed her career until she was lost to sight
amid sickness and distress. You all have friends among stationers
and newsdealers. You have seen them labor day in and day out, from
early morning until late at night; and have observed with sorrow the
small fruits of their many years of toil.

Why did they fail?

(4)

(_Illustrated Sunday Magazine_)

THE MAN WHO PUT THE "PEP" IN PRINTING

Look at your watch.

How long is a second? Gone as you look at the tiny hand, isn't it?
Yet within that one second it is possible to print, cut, fold and
stack sixteen and two-thirds newspapers!

Watch the second hand make one revolution--a minute. Within that minute it is possible to print, cut, fold and stack in neat piles one thousand big newspapers! To do that is putting "pep" in printing, and Henry A. Wise Wood is the man who did it.

CHAPTER VIII

STYLE

STYLE DEFINED. Style, or the manner in which ideas and emotions are expressed, is as important in special feature writing as it is in any other kind of literary work. A writer may select an excellent subject, may formulate a definite purpose, and may choose the type of article best suited to his needs, but if he is unable to express his thoughts effectively, his article will be a failure. Style is not to be regarded as mere ornament added to ordinary forms of expression. It is not an incidental element, but rather the fundamental part of all literary composition, the means by which a writer transfers what is in his own mind to the minds of his readers. It is a vehicle for conveying ideas and emotions. The more easily, accurately, and completely the reader gets the author's thoughts and feelings, the better is the style.

The style of an article needs to be adapted both to the readers and to the subject. An article for a boys' magazine would be written in a style different from that of a story on the same subject intended for a Sunday newspaper. The style appropriate to an entertaining story on odd superstitions of business men would be unsuitable for a popular exposition of wireless telephony. In a word, the style of a special article demands as careful consideration as does its subject, purpose, and structure.

Since it may be assumed that any one who aspires to write for newspapers and magazines has a general knowledge of the principles of composition and of the elements and qualities of style, only such points of style as are important in special feature writing will be discussed in this chapter.

The elements of style are: (1) words, (2) figures of speech, (3) sentences, and (4) paragraphs. The kinds of words, figures, sentences, and paragraphs used, and the way in which they are combined, determine the style.

WORDS. In the choice of words for popular articles, three points are important: (1) only such words may be used as are familiar to the average person, (2) concrete terms make a much more definite impression than general ones, and (3) words that carry with them associated ideas and feelings are more effective than words that lack such intellectual and emotional connotation.

The rapid reader cannot stop to refer to the dictionary for words that he does not know. Although the special feature writer is limited to terms familiar to the average reader, he need not confine himself to commonplace, colloquial diction; most readers know the meaning of many more words than they themselves use in everyday conversation. In treating technical topics, it is often necessary to employ some unfamiliar terms, but these may readily be explained the first time they appear. Whenever the writer is in doubt as to whether or not his readers will understand a certain term, the safest course is to explain it or to substitute one that is sure to be understood.

Since most persons grasp concrete ideas more quickly than abstract ones, specific words should be given the preference in popular articles. To create concrete images must be the writer's constant aim. Instead of a general term like "walk," for example, he should select a specific, picture-making word such as hurry, dash, run, race, amble, stroll, stride, shuffle, shamble, limp, strut, stalk. For the word "horse" he may substitute a definite term like sorrel, bay, percheron, nag, charger, steed, broncho, or pony. In narrative and descriptive writing particularly, it is necessary to use words that make pictures and that reproduce sounds and other sense impressions. In the effort to make his diction specific, however, the writer must guard against bizarre effects and an excessive use of adjectives and adverbs. Verbs, quite as much as nouns, adjectives, and adverbs, produce clear, vivid images when skillfully handled.

Some words carry with them associated ideas and emotions, while others do not. The feelings and ideas thus associated with words constitute their emotional and intellectual connotation, as distinct from their logical meaning, or denotation. The word "home," for example, denotes simply one's place of residence, but it connotes all the thoughts and feelings associated with one's own house and family circle. Such a word is said to have a rich emotional connotation because it arouses strong feeling. It also has a rich intellectual connotation since it calls up many associated images. Words and phrases that are peculiar to the Bible or to the church service carry with them mental images and emotions connected with religious worship. In a personality sketch of a spiritual leader, for example, such words and phrases would be particularly effective to create the atmosphere with which such a man might very appropriately be invested. Since homely, colloquial expressions have entirely different associations, they would be entirely out of keeping with the tone of such a sketch, unless the religious leader were an unconventional revivalist. A single word with the wrong connotation may seriously affect the tone of a paragraph. On the other hand, words and phrases rich in appropriate suggestion heighten immeasurably the effectiveness of an article.

The value of concrete words is shown in the following paragraphs taken from a newspaper article describing a gas attack:

> There was a faint green vapor, which swayed and hung under the lee of the raised parapet two hundred yards away. It increased in volume, and at last rose high enough to be caught by the wind. It strayed out in tattered yellowish streamers toward the English lines, half dissipating itself in twenty yards, until the steady outpour of the green smoke gave it reinforcement and it made headway. Then, creeping forward from tuft to tuft, and preceded by an acrid and parching whiff, the curling and tumbling vapor reached the English lines in a wall twenty feet high.

As the grayish cloud drifted over the parapet, there was a stifled call from some dozen men who had carelessly let their protectors drop. The gas was terrible. A breath of it was like a wolf at the throat, like hot ashes in the windpipe.

The yellowish waves of gas became more greenish in color as fresh volumes poured out continually from the squat iron cylinders which had now been raised and placed outside the trenches by the Germans. The translucent flood flowed over the parapet, linking at once on the inner side and forming vague, gauzy pools and backwaters, in which men stood knee deep while the lighter gas was blown in their faces over the parapet.

FAULTS IN DICTION. Since newspaper reporters and correspondents are called upon day after day to write on similar events and to write at top speed, they are prone to use the same words over and over again, without making much of an effort to "find the one noun that best expresses the idea, the one verb needed to give it life, and the one adjective to qualify it." This tendency to use trite, general, "woolly" words instead of fresh, concrete ones is not infrequently seen in special feature stories written by newspaper workers. Every writer who aims to give to his articles some distinction in style should guard against the danger of writing what has aptly been termed "jargon." "To write jargon," says Sir Arthur Quiller-Couch in his book, "On the Art of Writing," "is to be perpetually shuffling around in the fog and cotton-wool of abstract terms. So long as you prefer abstract words, which express other men's summarized concepts of things, to concrete ones which lie as near as can be reached to things themselves and are the first-hand material for your thoughts, you will remain, at the best, writers at second-hand. If your language be jargon, your intellect, if not your whole character, will almost certainly correspond. Where your mind should go straight, it will dodge; the difficulties it should approach with a fair front and grip with a firm hand it will be seeking to evade or circumvent. For the style is the man, and where a man's treasure is there his heart, and his brain, and his writing, will be also."

FIGURES OF SPEECH. To most persons the term "figure of speech" suggests such figures as metonymy and synecdoche, which they once learned to define, but never thought of using voluntarily in their own writing. Figures of speech are too often regarded as ornaments suited only to poetry or poetical prose. With these popular notions in mind, a writer for newspapers and magazines may quite naturally conclude that figurative expressions have little or no practical value in his work. Figures of speech, however, are great aids, not only to clearness and conciseness, but to the vividness of an article. They assist the reader to grasp ideas quickly and they stimulate his imagination and his emotions.

Association of ideas is the principle underlying figurative expressions. By a figure of speech a writer shows his readers the relation between a new idea and one already familiar to them. An unfamiliar object, for example, is likened to a familiar one, directly, as in the simile, or by implication, as in the metaphor. As the object brought into relation with the new idea is more familiar and more concrete, the effect of the figure is to simplify the subject that is being explained, and to make it more easy of comprehension.

A figure of speech makes both for conciseness and for economy of mental effort on the part of the reader. To say in a personality sketch, for example, that the person looks "like Lincoln" is the simplest, most concise way of creating a mental picture. Or to describe a smoothly running electric motor as "purring," instantly makes the reader hear the sound. Scores of words may be saved, and clearer, more vivid impressions may be given, by the judicious use of figures of speech.

As the familiar, concrete objects introduced in figures frequently have associated emotions, figurative expressions often make an emotional appeal. Again, to say that a person looks "like Lincoln" not only creates a mental picture but awakes the feelings generally associated with Lincoln. The result is that readers are inclined to feel toward the person so described as they feel toward Lincoln.

Even in practical articles, figurative diction may not be amiss. In explaining a method of splitting old kitchen boilers in order to make watering troughs, a writer in a farm journal happily described a cold chisel as "turning out a narrow shaving of steel and rolling it away much as the mold-board of a plow turns the furrow."

The stimulating effect of a paragraph abounding in figurative expressions is well illustrated by the following passage taken from a newspaper personality sketch of a popular pulpit orator:

> His mind is all daylight. There are no subtle half-tones, or sensitive reserves, or significant shadows of silence, no landscape fading through purple mists to a romantic distance. All is clear, obvious, emphatic. There is little atmosphere and a lack of that humor that softens the contours of controversy. His thought is simple and direct and makes its appeal, not to culture, but to the primitive emotions. * * * * His strenuousness is a battle-cry to the crowd. He keeps his passion white hot; his body works like a windmill in a hurricane; his eyes flash lightnings; he seizes the enemy, as it were, by the throat, pommels him with breathless blows, and throws him aside a miserable wreck.

SENTENCES. For rapid reading the prime requisite of a good sentence is that its grammatical structure shall be evident; in other words, that the reader shall be able at a glance to see the relation of its parts. Involved sentences that require a second perusal before they yield their meaning, are clearly not adapted to the newspaper or magazine. Short sentences and those of medium length are, as a rule, more easily grasped than long ones, but for rapid reading the structure of the sentence, rather than its length, is the chief consideration. Absolute clearness is of paramount importance.

In hurried reading the eye is caught by the first group of words at the beginning of a sentence. These words make more of an impression on the reader's mind than do those in the middle or at the end of the sentence. In all journalistic writing, therefore, the position of greatest emphasis is the beginning. It is there that the most significant idea should be placed. Such an arrangement does not mean that the sentence need trail off loosely in a series of phrases and clauses. Firmness of structure can and should be maintained even though the strongest emphasis is at the beginning. In revising his article a writer often finds that he may greatly increase the effectiveness of his sentences by so rearranging the parts as to bring the important ideas close to the beginning.

LENGTH OF THE SENTENCE. Sentences may be classified according to length as (1) short, containing 15 words or less; (2) medium, from 15 to 30 words; and (3) long, 30 words or more. Each of these types of sentence has its own peculiar advantages.

The short sentence, because it is easily apprehended, is more emphatic than a longer one. Used in combination with medium and long sentences it gains prominence by contrast. It makes an emphatic beginning and a strong conclusion for a paragraph. As the last sentence of an article it is a good "snapper." In contrast with longer statements, it also serves as a convenient transition sentence.

The sentence of medium length lends itself readily to the expression of the average thought; but when used continuously it gives to the style a monotony of rhythm that soon becomes tiresome.

The long sentence is convenient for grouping details that are closely connected. In contrast with the rapid, emphatic short sentence, it moves slowly and deliberately, and so is well adapted to the expression of dignified and impressive thoughts.

To prevent monotony, variety of sentence length is desirable. Writers who unconsciously tend to use sentences of about the same length and of the same construction, need to beware of this uniformity.

The skillful use of single short sentences, of series of short sentences, of medium, and of long sentences, to give variety, to express thoughts effectively, and to produce harmony between the movement of the style and the ideas advanced, is well illustrated in the selection below. It is the beginning of a personality sketch of William II, the former German emperor, published in the London _Daily News_ before the world war, and written by Mr. A.G. Gardiner, the editor of that paper.

> When I think of the Kaiser I think of a bright May morning at Potsdam. It is the Spring Parade, and across from where we are gathered under the windows of the old palace the household troops are drawn up on the great parade ground, their helmets and banners and lances all astir in the jolly sunshine. Officers gallop hither and thither shouting commands. Regiments form and reform. Swords flash out and flash back again. A noble background of trees frames the gay picture with cool green foliage. There is a sudden stillness. The closely serried ranks are rigid and moveless. The shouts of command are silenced.
>
> "The Kaiser."
>
> He comes slowly up the parade ground on his white charger, helmet and eagle flashing in the sunshine, sitting his horse as if he lived in the saddle, his face turned to his men as he passes by.
>
> "Morgen, meine Kinder." His salutation rings out at intervals in the clear morning air. And back from the ranks in chorus comes the response: "Morgen, Majestät."

And as he rides on, master of a million men, the most powerful
figure in Europe, reviewing his troops on the peaceful parade ground
at Potsdam, one wonders whether the day will ever come when he will
ride down those ranks on another errand, and when that cheerful
response of the soldiers will have in it the ancient ring of
doom--"Te morituri salutamus."

For answer, let us look at this challenging figure on the white
charger. What is he? What has he done?

By the three short sentences in the first paragraph beginning "Officers
gallop," the author depicts the rapid movement of the soldiers. By the
next three short sentences in the same paragraph beginning, "There is a
sudden stillness," he produces an impression of suspense. To picture the
Kaiser coming up "slowly," he uses a long, leisurely sentence. The
salutations "ring out" in short, crisp sentences. The more serious,
impressive thought of the possibility of war finds fitting expression in
the long, 64-word sentence, ending with the sonorous--"ring of doom,"
"Te morituri salutamus."

The transition between the introduction and the body of the sketch is
accomplished by the last paragraph consisting of three short sentences,
in marked contrast with the climactic effect with which the description
closed.

PARAGRAPHS. The paragraph is a device that aids a writer to convey to
readers his thoughts combined in the same groups in which they are
arranged in his own mind. Since a small group of thoughts is more easily
grasped than a large one, paragraphs in journalistic writing are usually
considerably shorter than those of ordinary English prose. In the narrow
newspaper column, there is room for only five or six words to a line. A
paragraph of 250 words, which is the average length of the literary
paragraph, fills between forty and fifty lines of a newspaper column.
Such paragraphs seem heavy and uninviting. Moreover, the casual reader
cannot readily comprehend and combine the various thoughts in so large a
group of sentences. Although there is no standard column width for
magazines, the number of words in a line does not usually exceed eight.
A paragraph of 250 words that occupies 30 eight-word lines seems less
attractive than one of half that length. The normal paragraph in
journalistic writing seldom exceeds 100 words and not infrequently is
much shorter. As such a paragraph contains not more than four or five
sentences, the general reading public has little difficulty in
comprehending it.

The beginning of the paragraph, like the beginning of the sentence, is
the part that catches the eye. Significant ideas that need to be
impressed upon the mind of the reader belong at the beginning. If his
attention is arrested and held by the first group of words, he is likely
to read on. If the beginning does not attract him, he skips down the
column to the next paragraph, glancing merely at enough words in the
paragraph that he skips to "get the drift of it." An emphatic beginning
for a paragraph will insure attention for its contents.

REVISION. It is seldom that the first draft of an article cannot be
improved by a careful revision. In going over his work, word by word and
sentence by sentence, the writer will generally find many opportunities

to increase the effectiveness of the structure and the style. Such revision, moreover, need not destroy the ease and naturalness of expression.

To improve the diction of his article, the writer should eliminate (1) superfluous words, (2) trite phrases, (3) general, colorless words, (4) terms unfamiliar to the average reader, unless they are explained, (5) words with a connotation inappropriate to the context, (6) hackneyed and mixed metaphors. The effectiveness of the expression may often be strengthened by the addition of specific, picture-making, imitative, and connotative words, as well as of figures of speech that clarify the ideas and stimulate the imagination.

Sentences may frequently be improved (1) by making their grammatical structure more evident, (2) by breaking up long, loose sentences into shorter ones, (3) by using short sentences for emphasis, (4) by varying the sentence length, (5) by transferring important ideas to the beginning of the sentence.

Every paragraph should be tested to determine whether or not it is a unified, coherent group of thoughts, containing not more than 100 words, with important ideas effectively massed at the beginning.

Finally, revision should eliminate all errors in grammar, spelling, punctuation, and capitalization. Every minute spent in improving an article adds greatly to its chances of being accepted.

CHAPTER IX

TITLES AND HEADLINES

IMPORTANCE OF HEAD AND TITLE. Headlines or titles, illustrations, and names of authors are the three things that first catch the eye of the reader as he turns over the pages of a newspaper or magazine. When the writer's name is unknown to him, only the illustrations and the heading remain to attract his attention.

The "attention-getting" value of the headline is fully appreciated not only by newspaper and magazine editors but by writers of advertisements. Just as the striking heads on the front page of a newspaper increase its sales, so, also, attractive titles on the cover of a magazine lead people to buy it, and so, too, a good headline in an advertisement arouses interest in what the advertiser is trying to sell.

A good title adds greatly to the attractiveness of an article. In the first place, the title is the one thing that catches the eye of the editor or manuscript reader, as he glances over the copy, and if the title is good, he carries over this favorable impression to the first page or two of the article itself. To secure such favorable consideration for a manuscript among the hundreds that are examined in editorial offices, is no slight advantage. In the second place, what is true of the editor and the manuscript is equally true of the reader and the printed article. No writer can afford to neglect his titles.

VARIETY IN FORM AND STYLE. Because newspapers and magazines differ in the size and the "make-up" of their pages, there is considerable variety in the style of headlines and titles given to special feature articles. Some magazine sections of newspapers have the full-size page of the regular edition; others have pages only half as large. Some newspapers use large eight-column display heads on their special articles, while others confine their headlines for feature stories to a column or two. Some papers regularly employ sub-titles in their magazine sections, corresponding to the "lines," "banks," and "decks" in their news headlines. This variety in newspapers is matched by that in magazines. Despite these differences, however, there are a few general principles that apply to all kinds of titles and headlines for special feature articles.

CHARACTERISTICS OF A GOOD TITLE. To accomplish their purpose most effectively titles should be (1) attractive, (2) accurate, (3) concise, and (4) concrete.

The attractiveness of a title is measured by its power to arrest attention and to lead to a reading of the article. As a statement of the subject, the title makes essentially the same appeal that the subject itself does; that is, it may interest the reader because the idea it expresses has timeliness, novelty, elements of mystery or romance, human interest, relation to the reader's life and success, or connection with familiar or prominent persons or things. Not only the idea expressed, but the way in which it is expressed, may catch the eye. By a figurative, paradoxical, or interrogative form, the title may pique curiosity. By alliteration, balance, or rhyme, it may please the ear. It permits the reader to taste, in order to whet his appetite. It creates desires that only the article can satisfy.

In an effort to make his titles attractive, a writer must beware of sensationalism and exaggeration. The lurid news headline on the front page of sensational papers has its counterpart in the equally sensational title in the Sunday magazine section. All that has been said concerning unwholesome subject-matter for special feature stories applies to sensational titles. So, too, exaggerated, misleading headlines on news and advertisements are matched by exaggerated, misleading titles on special articles. To state more than the facts warrant, to promise more than can be given, to arouse expectations that cannot be satisfied--all are departures from truth and honesty.

Accuracy in titles involves, not merely avoidance of exaggerated and misleading statement, but complete harmony in tone and spirit between title and article. When the story is familiar and colloquial in style, the title should reflect that informality. When the article makes a serious appeal, the title should be dignified. A good title, in a word, is true to the spirit as well as to the letter.

Conciseness in titles is imposed on the writer by the physical limitations of type and page. Because the width of the column and of the page is fixed, and because type is not made of rubber, a headline must be built to fit the place it is to fill. Although in framing titles for articles it is not always necessary to conform to the strict requirements as to letters and spaces that limit the building of news headlines, it is nevertheless important to keep within bounds. A study of a large number of titles will show that they seldom contain more than three or four important words with the necessary connectives and particles. Short words, moreover, are preferred to long ones. By analyzing the titles in the publication to which he plans to send his article, a writer can frame his title to meet its typographical requirements.

The reader's limited power of rapid comprehension is another reason for brevity. A short title consisting of a small group of words yields its meaning at a glance. Unless the reader catches the idea in the title quickly, he is likely to pass on to something else. Here again short words have an advantage over long ones.

Concreteness in titles makes for rapid comprehension and interest. Clean-cut mental images are called up by specific words; vague ones usually result from general, abstract terms. Clear mental pictures are more interesting than vague impressions.

SUB-TITLES. Sub-titles are often used to supplement and amplify the titles. They are the counterparts of the "decks" and "banks" in news headlines. Their purpose is to give additional information, to arouse greater interest, and to assist in carrying the reader over, as it were, to the beginning of the article.

Since sub-titles follow immediately after the title, any repetition of important words is usually avoided. It is desirable to maintain the same tone in both title and sub-title. Occasionally the two together make a continuous statement. The length of the sub-title is generally about twice that of the title; that is, the average sub-title consists of from ten to twelve words, including articles and connectives. The articles, "a," "an," and "the," are not as consistently excluded from sub-titles as they are from newspaper headlines.

SOME TYPES OF TITLES. Attempts to classify all kinds of headlines and titles involve difficulties similar to those already encountered in the effort to classify all types of beginnings. Nevertheless, a separation of titles into fairly distinct, if not mutually exclusive, groups may prove helpful to inexperienced writers. The following are the nine most distinctive types of titles: (1) label; (2) "how" and "why" statement; (3) striking statement, including figure of speech, paradox, and expression of great magnitude; (4) quotation and paraphrase of quotation; (5) question; (6) direct address, particularly in imperative form; (7) alliteration; (8) rhyme; (9) balance.

The label title is a simple, direct statement of the subject. It has only as much interest and attractiveness as the subject itself possesses. Such titles are the following:

(1)
RAISING GUINEA PIGS FOR A LIVING
One Missouri Man Finds a Ready Market for All He Can Sell

(2)
HUMAN NATURE AS SEEN BY A PULLMAN PORTER

(3)
THE FINANCIAL SIDE OF FOOTBALL

(4)
CONFESSIONS OF AN UNDERGRADUATE

(5)
BEE-KEEPING ON SHARES

(6)
A COMMUNITY WOOD-CHOPPING DAY

(7)
WHAT A WOMAN ON THE FARM THINKS OF PRICE FIXING

The "how-to-do-something" article may be given a "how" title that
indicates the character of the contents; for example:

(1)
HOW I FOUND HEALTH IN THE DENTIST'S CHAIR

(2)
HOW TO STORE YOUR CAR IN WINTER

(3)
HOW A FARMER'S WIFE MADE $55 EXTRA

(4)
HOW TO SUCCEED AS A WRITER
Woman Who "Knew She Could Write" Tells How She Began and
Finally Got on the Right Road

The "how" title may also be used for an article that explains some
phenomenon or process. Examples of such titles are these:

(1)
HOW A NETTLE STINGS

(2)
HOW RIPE OLIVES ARE MADE

(3)
HOW THE FREIGHT CAR GETS HOME

Articles that undertake to give causes and reasons are appropriately
given "why" titles like the following:

(1)
WHY CAVIAR COSTS SO MUCH

(2)
WHY I LIKE A ROUND BARN

(3)
WHY THE COAL SUPPLY IS SHORT

A title may attract attention because of the striking character of the
idea it expresses; for example:

                          (1)
                WANTED: $50,000 MEN

                          (2)
            200 BUSHELS OF CORN PER ACRE

                          (3)
            FIRE WRITES A HEART'S RECORD

                          (4)
          THE PSYCHOLOGY OF SECOND HELPINGS

The paradoxical form of title piques curiosity by seeming to make a
self-contradictory statement, as, for example, the following:

                          (1)
                    SHIPS OF STONE
      Seaworthy Concrete Vessels an Accomplished Fact

                          (2)
                  CHRISTIAN PAGANS

                          (3)
            A TELESCOPE THAT POINTS DOWNWARD

                          (4)
                SEEING WITH YOUR EARS

                          (5)
              MAKING SAILORS WITHOUT SHIPS

                          (6)
            HOW TO BE AT HOME WHILE TRAVELING

                          (7)
              CANAL-BOATS THAT CLIMB HILLS

A striking figure of speech in a title stimulates the reader's
imagination and arouses his interest; for example:

                          (1)
                PULLING THE RIVER'S TEETH

                          (2)
              THE OLD HOUSE WITH TWO FACES

                          (3)
              THE HONEY-BEE SAVINGS BANK

                          (4)
                  RIDING ON BUBBLES

                          (5)
                THE ROMANCE OF NITROGEN

A familiar quotation may be used for the title and may stand alone, but
often a sub-title is desirable to show the application of the quotation

to the subject, thus:

                    (1)
         THE SHOT HEARD 'ROUND THE WORLD
         America's First Victory in France

                    (2)
           "ALL WOOL AND A YARD WIDE"
What "All Wool" Really Means and Why Shoddy is Necessary

                    (3)
           THE SERVANT IN THE HOUSE
         And Why She Won't Stay in the House

A well-known quotation or common saying may be paraphrased in a novel
way to attract attention; for example:

                    (1)
           FORWARD! THE TRACTOR BRIGADE

                    (2)
           IT'S LO, THE RICH INDIAN

                    (3)
             LEARNING BY UNDOING

                    (4)
         THE GUILELESS SPIDER AND THE WILY FLY
Entomology Modifies our Ideas of the Famous Parlor

Since every question is like a riddle, a title in question form
naturally leads the reader to seek the answer in the article itself. The
directness of appeal may be heightened by addressing the question to the
reader with "you," "your," or by presenting it from the reader's point
of view with the use of "I," "we," or "ours." The sub-title may be
another question or an affirmation, but should not attempt to answer the
question. The following are typical question titles and sub-titles:

                    (1)
           WHAT IS A FAIR PRICE FOR MILK?

                    (2)
         HOW MUCH HEAT IS THERE IN YOUR COAL?

                    (3)
             WHO'S THE BEST BOSS?
   Would You Rather Work For a Man or For a Machine?

                    (4)
           "SHE SANK BY THE BOW"--BUT WHY?

                    (5)
         HOW SHALL WE KEEP WARM THIS WINTER?

                    (6)
             DOES DEEP PLOWING PAY?
         What Some Recent Tests Have Demonstrated

(7)
SHALL I START A CANNING BUSINESS?

The reader may be addressed in an imperative form of title, as well as in a question, as the following titles show:

(1)
BLAME THE SUN SPOTS
Solar Upheavals That Make Mischief on the Earth

(2)
EAT SHARKS AND TAN THEIR SKINS

(3)
HOE! HOE! FOR UNCLE SAM

(4)
DON'T JUMP OUT OF BED
Give Your Subconscious Self a Chance to Awake Gradually

(5)
RAISE FISH ON YOUR FARM

(6)
BETTER STOP! LOOK! AND LISTEN!

The attractiveness of titles may be heightened by such combinations of sounds as alliteration and rhyme, or by rhythm such as is produced by balanced elements. The following examples illustrate the use of alliteration, rhyme, and balance:

(1)
THE LURE OF THE LATCH

(2)
THE DIMINISHING DOLLAR

(3)
TRACING TELEPHONE TROUBLES

(4)
BOY CULTURE AND AGRICULTURE

(5)
A LITTLE BILL AGAINST BILLBOARDS

(6)
EVERY CAMPUS A CAMP

(7)
LABOR-LIGHTENERS AND HOME-BRIGHTENERS

(8)
THE ARTILLERY MILL AT OLD FORT SILL
How Uncle Sam is Training His Field Artillery Officers

(9)
SCHOLARS VS. DOLLARS

(10)
WAR ON PESTS
When the Spray Gun's Away, Crop Enemies Play

(11)
MORE HEAT AND LESS COAL

(12)
GRAIN ALCOHOL FROM GREEN GARBAGE

HOW TO FRAME A TITLE. The application of the general principles
governing titles may best be shown by means of an article for which a
title is desired. A writer, for example, has prepared a popular article
on soil analysis as a means of determining what chemical elements
different kinds of farm land need to be most productive. A simple label
title like "The Value of Soil Analysis," obviously would not attract the
average person, and probably would interest only the more enterprising
of farmers. The analysis of soil not unnaturally suggests the diagnosis
of human disease; and the remedying of worn-out, run-down farm land by
applying such chemicals as phosphorus and lime, is analogous to the
physician's prescription of tonics for a run-down, anæmic person. These
ideas may readily be worked out as the following titles show:

(1)
PRESCRIBING FOR RUN-DOWN LAND
What the Soil Doctor is Doing to Improve Our Farms

(2)
THE SOIL DOCTOR AND HIS TONICS
Prescribing Remedies for Worn-Out Farm Land

(3)
DIAGNOSING ILLS OF THE SOIL
Science Offers Remedies for Depleted Farms

Other figurative titles like the following may be developed without much
effort from the ideas that soil "gets tired," "wears out," and "needs to
be fed":

(1)
WHEN FARM LAND GETS TIRED
Scientists Find Causes of Exhausted Fields

(2)
FIELDS WON'T WEAR OUT
If the Warnings of Soil Experts Are Heeded

(3)
BALANCED RATIONS FOR THE SOIL
Why the Feeding of Farm Land is Necessary for Good Crops

CHAPTER X

PREPARING AND SELLING THE MANUSCRIPT

IMPORTANCE OF GOOD MANUSCRIPT. After an article has been carefully
revised, it is ready to be copied in the form in which it will be
submitted to editors. Because hundreds of contributions are examined
every day in editorial offices of large publications, manuscripts should
be submitted in such form that their merits can be ascertained as easily
and as quickly as possible. A neatly and carefully prepared manuscript
is likely to receive more favorable consideration than a badly typed
one. The impression produced by the external appearance of a manuscript
as it comes to an editor's table is comparable to that made by the
personal appearance of an applicant for a position as he enters an
office seeking employment. In copying his article, therefore, a writer
should keep in mind the impression that it will make in the editorial
office.

FORM FOR MANUSCRIPTS. Editors expect all manuscripts to be submitted in
typewritten form. Every person who aspires to write for publication
should learn to use a typewriter. Until he has learned to type his work
accurately, he must have a good typist copy it for him.

A good typewriter with clean type and a fresh, black, non-copying ribbon
produces the best results. The following elementary directions apply to
the preparation of all manuscripts: (1) write on only one side of the
paper; (2) allow a margin of about three quarters of an inch on all
sides of the page; (3) double space the lines in order to leave room for
changes, sub-heads, and other editing.

Unruled white bond paper of good quality in standard letter size, 8½
by 11 inches, is the most satisfactory. A high grade of paper not only
gives the manuscript a good appearance but stands more handling and
saves the recopying of returned manuscripts. A carbon copy should be
made of every manuscript so that, if the original copy goes astray in
the mail or in an editorial office, the writer's work will not have been
in vain. The carbon copy can also be used later for comparison with the
printed article. Such a comparison will show the writer the amount and
character of the editing that was deemed necessary to adapt the material
to the publication in which it appears.

A cover sheet of the same paper is a convenient device. It not only
gives the editorial reader some information in regard to the article,
but it protects the manuscript itself. Frequently, for purposes of
record, manuscripts are stamped or marked in editorial offices, but if a
cover page is attached, the manuscript itself is not defaced. When an
article is returned, the writer needs to recopy only the cover page
before starting the manuscript on its next journey. The form for such a
cover page is given on page 184.

The upper half of the first page of the manuscript should be left blank,
so that the editor may write a new title and sub-title if he is not
satisfied with those supplied by the author. The title, the sub-title,
and the author's name should be repeated at the beginning of the article
in the middle of the first page, even though they have been given on the
cover page. At the left-hand side, close to the top of each page after

the first, should be placed the writer's last name followed by a dash
and the title of the article, thus:

Milton--Confessions of a Freshman.

The pages should be numbered in the upper right-hand corner. By these
simple means the danger of losing a page in the editorial offices is
reduced to a minimum.

To be paid for at usual   Written for The Outlook
rates, or to be returned
with the ten (10) cents
in stamps enclosed, to
  Arthur W. Milton,
  582 Wilson Street,
  Des Moines, Iowa.

CONFESSIONS OF A FRESHMAN

Why I Was Dropped From College at the End of My
First Year

By Arthur W. Milton

(Note. This article is based on the writer's own experience in a
large Middle Western state university, and the statistics have been
obtained from the registrars of four state universities. It contains
2,750 words.)

Four (4) Photographs are Enclosed, as follows:

   1. How I Decorated My Room

   2. I Spent Hours Learning to Play My Ukelele

   3. When I Made the Freshman Team

   4. Cramming For My Final Exams

TYPOGRAPHICAL STYLE. Every newspaper and magazine has its own distinct
typographical style in capitalization, abbreviation, punctuation,
hyphenation, and the use of numerical figures. Some newspapers and
periodicals have a style book giving rules for the preparation and
editing of copy. A careful reading of several issues of a publication
will show a writer the salient features of its typographical style. It
is less important, however, to conform to the typographical
peculiarities of any one publication than it is to follow consistently
the commonly accepted rules of capitalization, punctuation,
abbreviation, and "unreformed" spelling. Printers prefer to have each
page end with a complete sentence. At the close of the article it is
well to put the end mark (#).

When a special feature story for newspaper publication must be prepared
so hastily that there is no time to copy the first draft, it may be

desirable to revise the manuscript by using the marks commonly employed
in editing copy. These are as follows:

american
=
-

Three short lines under a letter or a
word indicate that it is to be set in
capital letters; thus, American.

New York Times
 =   =   =
 -   -   -

Two short lines under a letter or a
word indicate that it is to be set in
small capital letters; thus, NEW
YORK TIMES.

sine qua non
indicates
---- --- ---

One line under a word or words

that it is to be set in italics;
thus, _sine qua non_.

He is a /Sophomore

indicates

An oblique line drawn from right to
left through a capital letter

that it is to be set in lower
case; thus, He is a sophomore.

There are |10| in a |bu.|
        ----   -----

A circle around numerical figures or
abbreviations indicates that they
are to be spelled out; thus, There
are ten in a bushel.

|Professor| A.B.Smith is |sixty|.
-----------   -------

A circle around words or figures
spelled out indicates that they are
to be abbreviated or that numerical
figures are to be used; thus,
Prof. A.B. Smith is 60.

        not   a
It is complimentry to him
     ^   ^
written

A caret is placed at the point in the
line where the letters or words

above the line are to be inserted;
thus, It is not complimentary
to him.

to |carefullyXstudy|
   ----------- ------
indicates

A line encircling two or more words
like an elongated figure "8"

that the words are to be transposed;
thus, to study carefully.

to[=()]morrow

Half circles connecting words or
letters indicate that they are to be
brought together; thus, tomorrow.

all/right

A vertical line between parts of a
word shows that the parts are to be
separated; thus, all right.

U S 4 per cent. bonds
  x x

A small cross or a period in a circle
may be used to show that a period

is to be used; thus, U.S. 4 per cent. bonds.

")Yes, ')Love laughs at lock-smiths(', you know(", he replied.

Quotation marks are often enclosed in half circles to indicate whether they are beginning or end marks.

¶"How old are you?" he asked.
_|"Sixteen", she said.
attontion

The paragraph mark (¶) or the sign [_|] may be used to call

to the beginning of a new paragraph.

MAILING MANUSCRIPTS. Since manuscripts are written matter, they must be sent sealed as first-class mail at letter rates of postage. For the return of rejected articles stamps may be attached to the cover page by means of a clip, or a self-addressed envelope with stamps affixed may be enclosed. The writer's name and address should always be given on the envelope in which the manuscript is sent to the publishers.

The envelope containing the article should be addressed to the "Editor" of a magazine or to the "Sunday Editor" of a newspaper, as nothing is gained by addressing him or her by name. If a writer knows an editor personally or has had correspondence with him in regard to a particular article, it may be desirable to send the manuscript to him personally. An accompanying letter is not necessary, for the cover page of the manuscript gives the editor and his assistants all the information that they need.

Articles consisting of only a few pages may be folded twice and mailed in a long envelope; bulkier manuscripts should be folded once and sent in a manila manuscript envelope. Photographs of sizes up to 5 x 7 inches may be placed in a manuscript that is folded once, with a single piece of stout cardboard for protection. When larger photographs, up to 8 x 10 inches, accompany the article, the manuscript must be sent unfolded, with two pieces of cardboard to protect the pictures. Manuscripts should never be rolled.

HOW MANUSCRIPTS ARE HANDLED. In order to handle hundreds of manuscripts as expeditiously as possible, most large editorial offices have worked out systems that, though differing slightly, are essentially the same. When a manuscript is received, a record is made of it on a card or in a book, with the name and address of the author, the title and character of the contribution, and the time of its receipt. The same data are entered on a blank that is attached to the manuscript by a clip. On this blank are left spaces for comments by each of the editorial assistants who read and pass upon the article.

After these records have been made, the manuscript is given to the first editorial reader. He can determine by glancing at the first page or two whether or not the article is worth further consideration. Of the thousands of contributions of all kinds submitted, a considerable proportion are not in the least adapted to the periodical to which they have been sent. The first reader, accordingly, is scarcely more than a skilled sorter who separates the possible from the impossible. All manuscripts that are clearly unacceptable are turned over to a clerk to be returned with a rejection slip.

When an article appears to have merit, the first reader looks over it a second time and adds a brief comment, which he signs with his initials. The manuscript is then read and commented on by other editorial readers before it reaches the assistant editor. The best of the contributions are submitted to the editor for a final decision. By such a system every meritorious contribution is considered carefully by several critics before it is finally accepted or rejected. Moreover, the editor and the assistant editor have before them the comments of several readers with which to compare their own impressions.

In newspaper offices manuscripts are usually sorted by the assistant Sunday editor, or assistant magazine editor, and are finally accepted or rejected by the Sunday or magazine editor.

REJECTED MANUSCRIPTS. In rejecting contributions, editorial offices follow various methods. The commonest one is to send the author a printed slip expressing regret that the manuscript is not acceptable and encouraging him to submit something else. Some ingenious editors have prepared a number of form letters to explain to contributors the various reasons why their manuscripts are unacceptable. The editorial assistant who rejects an unsuitable article indicates by number which of these form letters is to be sent to the author. A few editors send a personal letter to every contributor. Sometimes an editor in rejecting a contribution will suggest some publication to which it might be acceptable. If a manuscript has merit but is not entirely satisfactory, he may suggest that it be revised and submitted to him again.

KEEPING A MANUSCRIPT RECORD. Every writer who intends to carry on his work in a systematic manner should keep a manuscript record, to assist him in marketing his articles to the best advantage. Either a book or a card index may be used. The purpose of such a record is to show (1) the length of time required by various publications to make a decision on contributions; (2) the rate and the time of payment of each periodical; (3) the present whereabouts of his manuscript and the periodicals to which it has already been submitted.

It is important for a writer to know how soon he may expect a decision on his contributions. If he has prepared an article that depends on timeliness for its interest, he cannot afford to send it to an editor who normally takes three or four weeks to make a decision. Another publication to which his article is equally well adapted, he may find from his manuscript record, accepts or rejects contributions within a week or ten days. Naturally he will send his timely article to the publication that makes the quickest decision. If that publication rejects it, he will still have time enough to try it elsewhere. His experience with different editors, as recorded in his manuscript record, often assists him materially in placing his work to the best advantage.

The rate and the time of payment for contributions are also worth recording. When an article is equally well suited to two or more periodicals, a writer will naturally be inclined to send it first to the publication that pays the highest price and that pays on acceptance.

A manuscript record also indicates where each one of a writer's articles is at a given moment, and by what publications it has been rejected. For such data he cannot afford to trust his memory.

A writer may purchase a manuscript record book or may prepare his own book or card index. At the top of each page or card is placed the title of the article, followed by the number of words that it contains, the number of illustrations that accompany it, and the date on which it was completed. On the lines under the title are written in turn the names of the periodicals to which the manuscript is submitted, with (1) the dates on which it was submitted and returned or rejected; (2) the rate and the time of payment; and (3) any remarks that may prove helpful. A convenient form for such a page or card is shown on the next page:

Confessions of a Freshman. 2,750 Words. 4 Photos. Written, Jan. 18, 1919.						
	Sent	Returned	Accepted	Paid	Amount	Remarks
The Outlook	1/18/19	1/30/19				
The Independent	1/31/19	2/10/19				
The Kansas City Star	2/12/19		2/18/19	3/12/19	$9.50	$4 a col.

ACCEPTED MANUSCRIPTS. Contributions accepted for publication are paid for at the time of their acceptance, at the time of their publication, or at some fixed date in the month following their acceptance or publication. Nearly all well-established periodicals pay for articles when they are accepted. Some publications do not pay until the article is printed, a method obviously less satisfactory to a writer than prompt payment, since he may have to wait a year or more for his money. Newspapers pay either on acceptance or before the tenth day of the month following publication. The latter arrangement grows out of the practice of paying correspondents between the first and the tenth of each month for the work of the preceding month.

After a manuscript has been accepted, a writer usually has no further responsibility concerning it. Some magazines submit galley proofs to the author for correction and for any changes that he cares to make. It is desirable to make as few alterations as possible to avoid the delay and expense of resetting the type. Corrected proofs should be returned promptly.

Unless specific stipulations are made to the contrary by the author, an article on being accepted by a periodical becomes its property and cannot be republished without its consent. Usually an editor will grant an author permission to reprint an article in book or pamphlet form. By copyrighting each issue, as most magazines and some newspapers do, the publishers establish fully their rights to an author's work.

SYNDICATING ARTICLES. By sending copies of his articles to a number of newspapers for simultaneous publication, a writer of special feature stories for newspapers may add to his earnings. This method is known as syndicating. It is made possible by the fact that the circulation of newspapers is largely local. Since, for example, Chicago papers are not read in New York, or Minneapolis papers in St. Louis, these papers may well publish the same articles on the same day. Organized newspaper syndicates furnish many papers with reading matter of all kinds.

The same article must not, however, be sent to more than one magazine, but a single subject may be used for two entirely different articles intended for two magazines. If two articles are written on the same subject, different pictures should be secured, so that it will not be necessary to send copies of the same illustrations to two magazines. Agricultural journals with a distinctly sectional circulation do not object to using syndicated articles, provided that the journals to which the article is sent do not circulate in the same territory.

If a writer desires to syndicate his work, he must conform to several requirements. First, he must make as many good copies as he intends to send out and must secure separate sets of photographs to accompany each one. Second, he must indicate clearly on each copy the fact that he is syndicating the article and that he is sending it to only one paper in a city. A special feature story, for instance, sent to the _Kansas City Star_ for publication in its Sunday edition, he would mark, "Exclusive for Kansas City. Release for Publication, Sunday, January 19." Third, he must send out the copies sufficiently far in advance of the release date to enable all of the papers to arrange for the publication of the article on that day. For papers with magazine sections that are made up a week or more before the day of publication, articles should be in the office of the editor at least two weeks before the release date. For papers that make up their Sunday issues only a few days in advance, articles need be submitted only a week before the publication day.

SELLING ARTICLES TO SYNDICATES. The syndicates that supply newspapers with various kinds of material, including special feature stories, are operated on the same principle that governs the syndicating of articles by the writer himself. That is, they furnish their features to a number of different papers for simultaneous publication. Since, however, they sell the same material to many papers, they can afford to do so at a comparatively low price and still make a fair profit. To protect their literary property, they often copyright their features, and a line of print announcing this fact is often the only indication in a newspaper that the matter was furnished by a syndicate. Among the best-known newspaper syndicates are the Newspaper Enterprise Association, Cleveland, Ohio; the McClure Newspaper Syndicate, New York; and the Newspaper Feature Service, New York. A number of large newspapers, like the _New York Evening Post_, the _Philadelphia Ledger_, and the _New York Tribune_, syndicate their popular features to papers in other cities.

A writer may submit his special feature stories to one of the newspaper syndicates just as he would send it to a newspaper or magazine. These organizations usually pay well for acceptable manuscripts. It is not as easy, however, to discover the needs and general policy of each syndicate as it is those of papers and magazines, because frequently there is no means of identifying their articles when they are printed in newspapers.

CHAPTER XI

PHOTOGRAPHS AND OTHER ILLUSTRATIONS

VALUE OF ILLUSTRATIONS The perfecting of photo-engraving processes for making illustrations has been one of the most important factors in the development of popular magazines and of magazine sections of newspapers, for good pictures have contributed largely to their success. With the advent of the half-tone process a generation ago, and with the more recent application of the rotogravure process to periodical publications, comparatively cheap and rapid methods of illustration were provided. Newspapers and magazines have made extensive use of both these processes.

The chief value of illustrations for special articles lies in the fact that they present graphically what would require hundreds of words to describe. Ideas expressed in pictures can be grasped much more readily than ideas expressed in words. As an aid to rapid reading illustrations are unexcelled. In fact, so effective are pictures as a means of conveying facts that whole sections of magazines and Sunday newspapers are given over to them exclusively.

Illustrations constitute a particularly valuable adjunct to special articles. Good reproductions of photographs printed in connection with the articles assist readers to visualize and to understand what a writer is undertaking to explain. So fully do editors realize the great attractiveness of illustrations, that they will buy articles accompanied by satisfactory photographs more readily than they will those without illustrations. Excellent photographs will sometimes sell mediocre articles, and meritorious articles may even be rejected because they lack good illustrations. In preparing his special feature stories, a writer will do well to consider carefully the number and character of the illustrations necessary to give his work the strongest possible appeal.

SECURING PHOTOGRAPHS. Inexperienced writers are often at a loss to know how to secure good photographs. Professional photographers will, as a rule, produce the best results, but amateur writers often hesitate to incur the expense involved, especially when they feel uncertain about selling their articles. If prints can be obtained from negatives that photographers have taken for other purposes, the cost is so small that a writer can afford to risk the expenditure. Money spent for good photographs is usually money well spent.

Every writer of special articles should become adept in the use of a camera. With a little study and practice, any one can take photographs that will reproduce well for illustrations. One advantage to a writer of operating his own camera is that he can take pictures on the spur of the moment when he happens to see just what he needs. Unconventional pictures caught at the right instant often make the best illustrations.

The charges for developing films and for making prints and enlargements are now so reasonable that a writer need not master these technicalities in order to use a camera of his own. If he has time and interest, however, he may secure the desired results more nearly by developing and printing his own pictures.

Satisfactory pictures can be obtained with almost any camera, but one with a high-grade lens and shutter is the best for all kinds of work. A pocket camera so equipped is very convenient. If a writer can afford to make a somewhat larger initial investment, he will do well to buy a camera of the so-called "reflex" type. Despite its greater weight and bulk, as compared with pocket cameras, it has the advantage of showing the picture full size, right side up, on the top of the camera, until the very moment that the button is pressed. These reflex cameras are equipped with the fastest types of lens and shutter, and thus are particularly well adapted to poorly lighted and rapidly moving objects.

A tripod should be used whenever possible. A hastily taken snap shot often proves unsatisfactory, whereas, if the camera had rested on a tripod, and if a slightly longer exposure had been given, a good negative would doubtless have resulted.

REQUIREMENTS FOR PHOTOGRAPHS. All photographs intended for reproduction by the half-tone or the rotogravure process should conform to certain requirements.

First: The standard size of photographic prints to be used for illustrations is 5 x 7 inches, but two smaller sizes, 4 x 5 and 3½ x 5½, as well as larger sizes such as 6½ x 8½ and 8 x 10, are also acceptable. Professional photographers generally make their negatives for illustrations in the sizes, 5 x 7, 6½ x 8½, and 8 x 10. If a writer uses a pocket camera taking pictures smaller than post-card size (3½ x 5½), he must have his negatives enlarged to one of the above standard sizes.

Second: Photographic prints for illustrations should have a glossy surface; that is, they should be what is known as "gloss prints." Prints on rough paper seldom reproduce satisfactorily; they usually result in "muddy" illustrations. Prints may be mounted or unmounted; unmounted ones cost less and require less postage, but are more easily broken in handling.

Third: Objects in the photograph should be clear and well defined; this requires a sharp negative. For newspaper illustrations it is desirable to have prints with a stronger contrast between the dark and the light parts of the picture than is necessary for the finer half-tones and rotogravures used in magazines.

Fourth: Photographs must have life and action. Pictures of inanimate objects in which neither persons nor animals appear, seem "dead" and unattractive to the average reader. It is necessary, therefore, to have at least one person in every photograph. Informal, unconventional pictures in which the subjects seem to have been "caught" unawares, are far better than those that appear to have been posed. Good snap-shots of persons in characteristic surroundings are always preferable to cabinet photographs. "Action pictures" are what all editors and all readers want.

Fifth: Pictures must "tell the story"; that is, they should illustrate the phase of the subject that they are designed to make clear. Unless a photograph has illustrative value it fails to accomplish the purpose for which it is intended.

CAPTIONS FOR ILLUSTRATIONS. On the back of a photograph intended for reproduction the author should write or type a brief explanation of what it represents. If he is skillful in phrasing this explanation, or "caption," as it is called, the editor will probably use all or part of it just as it stands. If his caption is unsatisfactory, the editor will have to write one based on the writer's explanation. A clever caption adds much to the attractiveness of an illustration.

A caption should not be a mere label, but, like a photograph, should have life and action. It either should contain a verb of action or should imply one. In this and other respects, it is not unlike the newspaper headline. Instead, for example, of the label title, "A Large Gold Dredge in Alaska," a photograph was given the caption, "Digs Out a Fortune Daily." A picture of a young woman feeding chickens in a backyard poultry run that accompanied an article entitled "Did You Ever Think of a Meat Garden?" was given the caption "Fresh Eggs and Chicken Dinners Reward Her Labor." To illustrate an article on the danger of the pet cat as a carrier of disease germs, a photograph of a child playing with a cat was used with the caption, "How Epidemics Start." A portrait of a housewife who uses a number of labor-saving devices in her home bore the legend, "She is Reducing Housekeeping to a Science." "A Smoking Chimney is a Bad Sign" was the caption under a photograph of a chimney pouring out smoke, which was used to illustrate an article on how to save coal.

Longer captions describing in detail the subject illustrated by the photograph, are not uncommon; in fact, as more and more pictures are being used, there is a growing tendency to place a short statement, or "overline," above the illustration and to add to the amount of descriptive matter in the caption below it. This is doubtless due to two causes: the increasing use of illustrations unaccompanied by any text except the caption, and the effort to attract the casual reader by giving him a taste, as it were, of what the article contains.

DRAWINGS FOR ILLUSTRATIONS. Diagrams, working drawings, floor plans, maps, or pen-and-ink sketches are necessary to illustrate some articles. Articles of practical guidance often need diagrams. Trade papers like to have their articles illustrated with reproductions of record sheets and blanks designed to develop greater efficiency in office or store management. If a writer has a little skill in drawing, he may prepare in rough form the material that he considers desirable for illustration, leaving to the artists employed by the publication the work of making drawings suitable for reproduction. A writer who has had training in pen-and-ink drawing may prepare his own illustrations. Such drawings should be made on bristol board with black drawing ink, and should be drawn two or three times as large as they are intended to appear when printed. If record sheets are to be used for illustration, the ruling should be done with black drawing ink, and the figures and other data should be written in with the same kind of ink. Typewriting on blanks intended for reproduction should be done with a fresh record black ribbon. Captions are necessary on the back of drawings as well as on photographs.

MAILING PHOTOGRAPHS AND DRAWINGS. It is best to mail flat all photographs and drawings up to 8 x 10 in size, in the envelope with the manuscript, protecting them with pieces of stout cardboard. Only very large photographs or long, narrow panoramic ones should be rolled and mailed in a heavy cardboard tube, separate from the manuscript. The writer's name and address, as well as the title of the article to be illustrated, should be written on the back of every photograph and drawing.

As photographs and drawings are not ordinarily returned when they are used with an article that is accepted, writers should not promise to return such material to the persons from whom they secure it. Copies can almost always be made from the originals when persons furnishing writers with photographs and drawings desire to have the originals kept in good condition.

PART II

AN OUTLINE FOR THE ANALYSIS OF SPECIAL
FEATURE ARTICLES

I.   SOURCES OF MATERIAL

  1.   What appears to have suggested the subject to the writer?

  2.   How much of the article was based on his personal experience?

  3.   How much of it was based on his personal observations?

  4.   Was any of the material obtained from newspapers or periodicals?

  5.   What portions of the article were evidently obtained by interviews?

  6.   What reports, documents, technical periodicals, and books of
       reference were used as sources in preparing the article?

  7.   Does the article suggest to you some sources from which you might
       obtain material for your own articles?

II.   INTEREST AND APPEAL

  1.   Is there any evidence that the article was timely when it was
       published?

  2.   Is the article of general or of local interest?

  3.   Does it seem to be particularly well adapted to the readers of
       the publication in which it was printed? Why?

4. What, for the average reader, is the source of interest in the article?

5. Does it have more than one appeal?

6. Is the subject so presented that the average reader is led to see its application to himself and to his own affairs?

7. Could an article on the same subject, or on a similar one, be written for a newspaper in your section of the country?

8. What possible subjects does the article suggest to you?

III. PURPOSE

1. Did the writer aim to entertain, to inform, or to give practical guidance?

2. Does the writer seem to have had a definitely formulated purpose?

3. How would you state this apparent purpose in one sentence?

4. Is the purpose a worthy one?

5. Did the writer accomplish his purpose?

6. Does the article contain any material that seems unnecessary to the accomplishment of the purpose?

IV. TYPE OF ARTICLE

1. To which type does this article conform?

2. Is there any other type better adapted to the subject and material?

3. How far did the character of the subject determine the methods of treatment?

4. What other methods might have been used to advantage in presenting this subject?

5. Is the article predominantly narrative, descriptive, or expository?

6. To what extent are narration and description used for expository purposes?

7. Are concrete examples and specific instances employed effectively?

8. By what means are the narrative passages made interesting?

9. Do the descriptive parts of the article portray the impressions

vividly?

V. STRUCTURE

1. What main topics are taken up in the article?

2. Could any parts of the article be omitted without serious loss?

3. Could the parts be rearranged with gain in clearness, interest, or progress?

4. Does the article march on steadily from beginning to end?

5. Is the material so arranged that the average reader will reach the conclusion that the writer intended to have him reach?

6. Is there variety in the methods of presentation?

7. Is the length of the article proportionate to the subject?

8. What type of beginning is used?

9. Is the type of beginning well adapted to the subject and the material?

10. Would the beginning attract the attention and hold the interest of the average reader?

11. Is the beginning an integral part of the article?

12. Is the length of the beginning proportionate to the length of the whole article?

13. Is the beginning skillfully connected with the body of the article?

VI. STYLE

1. Is the article easy to read? Why?

2. Is the diction literary or colloquial, specific or general, original or trite, connotative or denotative?

3. Are figures of speech used effectively?

4. Do the sentences yield their meaning easily when read rapidly?

5. Is there variety in sentence length and structure?

6. Are important ideas placed at the beginning of sentences?

7. Are the paragraphs long or short?

8. Are they well-organized units?

9. Do the paragraphs begin with important ideas?

10. Is there variety in paragraph beginnings?

11. Is the tone well suited to the subject?

12. Do the words, figures of speech, sentences, and paragraphs
    in this article suggest to you possible means of improving
    your own style?

VII. TITLES AND HEADLINES

1. Is the title attractive, accurate, concise, and concrete?

2. To what type does it conform?

3. What is the character of the sub-title, and what relation
   does it bear to the title?

(_Boston Herald_)

TEACH CHILDREN LOVE OF ART THROUGH STORY-TELLING

"----And so," ended the story, "St. George slew the dragon."

A great sigh, long drawn and sibilant, which for the last five minutes
had been swelling 57 little thoraxes, burst out and filled the space of
the lecture hall at the Museum of Fine Arts.

"O-o-o-o-o-o-o-o-o!" said 27 little girls.

"Aw-w-w-w-w-w-w-w-w, gosh!" said 30 little boys. "Say, Mis' Cronan,
there wasn't no real dragon, was they?" A shock-headed youngster pushed
his way to the platform where Mrs. Mary C. Cronan, professional story
teller, stood smiling and wistfully looked up at her. "They wasn't no
really dragon, was they?"

"'Course they was a dragon! Whadd'ye think the man wanted to paint the
picture for if there wasn't a dragon? Certn'y there was a dragon. I
leave it to Mis' Cronan if there wasn't."

Steering a narrow course between fiction and truth, Mrs. Cronan told her
class that she thought there certainly must have been a dragon or the
picture wouldn't have been painted.

It was at one of the regular morning story hours at the Museum of Fine
Arts, a department opened three years ago at the museum by Mrs. Cronan
and Mrs. Laura Scales, a department which has become so popular that now
hundreds of children a week are entertained, children from the public
playgrounds and from the settlement houses.

On this particular day it was children from the Bickford street
playground under the guidance of two teachers from the Lucretia Crocker
School, Miss Roche and Miss Hayes, who had, in some mysterious manner,
convoyed these 57 atoms to the museum by car without mishap and who

apparently did not dread the necessity of getting them back again, although to the uninitiated it appeared a task beside which grasping a comet by the tail was a pleasant afternoon's amusement.

For the most part the story of St. George and the Dragon was a new thing to these children. They might stand for St. George, although his costume was a little out of the regular form at Jamaica Plain, but the Dragon was another thing.

"I don't believe it," insisted an 8-year-old. "I seen every animal in the Zoo in the park and I don't see any of them things." But the wistful little boy kept insisting that there must be such an animal or Mrs. Cronan wouldn't say so.

"That is the way they nearly always take it at first," said Mrs. Cronan. "Nearly all of these children are here for the first time. Later they will bring their fathers and mothers on Sunday and you might hear them explaining the pictures upstairs as if they were the docents of the museum.

"The object of the story hour is to familiarize the children with as many as possible of the pictures of the Museum and to get them into the way of coming here of themselves. When they go away they are given cards bearing a reproduction of the picture about which the story of the day has been told, and on these cards is always an invitation to them to bring their families to the Museum on Saturday and Sunday, when there is no entrance fee."

The idea of the story hour was broached several years ago and at first it was taken up as an experiment. Stereopticon slides were made of several of the more famous pictures in the Museum, and Mrs. Cronan, who was at the time achieving a well earned success at the Public Library, was asked to take charge of the story telling. The plan became a success at once.

Later Mrs. Scales was called in to take afternoon classes, and now more than 1000 children go to the Museum each week during July and August and hear stories told entertainingly that fix in their minds the best pictures of the world. Following the stories they are taken through the halls of the Museum and are given short talks on some art subject. One day it may be some interesting thing on Thibetan amulets, or on tapestries or on some picture, Stuart's Washington or Turner's Slave Ship, or a colorful canvas of Claude Monet.

It is hoped that the movement may result in greater familiarity with and love for the Museum, for it is intended by the officials that these children shall come to love the Museum and to care for the collection and not to think of it, as many do, as a cold, unresponsive building containing dark mysteries, or haughty officials, or an atmosphere of "highbrow" iciness.

"I believe," says Mrs. Cronan, "that our little talks are doing just this thing. And although some of them, of course, can't get the idea quite all at once, most of these children will have a soft spot hereafter for Donatello's St. George."

At least some of them were not forgetting it, for as they filed out the wistful little boy was still talking about it.

"Ya," he said to the scoffer, "you mightn't a seen him at the Zoo.
That's all right, but you never went over to the 'quarium. Probably they
got one over there. Gee! I wish I could see a dragon. What color are
they?"

But the smallest boy of all, who had hold of Miss Hayes's hand and who
had been an interested listener to all this, branched out mentally into
other and further fields.

"Aw," said he, "I know a feller what's got a ginny pig wit' yeller spots
on 'im and he--" And they all trailed out the door.

               *   *   *   *   *

(_Christian Science Monitor_)

One illustration, a half-tone reproduction of a photograph showing the
interior of the greenhouse with girls at work.

WHERE GIRLS LEARN TO WIELD SPADE AND HOE

To go to school in a potato patch; to say one's lessons to a farmer; to
study in an orchard and do laboratory work in a greenhouse--this is the
pleasant lot of the modern girl who goes to a school of horticulture
instead of going to college, or perhaps after going to college.

If ever there was a vocation that seemed specially adapted to many
women, gardening would at first glance be the one. From the time of

    "Mistress Mary, quite contrary,
    How does your garden grow?"

down to the busy city woman who to-day takes her recreation by digging
in her flowerbeds, gardens have seemed a natural habitat for womankind,
and garden activities have belonged to her by right.

In various parts of the country there have now been established schools
where young women may learn the ways of trees and shrubs, vegetables and
flowers, and may do experimental work among the growing things
themselves. Some of these schools are merely adjuncts of the state
agricultural colleges, with more or less limited courses of
instruction; but, just out of Philadelphia, there is a school, to which
women only are admitted, that is located on a real farm, and covers a
wide range of outdoor study.

One begins to feel the homely charm of the place the moment instructions
are given as to how to reach it.

"Out the old Lime-kiln road," you are told. And out the old Lime-kiln
road you go, until you come to a farm which spells the perfection of
care in every clump of trees and every row of vegetables. Some girls in
broad-brimmed hats are working in the Strawberry bed--if you go in
strawberry time--and farther on a group of women have gathered, with an
overalled instructor, under an apple tree the needs of which are being
studied.

Under some sedate shade trees, you are led to an old Pennsylvania stone farmhouse--the administration building, if you please. Beyond are the barns, poultry houses, nurseries and greenhouses, and a cottage which is used as a dormitory for the girls--as unlike the usual dormitory as the school is unlike the usual school. A bee colony has its own little white village near by.

Then the director, a trained woman landscape gardener, tells you all that this school of horticulture has accomplished since its founding five years ago.

"Women are naturally fitted for gardening, and for some years past there have been many calls for women to be teachers in school gardens, planners of private gardens, or landscape gardeners in institutions for women. Very few women, however, have had the practical training to enable them to fill such positions, and five years ago there was little opportunity for them to obtain such training. At that time a number of women in and about Philadelphia, who realized the need for thorough teaching in all the branches of horticulture, not merely in theory but in practice, organized this school. The course is planned to equip women with the practical knowledge that will enable them to manage private and commercial gardens, greenhouses or orchards. Some women wish to learn how to care for their own well-loved gardens; some young girls study with the idea of establishing their own greenhouses and raising flowers as a means of livelihood; still others want to go in for fruit farming, and even for poultry raising or bee culture.

"In other countries, schools of gardening for women are holding a recognized place in the educational world. In England, Belgium, Germany, Italy, Denmark and Russia, such institutions have long passed the experimental stage; graduates from their schools are managing large estates or holding responsible positions as directors of public or private gardens, as managers of commercial greenhouses, or as consulting horticulturists and lecturers. In this country there is a growing demand for supervisors of home and school gardens, for work on plantations and model farms, and for landscape gardeners. Such positions command large salaries, and the comparatively few women available for them are almost certain to attain success."

Already one of the graduates has issued a modest brown circular stating that she is equipped to supply ideas for gardens and personally to plant them; to expend limited sums of money to the best advantage for beauty and service; to take entire charge of gardens and orchards for the season and personally to supervise gardens during the owners' absence; to spray ornamental trees and shrubs, and prune them; and to care for indoor plants and window boxes.

"She is making a success of it, too. She has all she can do," comments one of the women directors, who is standing by.

A smiling strawberry student, who is passing, readily tells all that going to a garden school means.

"Each one of us has her own small plot of ground for which she is responsible. We have to plant it, care for it, and be marked on it. We all have special care of certain parts of the greenhouse, too, and each has a part of the nursery, the orchard and the vineyard. Even the work that is too heavy for us we have to study about, so that we can direct helpers when the time comes. We have to understand every detail of it all. We have to keep a daily record of our work. This is the way to learn how long it takes for different seeds to germinate, and thus we watch the development of the fruits and flowers and vegetables. You see, the attendance at the school is limited to a small number; so each one of us receives a great deal of individual attention and help.

"We learn simple carpentry, as part of the course, so that we shall be able to make window boxes, flats, cold frames and other articles that we need. We could even make a greenhouse, if we had to. We are taught the care and raising of poultry, we learn bee culture, and we have a course in landscape gardening. There is a course in canning and preserving, too, so that our fruits and berries can be disposed of in that way, if we should not be able to sell them outright, when we have the gardens of our own that we are all looking forward to."

In the cozy cottage that serves as a dormitory, there is a large classroom, where the lectures in botany, entomology, soils and horticultural chemistry are given. There is a staff of instructors, all from well-known universities, and a master farmer to impart the practical everyday process of managing fields and orchards. Special lectures are given frequently by experts in various subjects. In the cottage is a big, homelike living-room, where the girls read and sing and dance in the evening. Each girl takes care of her own bedroom.

The costumes worn by these garden students are durable, appropriate and most becoming. The school colors are the woodsy ones of brown and green, and the working garb is carried out in these colors. Brown khaki or corduroy skirts, eight inches from the ground, with two large pockets, are worn under soft green smocks smocked in brown. The sweaters are brown or green, and there is a soft hat for winter and a large shade hat for summer. Heavy working gloves and boots are provided, and a large apron with pockets goes with the outfit.

All in all, you feel sure, as you go back down the "old Lime-Kiln road," that the motto of the school will be fulfilled in the life of each of its students: "So enter that daily thou mayst become more thoughtful and more learned. So depart that daily thou mayst become more useful to thyself and to all mankind."

*   *   *   *   *

(_Boston Transcript_)

BOYS IN SEARCH OF JOBS

BY RAYMOND G. FULLER

One morning lately, if you had stood on Kneeland street in sight of the entrance of the State Free Employment Office, you would have seen a long line of boys--a hundred of them--waiting for the doors to open. They were of all sorts of racial extraction and of ages ranging through most of the teens. Some you would have called ragamuffins, street urchins, but some were too well washed, combed and laundered for such a designation. Some were eagerly waiting, some anxiously, some

indifferently. Some wore sober faces; some were standing soldierly
stiff; but others were bubbling over with the spirits of their age,
gossiping, shouting, indulging in colt-play. When they came out, some
hustled away to prospective employers and others loitered in the street.
Disappointment was written all over some of them, from face to feet; on
others the inscription was, "I don't care."

Two hundred boys applied for "jobs" at the employment office that day.
Half the number were looking for summer positions. Others were of the
vast army of boys who quit school for keeps at the eighth or ninth grade
or thereabouts. Several weeks before school closed the office had more
than enough boy "jobs" to go around. With the coming of vacation time
the ratio was reversed. The boy applicants were a hundred or two hundred
daily. For the two hundred on the day mentioned there were fifty places.

Says Mr. Deady, who has charge of the department for male minors:
"Ranging from fourteen to nineteen years of age, of all nationalities
and beliefs, fresh from the influence of questionable home environment,
boisterous and brimful of animation, without ideas and thoughtless to a
marked degree--this is the picture of the ordinary boy who is in search
of employment. He is without a care and his only thought, if he has one,
is to obtain as high a wage as possible. It is safe to say that of the
thousands of boys who apply annually at the employment office,
two-thirds are between sixteen and eighteen years of age. Before going
further, we can safely say that twenty per cent of the youngest lads
have left school only a few weeks before applying for work.
Approximately sixty per cent have not completed a course in the
elementary grammar schools."

The boy of foreign parentage seems to be more in earnest, more
ambitious, than the American boy (not to quibble over the definition of
the adjective "American"). Walter L. Sears, superintendent of the office
in Kneeland street, tells this story:

An American youngster came in.

"Gotta job?" he asked.

"Yes, here is one"--referring to the card records--"in a printing
office; four dollars a week."

"'Taint enough money. Got anything else?"

"Here's a place in a grocery store--six dollars a week."

"What time d'ye have to get to work in the morning?"

"Seven o'clock."

"Got anything else?"

"Here's something--errand boy--six a week, mornings at eight."

"Saturday afternoons off?"

"Nothing is said about it."

"W-ell-l, maybe I'll drop around and look at it."

American independence!

An Italian boy came in, looking for work. He was told of the printing office job.

"All right. I'll take it."

For what it is worth, it may be set down that a large proportion of the boy applicants carefully scrutinize the dollar sign when they talk wages. Moreover, they are not unacquainted with that phrase concocted by those higher up, "the high cost of living." The compulsion of the thing, or the appeal of the phrase--which?

The youthful unemployed, those who seek employment, would cast a good-sized vote in favor of "shoffer." A youngster comes to Mr. Sears. He wants to be a "shoffer."

"Why do you want to be a chauffeur?"

"I don't know."

"Haven't you any reasons at all?"

"No, sir."

"Isn't it because you have many times seen the man at the wheel rounding a corner in an automobile at a 2.40 clip and sailing down the boulevard at sixty miles an hour?"

The boy's eyes light up with the picture.

"Isn't that it?"

And the boy's eyes light up with discovery.

"Yes, I guess so."

"Well, have you ever seen the chauffeur at night, after being out all day with the car? Overalls on, sleeves rolled up, face streaming with perspiration? Repairing the mechanism, polishing the brass? Tired to death?"

"No, sir."

The boy applicants seldom have any clear idea of the ultimate prospects in any line of work they may have in mind--as to the salary limit for the most expert, or the opportunities for promotion and the securing of an independent position. Many of them have no preconceived idea even of what they want to do, to say nothing of what they ought to do.

Here is an instance.

"I want a position," says a boy.

"What kind of a position?"

"I don't know."

"Haven't you ever thought about it?"

"No."

"Haven't you ever talked it over at home or at school?"

"No."

"Would you like to be a machinist?"

"I don't know."

"Would you like to be a plumber?"

"I don't know."

Similar questions, with similar answers, continue. Finally:

"Would you like to be a doctor?"

"I don't know--is that a good position?"

Sometimes a boy is accompanied to the office by his father.

"My son is a natural-born electrician," the father boasts.

"What has he done to show that?"

"Why, he's wired the whole house from top to bottom."

It is found by further questions that the lad has installed a push-bell button at the front door and another at the back door. He had bought dry batteries, wire and buttons at a hardware store in a box containing full directions. It is nevertheless hard to convince the father that the boy may not be a natural-born electrician, after all.

In frequent cases the father has not considered the limitations and opportunities in the occupation which he chooses for his son.

Mr. Deady has this to say on the subject of the father's relation to the boy's "job": "The average boy while seeking employment in ninety-nine cases out of a hundred is unaccompanied by either parent. Such a condition is deplorable. It not only shows a lack of interest in the boy's welfare on the part of the parents, but also places the youthful applicant in an unfair position. Oftentimes, owing to inexperience, a boy accepts a position without inquiring into the details and nature of the same. His main thought is the amount of the wage to be received. Consequently there is but one obvious result. The hours are excessive, the work is beyond the boy's strength or is hazardous, and finally the lad withdraws without notice. It is this general apathy on the part of the parents of a boy, combined with over-zealousness on the part of an ordinary employer to secure boy labor for a mere trifle, that accounts for the instability of juvenile labor."

The coming of vacation invariably brings a great influx of boys to the State employment office, some looking for summer work, others for permanent employment. Most of them show lack of intelligent constructive thought on the matter in hand. Few of them have had any counsel, or any valuable counsel from their parents or others. To Mr. Sears and his assistants--and they have become very proficient at it--is left the task of vocational guidance, within such limitations as those of time and equipment. What can be done to get the boy and his sponsors to thinking intelligently about the question of an occupation for the boy, with proper regard to their mutual fitness?

Superintendent Sears has some suggestions to offer. In his opinion the subject of occupational choice should be debated thoroughly in the public schools. He favors the introduction of some plan embodying this idea in the upper grades of the grammar school, under conditions that would give each boy an opportunity to talk, and that would encourage him to consult his parents and teachers. The debates might be held monthly, and preparation should be required. Experts or successful men in various occupations might be called in to address the pupils and furnish authoritative information. The questions debated should involve the advisability of learning a trade and the choice of a trade, and the same considerations with respect to the professions, the mercantile pursuits, and so on. The pupils should be allowed to vote on the merits of each question debated. By such a method, thinks Mr. Sears, the boys would gain the valuable training which debating gives, would devote considerable thought to the question of their future employment, would acquire much information, and would get their parents more interested in the matter than many of them are.

                *   *   *   *   *

(_New York Evening Post_)

GIRLS AND A CAMP

NOW IT IS THAT MANY COVEYS OF STUDENTS ARE HEADED TOWARD LAKE AND MOUNTAIN--JUST HOW IT PAYS

With the sudden plunge into a muggy heat, more suggestive of July than of the rare June weather of poets, there has begun the exodus of summer camp folk, those men and women who add to the slender salary of the teaching profession the additional income made by running camps for boys and girls during the long vacation. They stretch, these camps, in rapidly extending area from Canada through Maine and northern New England, into the Adirondacks and the Alleghenies, and then across toward the Northwest and the Rockies. It is quite safe to assert that there is not a private school of importance that does not take under its protection and support at least one such institution, while large numbers of teachers either own camps or assist in their management as instructors.

One group, unmistakably the advance guard of a girls' camp, assembled at the Grand Central Station on Wednesday. There were two alert, dignified women, evidently the co-principals; a younger woman, who, at least so the tired suburban shopper decided, was probably the athletic instructor; two neat colored women, and a small girl of twelve, on tiptoe with excitement, talking volubly about the fun she would have when they got to the lake and when all the other girls arrived. Her excited chatter also revealed the fact that father and mother had just sailed for Europe, and, while she thought of them with regret, there was only pleasure in prospect as she started northward. There was much baggage to be attended to, and consultation over express and freight bills, with interesting references to tents, canoes, and tennis nets.

Success is an excellent testimonial, and there is no longer any need to point out the advantages of such camps for boys and girls. They fill a real place for the delicate, the lazy, or the backward, who must needs do extra work to keep up with their school grade, for those who otherwise would be condemned to hotel life, or for the children whose parents, because of circumstances, are compelled to spend the summer in cities. Even the most jealously anxious of mothers are among the converts to the movement. As one said the other day of her only son, "Yes, David will go to Mr. D.'s camp again this summer. It will be his third year. I thought the first time that I simply could not part with him. I pictured him drowned or ill from poor food or severe colds. Indeed, there wasn't a single terror I didn't imagine. But he enjoyed it so, and came home so well and happy, that I've never worried since."

From the child's point of view, summer camps are a blessing, and, as such, they have come to stay. But there are those who doubt their benefits, even the financial ones, for the teachers, who mortgage their vacations to conduct them. Unfortunately, as every one knows, almost every teacher has to mortgage her spare time in one way or another in order to make a more than bare living. Call the roll of those whom you may know, and you will be surprised--no, scarcely surprised; merely interested--to find that nine-tenths of them do some additional work. It may be extra tutoring, hack writing, translating, the editing of school texts or the writing of text-books, taking agencies for this, that, or the other commodity, conducting travel parties, lecturing at educational institutes, running women's clubs, or organizing nature classes. Some outside vocation is necessary if the teacher is to enjoy the advantages her training makes almost imperative, or the comforts her tired, nervous organism demands. So, as one philosopher was heard to remark, it is perhaps best to run a summer camp, since in the doing of it there is at least the advantage of being in the open and of leading a wholesomely sane existence.

Two good friends and fellow-teachers who have conducted a camp in northern Maine for the last five years have been extremely frank in setting forth their experiences for the benefit of those who are standing on the brink of a similar venture. And their story is worth while, because from every point of view they have been successful. Any pessimistic touches in their narrative cannot be laid at the door of failure. Indeed, in their first year they cleared expenses, and that is rare; and their clientèle has steadily increased until now they have a camp of forty or more girls, at the very topmost of camp prices. Again, as there were two of them and they are both versatile, they have needed little assistance; the mother of one has been house mother and general camp counsellor. With all this as optimistic preamble, let us hear their story.

Perhaps their first doubt arises with regard to the wear and tear of camp life upon those most directly responsible for its conduct. "For years we even refused to consider it," said the senior partner, "although urged by friends and would-be patrons, because we realized the unwisdom of working the year around and living continuously with school girls--but the inevitable happened. Our income did not keep pace with our expenses, and it was start a camp or do something less agreeable. Just at the psychological moment one of our insistent friends found the right spot, we concluded negotiations, and, behold, we are camp proprietors, not altogether sure, in our most uncompromisingly frank moments, that we have done the best thing."

That a girls' camp is a far more difficult proposition than one for boys is evident on the face of it. Mother may shed tears over parting with Johnny, but, after all, he's a boy, and sooner or later must depend upon himself. But Sister Sue is another matter. Can she trust any one else to watch over her in the matter of flannels and dry stockings? Do these well-meaning but spinster teachers know the symptoms of tonsilitis, the first signs of a bilious attack, or the peculiarities of a spoiled girl's diet? And will not Sue lose, possibly, some of the gentle manners and dainty ways inculcated at home, by close contact with divers other ways and manners? She is inclined to be skeptical, is mother. "And so," acknowledged the senior partner, "the first summer we were deluged by visits long and short from anxious ladies who could not believe on hearsay evidence that we knew how to care for their delicate daughters. They not only came, but they stayed, and as the nearest hotel was distant many devious miles of mountain road, we were forced to put them up; finally the maids had to sleep in the old barn, and we were camping on cots in the hall of the farmhouse which is our headquarters. Naturally we had to be polite, for we were under the necessity of making a good impression that first year, but it was most distracting, for while they stayed they were unconsciously but selfishly demanding a little more than a fair share of time and attention for their daughters."

And, indeed, all this maternal anxiety is not entirely misplaced. Sue is a good deal harder to take care of than Johnny. She needs a few more comforts, although camp life aims at eliminating all but the essentials of simple living. Her clothes, even at a minimum, are more elaborate, which increases the difficulty of laundering, always a problem in camping. She is infinitely more dependent upon her elders for direction in the veriest A B C's of daily existence. "Even the matter of tying a hair-ribbon or cleaning a pair of white canvas shoes is a mountain to a good many of my girls," said the successful camp counsellor.

Homesickness is "a malady most incident to maids." Boys may suffer from it, but they suffer alone. If tears are shed they are shed in secret, lest the other fellows find it out. Except in the case of the very little chaps, the masters are not disturbed. But girls have no such reserves; and the teachers in charge of twenty-five strange girls, many in the throes of this really distressing ailment, are not to be envied. "Frankly speaking," went on the confession, "there isn't a moment of the day when we can dismiss them from our thoughts. Are they swimming in charge of the director of athletics, a most capable girl, one of us must be there, too, because, should anything happen, we, and not she, are directly responsible. When the lesson hour is on, we not only teach, but must see that each girl's work is adapted to her needs, as they come from a dozen different schools. There are disputes to settle, plans for outings and entertainments to be made, games to direct, letters to the home folks to be superintended, or half the girls would never write at all, to say nothing of the marketing and housekeeping, and our own business correspondence, that has to be tucked into the siesta hour after luncheon. Indeed, in the nine weeks of camp last summer I never once had an hour that I could call my very own."

"And that is only the day's anxiety," sighed her colleague reflectively. "My specialty is prowling about at night to see that everybody is properly covered. Not a girl among them would have sense enough to get up and close windows in case of rain, so I sleep with one ear pricked for the first patter on the roof. Occasionally there are two or three who walk in their sleep, and I'm on pins and needles lest harm come to them, so I make my rounds to see that they're safe. Oh, it is a peacefully placid existence, I assure you, having charge of forty darling daughters. Some of them have done nothing for themselves in their entire lives, and what a splendid place camp is for such girls. But while they're learning we must be looking out for their sins of omission, such, for instance, as throwing a soaking wet bathing suit upon a bed instead of hanging it upon the line."

These are some of the few worries that attach to the care of sensitive and delicately brought up girls that the boys' camp never knows. But if the financial return is adequate there will naturally be some compensation for all these pinpricks. Here again the Senior Partner is inclined to hem and haw. "Given a popular head of camp," says she, "who has been fortunate enough to secure a desirable site and a paying clientèle, and she will certainly not lose money. Her summer will be paid for. However, that is not enough to reward her for the additional work and worry. Camp work does not confine itself to the nine weeks of residence. There are the hours and days spent in planning and purchasing equipment, the getting out of circulars, the correspondence entailed and the subsequent keeping in touch with patrons."

Her own venture has so far paid its own way, and after the first year has left a neat margin of profit. But this profit, because of expansion, has immediately been invested in new equipment. This year, for example, there has been erected a bungalow for general living purposes. A dozen new tents and four canoes were bought, and two dirt tennis courts made. Then each year there must be a general replenishing of dishes, table and bed linen, athletic goods, and furniture. The garden has been so enlarged that the semi-occasional man-of-all-work has been replaced by a permanent gardener.

Naturally, such extension does mean ultimate profit, and, given a few more years of continued prosperity, the summer will yield a goodly additional income. But the teacher who undertakes a camp with the idea that such money is easily made, is mistaken. One successful woman has cleared large sums, so large, indeed, that she has about decided to sever her direct connection with the private school where she has taught for years, and trust to her camp for a living. She has been so fortunate, it is but fair to explain, because her camp is upon a government reserve tract in Canada, and she has had to make no large investment in land; nor does she pay taxes. Desirable locations are harder to find nowadays and much more expensive to purchase. A fortunate pioneer in the movement bought seven acres, with five hundred feet of lake frontage, for three hundred dollars six years ago. That same land is worth ten times as much to-day.

And the kind of woman who should attempt the summer camp for girls as a means of additional income? First of all, the one who really loves outdoor life, who can find in woods and water compensation for the wear and tear of summering with schoolgirls. Again, she who can minimize the petty worries of existence to the vanishing point. And, last of all, she who has business acumen. For what does it profit a tired teacher if she fill her camp list and have no margin of profit for her weeks of hard labor?

                *   *   *   *   *

(Saturday Evening Post)

Two half-tone reproductions of wash-drawings by a staff artist.

YOUR PORTER

BY EDWARD HUNGERFORD

He stands there at the door of his car, dusky, grinning, immaculate--awaiting your pleasure. He steps forward as you near him and, with a quick, intuitive movement born of long experience and careful training, inquires:

"What space you got, guv'nor?"

"Lower five," you reply. "Are you full-up, George?"

"Jus' toler'bul, guv'nor."

He has your grips, is already slipping down the aisle toward section five. And, after he has stowed the big one under the facing bench and placed the smaller one by your side, he asks again:

"Shake out a pillow for you, guv'nor?"

That "guv'nor," though not a part of his official training, is a part of his unofficial--his subtlety, if you please. Another passenger might be the "kunnel"; still another, the "jedge." But there can be no other guv'nor save you on this car and trip. And George, of the Pullmans, is going to watch over you this night as a mother hen might watch over her solitary chick. The car is well filled and he is going to have a hard night of it; but he is going to take good care of you. He tells you so; and, before you are off the car, you are going to have good reason to believe it.

Before we consider the sable-skinned George of to-day, give a passing thought to the Pullman itself. The first George of the Pullmans--George M. Pullman--was a shrewd-headed carpenter who migrated from a western New York village out into Illinois more than half a century ago and gave birth to the idea of railroad luxury at half a cent a mile. There had been sleeping cars before Pullman built the Pioneer, as he called his maiden effort. There was a night car, equipped with rough bunks for the comfort of passengers, on the Cumberland Valley Railroad along about 1840.

Other early railroads had made similar experiments, but they were all makeshifts and crude. Pullman set out to build a sleeping car that would combine a degree of comfort with a degree of luxury. The Pioneer, viewed in the eyes of 1864, was really a luxurious car. It was as wide as the sleeping car of to-day and nearly as high; in fact, so high and so wide was it that there were no railroads on which it might run, and when Pullman pleaded with the old-time railroad officers to widen the clearances, so as to permit the Pioneer to run over their lines, they laughed at him.

"It is ridiculous, Mr. Pullman," they told him smilingly in refusal. "People are never going to pay their good money to ride in any such fancy contraption as that car of yours."

Then suddenly they ceased smiling. All America ceased smiling. Morse's telegraph was sobering an exultant land by telling how its great magistrate lay dead within the White House, at Washington. And men were demanding a funeral car, dignified and handsome enough to carry the body of Abraham Lincoln from Washington to Springfield. Suddenly somebody thought of the Pioneer, which rested, a virtual prisoner, in a railroad yard not far from Chicago.

The Pioneer was quickly released. There was no hesitation now about making clearances for her. Almost in the passing of a night, station platforms and other obstructions were being cut away, and the first of all the Pullman cars made a triumphant though melancholy journey to New York, to Washington, and back again to Illinois. Abraham Lincoln, in the hour of death--fifty years ago this blossoming spring of 1915--had given birth to the Pullman idea. The other day, while one of the brisk Federal commissions down at Washington was extending consideration to the Pullman porter and his wage, it called to the witness stand the executive head of the Pullman Company. And the man who answered the call was Robert T. Lincoln, the son of Abraham Lincoln.

When Pullman built the Pioneer he designated it A, little dreaming that eventually he might build enough cars to exhaust the letters of the alphabet. To-day the Pullman Company has more than six thousand cars in constant use. It operates the entire sleeping-car service and by far the larger part of the parlor-car service on all but half a dozen of the railroads of the United States and Canada, with a goodly sprinkling of routes south into Mexico. On an average night sixty thousand persons--a community equal in size to Johnstown, Pennsylvania, or South Bend, Indiana--sleep within its cars.

And one of the chief excuses for its existence is the flexibility of its service. A railroad in the South, with a large passenger traffic in the winter, or a railroad in the North, with conditions reversed and travel running at high tide throughout the hot summer months, could hardly afford to place the investment in sleeping and parlor cars to meet its high-tide needs, and have those cars grow rusty throughout the long, dull months. The Pullman Company, by moving its extra cars backward and forward over the face of the land in regiments and in battalions, keeps them all earning money. It meets unusual traffic demands with all the resources of its great fleet of traveling hotels.

Last summer, when the Knights Templars held their convention in Denver, it sent four hundred and fifty extra cars out to the capital of Colorado. And this year it is bending its resources toward finding sufficient cars to meet the demands for the long overland trek to the expositions on the Pacific Coast.

The transition from the Pioneer to the steel sleeping car of today was not accomplished in a single step. A man does not have to be so very old or so very much traveled to recall the day when the Pullman was called a palace ear and did its enterprising best to justify that title. It was almost an apotheosis of architectural bad taste. Disfigured by all manner of moldings, cornices, grilles and dinky plush curtains--head-bumping, dust-catching, useless--it was a decorative orgy, as well as one of the very foundations of the newspaper school of humor.

Suddenly the Pullman Company awoke to the absurdity of it all. More than ten years ago it came to the decision that architecture was all right in its way, but that it was not a fundamental part of car building. It separated the two. It began to throw out the grilles and the other knickknacks, even before it had committed itself definitely to the use of the steel car.

Recently it has done much more. It has banished all but the very simplest of the moldings, and all the hangings save those that are absolutely necessary to the operation of the car. It has studied and it has experimented until it has produced in the sleeping car of to-day what is probably the most efficient railroad vehicle in the world. Our foreign cousins scoff at it and call it immodest; but we may reserve our own opinion as to the relative modesty of some of their institutions.

        *   *   *   *   *

This, however, is not the story of the Pullman car. It is the story of that ebony autocrat who presides so genially and yet so firmly over it. It is the story of George the porter--the six thousand Georges standing to-night to greet you and the other traveling folk at the doors of the waiting cars. And George is worthy of a passing thought. He was born in the day when the negro servant was the pride of America--when the black man stood at your elbow in the dining rooms of the greatest of our hotels; when a colored butler was the joy of the finest of the homes along Fifth Avenue or round Rittenhouse Square. Transplanted, he quickly became an American institution. And there is many a man who avers that never elsewhere has there been such a servant as a good negro servant.

Fashions change, and in the transplanting of other social ideas the black man has been shoved aside. It is only in the Pullman service that he retains his old-time pride and prestige. That company to-day might almost be fairly called his salvation, despite the vexing questions of the wages and tips of the sleeping-car porters that have recently come to the fore. Yet it is almost equally true that the black man has been the salvation of the sleeping-car service. Experiments have been made in using others. One or two of the Canadian roads, which operate their own sleeping cars, have placed white men as porters; down in the Southwest the inevitable Mexicano has been placed in the familiar blue uniform. None of them has been satisfactory; and, indeed, it is not every negro who is capable of taking charge of a sleeping car.

The Pullman Company passes by the West Indians--the type so familiar to every man who has ridden many times in the elevators of the apartment houses of upper New York. It prefers to recruit its porters from certain of the states of the Old South--Georgia and the Carolinas. It almost limits its choice to certain counties within those states. It shows a decided preference for the sons of its employees; in fact, it might almost be said that to-day there are black boys growing up down there in the cotton country who have come into the world with the hope and expectation of being made Pullman car porters. The company that operates those cars prefers to discriminate--and it does discriminate.

That is its first step toward service--the careful selection of the human factor. The next step lies in the proper training of that factor; and as soon as a young man enters the service of the Pullmans he goes to school--in some one of the large railroad centers that act as hubs for that system. Sometimes the school is held in one of the division offices, but more often it goes forward in the familiar aisle of a sleeping car, sidetracked for the purpose.

Its curriculum is unusual but it is valuable. One moment it considers the best methods to "swat the fly"--to drive him from the vehicle in which he is an unwelcome passenger; the next moment the class is being shown the proper handling of the linen closet, the proper methods of folding and putting away clean linen and blankets, the correct way of stacking in the laundry bags the dirty and discarded bedding. The porter is taught that a sheet once unfolded cannot be used again. Though it may be really spotless, yet technically it is dirty; and it must make a round trip to the laundry before it can reenter the service.

All these things are taught the sophomore porters by a wrinkled veteran of the service; and they are minutely prescribed in the voluminous rule book issued by the Pullman Company, which believes that the first foundation of service is discipline. So the school and the rule book do not hesitate at details. They teach the immature porter not merely the routine of making up and taking down beds, and the proper maintenance of the car, but they go into such finer things as the calling of a passenger, for instance. Noise is tabooed, and so even a soft knocking on the top of the berth is forbidden. The porter must gently shake the curtains or the bedding from without.

When the would-be porter is through in this schoolroom his education goes forward out on the line. Under the direction of one of the grizzled autocrats he first comes in contact with actual patrons--comes to know their personalities and their peculiarities. Also, he comes to know the full meaning of that overused and abused word--service. After all, here is the full measure of the job. He is a servant. He must realize that. And as a servant he must perfect himself. He must rise to the countless opportunities that will come to him each night he is on the run. He must do better--he must anticipate them.

Take such a man as Eugene Roundtree, who has been running a smoking car on one of the limited trains between New York and Boston for two decades--save for that brief transcendent hour when Charles S. Mellen saw himself destined to become transportation overlord of New England and appropriated Roundtree for a personal servant and porter of his private car. Roundtree is a negro of the very finest type. He is a man who commands respect and dignity--and receives it. And Roundtree, as porter of the Pullman smoker on the Merchants' Limited, has learned to anticipate.

He knows at least five hundred of the big bankers and business men of
both New York and Boston--though he knows the Boston crowd best. He
knows the men who belong to the Somerset and the Algonquin Clubs--the
men who are Boston enough to pronounce Peabody "Pebbuddy." And they know
him. Some of them have a habit of dropping in at the New Haven ticket
offices and demanding: "Is Eugene running up on the Merchants'
to-night?"

"It isn't just knowing them and being able to call them by their names,"
he will tell you if you can catch him in one of his rarely idle moments.
"I've got to remember what they smoke and what they drink. When Mr.
Blank tells me he wants a cigar it's my job to remember what he smokes
and to put it before him. I don't ask him what he wants. I anticipate."

And by anticipating Roundtree approaches a sort of _n_th degree of
service and receives one of the "fattest" of all the Pullman runs.

George Sylvester is another man of the Roundtree type--only his run
trends to the west from New York instead of to the east, which means
that he has a somewhat different type of patron with which to deal.

Sylvester is a porter on the Twentieth Century Limited; and, like
Roundtree, he is a colored man of far more than ordinary force and
character. He had opportunity to show both on a winter night, when his
train was stopped and a drunken man--a man who was making life hideous
for other passengers on Sylvester's car--was taken from the train. The
fact that the man was a powerful politician, a man who raved the direst
threats when arrested, made the porter's job the more difficult.

The Pullman Company, in this instance alone, had good cause to remember
Sylvester's force and courage--and consummate tact--just as it has good
cause in many such episodes to be thankful for the cool-headedness of
its black man in a blue uniform who stands in immediate control of its
property.

Sylvester prefers to forget that episode. He likes to think of the nice
part of the Century's runs--the passengers who are quiet, and kind, and
thoughtful, and remembering. They are a sort whom it is a pleasure for a
porter to serve. They are the people who make an excess-fare train a
"fat run." There are other fat runs, of course: the Overland, the
Olympian, the Congressional--and of General Henry Forrest, of the
Congressional, more in a moment--fat trains that follow the route of the
Century.

It was on one of these, coming east from Cleveland on a snowy night in
February last, that a resourceful porter had full use for his store of
tact; for there is, in the community that has begun to stamp Sixth City
on its shirts and its shoe tabs, a bank president who--to put the matter
lightly--is a particular traveler. More than one black man, rising high
in porter service, has had his vanity come to grief when this crotchety
personage has come on his car.

And the man himself was one of those who are marked up and down the
Pullman trails. An unwritten code was being transmitted between the
black brethren of the sleeping cars as to his whims and peculiarities.
It was well that every brother in service in the Cleveland district

should know the code. When Mr. X entered his drawing-room--he never rides elsewhere in the car--shades were to be drawn, a pillow beaten and ready by the window, and matches on the window sill. X would never ask for these things; but God help the poor porter who forgot them!

So you yourself can imagine the emotions of Whittlesey Warren, porter of the car Thanatopsis, bound east on Number Six on the snowy February night when X came through the portals of that scarabic antique, the Union Depot at Cleveland, a redcap with his grips in the wake. Warren recognized his man. The code took good care as to that. He followed the banker down the aisle, tucked away the bags, pulled down the shades, fixed the pillow and placed the matches on the window sill.

The banker merely grunted approval, lighted a big black cigar and went into the smoker, while Warren gave some passing attention to the other patrons of his car. It was passing attention at the best; for after a time the little bell annunciator began to sing merrily and persistently at him--and invariably its commanding needle pointed to D.R. And on the drawing-room Whittlesey Warren danced a constant attention.

"Here, you nigger!" X shouted at the first response. "How many times have I got to tell all of you to put the head of my bed toward the engine?"

Whittlesey Warren looked at the bed. He knew the make-up of the train. The code had been met. The banker's pillows were toward the locomotive. But his job was not to argue and dispute. He merely said:

"Yas-suh. Scuse me!" And he remade the bed while X lit a stogy and went back to the smoker.

That was at Erie--Erie, and the snow was falling more briskly than at Cleveland. Slowing into Dunkirk, the banker returned and glanced through the car window. He could see by the snow against the street lamps that the train was apparently running in the opposite direction. His chubby finger went against the push button. Whittlesey Warren appeared at the door. The language that followed cannot be reproduced in THE SATURDAY EVENING POST. Suffice it to say that the porter remembered who he was and what he was, and merely remade the bed.

The banker bit off the end of another cigar and retired once again to the club car. When he returned, the train was backing into the Buffalo station. At that unfortunate moment he raised his car shade--and Porter Whittlesey Warren again reversed the bed, to the accompaniment of the most violent abuse that had ever been heaped on his defenseless head.

Yet not once did he complain--he remembered that a servant a servant always is. And in the morning X must have remembered; for a folded bill went into Warren's palm--a bill of a denomination large enough to buy that fancy vest which hung in a haberdasher's shop over on San Juan Hill.

If you have been asking yourself all this while just what a fat run is, here is your answer: Tips; a fine train filled with fine ladies and fine gentlemen, not all of them so cranky as X, of Cleveland--thank heaven for that!--though a good many of them have their peculiarities and are willing to pay generously for the privilege of indulging those peculiarities.

Despite the rigid discipline of the Pullman Company the porter's leeway is a very considerable one. His instructions are never to say "Against the rules!" but rather "I do not know what can be done about it"--and then to make a quick reference to the Pullman conductor, who is his arbiter and his court of last resort. His own initiative, however, is not small.

Two newspaper men in New York know that. They had gone over to Boston for a week-end, had separated momentarily at its end, to meet at the last of the afternoon trains for Gotham. A had the joint finances and tickets for the trip; but B, hurrying through the traffic tangle of South Station, just ninety seconds before the moment of departure, knew that he would find him already in the big Pullman observation car. He was not asked to show his ticket at the train gate. Boston, with the fine spirit of the Tea Party still flowing in its blue veins, has always resented that as a sort of railroad impertinence.

B did not find A. He did not really search for him until Back Bay was passed and the train was on the first leg of its journey, with the next stop at Providence. Then it was that A was not to be found. Then B realized that his side partner had missed the train. He dropped into a corner and searched his own pockets. A battered quarter and three pennies came to view--and the fare from Boston to Providence is ninety cents!

Then it was that the initiative of a well-trained Pullman porter came into play. He had stood over the distressed B while he was making an inventory of his resources.

"Done los' something, boss?" said the autocrat of the car.

B told the black man his story in a quick, straightforward manner; and the black man looked into his eyes. B returned the glance. Perhaps he saw in that honest ebony face something of the expression of the faithful servants of wartime who refused to leave their masters even after utter ruin had come upon them. The porter drew forth a fat roll of bills.

"Ah guess dat, ef you-all'll give meh yo' business cyard, Ah'll be able to fee-nance yo' trip dis time."

To initiative the black man was adding intuition. He had studied his man. He was forever using his countless opportunities to study men. It was not so much of a gamble as one might suppose.

A pretty well-known editor was saved from a mighty embarrassing time; and some other people have been saved from similarly embarrassing situations through the intuition and the resources of the Pullman porter. The conductor--both of the train and of the sleeping-car service--is not permitted to exercise such initiative or intuition; but the porter can do and frequently does things of this very sort. His recompense for them, however, is hardly to be classed as a tip.

The tip is the nub of the whole situation. Almost since the very day when the Pioneer began to blaze the trail of luxury over the railroads of the land, and the autocrat of the Pullman car created his servile but entirely honorable calling, it has been a mooted point. Recently a great Federal commission has blazed the strong light of publicity on it. Robert T. Lincoln, son of the Emancipator, and, as we have already said, the head and front of the Pullman Company, sat in a witness chair at Washington and answered some pretty pointed questions as to the division of the porter's income between the company and the passenger who employed him. Wages, it appeared, are twenty-seven dollars and a half a month for the first fifteen years of the porter's service, increasing thereafter to thirty dollars a month, slightly augmented by bonuses for good records.

The porter also receives his uniforms free after ten years of service, and in some cases of long service his pay may reach forty-two dollars a month. The rest of his income is in the form of tips. And Mr. Lincoln testified that during the past year the total of these tips, to the best knowledge and belief of his company, had exceeded two million three hundred thousand dollars.

The Pullman Company is not an eleemosynary institution. Though it has made distinct advances in the establishment of pension funds and death benefits, it is hardly to be classed as a philanthropy. It is a large organization; and it generally is what it chooses to consider itself. Sometimes it avers that it is a transportation company, at other times it prefers to regard itself as a hotel organization; but at all times it is a business proposition. It is not in business for its health. Its dividend record is proof of that. All of which is a preface to the statement that the Pullman Company, like any other large user of labor, regulates its wage scale by supply and demand. If it can find enough of the colored brethren competent and willing and anxious to man its cars at twenty-seven dollars and a half a month--with the fair gamble of two or three or four times that amount to come in the form of tips--it is hardly apt to pay more.

No wonder, then, the tip forms the nub of the situation. To-day all America tips. You tip the chauffeur in the taxi, the redcap in the station, the barber, the bootblack, the manicure, the boy or girl who holds your coat for you in the barber's shop or hotel. In the modern hotel tipping becomes a vast and complex thing--waiters, doormen, hat boys, chambermaids, bell boys, porters--the list seems almost unending.

The system may be abominable, but it has certainly fastened itself on us--sternly and securely. And it may be said for the Pullman car that there, at least, the tip comes to a single servitor--the black autocrat who smiles genially no matter how suspiciously he may, at heart, view the quarter you have placed within his palm.

A quarter seems to be the standard Pullman tip--for one person, each night he may be on the car. Some men give more; some men--alas for poor George!--less. A quarter is not only average but fairly standard. It is given a certain official status by the auditing officers of many large railroads and industrial corporations, who recognize it as a chargeable item in the expense accounts of their men on the road.

A man with a fat run--lower berths all occupied, with at least a smattering of riders in the uppers, night after night--ought to be able easily to put aside a hundred and fifty dollars a month as his income from this item. There are hundreds of porters who are doing this very thing; and there are at least dozens of porters who own real estate, automobiles, and other such material evidences of prosperity.

A tip is not necessarily a humiliation, either to the giver or to the taker. On the contrary, it is a token of meritorious service. And the smart porter is going to take good care that he gives such service. But how about the porter who is not so smart--the man who has the lean run? As every butcher and every transportation man knows, there is lean with the fat. And it does the lean man little good to know that his fat brother is preparing to buy a secondhand automobile. On the contrary, it creates an anarchist--or at least a socialist--down under that black skin.

Here is Lemuel--cursed with a lean run and yet trying to maintain at least an appearance of geniality. Lemuel runs on a "differential" between New York, Chicago and St. Louis. Every passenger-traffic man knows that most of the differentials--as the roads that take longer hours, and so are permitted to charge a slightly lower through fare between those cities, are called--have had a hard time of it in recent years. It is the excess-fare trains, the highest-priced carriers--which charge you a premium of a dollar for every hour they save in placing you in the terminal--that are the crowded trains. And the differentials have had increasing difficulty getting through passengers.

It seems that in this day and land a man who goes from New York to Chicago or St. Louis is generally so well paid as to make it worth dollars to him to save hours in the journey. It is modern efficiency showing itself in railroad-passenger travel. But the differentials, having local territory to serve, as well as on account of some other reasons, must maintain a sleeping-car service--even at a loss. There is little or no loss to the Pullman Company--you may be sure of that! The railroad pays it a mileage fee for hauling a half or three-quarter empty car over its own line--in addition to permitting the Pullman system to take all the revenue from the car; but Lemuel sees his end of the business as a dead loss.

He leaves New York at two-thirty o'clock on Monday afternoon, having reported at his car nearly three hours before so as to make sure that it is properly stocked and cleaned for its long trip. He is due at St. Louis at ten-fifteen on Tuesday evening--though it will be nearly two hours later before he has checked the contents of the car and slipped off to the bunking quarters maintained there by his company.

On Wednesday evening at seven o'clock he starts east and is due in New York about dawn on Friday morning. He cleans up his car and himself, and gets to his little home on the West Side of Manhattan Island sometime before noon; but by noon on Saturday he must be back at his car, making sure that it is fit and ready by two-thirty o'clock--the moment the conductor's arm falls--and they are headed west again.

This time the destination is Chicago, which is not reached until about six o'clock Sunday night. He bunks that night in the Windy City and then spends thirty-two hours going back again to New York. He sees his home one more night; then he is off to St. Louis again--started on a fresh round of his eternal schedule.

Talk of tips to Lemuel! His face lengthens. You may not believe it, white man, but Lemuel made fifty-three cents in tips on the last trip from New York to Chicago. You can understand the man who gave him the Columbian antique; but Lemuel believes there can be no future too warm for that skinny man who gave him the three pennies! He thinks the gentleman might at least have come across with a Subway ticket. It is all legal tender to him.

All that saves this porter's bacon is the fact that he is in charge of the car--for some three hundred miles of its eastbound run he is acting as sleeping-car conductor, for which consolidated job he draws down a proportionate share of forty-two dollars a month. This is a small sop, however, to Lemuel. He turns and tells you how, on the last trip, he came all the way from St. Louis to New York--two nights on the road--without ever a "make-down," as he calls preparing a berth. No wonder then that he has difficulty in making fifty dollars a month, with his miserable tips on the lean run.

Nor is that all. Though Lemuel is permitted three hours' sleep--on the bunk in the washroom on the long runs--from midnight to three o'clock in the morning, there may come other times when his head begins to nod. And those are sure to be the times when some lynx-eyed inspector comes slipping aboard. Biff! Bang! Pullman discipline is strict. Something has happened to Lemuel's pay envelope, and his coffee-colored wife in West Twenty-ninth Street will not be able to get those gray spats until they are clean gone out of style.

What can be done for Lemuel? He must bide his time and constantly make himself a better servant--a better porter, if you please. It will not go unnoticed. The Pullman system has a method for noticing those very things--inconsequential in themselves but all going to raise the standard of its service.

Then some fine day something will happen. A big sleeping-car autocrat, in the smugness and false security of a fat run, is going to err. He is going to step on the feet of some important citizen--perhaps a railroad director--and the important citizen is going to make a fuss. After which Lemuel, hard-schooled in adversity, in faithfulness and in courtesy, will be asked in the passing of a night to change places with the old autocrat.

And the old autocrat, riding in the poverty of a lean run, will have plenty of opportunity to count the telegraph poles and reflect on the mutability of men and things. The Pullman Company denies that this is part of its system; but it does happen--time and time and time again.

George, or Lemuel, or Alexander--whatever the name may be--has no easy job. If you do not believe that, go upstairs some hot summer night to the rear bedroom--that little room under the blazing tin roof which you reserve for your relatives--and make up the bed fifteen or twenty times, carefully unmaking it between times and placing the clothes away in a regular position. Let your family nag at you and criticize you during each moment of the job--while somebody plays an obbligato on the electric bell and places shoes and leather grips underneath your feet. Imagine the house is bumping and rocking--and keep a smiling face and a courteous tongue throughout all of it!

Or do this on a bitter night in midwinter; and between every two or
three makings of the bed in the overheated room slip out of a linen coat
and into a fairly thin serge one and go and stand outside the door from
three to ten minutes in the snow and cold. In some ways this is one of
the hardest parts of George's job. Racially the negro is peculiarly
sensitive to pneumonia and other pulmonary diseases; yet the rules of a
porter's job require that at stopping stations he must be outside of the
car--no matter what the hour or condition of the climate--smiling and
ready to say:

"What space you got, guv'nor?"

However, the porter's job, like nearly every other job, has its glories
as well as its hardships--triumphs that can be told and retold for many
a day to fascinated colored audiences; because there are special
trains--filled with pursy and prosperous bankers from Hartford and
Rochester and Terre Haute--making the trip from coast to coast and back
again, and never forgetting the porter at the last hour of the last day.

There are many men in the Pullman service like Roger Pryor, who has
ridden with every recent President of the land and enjoyed his
confidence and respect. And then there is General Henry Forrest, of the
Congressional Limited, for twenty-four years in charge of one of its
broiler cars, who stops not at Presidents but enjoys the acquaintance
of senators and ambassadors almost without number.

The General comes to know these dignitaries by their feet. When he is
standing at the door of his train under the Pennsylvania Terminal, in
New York, he recognizes the feet as they come poking down the long
stairs from the concourse. And he can make his smile senatorial or
ambassadorial--a long time in advance.

Once Forrest journeyed in a private car to San Francisco, caring for a
Certain Big Man. He took good care of the Certain Big Man--that was part
of his job. He took extra good care of the Certain Big Man--that was his
opportunity. And when the Certain Big Man reached the Golden Gate he
told Henry Forrest that he had understood and appreciated the countless
attentions. The black face of the porter wrinkled into smiles. He dared
to venture an observation.

"Ah thank you, Jedge!" said he. "An' ef it wouldn't be trespassin' Ah'd
lak to say dat when yo' comes home you's gwine to be President of dese
United States."

The Certain Big Man shook his head negatively; but he was flattered
nevertheless. He leaned over and spoke to Henry Forrest.

"If ever I am President," said he, "I will make you a general."

And so it came to pass that on the blizzardy Dakota-made day when
William Howard Taft was inaugurated President of these United States
there was a parade--a parade in which many men rode in panoply and
pride; but none was prouder there than he who, mounted on a magnificent
bay horse, headed the Philippine Band.

A promise was being kept. The bay horse started three times to bolt from
the line of march, and this was probably because its rider was better

used to the Pompeian-red broiler car than to a Pompeian-red bay mare.
But these were mere trifles. Despite them--partly because of them
perhaps--the younger brethren at the terminals were no longer to address
the veteran from the Congressional merely as Mr. Forrest. He was General
Forrest now--a title he bears proudly and which he will carry with him
all the long years of his life.

What becomes of the older porters?

Sometimes, when the rush of the fast trains, the broken nights, the
exposure and the hard, hard work begin to be too much for even sturdy
Afric frames, they go to the "super" and beg for the "sick man's run"--a
leisurely sixty or a hundred miles a day on a parlor car, perhaps on a
side line where travel is light and the parlor car is a sort of
sentimental frippery; probably one of the old wooden cars: the Alicia,
or the Lucille, or the Celeste, still vain in bay windows and grilles,
and abundant in carvings. For a sentimental frippery may be given a
feminine name and may bear her years gracefully--even though she does
creak in all her hundred joints when the track is the least bit uneven.

As to the sick man's tips, the gratuity is no less a matter of keen
interest and doubt at sixty than it is at twenty-six. And though there
is a smile under that clean mat of kinky white hair, it is not all
habit--some of it is still anticipation. But quarters and half dollars
do not come so easily to the old man in the parlor car as to his younger
brother on the sleepers, or those elect who have the smokers on the fat
runs. To the old men come dimes instead--some of them miserable affairs
bearing on their worn faces the faint presentments of the ruler on the
north side of Lake Erie and hardly redeemable in Baltimore or
Cincinnati. Yet even these are hardly to be scorned--when one is sixty.

After the sick man's job? Perhaps a sandy farm on a Carolina
hillside, where an old man may sit and nod in the warm sun, and dream
of the days when steel cars were new--perhaps of the days when the
platform-vestibule first went bounding over the rails--may dream and
nod; and then, in his waking moments, stir the pickaninnies to the
glories of a career on a fast train and a fat run. For if it is true
that any white boy has the potential opportunity of becoming President
of the United States, it is equally true that any black boy may become
the Autocrat of the Pullman Car.

             *   *   *   *   *

(The Independent)

THE GENTLE ART OF BLOWING BOTTLES
And the Story of How Sand is Melted into Glass

BY F. GREGORY HARTSWICK

Remedies for our manifold ills; the refreshment that our infant lips
craved; coolness in time of heat; yes--even tho July 1st has come and
gone--drafts to assuage our thirst; the divers stays and supports of our
declining years--all these things come in bottles. From the time of its
purchase to the moment of its consignment to the barrel in the cellar or
the rapacious wagon of the rag-and-bone man the bottle plays a vital
part in our lives. And as with most inconspicuous necessities, but

little is known of its history. We assume vaguely that it is blown--ever since we saw the Bohemian Glass Blowers at the World's Fair we have known that glass is blown into whatever shape fancy may dictate--but that is as far as our knowledge of its manufacture extends.

As a matter of fact the production of bottles in bulk is one of the most important features of the glass industry of this country today. The manufacture of window glass fades into insignficance before the hugeness of the bottle-making business; and even the advent of prohibition, while it lessens materially the demand for glass containers of liquids, does not do so in such degree as to warrant very active uneasiness on the part of the proprietors of bottle factories.

The process of manufacture of the humble bottle is a surprizingly involved one. It includes the transportation and preparation of raw material, the reduction of the material to a proper state of workability, and the shaping of the material according to design, before the bottle is ready to go forth on its mission.

The basic material of which all glass is made is, of course, sand. Not the brown sand of the river-bed, the well remembered "sandy bottom" of the swimmin' hole of our childhood, but the finest of white sand from the prehistoric ocean-beds of our country. This sand is brought to the factory and there mixed by experts with coloring matter and a flux to aid the melting. On the tint of the finished product depends the sort of coloring agent used. For clear white glass, called flint glass, no color is added. The mixing of a copper salt with the sand gives a greenish tinge to the glass; amber glass is obtained by the addition of an iron compound; and a little cobalt in the mixture gives the finished bottle the clear blue tone that used to greet the waking eye as it searched the room for something to allay that morning's morning feeling. The flux used is old glass--bits of shattered bottles, scraps from the floor of the factory. This broken glass is called "cullet," and is carefully swept into piles and kept in bins for use in the furnaces.

The sand, coloring matter, and cullet, when mixed in the proper proportions, form what is called in bottle-makers' talk the "batch" or "dope." This batch is put into a specially constructed furnace--a brick box about thirty feet long by fifteen wide, and seven feet high at the crown of the arched roof. This furnace is made of the best refractory blocks to withstand the fierce heat necessary to bring the batch to a molten state. The heat is supplied by various fuels--producer-gas is the most common, tho oil is sometimes used. The gas is forced into the furnace and mixed with air at its inception; when the mixture is ignited the flame rolls down across the batch, and the burnt gases pass out of the furnace on the other side. The gases at their exit pass thru a brick grating or "checkerboard," which takes up much of the heat; about every half hour, by an arrangement of valves, the inlet of the gas becomes the outlet, and vice versa, so that the heat taken up by the checkerboard is used instead of being dissipated, and as little of the heat of combustion is lost as is possible. The batch is put into the furnace from the rear; as it liquefies it flows to the front, where it is drawn off thru small openings and blown into shape.

The temperature in the furnace averages about 2100 degrees Fahrenheit; it is lowest at the rear, where the batch is fed in, and graduates to its highest point just behind the openings thru which the glass is drawn off. This temperature is measured by special instruments called thermal couples--two metals joined and placed in the heat of the flame. The heat sets up an electric current in the joined metals, and this current is read on a galvanometer graduated to read degrees Fahrenheit instead of volts, so that the temperature may be read direct.

All furnaces for the melting of sand for glass are essentially the same in construction and principle. The radical differences in bottle manufacturing appear in the methods used in drawing off the glass and blowing it into shape.

Glass is blown by three methods: hand-blowing, semi-automatic blowing, and automatic blowing. The first used was the hand method, and tho the introduction of machines is rapidly making the old way a back number, there are still factories where the old-time glass blower reigns supreme.

One of the great centers of the bottle industry in the United States is down in the southern end of New Jersey. Good sand is dug there--New Jersey was part of the bed of the Atlantic before it literally rose to its present state status--and naturally the factories cluster about the source of supply of material. Within a radius of thirty miles the investigator may see bottles turned out by all three methods.

The hand-blowing, while it is the slowest and most expensive means of making bottles, is by far the most picturesque. Imagine a long, low, dark building--dark as far as daylight is concerned, but weirdly lit by orange and scarlet flashes from the great furnaces that crouch in its shelter. At the front of each of these squatting monsters, men, silhouetted against the fierce glow from the doors, move about like puppets on wires--any noise they may make is drowned in the mastering roar of the fire. A worker thrusts a long blowpipe (in glassworkers' terminology a wand) into the molten mass in the furnace and twirls it rapidly. The end of the wand, armed with a ball of refractory clay, collects a ball of semi-liquid glass; the worker must estimate the amount of glass to be withdrawn for the particular size of the bottle that is to be made. This ball of glowing material is withdrawn from the furnace; the worker rolls it on a sloping moldboard, shaping it to a cylinder, and passes the wand to the blower who is standing ready to receive it. The blower drops the cylinder of glass into a mold, which is held open for its reception by yet another man; the mold snaps shut; the blower applies his mouth to the end of the blowpipe; a quick puff, accompanied by the drawing away of the wand, blows the glass to shape in the mold and leaves a thin bubble of glass protruding above. The mold is opened; the shaped bottle, still faintly glowing, is withdrawn with a pair of asbestos-lined pincers, and passed to a man who chips off the bubble on a rough strip of steel, after which he gives the bottle to one who sits guarding a tiny furnace in which oil sprayed under pressure roars and flares. The rough neck of the bottle goes into the flame; the raw edges left when the bubble was chipped off are smoothed away by the heat; the neck undergoes a final polishing and shaping twirl in the jaws of a steel instrument, and the bottle is laid on a little shelf to be carried away. It is shaped, but not finished.

The glass must not be cooled too quickly, lest it be brittle. It must be annealed--cooled slowly--in order to withstand the rough usage to which it is to be subjected. The annealing process takes place in a long, brick tunnel, heated at one end, and gradually cooling to atmospheric temperature at the other. The bottles are placed on a moving platform, which slowly carries them from the heated end to the cool end. The process takes about thirty hours. At the cool end of the annealing furnace the bottle is met by the packers and is made ready for shipment. These annealing furnaces are called "lehrs" or "leers"--either spelling is correct--and the most searching inquiry failed to discover the reason for the name. They have always been called that, and probably always will be.

In the hand-blowing process six men are needed to make one bottle. There must be a gatherer to draw the glass from the furnace; a blower; a man to handle the mold; a man to chip off the bubble left by the blower; a shaper to finish the neck of the bottle; and a carrier-off to take the completed bottles to the lehr. Usually the gatherer is also the blower, in which case two men are used, one blowing while the other gathers for his turn; but on one platform I saw the somewhat unusual sight of one man doing all the blowing while another gathered for him. The pair used two wands, so that their production was the same as tho two men were gathering and blowing. This particular blower was making quart bottles, and he was well qualified for the job. He weighed, at a conservative estimate, two hundred and fifty pounds, and when he blew something had to happen. I arrived at his place of labor just as the shifts were being changed--a glass-furnace is worked continuously, in three eight-hour shifts--and as the little whistle blew to announce the end of his day's toil the giant grabbed the last wand, dropped it into the waiting mold, and blew a mighty blast. A bubble of glass sprang from the mouth of the mold, swelled to two feet in diameter, and burst with a bang, filling the air with shimmering flakes of glass, light enough to be wafted like motes. When the shining shower had settled and I had opened my eyes--it would not be pleasant to get an eyeful of those beautiful scraps--the huge blower was diminishing in perspective toward his dinner, and the furnace door was, for the moment, without its usual hustling congregation of workers. I made bold to investigate the platform.

Close to me glared the mouth of the furnace, with masses of silver threads depending from it like the beard of some fiery gulleted ogre--the strings of glass left by the withdrawal of the wand. The heat three feet away was enough to make sand melt and run like water, but I was not unpleasantly warm. This was because I stood at the focus of three tin pipes, thru which streams of cold air, fan-impelled, beat upon me. Without this cooling agent it would be impossible for men to work so close to the heat of the molten glass.

Later, in the cool offices of the company, where the roar of the furnaces penetrated only as a dull undertone, and electric fans whizzed away the heat of the summer afternoon, I learned more of the technique of the bottle industry. Each shape demanded by the trade requires a special mold, made of cast iron and cut according to the design submitted. There are, of course, standard shapes for standard bottles; these are alluded to (reversing the usual practise of metonymy) by using thing contained for container, as "ginger ales," "olives," "mustards," "sodas" and (low be it spoken) "beers." But when a firm places an order for bottles of a particular shape, or ones with lettering in relief on the glass, special molds must be made; and after the lot is finished the molds are useless till another order for that particular design comes in. A few standard molds are made so that plates with lettering can be

inserted for customers who want trademarks or firm names on their
bottles; but the great majority of the lettered bottles have their own
molds, made especially for them and unable to be used for any other lot.

All bottles are blown in molds; it is in the handling of the molten
glass and the actual blowing that machinery has come to take the place
of men in the glass industry. The first type of machine to be developed
was for blowing the bottle and finishing it, thus doing away with three
of the six men formerly employed in making one bottle. In appearance the
bottle-blowing machine is merely two circular platforms, revolving in
the same horizontal plane, each carrying five molds. One of the
platforms revolves close to the furnace door, and as each mold comes
around it automatically opens and the gatherer draws from the furnace
enough glass for the bottle which is being made at the time, and places
it in the mold. The mold closes, and the platform turns on, bringing
around another mold to the gatherer. Meanwhile a nozzle has snapped down
over the first mold, shaping the neck of the bottle, and beginning the
blowing. As the mold comes to a point diametrically opposite the furnace
door it opens again, and a handler takes the blank, as the bottle is
called at this stage, and places it in a mold on the second revolving
platform. This mold closes and compressed air blows out the bottle as
the platform revolves. As the mold comes around to the handler again it
opens and the handler takes out the finished bottle, replacing it with a
new blank drawn from the mold on the first platform. This operation
necessitates only three men--a gatherer, a handler, and a carrier-off.
It is also much faster than the old method--an average of about forty
bottles per minute as against barely twenty.

A newer development of this machine does away with the gatherer. A long
rod of refractory clay is given a churning movement in the mouth of the
furnace, forcing the molten glass thru a tube. As enough glass for one
bottle appears at the mouth of the tube a knife cuts the mass and the
blob of glass falls into a trough which conveys it to the blank mold. By
an ingenious device the same trough is made to feed three or four
machines at one time. As many as fifty bottles a minute can be turned
out by this combination blowing machine and feeder.

But the apotheosis of bottle-making is to be seen in another factory in
the south Jersey district. Here it is the boast of the superintendents
that from the time the sand goes out of the freight cars in which it is
brought to the plant till the finished bottle is taken by the packer, no
human hand touches the product; and their statement is amply confirmed
by a trip thru the plant. The sand, coloring matter and cullet are in
separate bins; an electrical conveyor takes enough of each for a batch
to a mixing machine; from there the batch goes on a long belt to the
furnace. At the front of the furnace, instead of doors or mouths, is a
revolving pan, kept level full with the molten glass. Outside the
furnace revolves a huge machine with ten arms, each of which carries its
own mold and blowpipe. As each arm passes over the pan in the furnace
the proper amount of glass is sucked into the mold by vacuum; the bottle
is blown and shaped in the course of one revolution, and the mold,
opening, drops the finished bottle into a rack which carries it to the
lehr on a belt. It passes thru the lehr to the packers; and as each rack
is emptied of its bottles the packers place it again on the belt, which
carries it up to the machine, where it collects its cargo of hot bottles
and conducts it again thru the lehr. The entire plant--mixing, feeding,
actually making the bottles, delivery to the lehr, and packing--is

synchronized exactly. Men unload the cars of sand--men pack the bottles.
The intermediate period is entirely mechanical. The plant itself is as
well lighted and ventilated as a department store, and except in the
immediate vicinity of the furnace there is no heat felt above the daily
temperature. The machines average well over a bottle a second, and by an
exceedingly clever arrangement of electrical recording appliances an
accurate record of the output of each machine, as well as the
temperatures of the furnaces and lehrs, is kept in the offices of the
company. The entire equipment is of the most modern, from the boilers
and motors in the power-plant and producer-gas-plant to the packing
platforms. In addition, the plant boasts a complete machine shop where
all the molds are made and the machines repaired.

It is a far cry from human lung-power to the super-efficient machinery
of the new plants; but it is the logical progress of human events,
applying to every product of man's hands, from battleships to--bottles.

              *   *   *   *   *

SPECIAL FEATURE ARTICLES

(_New York World_)

One illustration, a half-tone reproduction of a photograph of the
exterior of the theater.

THE NEIGHBORHOOD PLAYHOUSE

A GIFT TO THE EAST SIDE--HOW THE SETTLEMENT WORK OF MISSES IRENE AND
ALICE LEWISOHN HAS CULMINATED AT LAST IN A REAL THEATRE--ITS ATTRACTIONS
AND EDUCATIONAL VALUE

The piece is the Biblical "Jephthah's Daughter," adapted from the Book
of Judges. The hero, "a mighty man of valor," has conquered the enemies
of his people. There is great rejoicing over his victory, for the tribe
of Israel has been at its weakest. But now comes payment of the price of
conquest. The leader of the victorious host promised to yield to God as
a burnt sacrifice "whatsoever cometh forth from the doors of my house to
meet me when I return from battle." And his daughter came forth.

In the last act, the girl herself, young and beautiful, advances toward
the altar on which fagots have been piled high. In her hand is the
lighted torch which is to kindle her own death fire.

The chorus chants old Hebraic melodies. Even the audience joins in the
singing. The play takes on the aspect of an ancient religious
ceremonial. Old men and women are in tears, moved by the sad history of
their race, forgetful of the horror of human sacrifice in the intensity
of their religious fervor.

Such is the artistry of the piece; such the perfection of its
production.

Yet this is no professional performance, but the work of amateurs. It is the opening night of the new community theatre of New York's densely populated East Side.

At No. 466 Grand Street it stands, far away from Broadway's theatrical district--a low-lying, little Georgian building. It is but three stories high, built of light red brick, and finished with white marble. All around garish millinery shops display their showy goods. Peddlers with pushcarts lit by flickering flames, vie with each other in their array of gaudy neckties and bargain shirtwaists. Blazing electric signs herald the thrills of movie shows. And, salient by the force of extreme contrast, a plain little white posterboard makes its influence felt. It is lit by two iron lanterns, and reads simply, "The Neighborhood Playhouse."

The Misses Irene and Alice Lewisohn of No. 43 Fifth Avenue have built this theatre. It is their gift to the neighborhood, and symbolizes the culmination of a work which they have shared with the neighborhood's people.

Eight years ago the Henry Street Settlement started its scheme of festivals and pantomimes, portraying through the medium of color, song, and dance such vague ideas as "Impressions of Spring." It was the boys and girls of the Settlement who performed in these pantomimes. It was they who made the costumes, painted the necessary scenery, sang and danced.

And both daughters of the late Leonard Lewisohn were always interested and active in promoting this work.

Out of it, in due time, there developed, quite naturally, a dramatic club. Plays were given in the Settlement gymnasium--full-grown pieces like "The Silver Box," by John Galsworthy, and inspiring dramas like "The Shepherd," a plea for Russian revolutionists, by an American author, Miss Olive Tilford Dargan. Such was the emotional response of the neighborhood to this drama that four performances had to be given at Clinton Hall; and as a result a substantial sum of money was forwarded to "The Friends of Russian Freedom."

Then, in 1913, came the famous Pageant, which roused the entire district to a consciousness of itself--its history, its dignity and also its possibilities.

That portion of the East Side which surrounds the Henry Street Settlement has seen many an invasion since the days when the Dutch first ousted the Indians. English, Quakers, Scotch have come and gone, leaving traces more or less distinct. The Irish have given place to the Italians, who have been replaced by the Russians. In the Pageant of 1913 all these settlers were represented by artistically clad groups who paraded the streets singing and dancing. No hall could have held the audience which thronged to see this performance; no host of matinée worshippers could have rivalled it in fervor of appreciation.

When the Misses Lewisohn, then, built their new playhouse in Grand Street, it was not with the intention of rousing, but rather of satisfying, an artistic demand among the people of the neighborhood. And in the new home are to be continued all the varied activities of which the Henry Street Settlement festival and dramatic clubs were but the

centre. It is to be a genuine community enterprise in which each boy and
girl will have a share. Miss Alice Lewisohn herself thus expresses its
many-sided work:

"The costume designers and makers, fashioners of jewelry, painters and
composers, musicians and seamstresses, as well as actors and directors,
will contribute their share in varying degree.

"Putting aside for a moment the higher and artistic development which
such work must bring, there is the craftsman side, too, which has
practical value. The young men will become familiar with all the
handiwork of the theatre, the construction and handling of scenery, the
electrical equipment and its varied uses. It will be conceded, I think,
that in this respect the community playhouse is really a college of
instruction in the craft of the stage."

It is a college with a very efficient and well-trained staff of
professors. Mrs. Sarah Cowell Le Moyne, already well known as a teacher
of elocution and acting, will be one of its members. Miss Grace
Griswold, an experienced co-worker of the late Augustine Daly, will act
as manager.

The pupils of this novel school are to have amusement as well as work.
The third floor has been planned to meet many more requirements than are
usually considered in a theatre. Across the front runs a large rehearsal
room, large enough to make a fine dance hall when occasion demands.
Here, too, is a kitchenette which will be used to serve refreshments
when social gatherings are in progress or when an over-long rehearsal
tires out the cast. In warm weather the flat-tiled roof will be used as
a playground. It will be the scene, too, of many open air performances.

The Neighborhood Playhouse has been open only a few weeks. Already it is
in full swing. On the nights when the regular players do not appear the
programme consists of motion pictures and music. There is a charming
informality and ease about these entertainments; there is also genuine
art, and a whole-hearted appreciation on the part of the neighborhood's
people.

           *   *   *   *   *

(_New York Evening Post_)

THE SINGULAR STORY OF THE MOSQUITO MAN

BY HELEN BULLITT LOWRY

"Now you just hold up a minute"--the bungalow-owner waved an indignant
hand at the man in the little car chug-chugging over the bumpy road.
"Now I just want to tell you," he protested, "that a mosquito got into
my room last night and bit me, and I want you to know that this has
happened three times this week. I want it to stop."

The man in the car had jumped out, and was turning an animated, and
aggressive, but not at all provoked, face on the complainer.

"Are you certain your drains are not stopped up?" he asked.

"Oh, those drains are all right. It's that damp hollow over in Miss K's woods that's making the trouble."

"I'll go there immediately," said the aggressive one. "She promised me she would fill that place this week."

"All right, then," answered the placated bungalow-owner, "I thought you'd fix it up if you found out about it. I certainly wouldn't have bought around Darien if you had not cleared this place of mosquitoes."

The aggressive one plunged into the Connecticut woods and began his search for possible mosquito-breeding spots. He was the "Mosquito Man," the self-appointed guardian of the Connecticut coast from Stamford to Westport.

He was not born a Mosquito Man at all--in fact, he did not become one until he was forty years old and had retired from business because he had made enough money to rest and "enjoy life." But he did not rest, and did not get enjoyment, for the mosquitoes had likewise leased his place on the Sound and were making good their title.

Came then big fat mosquitoes from the swamp. Came mosquitoes from the salt marshes. Some lighted on the owner's nose and some looked for his ankles, and found them. Three days of this sort of rest made him decide to move away. Then, because he was aggressive, he became the Mosquito Man. The idea occurred to him when he had gone over to a distant island and was watching the building of houses.

"This place," he said to the head carpenter, "is going to be a little heaven."

"More like a little other place," growled the head carpenter. "Here they've dug out the centre of the island and carted it to the beach to make hills for the houses to be built on. One good rain will fill their little heaven with mosquitoes. Why don't the people around here drain their country?"

That night the Mosquito Man telephoned to a drainage expert in New York and demanded that he come out the next day.

"I don't like to work on Sunday," the expert objected.

"It is absolutely essential that you come at once," he was told. "Can you take the first train?"

The first train and the expert arrived in Darien at 5:51. Before the day was over a contract had been drawn up to the purport that the expert would drain the salt marshes between Stamford and South Norwalk for $4,000.

The Mosquito Man now began to talk mosquitoes to every one who would listen and to many who did not want to listen. "That bug," the old settlers called him at the time--for old settlers are very settled in their ways. The young women at the Country Club, whenever they saw him coming, made bets as to whether he would talk mosquitoes--and he always did. Every property-owner in the township was asked for a subscription, and some gave generously and some gave niggardly and some did not give at all. The subscriptions were voluntary, for no one could be forced to remove a mosquito-breeding nuisance from his property. This was in 1911, and only in 1915 has a mosquito law been passed in Connecticut. The Mosquito Man was forced to use "indirect influence," which does not expedite matters.

A subscription of $1,000 came from the big land corporation of the neighborhood, after the "indirect influence" had rather forcibly expressed itself.

"I want $1,000 from you," said the Mosquito Man to the representative of the president--the president was in South America. The representative laughed, so the Mosquito Man spent several days explaining to him why property is more valuable when it is not infested with pests. But every time that the $1,000 was mentioned, the representative could not restrain the smile.

"Well," the Mosquito Man said, at last, "I will make the drainage on your property anyway, and it will cost me $2,000. If you want it left you will have to pay me every cent of the $2,000, not just the $1,000 that I am asking now. Otherwise I shall fill up my ditches and let you enjoy your mosquitoes."

The representative did not laugh at this, but cabled the president in South America. As the president had just been at Panama, and had seen the mosquito extermination work, the $1,000 subscription came back by return cable.

The Darien Board of Health also was a spot against which in direct influence was knocking, for it was a rich Board of Health with $150 at its disposal--and the Mosquito Man wanted that appropriation to flaunt in the faces of the old settlers.

"God sent mosquitoes," objected one member of the Board of Health, "and it is going in the face of Providence to try to get rid of them."

All in all, the money was raised. Some whom he asked for $100 gave $25, and some whom he asked for $25 gave $100, and some millionaires did not give at all--but a sail-maker is still telling proudly of how he gave $5, and "I haven't regretted a cent of it since."

The draining now commenced, and the expert and the Mosquito Man were of the same stripe. The work was completed in six weeks. Just about this time people stopped calling the Mosquito Man "a bug," and the members of the Country Club even tried to make him talk mosquitoes to them, while the sail-maker felt sure that his $5 had done the whole job. Hammocks were swung out in the yards--and a hammock hung outside of the screens is the barometer of the mosquito condition.

The Mosquito Man was feeling very satisfied the night he went to a dance at the Country Club. But the east wind blew in the mosquitoes from the Norwalk marshes.

"It was the most embarrassing experience I have ever had," said the Mosquito Man. "I sat right behind a big fat lady whose dress was very low and I watched the mosquitoes bite her; her whole back was covered with red lumps. That night I telegraphed to the man who had done the draining and he telegraphed back that all of Norwalk township must be drained."

Norwalk proved to be a much severer task than Darien. In Darien the Mosquito Man had found only indifference and prejudice; in Norwalk he met active opposition. Property owners and city councils seem to be afraid that the value of property will be brought down if any sanitation scandal is advertised. It really appeared to be simpler and better business to ignore the fact.

To do away with this opposition, the Mosquito Man handled his campaign in a popular manner. The cooperation of the newspapers was gained and every day he published articles on the mosquito question; some of the articles were educational and others were facetious--while one came out that brought the property owners crying "murder" about his ears. This was the article in which he gave the statistics of Norwalk's health rate in comparison with other Connecticut towns. The smallest subscriptions were encouraged, for, after a man has given a dollar to a cause, that cause is his. Many a child was received with a welcoming smile when he brought to the campaign offices a ten-cent donation.

True, ten-cent donations were not suggested to adult contributors, and the Mosquito Man did much to induce the well-to-do citizens to subscribe according to their means. He still tells with relish of the club of women which took up a collection, after his talk, and presented him with two dollars, in small change.

"The women, though, were my greatest help," he adds; "I found that the women are as a rule better citizens than the men and are glad to be organized to fight the mosquito and fly menace. Of course, I found some uneducated ones that owned a piece of property a foot square, and were afraid that I would walk off with it in my pocket if I came to look it over--but, as for the educated women, I could not have managed my campaign without them."

A large contributor to the fund was the monastery at Kaiser Island. For years this had been a summer resort for the monks, who filled the dormitories in the old days before the mosquitoes took the island. Only one priest was there when the Mosquito Man visited the place to ask for a subscription.

"Very few come any more," said the priest. "It is because of the mosquitoes."

"Will you contribute $500 to get rid of them?" asked the Mosquito Man.

Briefly, the Mosquito Man offered to repay the $500 himself if he did not exterminate the mosquitoes. The mosquitoes went; the monks came back to Kaiser Island.

Yet, in spite of the occasional generous giver, the $7,500 was never quite raised, and the Mosquito Man himself had to make up the deficit. The citizens of Norwalk, for instance, contributed only $150.

This all happened three years ago, and now not a child in the twelve miles but can tell you all about mosquitoes and how a community can avoid having them. The Mosquito Man is appreciated now, and the community understands what he has done for them and what he is still doing--for the contract merely drained the salt marshes, doing away with the salt-water mosquitoes. There were still the fresh-water mosquitoes, and there was still much work for some one to do. That some one has been the Mosquito Man.

During the three years, he has made it his business to drain every inland marsh within his territory, to turn over every tub which may collect water, to let the plug out of every old boat which is breeding mosquitoes, and to convince every ancestor-encumbered autocrat that his inherited woods can breed mosquitoes just as disastrously as do the tin cans of the Hungarian immigrant down the road. The Mosquito Man has an assistant, paid by the towns of Darien and Norwalk--and together they traverse the country.

"It was difficult finding a man who would go into mud to the waist when need was," said the Mosquito Man, "but I finally found a good man with the proper scorn of public opinion on the clothes question, and with a properly trained wife who cleaned without scolding."

You can find traces of the two men any place you go in the woods of Darien or Norwalk. In a ferned dell where you are quite sure that yours is the first human presence, you come upon a ditch, as clean and smooth as a knife--or you find new grass in a place which you remember as a swamp. Perhaps you may even be lucky enough to come on the two workers themselves, digging with their pick and spade--for all summer long the Mosquito Man is working eight hours a day at his self-appointed task.

You might even find him in New York some off-day--and you will know him, for surely he will be telling some rebellious apartment-house owner that the tank on his roof is unscreened. For they do say that he carries his activities into any part of the world where he may chance to be; they do say that, when he was in Italy not so very long ago, he went out to investigate the mosquitoes which had disturbed his rest the night before.

"Now you must oil your swamp," said he to the innkeeper.

That night there was no salad for dinner, for the innkeeper had obeyed the order to the best of his ability. He had poured all of his best olive oil on the mosquito marsh.

       *   *   *   *   *

(Country Gentleman)

Five half-tone illustrations, with the following captions:
1. "A Traction Ditcher at Work Digging Trench for Tile."
2. "Ditch Dug With Dynamite Through Woods."
3. "Apple Packing House and Cold Storage at Ransomville."
4. "Nelson R. Peet, County Agent and Manager of the Niagara County Farm Bureau, New York."
5. "Part of the Crowd Listening to the Speakers."

A COUNTY SERVICE STATION

WHERE NEW YORK FARMERS GET HELP IN THEIR FRUIT GROWING AND MARKETING
PROBLEMS

BY D. H. WILLIAMS

You've got to look into the family closet of a county and study its
skeletons before you can decide whether that county's farming business
is mostly on paper or on concrete. You've got to know whether it
standardizes production and marketing, or just markets by as many
methods as there are producers.

As a living example of the possibility of tightening up and retiming the
gears of a county's economic machinery to the end of cutting out power
losses, Niagara County, New York, stands in a distinct class by itself.

Here is an area of 558 square miles, with Lake Ontario spraying its
northern line. A network of electric and steam railways and hundreds of
miles of splendid state highways make up a system of economic arteries
through which the industrial life-blood of the county circulates.

Forty-eight hours to Chicago's markets, the same distance to New York's;
three wealthy industrial and agricultural cities within the county
itself--Lockport, Niagara Falls and North Tonawanda--operating with a
wealth of cheap electric power generated at Niagara Falls--these are
some of the advantages within and without the county, the value of which
is self-evident.

Beginning with the southern plain section, Niagara's agriculture changes
in type from general hay and grain farming to a more intense
fruit-growing industry as the northern plain section is approached,
until within the zone of Lake Ontario's tempering influence the fruit
industry almost excludes all other types of farming.

There is hardly a more favored fruit section in the country than the
northern half of Niagara County. Apples, pears, peaches, plums, grapes,
cherries, quinces make up the county's horticultural catalogue. The
latest available figures rank Niagara County first among the counties of
New York in the number of fruit trees; second in the total number of
bushels of fruit produced; first in the quantity of peaches, pears,
plums and prunes, quinces and cherries; third in the number of bushels
of apples.

Yet there are things about the county which no statistics will ever
show, such things, for instance, as the condition of the orchards, the
market value of the fruit, the earning capacity of the land as a
whole--in other words, the bedrock rating of the county. You have to get
at these things by a different avenue of approach.

A rather close auditing during 1914 of the accounts of some eighty-seven
typical good farms in perhaps the best section of Niagara County brought
out the fact that labor incomes from these farms, on the whole, could
not be classed as strictly giltedge. One diagnosis made by a Niagara
County investigator is recorded in these words:

"Though Niagara County has many of the best fruit farms in New York
State, there are numbers of orchards that have been abandoned to the

ravages of insects and disease. There is also a tendency toward
extensive rather than intensive fruit growing, which has resulted in
many large plantings being made.

"Niagara County does not need more orchards, but rather cultivation and
spraying of the present orchards; it does not need to produce more
fruit, but rather to insure better grading and marketing of the present
production."

This observation is dated 1914, one year after leading farmers and
business men of the county, convinced that all was not so well with them
as the lifeless census figures would have one believe, made the move to
set up and operate for the county a farm bureau. New York is the
national hotbed of farm-bureau enthusiasm and propaganda.

Almost six years to the day after the inauguration of this bureau, I
went into Niagara County. And before I left I was able to sketch a
rather vivid mental picture of what a farm bureau really can do for a
county, be the raw material with which it must work good, bad or
indifferent.

Up in the office of the Niagara County Farm Bureau at Lockport I waited
some two hours for an interview with its manager, Nelson R. Peet. That
wait was an eye-opener.

Three women clerks and stenographers and the assistant manager occupied
this room. The clerks were trying to typewrite, answer the continuous
ringing of the phone, respond to buzzer summons from Manager Peet's
private office and talk with a stream of visitors, all at the same time.

I spent two whole days and half a night in these offices and not once
save at night was there a let-up in this sort of thing. It was business
all the time; the business of service! Niagara County farmers are using
the bureau.

Nelson Peet, manager, is a spectacled human magneto. His speech and his
movements fairly crackle with energy; his enthusiasm is as communicable
as a jump spark. A young man in years, yet mature in the knowledge of
men and the psychology of service, he never wastes a minute dilating
upon the philosophy of farm management; but he has worked twenty hours a
day to see that Niagara County farmers got all the labor they needed
during rush seasons.

This man has been with the bureau three years. When he came to it the
bureau had a paid-up membership of 325. In March this year, when I was
in Niagara County, the membership stood at 2185, and was increasing
daily. It led by a good margin, I was told, the fifty-five New York
county farm bureaus. These, in 1918, had a total membership of 60,000.
More than half the farmers in Niagara County are members of the Niagara
Bureau.

When Peet first took charge there were two broad courses open to him. He
might have planned a program of paternalistic propaganda in behalf of
the farmers of the county. Such a program calls for a tremendous amount
of talking and writing about coöperation and community interests, better
economics and better social conditions, but too often results in the
propagandist doing the "coing," while the "operating" is left to

somebody else.

The other course was to find out what the farms and farmers in the
county needed most and then set to work with little ado to get those
things. Peet chose the latter course. And in so doing he has staged one
of the best demonstrations in rural America. He has shown that a farm
bureau can be made into a county service station and actually become the
hub of the county's agricultural activities.

With the aid of state-college men, one of Peet's foremost lines of
bureau work has been that of taking inventories of the farming business
of Niagara County. For four years these records have been taken on some
100 typical farms. Group meetings are regularly held at the homes of the
bureau's community committeemen. Here, with the records they have been
keeping, the farmers assemble. Here they work out their own labor
incomes and compare notes with their neighbors. The farm bureau helps
the men make these business analyses--it does not do the work for them.
Now the farmers ask for the blank forms and are themselves as
enthusiastic over farm-management records as the men who specialize in
such.

These figures serve the bureau as an index to the county's progress.
More than once Peet has referred to them and discovered where leaks
could be plugged. For example, these records showed an average labor
income of $182 a farm for the four years ending 1916.

"This fact," Mr. Peet explained, "we put to work as the reason for doing
something to benefit the fruit industry. What could be done? The answer
in other highly specialized fruit sections seems to have been central
packing houses. We held a meeting, inviting one very influential fruit
grower from each loading station in the county. We showed charts of the
farm-management records. It didn't take long for the meeting to go on
record as favoring the central-packing-house plan.

"Later meetings were held in each community, the farm-management charts
were again shown, and at every loading station the meetings went on
record as favoring central packing houses. To make a long story short,
sites and methods of financing these houses were worked out. There were
already two old central packing houses in operation. They took on new
life. Five new ones have been formed. All were incorporated and
federated into a central parent association, which owns the brand
adopted and makes the rules and regulations under which the fruit is
packed.

"From the very beginning the proposition has been pushed not as a means
of beating the selling game by selling coöperatively, but as a means of
securing the confidence of the consuming public, which must ultimately
result in a wider distribution and better prices. In fact, the matter of
selling has not been fostered from the farm-bureau office. We have
concerned ourselves solely with uniform grading and central packing. We
believed from the start that the selling of properly graded and packed
fruit will take care of itself, and this stand has been justified.

"Each association makes its own arrangements for selling, and in every
case has secured better prices than the growers who sold under the old
system. The most satisfactory feature of this work centers round the
fact that the best and most influential growers are heart and soul

behind the proposition. The personnel of coöperative movements, I believe, is the main feature."

When I visited Niagara County the seven central packing associations were doing a splendid business, handling about $1,000,000 worth of apples between them. Only two of the associations were more than one year old. Many of the associations were dickering for additional space for packing and for extensions for their refrigerator service. Other communities in Niagara and in other counties were writing in for details of the plan, to the end of getting the same thing started in their sections. And inquiries were coming in from states outside of New York.

Even with the best of selling methods, no commodity will bring a profit to the producer unless the greater portion of it is eligible to the A-1 class. Too many seconds or culls will throw any orchard venture on the rocks of bankruptcy. It came to Manager Peet's attention early in 1917 that the farm bureau had a golden opportunity to put on another service, which alone, if it worked out in practice as well as it did on paper, would justify the existence of the bureau.

He noticed that though orchardists were following spraying schedules--the best they could find--some had splendid results in controlling apple scab and other pests, but others got results ranging between indifferent and poor. This seemed paradoxical, in view of the fact that one man who followed the same spraying schedule as his neighbor would have more scabby apples than the other.

At that time L.F. Strickland, orchard inspector for the state department of agriculture, had paid particular attention to a limited number of apple orchards in Niagara County with a view to controlling scab by spraying. He discovered that, though the average spraying calendar is all right, climatic conditions in different parts of the same county often upset these standard calculations, so that a difference of one day or even a few hours in time of spraying often meant the difference between success and failure. In other words, it was necessary to study all contributing factors, watch the orchards unremittingly and then decide on the exact day or even hour when conditions were right for a successful spray treatment. He found that one must strike the _times between times_ to get the optimum of results.

So Mr. Strickland, in conjunction with his regular work, kept an eagle eye on a few orchards and would notify the owners when it seemed the moment for spraying had come. It worked out that those favored orchardists had magnificent yields of A-1 fruit; others in the same sections, following the rather flexible spraying calendars, didn't do nearly so well.

All this set Manager Peet to thinking. "Strickland hasn't got an automobile and has lots of other work to do," he reasoned; "but why, if he had a car and could give all the time necessary to such work, couldn't the same results be had in orchards all over the county? Why can't this farm bureau put on a spraying service?"

He put the idea up to the executive committee of the bureau. The idea was good, they agreed, but it would cost at least $500 to try it out the first year. The bureau didn't have the available funds.

"Tell you what," they finally said: "If you want to get out and rustle up 500 new members at one dollar each to pay for this thing, we'll authorize it."

Peet was telling me about it. "Here the bureau had been working for four years with a paid-up membership of about 375," he said, "and if I believed in my idea I had to get 500 more by spring. It was February eighth when the committee gave me this decision. Well, I did it in time to start the ball that spring!"

He got the new members because he had a service to sell them. Arrangements were made whereby the county was divided into six zones, varying in soil and topographic conditions. Criterion orchards were selected in each zone. The inspector, with the aid of daily telegraphic weather reports and through constant inspection of the criterion orchards, decided when the hour struck for the most effective spraying of these orchards.

In the meantime Manager Peet and the inspector had worked out a code system for spraying instructions and put this into the hands of the growers in the six zones. When it came time to spray, the telephones from headquarters in Lockport were put to work and the code message sent to certain orchardists; these in turn repeated the instructions to a number of other orchardists agreed upon, until every member had received the message.

The scheme has worked. The first year there were 800 members who took this service; the second year--1918--there were 900; this year there are 1500. It is paying for itself many times over. One central packing house with nine grower members reports that eight of the members used the spraying service and that none of these had more than five per cent of their fruit to cull out. The ninth member sprayed, but not through the service. He culled forty-five per cent of his crop. There are scores of similar instances.

Seeing how quickly he could get the support of the Niagara farmers for any move which had practice and not theory to recommend it, Manager Peet next began to agitate for an improvement in city-marketing conditions in Lockport. Up to August, 1915, the system--if system it might be called--of distributing farm produce for Lockport's consumption consisted of sporadic visits by producers to the city with produce to be sold at prices largely controlled by the local grocerymen. Likewise retail prices to consumers were chiefly regulated by the same standard.

A grower might drive into Lockport with 100 quarts of strawberries. He would stop at a grocery and offer them.

"No," the grocer would say, "I don't want any. Say, how much do you want for them anyhow?"

"Ten cents a quart."

"Too high; I'll give you six."

Whereupon the man would drive on to see the next grocer. But the man who offered six cents might go straight to his phone, call up the rest of the trade and inform it that there were 100 quarts of strawberries on the streets for which he had offered six cents against ten asked. The result would be that the farmer would get no better offer than six cents.

So Manager Peet joined hands with the Lockport Board of Commerce and went at the job of righting this condition. He proposed a city market for farmers. The nearest approach to a market was a shelter for teams which the local food dealers had rented.

To 700 farmers in the vicinity of Lockport Manager Peet wrote letters, calling their attention to these conditions and offering the city-market idea as a remedy. And he used publicity among Lockport's population of consumers, showing them the economy of such a move. The farmers held a get-together meeting, decided on a location for a market in Lockport, decided on market days and market hours. After this the farm bureau got the city's common council to pass an ordinance prohibiting the huckstering of farm produce on the streets during market hours; also an ordinance setting the market hours, marking off a street section which should be used as a market stand, and putting the superintendent of streets in charge.

That was all. Not a cent of appropriation asked for. The market opened August 10, 1917, with fifty farm wagons in place. Before the summer was over it was common to find more than 100 at their stands. The local war-garden supervisor acted as inspector. He looked over the produce, advised the farmers how to pack and display it, and used every energy in the direction of popularizing the market among producers and consumers alike.

Between Manager Peet and the inspector a scheme was worked out whereby every Thursday was bargain day in market. They would get a certain number of farmers to agree to pack and offer for sale on those days a limited number of baskets of their finest tomatoes, say. Or it might be corn. In the case of tomatoes the bargain price would be ten cents for baskets which that day were selling regularly for eighteen to twenty-five cents. To each of these baskets--no farmer was asked to sacrifice more than ten--was attached a green tag noting that it was a bargain.

Each bargain day was advertised in advance among Lockport consumers. Thursday mornings would see an early rush to the market. The bargains would be cleaned out and then business at normal prices would continue at a brisker rate than usual.

The first year of its operation this market was held on fifty-one days. During this period 1300 rigs sold out their produce for a total of $13,000. This simple move has resulted in stabilizing prices in Lockport and has encouraged the bringing in of farm produce. Prices automatically regulate themselves. If they begin to get too low in Lockport, the supply in sight is immediately reduced through action by the producers in shipping the stuff to Niagara Falls or Buffalo by motor trucks.

The distribution of Lockport's milk supply, as happens in hundreds of cities, has been attended by considerable waste and expense as a result of duplication of delivery routes, breakage of bottles and uneconomic schedules.

The first night I was in Lockport, Manager Peet was holding a meeting of the milk producers supplying the city for the purpose of settling this inequity once and for all. A little agitation had been carried on ahead of this meeting, but only a little. Peet had a plan.

"It's all wrong to plan for a municipally owned central distributing system," he was explaining to me the next morning; "these are too likely to get mixed up in politics. So last night we just about clinched our arrangement for having our city distributing system owned by the producers themselves. In the past we have had eight distributors with fifteen wagons handling the milk supplied from fifty dairy farms. There has been a big loss in time and money as a result of this competition.

"The farm bureau got the producers together on the plan of securing options on these distributors' interests, and last night we just about wound up all the preliminaries. We already have our limited liability corporation papers. We're incorporating under the Membership Corporation Law. Our organization comes under the amendment to the Sherman Antitrust Law, you know, following closely the California law under which the California fruit growers' associations operate.

"We figure that we will need between $20,000 and $30,000 for the purchase of buildings, wagons, equipment and good-will now in the hands of the distributors. At first we thought it would be a good plan to have every member of the association subscribe to the amount proportioned by the number of cows he keeps or the amount of milk he has for sale. But for several reasons this wouldn't work. So we hit on the scheme of having each man subscribe to the amount he personally is able to finance.

"We already have $24,000 subscribed in sums between set limits of $100 and $1000. We're issuing five-year certificates of indebtedness bearing six per cent interest. Our producers will have about $9000 worth of milk a month to distribute. We plan to deduct five per cent every month from these milk checks to pay off the certificates. Then later we'll create a new set of certificates and redistribute these in proportion to the amounts of milk produced on the members' farms."

Manager Peet and the producers are making it perfectly plain to Lockport consumers that this is no move contemplating price control. In fact, they expect to sell milk for a cent a quart under the old price.

The farm-labor shortage which antedated our entrance into the war became a national menace about the time our selective draft began to operate. New York farmers were as hard hit as any other farmers, particularly in the fruit sections, where a tremendous labor supply falls suddenly due at harvest time. Niagara County came in for its full share of this trouble and the Niagara County Farm Bureau went its length to meet the emergency.

In 1917 Western New York produced the biggest crop of peaches in its history, and in the face of the greatest labor famine. There were nearly 8000 cars of the fruit in danger of spoiling on the trees and on the ground. Peet anticipated the crisis by converting the farm bureau into a veritable county labor department. He was promised a good number of high-school boys who were to help in the peach harvest and who were to be cleared through a central office in Buffalo.

Manager Peet worked out arrangements for the care of these boys in forty-two camps strategically located. The camps were to accommodate thirty boys each. The farmers had asked Peet for 4500 hands. He applied for 1500 boys and had every reason to expect these. But at the critical moment something went wrong in Buffalo headquarters and of the 1500 asked for he got only 200!

"I was in Buffalo at the time the news was broken," Manager Peet was saying to me, "and my first impulse was to jump off one of the docks!"

Here was a nice kettle of fish! The fruit was ripening on the trees, and the phones in the bureau offices were ringing their plating off with calls from frantic farmers. Peet didn't jump off a Buffalo dock; he jumped out of his coat and into the fray. He got a Federal Department of Labor man to help him. They plastered appeals for help all over Western New York--on the walls of post offices, railroad stations, on boarding houses. They worked on long-distance phones, the telegraph, the mails. They hired trucks and brought city men and boys and women and girls from cities to work in the orchards over week-ends. Labor, attracted by the flaring posters, drifted into the bureau's offices in Lockport and immediately was assigned to farms; and hundreds of laborers whom Peet never saw also came.

By working seven days a week and often without meals and with cat naps for sleep the bureau cleared 1200 laborers through its office, to say nothing of the loads brought overland by motor truck and which never came near the office. Business houses in the towns closed down and sent their help to the orchards. Lockport's organization of "live wires"--lawyers, doctors, bankers--went out and worked in the orchards.

"Well," was Peet's comment, "we saved the crop, that's all!"

Last year the bureau placed 1095 men and four women on farms in Niagara County. In addition, 1527 soldiers were secured on two-day furloughs from Fort Niagara to help harvest the fruit crops. "We did this," said Manager Peet, "mainly by starting early and keeping persistently at it with the War Department, in order to cut the red tape."

This fall there will go into effect in New York State an amendment to its drainage law which is going to do more properly to drain the state than all the steam diggers that could have been crowded on its acres under former conditions. This action came out of Niagara County, through the farm bureau.

To realize the importance of drainage in this county one must remember that it lies in two levels broken by the ridge which forms the locks at Lockport, the falls at Niagara Falls, and which extends across the county from east to west. In each plateau the land is very level, there being but few places in the county having a difference in elevation of twenty feet within a radius of a mile. Good drainage is very necessary and in the past has been very hard to secure.

"Practically no man can secure adequate drainage without being concerned in the drainage of his neighbor's land," said Mr. Peet. "If the neighbor objects the situation is complicated. And our drainage laws have been woefully inadequate to handle these problems."

But recently the farm bureau put it up to a conference of county agents of New York to get the "state leader" to appoint a state committee to work this thing out and persuade the state legislature to make the necessary amendments to the drainage law. The plan went through, and one of the laws passed compels an objecting property owner to open drains which are necessary for the relief of his neighbors. This law goes into effect next fall.

Farmers are looking to the farm bureau for help in the cleaning and repairing of some sixty drainage ditches constructed in the past under the county-commissioner plan. But the records on file in the county clerk's office are in bad shape. The farm bureau has taken it upon itself to arrange all this material so that it is available on a minute's notice, and as a result has drawn up petitions to the supervisors for the cleaning out of three of these ditches.

Cooperating with the New York State Food Commission, the farm bureau had a power-tractor ditcher placed in the county last summer. Peet placed his assistant in full charge, and the machine never lost a single day as a result of lack of supervision. It has dug over 4000 rods of ditch for tile on twenty-eight farms.

For four years Niagara County farmers had not made expenses in growing tomatoes for the canneries. The farm bureau called a meeting of some fourteen growers and together they figured the cost of production. The average cost for 1917 was found to be $85 an acre; the estimated cost for 1918 was $108 an acre. The average crop was set at six tons to the acre. A joint committee went out of the conference and laid these facts before the canners. The result was that the growers got $20 a ton for their crops in 1918.

These are some outstanding features of the service rendered its farmers by the Niagara bureau. Here are some of its "lesser" activities:

Taking an agricultural census by school districts of each farm in the county and completing the job in one week.

Effecting an interchange of livestock and seed.

Distributing 1000 bushels of seed corn among 383 farmers, twenty-two tons of nitrate of soda at cost among sixty-two farmers, and securing and distributing six tons of sugar to fifty beekeepers for wintering bees.

Indorsing 200 applications for military furloughs.

Assisting in organizing Liberty Loan campaigns, especially the third.

Assisting in the delivery of twenty carloads of feed, fertilizer, farm machinery and barrels, which had been delayed.

Holding twelve demonstration meetings, attended by 602 farmers.

Conducting two tractor schools, attended by 125 farmers.

Arranging eight farmers' institutes, attended by 900 farmers.

Organizing a Federal Farm Loan Association which has loaned $125,000 to nineteen farmers.

The bureau keeps its members posted on what is going on in the county and what the bureau is doing through the medium of a well-edited monthly "News" of eight pages. The best feature of the handling of this publication is that it costs neither bureau nor members a cent. The advertisements from local supply dealers pay for it, and two pages of ads in each issue settles the bill.

The bureau's books show that last year it spent five dollars in serving each member. The membership fee is only one dollar. The difference comes from Federal, state and county appropriations.

The success of this bureau comes from having at the head of it the right man with the right view of what a farm bureau should do. Manager Peet sees to it that the organization works with the local chamber of commerce--the one in Lockport has 700 members--which antedates the farm bureau and which always has supported the bureau. Peet's policy has been to keep the bureau not only before the farmers but before the city people as well.

The "live-wire" committee of the Lockport chamber, composed of lawyers, doctors, bankers, merchants, and the like, has made Manager Peet an _ex-officio_ member. The Niagara Falls and Tonawanda Chambers of Commerce get together with the Lockport chamber and the farm bureau and talk over problems of inter-county importance. These conferences have worked out a unified plan for road development, for instance. The Niagara Farm Bureau helped the Niagara Falls city administration to secure the services of a Federal market inspector. In this way all rivalry between different sections and towns in Niagara County is freed of friction.

About the only criticism I heard against the farm bureau of Niagara County was that Peet was the wrong man. The farmers want a man who will _stay_ manager. But some of the best members hinted that Peet will not stay because he's just a bit too efficient. They seem to fear that some business corporation is going to get him away. And when you look over the record of his work as organizer and executive, you must admit there's something in this.

                *   *   *   *   *

(Detroit News)

Four half-tone illustrations:
  1. The Settling Basin at the Water Works.
  2. Interior of the Tunnel Through which the Water is Pumped.
  3. Where Detroit's Water Comes From.
  4. Water Rushing into the Settling Basin.

GUARDING A CITY'S WATER SUPPLY

HOW THE CITY CHEMIST WATCHES FOR THE APPEARANCE OF DEADLY BACILLI; WATER MADE PURE BY CHEMICALS

BY HENRY J. RICHMOND

"COLON." The city chemist spoke the one significant word as he set down
the test tube into which he had been gazing intently. The next morning
the front page of all the city papers displayed the warning, "Citizens
should boil the drinking water."

Every morning, as the first task of the day, the city chemist uncorks a
curious little crooked tube containing a few spoonsful of very ordinary
bouillon, akin to that which you might grab at the quick lunch, but
which has been treated by the admixture of a chemical. This tube begins
in a bulb which holds the fluid and terminates in an upturned crook
sealed at the end. Into this interesting little piece of apparatus, the
chemist pours a small quantity of the city drinking water, and he then
puts the whole into an incubator where it is kept at a temperature
favorable to the reactions which are expected if the water is
contaminated.

After a sufficient time the tube is inspected. To the untrained eye
nothing appears. The bouillon still remains in the little bulb
apparently unchanged. Its color and clearness have not been affected.
But the chemist notices that it does not stand so high in the closed end
of the tube as it did when placed in the incubator. The observation
seems trivial, but to the man of science it is significant.

What has happened? The water contained some minute organisms which when
acted upon by the chemical in the tube have set up a fermentation.
Gradually, one by one in the little bulb, bubbles of gas have formed and
risen to the surface of the liquid in the closed upper end of the tube.
As this gas was liberated, it took the place of the liquid in the tube,
and the liquid was forced downward until there was quite a large space,
apparently vacant but really filled with gas.

It was this phenomenon that had attracted the attention of the chemist.
What did it mean? It was the evidence that the water which was being
furnished to the city for half a million people to drink contained some
living organism.

Now that, in itself, was enough to make an official of the health
department begin to take an interest. It was not, however, in itself a
danger signal.

Not all bacterial life is a menace to health, the chemist will tell you.
Indeed, humanity has come to live on very peaceable terms with several
thousand varieties of bacteria and to be really at enmity with but a
score or more. Without the beneficent work of a certain class of
bacteria the world would not be habitable. This comes about through a
very interesting, though rather repulsive condition--the necessity of
getting rid of the dead to make room for the living.

What would be the result if no provision had been made for the
disintegration of the bodies of all the men and animals that have
inhabited the earth since the beginning? Such a situation is
inconceivable. But very wisely providence has provided that myriads and
myriads of tiny creatures are ever at work breaking up worn-out and dead
animal matter and reducing it to its original elements. These elements
are taken up by plant life, elaborated into living vegetable growth and

made fit again for the nourishment of animal life, thus completing the marvelous cycle. And so we must not get the notion that all bacteria are our mortal foes. We could not live without them, and our earth, without their humble services, would no longer be habitable.

Neither need we fear the presence of bacterial life in our drinking water. Drinking water always contains bacteria. We, ourselves, even when in the best of health, are the hosts of millions upon millions of them, and it is fair to suppose that they serve some useful purpose. At any rate, it has never been demonstrated that they do us any harm under normal conditions.

And so, the chemist was not alarmed when he discovered that the formation of gas in his crooked tube gave indication of bacteria in the drinking water. He must ascertain what type of bacteria he had entrapped. To this end, he analyzed the gas, and when he determined that the fermentation was due to the presence of colon bacilli in the water, he sent out his warning. Not that the colon bacilli are a menace to health. The body of every human being in the world is infested with millions of them. But the presence of colon bacilli in drinking water is an indication of the presence of a really dangerous thing--sewage.

Thus, when the city chemist turned from his test tube with the exclamation, "Colon!" he did not fear the thing that he saw, but the thing that he knew might accompany it.

There has been much discussion of late of the possibility that the great lakes cities may suffer a water famine. The rapid increase of population along the borders of these great seas, it has been said, might render the water unfit for use. This fear is based upon the assumption that we shall always continue the present very foolish practice of dumping our sewage into the source of our water supply. The time may come when we shall know better how to protect the public health and at the same time husband the public resources. But even at that, the city chemist says that he hardly expects to see the time when the present intake for water near the head of Belle Isle will not be both safe and adequate.

No doubt he makes this statement because he has confidence that the purification of water is both simple and safe. There are two principal methods. The first, and most expensive, is nature's own--the filter. The application of this method is comparatively simple though it involves considerable expense. The trick was learned from the hillside spring which, welling up through strata of sand and gravel, comes out pure and clear and sparkling. To make spring water out of lake water, therefore, it is merely necessary to excavate a considerable area to the desired depth and lead into it the pipes connected with the wells from which water is to be pumped. Then the pit is filled with successive layers of crushed stone graduated in fineness to the size of gravel and then covered with a deep layer of fine sand. This area is then flooded with the water to be filtered, which slowly percolates and comes out clear and pure. The best results in purification of contaminated water supplies have probably been attained in this way; that is, as measured by the improvement of health and the general reduction of the death rate from those diseases caused by the use of contaminated water.

But when the alarm was given this spring by the city chemist there was no time to excavate and build an extensive filtering plant. The dreaded

typhoid was already making its appearance and babies were dying.
Something had to be done at once.

If some afternoon you take a stroll through Gladwin park your attention
may be attracted to a little white building at the lower end of the
settling basin. It is merely a temporary structure yet it is serving a
very important purpose. Approach the open door and your nostrils will be
greeted by a pungent odor that may make you catch your breath. The
workmen, too, you will notice, do not stay long within doors, but take
refuge in a little shelter booth outside. Strewn about here and there
are traces of a white, powdery substance which seems to have been
tracked down from a platform erected on the roof. This is hypochlorite
of lime, the substance used for sterilizing the city drinking water.

This is so powerful a disinfectant that it destroys all bacteria in
water even in an extremely dilute solution. The method of applying it is
interesting. The city water comes in from the river through a great
tunnel about 10 feet in diameter. The little chlorinating plant is
situated on the line of this tunnel so that the solution is readily
introduced into the water before it reaches the pool called a settling
basin.

The hypochlorite reaches the plant in iron cylinders containing 100
pounds. These are carried up to the roof and poured into the first
mixing tank through a hopper fixed for the purpose. There are within the
building four of these mixing tanks. In the first, up near the roof, a
very strong solution is first made. This is drawn off into a second tank
with a greater admixture of water and thence passes into the third and
fourth. From the last it is forced out into the main tunnel by a pipe
and mingles with the great flood that is pouring constantly into the
wells beneath pumping engines. And this is the strength of the chemical:
five pounds of it mingled with one million gallons of water is
sufficient to render the water fit for drinking purposes. Nearly 98 per
cent of the bacteria in the water is destroyed by this weak solution.
The water is tasteless and odorless. Indeed, probably very few of the
citizens of Detroit who are using the city water all the time, know that
the treatment is being applied.

But the chemist continues his tests every morning. Every morning the
little crooked tubes are brought out and filled and carefully watched to
ascertain if the telltale gas develops which is an index of "death in
the cup." Thus is the city's water supply guarded.

No more important work can devolve on the board of health. Before
science had learned to recognize the tiny enemies which infest drinking
water, typhoid and kindred diseases were regarded as a visitation of
divine providence for the sins of a people. We now know that a rise in
the death rate from these diseases is to be laid rather to the sins of
omission on the part of the board of health and the public works
department.

        *   *   *   *   *

(The Outlook)

THE OCCUPATION AND EXERCISE CURE

BY FRANK MARSHALL WHITE

The nerve specialist leaned back in his chair behind the great mahogany desk in his consulting-room and studied the features of the capitalist as that important factor in commerce and industry explained the symptoms that had become alarming enough to drive him, against his will, to seek medical assistance. The patient was under fifty years of age, though the deep lines in his face, with his whitening hair--consequences of the assiduity with which he had devoted himself to the accumulation of his millions and his position in the Directory of Directors--made him appear ten years older. An examination had shown that he had no organic disease of any kind, but he told the physician that he was suffering from what he called "inward trembling," with palpitation of the heart, poor sleep, occasional dizziness, pain in the back of the neck, difficulty in concentrating his attention, and, most of all, from various apprehensions, such as that of being about to fall, of losing his mind, of sudden death--he was afraid to be alone, and was continually tired, worried, and harassed.

"You present merely the ordinary signs of neurasthenia," said the specialist. "These symptoms are distressing, but not at all serious or dangerous. You have been thinking a great deal too much about yourself and your feelings. You watch with morbid interest the perverted sensations that arise in various parts of your body. You grow apprehensive about the palpitation of your heart, which is not at all diseased, but which flutters a little from time to time because the great nerve of the heart is tired, like the other great nerves and nerve-centers of your body. You grow apprehensive over the analogous tremor which you describe as 'inward trembling,' and which you often feel all through your trunk and sometimes in your knees, hands, and face, particularly about the eyes and mouth and in the fingers."

The capitalist had started at the mention of the word neurasthenia, and had seemed much relieved when the physician had declared that the symptoms were not dangerous. "I had been under the impression that neurasthenia was practically an incurable disease," he said. "However, you have described my sensations exactly."

"One hundred per centum of cases of neurasthenia are curable," responded the specialist. "Neurasthenia is not, as is usually supposed, an equally diffused general exhaustion of the nervous system. In my opinion, it is rather an unequally distributed multiple fatigue. Certain more vulnerable portions of the nervous system are affected, while the remainder is normal. In the brain we have an overworked area which, irritated, gives rise to an apprehension or imperative idea. By concentration of energy in some other region of the brain, by using the normal portions, we give this affected part an opportunity to rest and recuperate. New occupations are therefore substituted for the old habitual one. A change of interests gives the tired centers rest."

"I have heard the 'rest cure' advocated in cases like mine," suggested the capitalist.

"In the treatment of neurasthenia we must take the whole man into consideration," said the physician. "We must stimulate nutrition, feed well the tired and exhausted organism, and, above all, provide some sort of rest and distraction for the mind. The mind needs feeding as well as

the body. The rest cure is a kind of passive, relaxing, sedative
treatment. The field is allowed to lie fallow, and often to grow up with
weeds, trusting to time to rest and enrich it. The 'exercise and
occupation cure,' on the other hand, is an active, stimulating, and
tonic prescription. You place yourself in the hands of a physician who
must direct the treatment. He will lay out a scheme with a judicious
admixture of exercise which will improve your general health, soothe
your nervous system, induce good appetite and sleep, and of occupation
which will keep your mind from morbid self-contemplation. One of the
best means to this end is manual occupation--drawing, designing,
carpentry, metal-work, leather-work, weaving, basket-making,
bookbinding, clay-modeling, and the like--for in all these things the
hands are kept busy, requiring concentration of attention, while new
interests of an artistic and æsthetic nature are aroused. The outdoor
exercise, taken for a part of each day, if of the right sort, also
distracts by taking the attention and creating interest."

The capitalist had called upon the specialist braced for a possible
sentence of death, prepared at the least to be informed that he was
suffering from a progressive mental malady. Now, while a tremendous
weight was lifted from his mind with the information that he might
anticipate a complete return to health, the idea of devoting his trained
intelligence, accustomed to cope with great problems of trade and
finance, to such trivialities as basket-making or modeling in clay
appeared preposterous. Nevertheless, when the physician told him of a
resort near at hand, established for the treatment of cases just such as
his, where he might be under continuous medical supervision, without
confinement indoors or being deprived of any of the comforts or luxuries
of life, he decided to put himself in the other's hands unreservedly.
The specialist informed him that the length of time required for his
cure would depend largely upon himself. He might, for instance, even
keep in touch with his office and have matters of import referred to
him while he was recuperating his mental and physical strength, but such
a course would inevitably retard his recovery, and possibly prevent it.
To get the best results from the treatment he ought to leave every
business interest behind him, he was told.

The fee that the capitalist paid the specialist made his advice so
valuable that the other followed it absolutely. The next evening saw the
patient in the home of the "occupation and exercise cure." He arrived
just in time to sit down to dinner with a score of other patients, not
one of whom showed any outward sign of illness, though all were taking
the cure for some form of nervous trouble. There were no cases of
insanity among them, however, none being admitted to the institution
under any circumstances. The dinner was simple and abundant, and the
conversation at the tables of a lively and cheerful nature. As everybody
went to bed by ten o'clock--almost every one considerably before that
hour, in fact--the newcomer did likewise, he having secured a suite with
a bath in the main building. Somewhat to the surprise of the capitalist,
who was accustomed to be made much of wherever he happened to be, no
more attention was paid to him than to any other guest of the
establishment, a condition of affairs that happened to please him. He
was told on retiring that breakfast would be served in the dining-room
from 7:30 to 8:30 in the morning, but that, if he preferred to remain in
his room, it would be brought to him there at nine o'clock.

The capitalist had a bad night, and was up to breakfast early. After he had concluded that repast the medical superintendent showed him about the place, but did not encourage him to talk about his symptoms. The grounds of the "occupation and exercise cure" comprised a farm of forty acres located among the hills of northern Westchester County in the Croton watershed, with large shade trees, lawns, flower gardens, and an inexhaustible supply of pure spring water from a well three hundred feet deep in solid rock. The main building, situated on a knoll adjacent to a grove of evergreen trees, contained a great solarium, which was the favorite sitting-room of the patients, and the dining-room was also finished with two sides of glass, both apartments capable of being thrown open in warm weather, and having the advantage of all the sun there was in winter. In this building were also the medical offices, with a clinical laboratory and hydro- and electro-therapeutic equipment, and accommodations for from twelve to fifteen guests. Two bungalows under the trees of the apple orchard close at hand, one containing two separate suites with baths, and the other two living-rooms with hall and bath-room, were ideal places for quiet and repose. Situated at the entrance to the grounds was a club-house, with a big sitting-room and an open fireplace; it also contained a solarium, billiard-room, bowling alleys, a squash court, a greenhouse for winter floriculture, and the arts and crafts shops, with seven living-rooms. Every living-room in the main building, the club-house, and the bungalows was connected with the medical office by telephone, so that in case of need patients might immediately secure the services of a physician at any hour of the day or night.

The arts and crafts shops being the basic principle of the "occupation and exercise cure," the capitalist was introduced to an efficient and businesslike young woman, the instructress, who explained to him the nature of the avocations in which he might choose to interest himself. Here he found his fellow-patients busily and apparently congenially employed. In one of the shops a recent alumnus of one of the leading universities, who had undergone a nervous breakdown after graduation, was patiently hammering a sheet of brass with a view to converting it into a lampshade; a matron of nearly sixty, who had previously spent eight years in sanatoriums, practically bedridden, was setting type in the printing office with greater activity than she had known before for two decades; two girls, one sixteen and the other twelve, the latter inclined to hysteria and the former once subject to acute nervous attacks, taking the cure in charge of trained nurses, were chattering gayly over a loom in the construction of a silk rug; a prominent business man from a Western city, like the New York capitalist broken down from overwork, was earnestly modeling in clay what he hoped might eventually become a jardiniere; one of last season's debutantes among the fashionables, who had been leading a life of too strenuous gayety that had told on her nerves, was constructing a stamped leather portfolio with entire absorption; and half a dozen others, mostly young women, were engaged at wood-carving, bookbinding, block-printing, tapestry weaving, or basket-making, each one of them under treatment for some nervous derangement.

The new patient decided to try his hand at basket-making; and, although he figured out that it would take him about four days to turn out a product that might sell for ten cents, he was soon so much interested in mastering the manual details of the craft that he was disinclined to put the work aside when the medical superintendent suggested a horseback ride. When, at the advice of the specialist, the capitalist had decided

to try the occupation and exercise cure, he did so with little faith
that it would restore him to health, though he felt that there was
perhaps a slight chance that it might help him. The remedy seemed to him
too simple to overcome a disease that was paralyzing his energies. To
his great surprise, he began to improve at once; and though for the
first week he got little sleep, and his dizziness, with the pain in the
back of his neck and his apprehensions, continued to recur for weeks,
they did so at always increasing intervals.

He learned bookbinding, and sent to his library for some favorite
volumes, and put them into new dress; he made elaborate waste-paper
baskets, and beat brass into ornamental desk-trays, which he proudly
presented to his friends in the city as specimens of his skill. Work
with him, as with the others of the patients, was continually varied by
recreation. In the summer months there were lawn-tennis, golf, croquet,
canoeing, rowing, fishing, riding, and driving. In winter, such outdoor
sports as skating, tobogganing, coasting, skeeing, snowshoeing, and
lacrosse were varied by billiards, bowling, squash, the medicine ball,
and basket and tether ball. The capitalist was astonished to discover
that he could take an interest in games. The specialist, who called upon
his patient at intervals, told him that a point of great importance in
the cure was that exercise that is _enjoyed_ is almost twice as
effective in the good accomplished as exercise which is a mere
mechanical routine of movements made as a matter of duty.

The net result was that, after four months of the "occupation and
exercise cure," the capitalist returned to New York sound in mind and
body, and feeling younger than he had before in years. Complete cures
were effected in the cases of the other patients also, which is the less
remarkable when the circumstance is taken into consideration that only
patients capable of entire recovery are recommended to take the
treatment.

Of course the institution that has been described is only for the
well-to-do, and physicians are endeavoring to bring the "occupation and
exercise cure" within the reach of the poor, and to interest
philanthropists in the establishment of "colony sanatoriums," such as
already exist in different parts of Europe, for those suffering from
functional nervous disorders who are without means. Contrary to the
general opinion, neurasthenia, particularly among women, is not confined
to the moneyed and leisure class; but, owing to the fact that women have
taken up the work of men in offices and trades as well as in many of
the professions, working-women are continually breaking down under
nervous strain, and many, under present conditions, have little chance
for recovery, because they cannot afford the proper treatment. As a
speaker at the last annual meeting of the American Medical Association
declared, "Idiots and epileptics and lunatics are many; but all together
they are less numerous than the victims of nervousness--the people
afflicted with lesser grades of psychasthenic and neurasthenic
inadequacy, who become devoted epicures of their own emotions, and who
claim a large share of the attention of every general practitioner and
of every specialist."

Scientists declare that this premature collapse of nerve force is
increasing to such an extent as to become a positive menace to the
general welfare. The struggle for existence among the conditions of
modern life, especially among those found in the large centers of

industrial and scientific activity, and the steady, persistent work, with its attendant sorrows, deprivations, and over-anxiety for success, are among the most prolific causes--causes which are the results of conditions from which, for the large mass of people, according to a leading New York alienist, there has been no possibility of escape.

"Especially here in America are people forced into surroundings for which they have never been fitted," the alienist asserts, "and especially here are premature demands made upon their nervous systems before they are mature and properly qualified. The lack of proper training deprives many of the workers, in all branches, of the best protection against functional nervous diseases which any person can have, namely, a well-trained nervous system. This struggle for existence by the congenital neuropath or the educationally unfit forces many to the use, and then to the abuse, of stimulants and excitants, and herein we have another important exciting cause. This early and excessive use of coffee, tea, alcohol, and tobacco is especially deleterious in its action upon the nervous system of those very ones who are most prone to go to excess in their use.

"Therefore, predisposition, aided by the storm and stress of active competition and abetted by the use of stimulants, must be looked upon as the main cause for the premature collapse of nerve force which we call neurasthenia; so it will be found that the majority of neurasthenics are between twenty-five and fifty years of age, and that their occupations are those which are attended by worry, undue excitement, uncertainty, excessive wear and tear, and thus we find mentally active persons more easily affected than those whose occupation is solely physical. Authors, actors, school-teachers, governesses, telegraph and telephone operators, are among those most frequently affected, and the increase of neurasthenia among women dates from the modern era which has opened to them new channels of work and has admitted them more generally into the so-called learned professions. But whatever may be the occupation in which persons have broken down, it is never the occupation alone which has been the cause.

"This cannot be too often repeated. The emotional fitness or unfitness of an individual for his occupation is of the utmost importance as a causative factor, and overwork alone, without any emotional cause and without any errors in mode of life, will never act to produce such a collapse. It is therefore not astonishing that this class of functional nervous diseases is not confined to the wealthy, and that the rich and the poor are indiscriminately affected. But certain causes are of greater influence in the one class, while different ones obtain in the other. Poverty in itself, with its limitations of proper rest and recuperation, is a very positive cause. Years of neurological dispensary work among the poor have convinced me that nervousness, neurasthenia, hysteria, etc., are quite as prevalent among the indigent as among the well-to-do."

Physicians agree that the prime requisite in the treatment of these disorders is the removal of the patient from his or her habitual surroundings, where recognition of the existence of actual disease is generally wanting, where the constant admonitions of well-meaning friends to "brace up" and to "exert your will power" force the sick man or woman to bodily and mental over-exertion, and where the worries about a livelihood are always dominant. Such a change alone, however, the experts say, will help but few, for it is being recognized more and more that these functional diseases of the nervous system can receive satisfactory treatment only in institutions, where constant attention may be had, with expert supervision and trained attendants.

The "occupation and exercise cure" is applicable also to epilepsy, and is the therapeutic principle of the Craig Colony for Epileptics at Sonyea, in Livingston County, supported by the State, and that institution furnishes a general model for the "colony sanatoriums" suggested for indigent patients suffering from functional nervous disorders. The Craig Colony was the idea of Dr. Frederick Peterson, Professor of Psychiatry at Columbia University, and former President of the New York State Commission of Lunacy and of the New York Neurological Society, which he based upon the epileptic colony at Beilefeld, Germany, that was founded in 1867. The Craig Colony was founded in 1894, and there are now being cared for within its confines more than thirteen hundred patients, who have turned out this year agricultural products, with bricks, soap, and brooms, to the value of $60,000. The colony is named after the late Oscar Craig, of Rochester, who, with William P. Letchworth, of Buffalo, purchased the two-thousand-acre tract of land on which it is situated from the Shaker colony at Sonyea and presented it to the State, Dr. Peterson devoting several months of each year for nine years to getting the institution into working order. The first patients were housed in the old Shaker buildings, which were well constructed and fairly well arranged for the purpose, but as additional applications for admission have been made new buildings have been erected. To-day there are eighty buildings in the colony, but a thousand patients are waiting for admission, eight hundred of whom are in New York City.

Epilepsy, the "falling sickness," is a most difficult malady to treat even in an institution for that purpose, and it is impossible to treat it anywhere else. An epileptic in a family is an almost intolerable burden to its other members, as well as to himself. The temperamental effect of the disease takes the form in the patient of making frequent and unjust complaints, and epileptics invariably charge some one with having injured them while they have been unconscious during an attack. Then, too, living at home, they are often dangerous to younger members of a family, and they are fault-finding, exacting, and irritable generally. The seizures frequently come on without warning, and the patient drops where he stands, often injuring himself severely. The last annual report of the Craig Colony records more than four hundred injuries within the year to patients during seizures which required a surgeon's attention, the injuries varying from severe bruises to fractures of the skull.

The object of the Craig Colony is to remove the burden of the epileptic in the family from the home without subjecting the patient to the hardship of confinement with the insane. "Very few epileptics suffer permanent insanity in any form except dementia," says the medical superintendent of the Colony. "Acute mania and maniac depressive insanity not infrequently appear as a 'post-convulsive' condition, that generally subsides within a few hours, or at most a few days. Rarely the state may persist a month. Melancholia is extremely infrequent. Delusions of persecution, hallucinations of sight or hearing, systematized in character, are almost never encountered in epilepsy."

Only from six to fifteen per cent of epileptics are curable, and hence the work of the Craig Colony is largely palliative of the sufferings of the patients. Each individual case is studied with the utmost care, however, and patients are given their choice of available occupations. The Colony is not a custodial institution. There are no bars on the windows, no walls or high fences about the farm. The patients are housed in cottages, men and women in separate buildings some distance apart, about thirty to each cottage. In charge of each of these families are a man and his wife, who utilize the services of some of the patients in the performance of household work, while the others have their duties outside. Kindness to the unfortunates under their care is impressed upon every employee of the Colony, and an iron-bound rule forbids them to strike a patient even in case of assault.

Besides the agricultural work in the Craig Colony, and that in the soap and broom factories and the brick-yard, the patients are taught blacksmithing, carpentry, dressmaking, tailoring, painting, plumbing, shoemaking, laundrying, and sloyd work. It is insisted on that all patients physically capable shall find employment as a therapeutic measure. The records show that on Sundays and holidays and on rainy days, when there is a minimum of physical activity among the patients, their seizures double and sometimes treble in number. Few of the patients know how to perform any kind of labor when they enter the Colony, but many of them learn rapidly. It has been repeatedly demonstrated that boys from eighteen to twenty years of age can spend two years in the sloyd shop and leave it fully qualified as cabinet-makers, and capable of earning a journeyman's wages.

There are about two hundred children in the colony of epileptics at Sonyea, more than half of whom are girls. As children subject to epileptic seizures are not received in the public schools of the State, the only opportunity for any education among these afflicted little ones whose parents are unable to teach them themselves or provide private tutors for them is in the schools of the Colony. Some of the children are comparatively bright scholars, while the attempt to teach others seems a hopeless task. For instance, it took one girl ninety days to learn to lay three sticks in the form of a letter A.

Every effort is made to encourage recreation among the patients in the Craig Colony, both children and adults. The men have a club of 250 members, with billiards, chess, checkers, cards, and magazines and newspapers. The boys have their baseball and football, and play match games among themselves or with visiting teams. The women and girls play croquet, tennis, and other outdoor games. There is a band composed of patients that gives a concert once a week, and there are theatricals and dancing, with occasional lectures by visiting celebrities. As the Colony, with the medical staff, nurses, and other employees, has a population of 2,000, there is always an audience for any visiting attraction. The maintenance of the Colony is costing the State $225,000 the present year.

Since the founding of the Craig Colony similar institutions have been established in Massachusetts, Texas, Michigan, Ohio, New Jersey, Pennsylvania, Illinois, and Kansas, and other States are preparing to follow their example. There are other private sanatoriums throughout the country similar to the one in Westchester County, where the nervous or neurasthenic patient who is well-to-do may obtain relaxation and supervision, but there is no place at all to-day where the man or woman

suffering from curable nervous disorders who is without means can go for
treatment.

                 *   *   *   *   *

(McClure's Magazine)

Five illustrations: two wash drawings by André Castaigne showing
mono-rail trains in the future, five half-tone reproductions of
photographs
of the car on its trial trip, and one pen-and-ink diagram of the
gyroscopes.

THE BRENNAN MONO-RAIL CAR

BY PERCEVAL GIBBON

It was November 10, 1909--a day that will surely have its place in
history beside that other day, eighty-five years ago, when George
Stephenson drove the first railway locomotive between Stockton and
Darlington. In the great square of the Brennan torpedo factory at
Gillingham, where the fighting-tops of battleships in the adjacent
dockyard poise above the stone coping of the wall, there was a track
laid down in a circle of a quarter of a mile. Switches linked it up with
other lengths of track, a straight stretch down to a muddy cape of the
Medway estuary, and a string of curves and loops coiling among the
stone and iron factory sheds. The strange thing about it was that it was
single--just one line of rail on sleepers tamped into the unstable
"made" ground of the place.

And there was Brennan, his face red with the chill wind sweeping in from
the Nore, his voice plaintive and Irish, discoursing, at slow length, of
revolutions per minute, of "precession," and the like. The journalists
from London, who had come down at his invitation, fidgeted and shivered
in the bitter morning air; the affair did not look in the least like an
epoch in the history of transportation and civilization, till--

"Now, gentlemen," said Brennan, and led the way across the circle of
track.

And then, from its home behind the low, powder-magazine-like sheds,
there rode forth a strange car, the like of which was never seen before.
It was painted the businesslike slatyblue gray of the War Department. It
was merely a flat platform, ten feet wide by forty feet long, with a
steel cab mounted on its forward end, through the windows of which one
could see a young engineer in tweeds standing against a blur of moving
machine-parts.

It ran on the single rail; its four wheels revolved in a line, one
behind another; and it traveled with the level, flexible equilibrium of
a ship moving across a dock. It swung over the sharp curves without
faltering, crossed the switch, and floated--floated is the only word for
the serene and equable quality of its movement--round and round the
quarter-mile circle. A workman boarded it as it passed him, and sat on
the edge with his legs swinging, and its level was unaltered. It was
wonderful beyond words to see. It seemed to abolish the very principle

of gravitation; it contradicted calmly one's most familiar instincts.

Every one knows the sense one gains at times while watching an ingenious machine at its work--a sense of being in the presence of a living and conscious thing, with more than the industry, the pertinacity, the dexterity, of a man. There was a moment, while watching Brennan's car, when one had to summon an effort of reason to do away with this sense of life; it answered each movement of the men on board and each inequality in the makeshift track with an adjustment of balance irresistibly suggestive of consciousness. It was an illustration of that troublous theorem which advances that consciousness is no more than the co-relation of the parts of the brain, and that a machine adapted to its work is as conscious in its own sphere as a mind is in its sphere.

The car backed round the track, crossed to the straight line, and halted to take us aboard. There were about forty of us, yet it took up our unequally distributed weight without disturbance. The young engineer threw over his lever, and we ran down the line. The movement was as "sweet" and equable as the movement of a powerful automobile running slowly on a smooth road; there was an utter absence of those jars and small lateral shocks that are inseparable from a car running on a double track. We passed beyond the sheds and slid along a narrow spit of land thrusting out into the mud-flanked estuary. Men on lighters and a working-party of bluejackets turned to stare at the incredible machine with its load. Then back again, three times round the circle, and in and out among the curves, always with that unchanging stateliness of gait. As we spun round the circle, she leaned inward like a cyclist against the centrifugal pull. She needs no banking of the track to keep her on the rail. A line of rails to travel on, and ground that will carry her weight--she asks no more. With these and a clear road ahead, she is to abolish distance and revise the world's schedules of time.

"A hundred and twenty miles an hour," I hear Brennan saying, in that sad voice of his; "or maybe two hundred. That's a detail."

In the back of the cab were broad unglazed windows, through which one could watch the tangle of machinery. Dynamos are bolted to the floor, purring under their shields like comfortable cats; abaft of them a twenty-horse-power Wolseley petrol-engine supplies motive power for everything. And above the dynamos, cased in studded leather, swinging a little in their ordered precession, are the two gyroscopes, the soul of the machine. To them she owes her equilibrium.

Of all machines in the world, the gyroscope is the simplest, for, in its essential form, it is no more than a wheel revolving. But a wheel revolving is the vehicle of many physical principles, and the sum of them is that which is known as gyroscopic action. It is seen in the ordinary spinning top, which stands erect in its capacity of a gyroscope revolving horizontally. The apparatus that holds Brennan's car upright, and promises to revolutionize transportation, is a top adapted to a new purpose. It is a gyroscope revolving in a perpendicular plane, a steel wheel weighing three quarters of a ton and spinning at the rate of three thousand revolutions to the minute.

Now, the effect of gyroscopic action is to resist any impulse that tends to move the revolving wheel out of the plane in which it revolves. This resistance can be felt in a top; it can be felt much more strongly

in the beautiful little gyroscopes of brass and steel that are sold for
the scientific demonstration of the laws governing revolving bodies.
Such a one, only a few inches in size, will develop a surprising
resistance. This resistance increases with the weight of the wheel and
the speed at which it moves, till, with Brennan's gyroscopes of three
quarters of a ton each, whirling in a vacuum at three thousand
revolutions per minute, it would need a weight that would crush the car
into the ground to throw them from their upright plane.

Readers of MCCLURE'S MAGAZINE were made familiar with the working of
Brennan's gyroscope by Mr. Cleveland Moffett's article in the issue of
December, 1907. The occasion of that article was the exhibition of
Brennan's model mono-rail car before the Royal Society and in the
grounds of his residence at Gillingham. For a clear understanding of the
first full-sized car, it may be well to recapitulate a few of the
characteristics of the gyroscope.

When Brennan made his early models, he found that, while the little cars
would remain upright and run along a straight rail, they left the track
at the first curve. The gyroscope governed their direction as well as
their equilibrium. It was the first check in the evolution of the
perfect machine. It was over ten years before he found the answer to the
problem--ten years of making experimental machines and scrapping them,
of filing useless patents, of doubt and persistence. But the answer was
found--in the spinning top.

A spinning top set down so that it stands at an angle to the floor will
right itself; it will rise till it stands upright on the point of equal
friction. Brennan's resource, therefore, was to treat his gyroscope as a
top. He enclosed it in a case, through which its axles projected, and at
each side of the car he built stout brackets reaching forth a few inches
below each end of the axle.

The result is not difficult to deduce. When the car came to a curve, the
centrifugal action tended to throw it outward; the side of the car that
was on the inside of the curve swung up and the bracket touched the axle
of the gyroscope. Forthwith, in the manner of its father, the top, the
gyroscope tried to stand upright on the bracket; all the weight of it
and all its wonderful force were pressed on that side of the car,
holding it down against the tendency to rise and capsize. The thing was
done; the spinning top had come to the rescue of its posterity. It only
remained to fit a double gyroscope, with the wheels revolving in
opposite directions, and, save for engineering details, the mono-rail
car was evolved.

Through the window in the back of the cab I was able to watch them at
then; work--not the actual gyroscopes, but their cases, quivering with
the unimaginable velocity of the great wheels within, turning and
tilting accurately to each shifting weight as the men on board moved
here and there. Above them were the glass oilcups, with the opal-green
engine-oil flushing through them to feed the bearings. Lubrication is a
vital part of the machine. Let that fail, and the axles, grinding and
red-hot, would eat through the white metal of the bearings as a knife
goes through butter. It is a thing that has been foreseen by the
inventor: to the lubricating apparatus is affixed a danger signal that
would instantly warn the engineer.

"But," says Brennan, "if one broke down, the other gyroscope would hold her up--till ye could run her to a siding, anyway."

"But supposing the electric apparatus failed?" suggests a reporter--with visions of headlines, perhaps. "Supposing the motor driving the gyroscopes broke down; what then?"

"They'd run for a couple of days, with the momentum they've got," answers the inventor. "And for two or three hours, that 'ud keep her upright by itself."

On the short track at Gillingham there are no gradients to show what the car can do in the way of climbing, but here again the inventor is positive. She will run up a slope as steep as one in six, he says. There is no reason to doubt him; the five-foot model that he used to exhibit could climb much steeper inclines, run along a rope stretched six feet above the ground, or remain at rest upon it while the rope was swung to and fro. It would do all these things while carrying a man; and, for my part, I am willing to take Brennan's word.

Louis Brennan himself was by no means the least interesting feature of the demonstration. He has none of the look of the visionary, this man who has gone to war with time and space; neither had George Stephenson. He is short and thick-set, with a full face, a heavy moustache hiding his mouth, and heavy eyebrows. He is troubled a little with asthma, which makes him somewhat staccato and breathless in speech, and perhaps also accentuates the peculiar plaintive quality of his Irish voice. There is nothing in his appearance to indicate whether he is thirty-five or fifty-five. As a matter of fact, he is two years over the latter age, but a man ripe in life, with that persistence and belief in his work which is to engineers what passion is to a poet.

The technicalities of steel and iron come easily off his tongue; they are his native speech, in which he expresses himself most intimately. All his life he has been concerned with machines. He is the inventor of the Brennan steerable torpedo, whose adoption by the Admiralty made him rich and rendered possible the long years of study and experiment that went to the making of the mono-rail car. He has a touch of the rich man's complacency; it does not go ill with his kindly good humor and his single-hearted pride in his life work.

It is characteristic, I think, of his honesty of purpose and of the genius that is his driving force that hitherto he has concerned himself with scientific invention somewhat to the exclusion of the commercial aspects of his contrivance. He has had help in money and men from the British Government, which likewise placed the torpedo factory at his disposal; and the governments of India and--of all places--Kashmir have granted him subsidies. Railroad men from all parts of the world have seen his model; but he has not been ardent in the hunt for customers. Perhaps that will not be necessary; the mono-rail car should be its own salesman; but, in the meantime, it is not amiss that a great inventor should stand aloof from commerce.

But, for all the cheerful matter-of-factness of the man, he, too, has seen visions. There are times when he talks of the future as he hopes it will be, as he means it to be, when "transportation is civilization." Men are to travel then on a single rail, in great cars like halls, two hundred feet long, thirty to forty feet wide, whirling across continents at two hundred miles an hour--from New York to San Francisco between dawn and dawn.

Travel will no longer be uncomfortable. These cars, equipped like a hotel, will sweep along with the motion of an ice-yacht. They will not jolt over uneven places, or strain to mount the track at curves; in each one, the weariless gyroscopes will govern an unchanging equilibrium. Trustful Kashmir will advance from its remoteness to a place accessible from anywhere. Streetcar lines will no longer be a perplexity to paving authorities and anathema to other traffic; a single rail will be flush with the ground, out of the way of hoofs and tires. Automobiles will run on two wheels like a bicycle. It is to be a mono-rail world, soothed and assured by the drone of gyroscopes. By that time the patient ingenuity of inventors and engineers will have found the means to run the gyroscopes at a greater speed than is now possible, thus rendering it feasible to use a smaller wheel. It is a dream based on good, solid reasoning, backed by a great inventor's careful calculations; H.G. Wells has given a picture of it in the last of his stories of the future.

Practical railroad men have given to the mono-rail car a sufficiently warm welcome. They have been impressed chiefly by its suitability to the conditions of transportation in the great new countries, as, for instance, on that line of railway that is creeping north from the Zambesi to open up the copper deposits of northwestern Rhodesia, and on through Central Africa to its terminus at Cairo. Just such land as this helped to inspire Brennan. He was a boy when he first saw the endless plains of Australia, and out of that experience grew his first speculations about the future of railway travel. Such lands make positive and clear demands, if ever they are to be exploited for their full value to humanity. They need railways quickly laid and cheaply constructed; lines not too exacting in point of curves and gradients; and, finally, fast travel. It is not difficult to see how valuable the mono-rail would have been in such an emergency as the last Sudan War, when the army dragged a line of railway with it down toward Omdurman. Petrol-driven cars to replace the expensive steam locomotives, easy rapid transit instead of the laborious crawl through the stifling desert heat--a complete railway installation, swiftly and cheaply called into being, instead of a costly and cumbersome makeshift.

The car went back to her garage, or engine-shed, or stable, or whatever the railway man of the future shall decide to call it. Struts were pulled into position to hold her up, the motors were switched off, and the gyroscopes were left to run themselves down in forty-eight hours or so. When the mono-rail comes into general use, explained Brennan, there will be docks for the cars, with low brick walls built to slide under the platforms and take their weight.

While his guests assembled in a store-shed to drink champagne and eat sandwiches, he produced a big flat book, sumptuously bound, and told us how his patents were being infringed on in Germany. On that same day there was an exhibition of a mono-rail car on the Brennan principle taking place at the Zoölogical Gardens in Berlin; the book was its catalogue. It was full of imaginative pictures of trains fifty years hence, and thereto was appended sanguine letter-press. While there sounded in our ears the hum of the gyroscopes from the car housed in the rear, I translated one paragraph for him. It was to the effect that one

Brennan, an Englishman, had conducted experiments with gyroscopes ten
years ago, but the matter had gone no further.

"There, now," said Brennan.

        *   *   *   *   *

(_Everybody's Magazine_)

A NEW POLITICAL WEDGE

THE WAY ST. LOUIS WOMEN DROVE A NINE-HOUR DAY INTO THE LAW

BY INIS H. WEED

It was the evening before the state primaries--a sweltering
first of August night in the tenement district of St. Louis, where
the factory people eat their suppers and have their beds. Men
in shirt-sleeves and women with babies sat on the steps for a
breath of air, and the streets were a noisy welter of children.

Two of the most enthusiastic girls in the Women's Trade
Union League stopped before the group silhouetted in the gaslight
at No. 32 and handed the men in the group this card:

                         REPUBLICAN VOTERS

It is the Women and Children that are the Victims of Manufacturers
                 and Manufacturers Associations
                       and it is the
                 WORKING WOMAN AND CHILD
              that demands your protection at the
              PRIMARIES, TUESDAY, AUGUST 2nd
                          Scratch

                         E.J. Troy
Secretary St. Louis Manufacturers Association and run by them on the
Republican Ticket for the Legislature in the 1st District Comprising
WARDS 10, 11, 2,13, and 24. Precincts 14 of the 15th WARD. Precincts 1,
2, 3 of the 23rd WARD. Precincts 1, 2 of the 15th WARD. Precincts 6, 7,
10, 11, 12, 13 of the 14th WARD. Precincts 1, 4, 5 of the 9th Ward

"So yez would be afther havin' me scratch Misther Troy?" Mike Ryan ran
his fingers through his stubby crop with a puzzled air. "Oi'm always fur
plazin' the loidies, but Misther Troy, he's a frind o' mine. Shure, he
shmokes a grand cigar, an' he shakes yer hand that hearty."

So Mike belonged to the long, long glad-hand line. Well, _personal_
arguments were necessary in his case then. That was the way the girls
sized up Mike Ryan.

"But this ticket has something to do with your oldest girl."

"With Briddie?"

"It sure does, Mr. Ryan. Didn't I hear your wife tellin' what with the hard times an' all, you'd be puttin' Briddie in the mill this winter as soon as ever she's turned fourteen? Wouldn't you rather they worked her nine hours a day instead o' ten--such a soft little kid with such a lot o' growin' to do? There's a lot of us goin' to fight for a Nine-Hour Bill for the women and children this winter, an' do you think a manufacturers' representative, like Troy, is goin' to help us? Look at his record! See how he's fought the employees' interests in the legislature! That's a part of his job! _He_ won't vote for no Nine-Hour Bill!"

And the two girls went on to the next tenement.

They were only two of the hundreds of Trade Union girls who were "doing" the First Electoral District (about one-third of St. Louis) on the eve of the primaries. They were thorough. They had the whole district organized on the block system, and they went over each block house by house.

A new move, is it not, this carefully organized effort of factory women to secure justice through the ballot-box?

How have St. Louis women attained this clear vision that their industrial future is bound up in politics? It is a three years' story. Let us go back a little.

St. Louis is essentially a conservative city. First, it was an old French town; then a Southern town; then a German tradesman's town. With such strata superimposed one above the other, it could hardly be other than conservative. In addition, St. Louis was crippled in the war between the states. She lost her market. This made her slow.

In the 'eighties, this old French-Southern-German city began to recover from the ruin of her Southern trade. Little by little she took heart, for the great Southwest was being settled. There was a new field in which to build up trade. To-day St. Louis is _the_ great wholesale and jobbing depot, _the_ manufacturing city for that vast stretch of territory known as the Southwest.

Since 1890, great fortunes have been amassed--most of them, indeed, in the past ten years. There has been a rapid growth of industry. The old Southern city has become a soft-coal factory center. A pall of smoke hangs over the center of the city where the factories roar and pound. In the midst of this gloom the workfolk are creating rivers of beer, carloads of shoes and woodenware, millions of garments and bags, and the thousand and one things necessary to fill the orders of hundreds of traveling salesmen in the Southwest territory--and in the South, too, for St. Louis is winning back some of her old-time trade.

And the toil of their lifting hands and flying fingers has wrought a golden age for the men who control the capital and the tools. The men who manage have been shaking hands in their clubs for the past decade and congratulating themselves and each other over their drinks. "Yes, St. Louis is a grand old business town. Solid! No mushroom real-estate booms, you know, but a big, steady growth. New plants starting every month and the old ones growing. Then, when we get our deep waterway, that's going to be another big shove toward prosperity.

"Nice town to live in, too! Look at our handsome houses and clubs and public buildings. Never was anything like our World's Fair in the history of men--never! Look at our parks, too. When we get 'em linked together with speedways, where'll you find anything prettier?" Thus the money-makers in this heavy German town.

But what about the employees--the clerks and the factory workers? Have they been "in" on this "big shove toward prosperity?" Have they found it a "nice" town to live in?

No, to each count. For the people at the bottom of the ladder--for the people who tend machines, dig ditches, and stand behind the notion counter--St. Louis is a smoky town, where people have gray lungs instead of pink; a town where franchise grabbing and an antiquated system of taxation have their consequence of more than New York city rents. A town whose slums, says Lee Frankel, are the worst in the country. A town where wages are low (in some occupations twenty-five per cent lower than in New York City); where employment is irregular, the speeding-up tremendous, the number of women entering industry steadily increasing, and where the influx of immigrant labor is pulling down the wage scale and the standard of living.

The average wage of the shoe-workers in the East is $550 per year. In St. Louis it is $440 if work is steady--and rents are higher than in New York City.

It must be remembered that this sum is an average, and that thousands of shoe-workers earn, less than $440, for full-time work. The same is true of thousands engaged in other kinds of manufacture and in department stores.

Somehow the town looks different from the two ends of the ladder.

The government of Missouri and St. Louis has been about as little adapted to the needs of the industrial worker as it well could be. Men have been concerned not so much with social justice as with government protection for money-making schemes.

Business opportunity has depended much on _pliable state and municipal laws_. How the interests fought to keep them pliable; how St. Louis and Missouri became a world scandal in this steady growth to riches, we all know.

We know, too, the period of political reform. People thought the killing trouble in Missouri lay largely with the governmental machinery; and the optimists' faith in a state primary law, in the initiative and referendum as panacea, was white and shining. _They did not see that the underlying problem is industrial_.

After the reform wave had spent itself, the crooked people who had kept out of jail crept from their holes and went back to their old job of beating the game. The only essential difference is that their methods to-day are less raw and crude. They play a more gentlemanly game; but the people are still robbed of their rights.

Thus it came to pass that when the cheerful optimist went to the cupboard to get his poor dog a bone, why, lo! the cupboard was bare.

Meantime the dog has taken up the struggle for social justice on his own account, not singly but in groups and packs. As yet, although a deal of snuffing, running to and fro, barking, yelping, and fighting has been done, little has been accomplished; for one reason, because labor has lacked great organizers in St. Louis.

It has remained for the working women of St. Louis to make the industrial idea effective and to reach out with united single purpose to bend the political bow for their protection.

The Women's Trade Union League, whose real general is Cynthelia Isgrig Knefler, the most dynamic woman in St. Louis, received its first impetus only three years ago in the idealism of a brilliant young Irish girl, Hannah Hennessy, who died at Thanksgiving, 1910, a victim of exhausting work in a garment shop and of her own tireless efforts to organize the working girls of her city.

Hannah Hennessy was sent by the Garment Workers' Union to the National Labor Convention of 1907 at Norfolk, Virginia.

There she glimpsed for the first time the inevitable great world march of women following industry as machinery takes it out of the home and into the shop--saw these women, blind, unorganized, helpless to cope with the conditions offered by organized capital. The vision fired this Irish girl to a pitch of enthusiasm peculiar to the Celtic temperament. Back she came to St. Louis with the spirit of the Crusaders, her vision "the eight-hour day, the living wage to guard the home."

For the first time she saw the broken physical future of women who label three thousand five hundred bottles of beer an hour, and accept their cuts and gashes from the bursting bottles as inevitable; of women who put eyelets on a hundred cases of shoes a day, twenty-four pairs to the case; of women who must weave one thousand yards of hemp cloth a day to hold their job in a mill where the possible speed of woman and machine is so nicely calculated that the speediest person in the factory can weave only twelve hundred and sixty yards a day; where the lint from this hemp fills the air and is so injurious to eyes and throat that the company furnishes medical attendance free.

To undertake the huge task of organizing these thousands of St. Louis women would require not only vision but time and energy. Hannah's return meant being engulfed in the vast roar made by rows of throbbing, whirring machines, into one of which she sewed her vitality at dizzy speed ten hours a day. Vision she had, but training, time, energy--no!

It was at this point that she met Cynthelia Isgrig Knefler, a leisure-class young woman, who had been gripped by a sense of the unevenness of the human struggle. Cynthelia Knefler was groping her way through the maze of settlement activities to an appreciation of their relative futility in the face of long hours, low wages, and unsanitary shops.

Then the idealism of these two young women, born on the one hand of hard experience, on the other of a gentle existence, fused, and burned with a white light whose power is beginning to touch the lives of the women who toil and spin for the great Southwest.

Both women possessed fire and eloquence. Hannah's special contribution was first-hand experience; Mrs. Knefler's the knowledge of economic conditions necessary to an understanding of our complicated labor problems. Wise, sane, conservative, Mrs. Knefler not only helped Hannah to organize branch after branch of the Women's Trade Union League in the different industries, but set out at once to train strong, intelligent leaders. She stimulated them to a critical study of labor laws with the evolution of industry for background.

Night after night for two years Mrs. Knefler and Hannah were out organizing groups of girls. Mrs. Knefler's friends finally stopped remonstrating with her. Hannah, utterly self-forgetful despite ten hours a day in the mills, hurled herself into the new work. Evening after evening her mother protested anxiously, but Hannah, heedless of her own interest, would eat her supper and hurry across the city to help groups of new girls--American, Russian, Roumanian--a confused mass, to find themselves and pull together.

One June morning in 1910 the papers announced that the Manufacturers' Association and the Business Men's League had decided on E.J. Troy as their candidate to the State Legislature for the First District. His candidacy was also backed by the Republican machine. The papers went on to say that E.J. Troy was one of "our ablest and most popular fellow townsmen," that he had grown up in his district, had a host of friends, and might be expected to carry the primaries by a big majority.

That evening at the weekly dinner of the officers of the Women's Trade Union League at the Settlement, Mrs. Knefler hurried in: "Girls, have you seen the morning papers? Do you know that we've got E.J. Troy to contend with again?"

At the same moment in dashed Hannah Hennessy by another door, calling out, "Girls, they're goin' to put Troy on the carpet again!"

To both speeches came half a dozen excited replies that that's just what they were talking about!

Over the potatoes and meat and bread-pudding the situation was discussed in detail.

"Yes, 'twas him, all right, that thought up most of those tricky moves when we was tryin' to get our Nine-Hour Bill before," reflected a wiry, quick-motioned girl during a second's pause.

"Don't it just make you boil," began another, "when you think how he riled 'em up at every four corners in Missouri! He had every old country storekeeper standin' on end about that Nine-Hour Bill. He had 'em puttin' on their specs and callin' to mother to come and listen to this information the manufacturers had sent him:--how the labor unions was tryin' to get a Nine-Hour Bill for women passed; how it would keep their youngest girl, Bessie, from helping in the store when the farmers drove in of a Saturday night; and how it was a blow at American freedom."

"E.J. Troy's got to be squenched at the primaries," said a third, quietly and decisively.

"But how?" asked a more timid officer.

Bing! Mrs. Knefler got into action. There never was a woman for whom a difficult situation offered a more bracing tonic quality. The business meeting that followed fairly bristled with plans.

The girls' first move was to go before the Central Labor Body and ask them to indorse their objections to E.J. Troy. Definite action beyond indorsement the girls did not ask or expect. This much they got.

One day a little later, when Mrs. Knefler's campaign was beginning to take form, a representative of E.J. Troy called Mrs. Knefler on the telephone. The voice was bland, smooth, and very friendly. Wouldn't she--that is--ah--er--wouldn't her organization confer with Mr. E.J. Troy? He felt sure they would come to a pleasant and mutually helpful understanding.

Mrs. Knefler explained to the mouthpiece (take it either way) that it would be quite useless; that the stand of the League was taken on Mr. Troy's previous record and on the "interests" he represented; that while they had nothing against him in his private capacity, as a public servant they must oppose him. All this in Mrs. Knefler's suavest fashion. She feels intensely, but she never loses her self-possession. That's why she is such a formidable antagonist.

It was the last week in June--they had just a month before the primaries in which to rouse public opinion. The newspapers must help, of course.

Mrs. Knefler went to the editors. They were polite, they admitted the justice of her stand, but they were evasive. Mrs. Knefler opened her paper the next morning after she had made the rounds, to find not a single word about the danger to the working woman's interests.

What could the papers do? Weren't they in the hands of the "big cinch," as a certain combination of business men in St. Louis is known? Naturally they refused to print a line. You never step on your own toe, do you, or hit yourself in the face--if you can help it?

One must admit that things looked bad for the League. How were girls who raced at machines all day, who had neither money nor the voice of the press, to rouse this sluggish, corrupt city to the menace of sending to the legislature men like E.J. Troy, pledged body and soul to the manufacturers? How could they waken the public to woman's bitter necessity for shorter hours? The case looked hopeless, but Mrs. Knefler merely set her teeth, and got busy--decidedly busy.

She planned a campaign that no other St. Louis woman in her class would have had the courage to tackle. Mrs. Knefler is a member of the club that is the St. Louis clubwomen's "holy of holies." They have a club-house that just drips art, and they steep themselves in self-culture. As a group their consciousness of the city's industrial problems is still nebulous. The high light in which Mrs. Knefler's work must inevitably stand out is intensified by this background of self-culture women, with a few--only a few--rash daughters shivering around preparatory to taking their first cold plunge in the suffrage pool.

In such an atmosphere Cynthelia Knefler planned and carried out the biggest, the most modern and strategic campaign for the working woman ever waged outside a suffrage state. It was done simply because her heart was filled with the need of the thousands of helpless, unorganized girls for protection from the greed of organized capital.

There are moments when love gives vision and raises us head and shoulders above our group. So it was with Cynthelia Knefler, brought up in this conservative city, educated in a prunes-and-prisms girls' school, steeped in the Southern idea that no "lady" would ever let her picture or her opinions get into the newspapers, and that making public speeches was quite unthinkable!

The press was silent, but at least Mrs. Knefler could speak to the labor unions. She and two other women appealed to every labor union in St. Louis with a speech against E.J. Troy. They fought him--not as a man, but as a representative of the "big interests." Mrs. Knefler made seventy-six speeches in that one month before the primaries. That meant hurrying from hall to hall on hot summer nights and making two speeches, and sometimes three and four, while her friends were wearing white muslin and sitting on the gallery, to get the cool of the evening.

Mrs. Knefler's mind was working like a trip-hammer that month; seeking ways and means for rousing the busy, unthinking, conglomerate mass of people to the real issue. Money in the League was scarce. There are no rich members. But out of their wages and out of raffles and entertainments the League had a small reserve. Part of this they used to print sixty thousand cards. So that when you went in to get a shave your glance was caught, as the barber turned your head, by this red ticket "Scratch E.J. Troy." When you stopped in for a loaf of bread, a red ticket behind the glass of the case advised you to "Scratch E.J. Troy." When you went in for a drink, there leaped into sight dozens of little red tickets: "Scratch E.J. Troy."

There are always some men, though, who are moved only by the big, noisy things of life. Only Schneider's band sounds like music to them; only "Twenty Buckets of Blood, or Dead Man's Gulch" appeals to them as literature; and the only speaker is the man who rips out Old Glory and defies forked lightning. In a political campaign the little red ticket is lost on that kind of man. Mrs. Knefler understood this. So one hot July day huge posters in high, wood-block letters screamed from billboards and the walls of saloons and barber shops and labor halls: "Union men and friends, Scratch E.J. Troy."

All this printing and bill-posting was expensive for working girls. They came back at the Central Labor body again. "Your sympathy is great, but your funds are better," they said.

"You've tackled too big a job," the Labor leaders told the girls, with a benevolent air. "He's the candy around this town--E.J. Troy is. It would take a mint of money to beat E.J. Troy."

However, the Central body instructed the legislative committee of five to give the girls every help, and they did good service. But the Central Body didn't instruct the Committee to go down very far into the treasury.

July was wearing on. The League hurled itself upon the press once more. Surely after so much speech-making and bill-posting the editors would accord them some recognition merely as news. Silence--absolute silence in the next day's papers, and the next.

How did they accomplish the next move? That is one of the secrets. Their money was gone, the silence of the press had crushed them with an overwhelming sense of helplessness, but nevertheless they turned the trick. They reached the upper and middle class readers of the South Side District, Troy's district, which the papers were determined to keep as much in ignorance as possible. All one night, silent, swift-moving men whipped the paste across the billboards of that section and slapped on huge posters, so that when Papa Smith and young Mr. Jones and Banker Green came out of their comfortable houses next morning on their way to business, they neglected their papers to find out why they should "scratch E.J. Troy."

The day of the primaries was almost come. Now to reach the dull fellows who hadn't seen the cards and the huge posters, who use their eyes only to avoid obstacles. One night, as the factory whistles blew the signal of dismissal, the men in the lines of operators who filed out of shop and mills found themselves mechanically taking and examining this ticket handed them by League girls, who had gone off their job a bit early and had their wages docked in order to work for the larger good.

The Committee of the Central Body was now openly active in their behalf. Men as well as women were passing out the tickets.

Then came the eve of the election. Busy pairs of girls who had already done ten hours' work were going over E.J. Troy's district, with its sections of rich and poor and well-to-do. Throbbing feet that had carried the body's weight ten hot, fatiguing hours hurried up and down the blocks, climbed flight after flight of stairs, and stood at door after door.

"Say, kid, ain't it the limit that a woman can't vote on her own business?" said one girl too another after they had finished the one hundred and forty-fifth family and tried to explain their stake in the election to a bigoted "head of the house."

On the morning of the primaries Mrs. Schurz, as she took the coffee off the stove, remonstrated with her oldest daughter, Minna. "Vat, Minna, you ain't goin' to stay out of de mill today and lose your pay?

"Yes, I be, _Mutter_," retorted Minna, with a tightening of the lips and a light in her eyre. "I'm goin' to the polls to hand out cards to the voters. I'm goin'. I don't care if I lose my job even."

"Oh, Minna, dat is bad, and me wid four _kinder_ to eat de food. Where is de _fleisch_ and de _brot_ widout your wages?" Mrs. Schurz's heavy face wore the anxious despondence so common to the mothers of the poor.

The girl hesitated, then tightened her lips once more. "I've got to take the risk, _Mutter_. It'll come out right--it's got to. Do you want the rest of the children workin' ten hours a day too? Look at me! I ain't

got no looks any more. I'm too dead tired to go out of a Saturday night.
I can't give nobody a good time any more. I guess there won't be no
weddin' bells for mine--ever. But the kids"--pointing to the inside
bedroom, where the younger girls were still asleep--"the kids is a-goin'
to keep their looks."

So at six o'clock Minna joined the relays of working girls who--many of
them, like Minna, at personal risk and sacrifice--handed out cards all
day to each man who entered. Thus the men were reminded at the last
moment of the working woman's stake in the election. "Scratch E.J. Troy"
was before their eyes as they crossed their tickets.

Every moment of the day there were alert girls to make this final quiet
appeal for justice. They were serious, dignified. There was no jeering,
no mirth on the part of the men at the novelty of this campaign--nothing
to make any woman self-conscious.

The girls were quiet enough outwardly, but the inner drama was keyed
high. Had all their speech-making, placarding, bill-posting and the
canvassing of factories, blocks, and primaries--had all their little
savings, their risk and personal sacrifice accomplished anything? That
was what the girls asked themselves. The thermometer of their hope rose
and fell with the rumors of the day. The fathers of the Central Labor
Body patted them on the head benevolently and tried to ease their fall,
if they were to fall, by saying that anyway it would be something to
make Troy run third on his ticket.

Seven o'clock, and the girls were leaving the primaries in twos and
threes, tired but excitedly discussing the situation. Between hope and
despondency the comment varied on the streets, at the supper-tables, and
in the eager, waiting groups of girls on tenement steps and stairs.

At last came the authentic returns. E.J. Troy ran _3,338 votes behind
his ticket. With a silent press and practically no money, the working
women had defeated one of the most popular men in St. Louis._

A man pledged to the interests of labor legislation won his place. That
made the outlook better for the Women's Nine-Hour Bill, and thousands of
working girls tumbled into bed, tired, but with new hope.

Every newspaper in St. Louis failed to comment on the victory. The
slaves who sit at the editorial desk said they couldn't--they weren't
"let." _So the most hopeful feature in St. Louis politics has never been
commented on by the American press._

As for Hannah Hennessy--she had been too ill to share in the active
work of the campaign, but her influence was everywhere--a vital force, a
continual inspiration.

Week by week her cheeks grew thinner, her cough more rasping. But after
the campaign against Troy was over, she turned with the same intensity
of interest to the National Convention of the American Federation of
Labor which was to meet there in November. For a year she had been
making plans, eager to make this convention a landmark in the history of
women's labor. But in November she was in bed by the little grate fire
in the family sitting-room. And when convention week came with its
meetings a scant three blocks from her home, she could be there in

spirit only; she waited restlessly for the girls to slip in after the daily sessions and live them over again for her.

On Thanksgiving Day, between the exhausting strain of high-tension work and the zeal of the young reformer, her beautiful life and brilliant fire were burned out. The committee for the prevention of tuberculosis added her case to their statistics, and the League girls bore her into the lighted church.

In the winter of 1910-11 the leaders of all the labor and social forces of St. Louis, all the organizations for various forms of uplift, united under an able secretary and began their custom of lunching together once a week to discuss the pending social legislation. They played a good game. First, there was the educational effect of their previous legislative campaign to build on. Then there was all the economy and impetus gained from consolidation. They knew the rules of the game better, too. Their plans were more carefully laid and executed.

With a more wary and sophisticated eye on the Manufacturers' Association and a finger in the buttonhole of every legislator, the socially awake of St. Louis have secured _more humane child labor legislation, and the Nine-Hour Day for women and children with no exception in favor of shop-keepers_.

Knowing the sickening fate of industrial legislation in certain other states when tried before judges whose social vision is fifty years behind the times, the winners of this new bill began to wait tensely enough for its testing. So far, however, the Women's Nine-Hour law has not been contested. It has also been exceptionally well enforced, considering that there are only four factory inspectors for all the myriad shops and mills of this manufacturing city of the Southwest, and only seven factory inspectors for the whole state of Missouri.

Meanwhile St. Louis's new political wedge, the Women's Trade Union League, continues to be a perfectly good political wedge. When there is legislation wanted, all kinds of organizations invariably call upon this league of the working women, whose purpose is a wider social justice.

St. Louis is another American city where the working women are discovering that they can do things if they only think so.

      *   *   *   *   *

(_The Delineator_)

Illustrated by two pen-and-ink sketches made by a staff artist.

THE JOB LADY

GIVES THE YOUNG WAGE-EARNER A FAIR WORKING CHANCE

BY MARY E. TITZEL

The Jones School, the oldest public school building in Chicago, is at Harrison Street and Plymouth Court. When it was new, it was surrounded by "brown-stone fronts," and boys and girls who to-day are among the city's most influential citizens learned their A-B-C's within its walls.

Now, the office-buildings and printing-houses and cheap hotels and
burlesque shows that mark the noisy, grimy district south of the "loop"
crowd in upon it; and only an occasional shabby brown-stone front
survives in the neighborhood as a tenement house. But in the Jones
School, the process of making influential citizens is still going on.
For there the "Job Lady" has her office, her sanctum.

Job Lady is a generic term that includes Miss Anne Davis, director of
the Bureau of Vocational Supervision, and her four assistants. The
Bureau--which is the newest department of Chicago's school system--is
really an employment agency, but one that is different from any other
employment agency in the United States. It is concerned solely with a
much-neglected class of wage-earners--children from fourteen to sixteen
years of age; and its chief purpose is, not to find positions for its
"patrons," but to keep them in school.

It was founded as a result of the discovery that there were not nearly
enough jobs in Chicago to go around among the twelve or fifteen thousand
children under sixteen years of age who left school each year to go to
work; also that, though a statute of the State required a child either
to work or to go to school, there were about twenty-three thousand
youngsters in the city who were doing neither. The law had made no
provision for keeping track of the children once they had left school.
No one knew what had become of them. So Miss Davis, acting as special
investigator for the School of Civics and Philanthropy and the Chicago
Women's Club, set to work to find out.

She discovered--and she can show you statistics to prove it--that
"bummin'" around, looking aimlessly for work, brought many a boy and
girl, unable to withstand the temptations of the street, into the
Juvenile Court. And she found, as other statistics bear witness, that
the fate of the children who found jobs was scarcely better than that of
their idle brothers and sisters. Undirected, they took the first
positions that offered, with the result that most of them were engaged
in "blind-alley" occupations, unskilled industries that offered little,
if any, chance for advancement and that gave no training for the future.
The pay was poor; it averaged two dollars a week. Working conditions
were frequently unhealthful. Moral influences of shop and factory and
office were often bad. For the most part, the industries that employed
children were seasonal; and many boys and girls were forced into long
periods of inactivity between positions. This state of affairs, combined
with a natural tendency to vary the monotony of life by shifting, on the
slightest pretext, from one job to another, was making of many children
that bane of modern industry, the "casual" laborer.

The Bureau--started informally in the course of initial investigations
and kept alive through the grace of the Women's Club, until the Board of
Education was ready to adopt it--has been able to do much in
amelioration of the lot of the fourteen-to-sixteen-year-old worker. But
no statistics it can produce are as telling as the sight of the Bureau
in operation. Sit with your eyes and ears open, in a corner of the
office in the Jones School and you will make the acquaintance of one of
the humanest employment agencies in the world; also you will learn more
about such grave subjects as the needs of our educational system and the
underlying causes of poverty than you can learn out of fat treatises in
a year.

"Why do you want to leave school?" That is the first question the Job
Lady asks of each new applicant who comes to the Bureau for work.
Perhaps the child has heard that question before; for in those schools
from which the greatest numbers of children go out at the age of
fourteen, Miss Davis and her assistants hold office hours and interview
each boy or girl who shows signs of restlessness. They give informal
talks to the pupils of the sixth and seventh grades about the
opportunities open to boys and girls under sixteen; they discuss the
special training offered by the schools and show the advisability of
remaining in school as long as possible; they try to find an opportunity
of talking over the future with each member of the graduating class.

But even when the way has been paved for it, the question, "Why do you
want to leave school?" brings to light the most trivial of reasons. In
very few cases is it economic necessity that drives a child to work.

"I ain't int'rusted," explained one boy to Miss Davis. "I jest sits."

The Job Lady is often able to convince even the sitters that school is,
after all, the best place for boys and girls under sixteen. She
persuaded between twenty-five and thirty per cent. of the children that
applied at the Bureau last year to return to school. Sometimes all she
had to do was to give the child a plain statement of the facts in the
case--of the poor work and poor pay and lack of opportunity in the
industries open to the fourteen-year-old worker. Often she found it
necessary only to explain what the school had to offer. One boy was sent
to Miss Davis by a teacher who had advised him to go to work, although
he had just completed the seventh grade, because he had "too much
energy" for school! He was a bright boy--one capable of making something
of himself, if the two important, formative years that must pass before
he was sixteen were not wasted; so he was transferred from his school to
one where vocational work was part of the curriculum--where he could
find an outlet for his superfluous energy in working with his hands. Now
he is doing high-school work creditably; and he has stopped talking
about leaving school.

But it isn't always the whim of the child that prompts him to cut short
his education. Sometimes he is driven into the industrial world by the
ignorance or greed of his parents. Miss Davis tells of one little girl
who was sacrificed to the great god Labor because the four dollars she
brought home weekly helped to pay the instalments on a piano, and of a
boy who was taken from eighth grade just before graduation because his
father had bought some property and needed a little extra money.
Frequently boys and girls are put to work because of the impression
that schools have nothing of practical value to offer.

Still, even the most miserly and most stubborn and most ignorant of
parents can sometimes be made to see the wisdom of keeping a child in
school until he is sixteen. They are won to the Job Lady's point of view
by a statement of the increased opportunity open to the child who is
sixteen. Or they are brought to see that the schools are for _all_
children, and that work, on the contrary, is very bad for some children.

But often all the Job Lady's efforts fail. The child is incurably sick
of school, the parent remains obdurate. Or, perhaps, there is a very
real need of what little the son or daughter can earn. Often some one
can be found who will donate books, or a scholarship ranging from

car-fare to a few dollars a week. Over four hundred dollars is being
given out in scholarships each month, and every scholarship shows good
returns. But often no scholarship is forthcoming; and there is nothing
for the Job Lady to do but find a position for the small applicant.

Then begins the often difficult process of fitting the child to some
available job. The process starts, really, with fitting the job to the
child, and that is as it should be. The Job Lady always tries to place
the boys and girls that come to her office where there will be some
chance for them to learn something. But jobs with a "future" are few for
the fourteen-year-old worker. The trades will not receive apprentices
under the age of sixteen; business houses and the higher-grade factories
won't bother with youngsters, because they are too unreliable; as one
man put it, with unconscious irony, too "childish." So the Job Lady must
be content to send the boys out as office and errand boys or to find
employment for the girls in binderies and novelty shops. But she
investigates every position before a child is sent to fill it; and if it
is found to be not up to standard in wages or working conditions, it is
crossed off the Bureau's list.

The Job Lady has established a minimum wage of four dollars a week. No
children go out from the Bureau to work for less than that sum,
excepting those who are placed in the part-time schools of some printing
establishments, or in dressmaking shops, where they will be learning a
useful trade. This informal minimum-wage law results in a raising of the
standard of payment in a shop.

In such manner, the Bureau makes over many a job to fit the worker. But
the fitting process works both ways. The Job Lady knows that it is
discouraging, often demoralizing, for a child to be turned away, just
because he is not the "right person" for a place. So she tries to make
sure that he _is_ the right person. That she succeeds very often, the
employers who have learned to rely on the Bureau will testify.

"If you haven't a boy for me now," one man said to Miss Davis, "I'll
wait until you get one. It will save time in the end, for you always
send just the boy I want."

The secret of finding the right boy lies, first of all, in discovering
what he wants to do; and, next, in judging whether or not he can do it.
Very often, he has not the least idea of what he wants to do. He has
learned many things in school, but little or nothing of the industrial
world in which he must live. To many boys and girls, especially to those
from the poorest families, an "office job" is the acme of desire. It
means to them, pitifully enough, a respectability they have never been
quite able to encompass. As a result, perhaps, of our slow-changing
educational ideals, they scorn the trades.

Into the trades, however, Miss Davis finds it possible to steer many a
boy who is obviously unfitted for the career of lawyer, bank clerk, or,
vaguely, "business man." And she is able to place others in the coveted
office jobs, with their time-honored requirement: "only the neat,
honest, intelligent boy need apply."

Often, given the honesty and intelligence, she must manufacture a child
to fit the description. Sometimes all that is necessary is a hint about
soap and water and a clean collar. Sometimes the big cupboard in her

office must yield up a half-worn suit or a pair of shoes that some
luckier boy has outgrown. Occasionally, hers is the delicate task of
suggesting to a prematurely sophisticated little girl that some
employers have an unreasonable prejudice against rouge and earrings; or
that even the poorest people can wash their underwear. Manners
frequently come in for attention.

When the boys or girls are placed, the Bureau, unlike most employment
agencies, does not wash its hands of them. Its work has only begun. Each
child is asked to report concerning his progress from time to time; and
if he does not show up, a vocational supervisor keeps track of him by
visits to home or office, or by letters, written quarterly. The Job Lady
is able to observe by this method, whether or not the work is suitable
for the child, or whether it offers him the best available chance; and
she is often able to check the habit of "shifting" in its incipient
stages. She is continually arbitrating and making adjustments, always
ready to listen to childish woes and to allay them when she can.

Not long ago, I went to a conference on Vocational Guidance. There I
heard, from the mouths of various men, what hope the work being done by
the Bureau held for the future. One showed how it had infused new blood
into the veins of an anemic educational system, how it was making the
schools a more efficient preparation for life--the life of factory and
shop and office--than they ever had been before.

Another man pointed out that the Bureau, through the schools, would
strike at one of the deep roots of poverty--incompetency. More people
are poor for lack of proper equipment to earn a living and proper
direction in choosing a vocation, he said, than for any other one
reason.

A third man saw in the Vocational Bureau a means of keeping a control
over employing interests. "You treat our children well, and you pay them
well," the schools of the future, he declared, would be able to say to
the employer, as the Bureau was already saying, "or we won't permit our
children to work for you." A fourth had a vision of what the Bureau and
the new education it heralded could do toward educating the men and
women of the future to a knowledge of their rights as workers.

And then there came a man with a plea. "All of these things," he said,
"the Bureau can accomplish--must accomplish. But let us not forget, in
our pursuance of great ends, that it is the essential _humanness_ of the
Bureau that has made it what it is."

Here was the final, immeasurable measure of its success. It counts, of
course, that the Job Lady helps along big causes, drives at the roots of
big ills; but, somehow it counts more that an anxious-faced youngster I
saw at the Bureau should have brought his woes to her. His employer had
given him a problem to solve--and he couldn't do it. He was afraid he'd
lose his job. He had never been to the Bureau before, but "a boy you got
a job for said you'd help me out," he explained--and he was sent off
happy, the problem solved.

It counts too, that Tillie, who had once found work through the Bureau,
but was now keeping house for her father, should turn to the Bureau for
aid. Her father had been sick and couldn't afford to buy her anything
new to wear. "My dress is so clumsy," she wrote, "that the boys laugh at

me when I go out in the street." She was confident that the Job Lady would help her--and her confidence was not misplaced. It counts that the Jameses and Henrys and Johns and Marys and Sadies come, brimming over with joy, to tell the Job Lady of a "raise" or of a bit of approbation from an employer. All the funny, grateful, pathetic letters that pour in count unspeakably!

To hundreds of boys and girls and parents the Job Lady has proved a friend. There has been no nonsense about the matter. She has not sentimentalized over her work; she has not made it smack of charity. Indeed, there is no charity about it. The boys and girls and parents who come to the Job Lady are, for the most part, just average boys and girls and parents, as little paupers as millionaires. They are the people who are generally lost sight of in a democracy, where one must usually be well-to-do enough to, buy assistance, or poor enough to accept it as alms, if he is to have any aid at all in solving the problems of life.

It is a great thing for the schools, through the Bureau, to give to these average men and women and children practical aid in adjusting their lives to the conditions under which they live and work, and to do it with a sympathy and an understanding--a humanness that warms the soul.

           *   *   *   *   *

(Kansas City Star)

Two illustrations with the captions:
   1. "Tom Sawyer and Becky Thatcher," an Illustration in
      the "Adventures of Tom Sawyer" (Harpers), which met the
      Author's Approval.

   2. Mrs. Laura Frazer, the Original "Becky Thatcher," Pouring
      Tea at Mark Twain's Boyhood Home in Hannibal, Mo.,
      on the Anniversary of the Author's Birth.

MARK TWAIN'S FIRST SWEETHEART, BECKY THATCHER, TELLS OF THEIR CHILDHOOD COURTSHIP

To Mrs. Laura Frazer of Hannibal, Mo., Mark Twain's immortal "Adventures of Tom Sawyer" is a rosary, and the book's plot is the cord of fiction on which beads of truth are strung. In the sunset of her life she tells them over, and if here and there among the roseate chaplet is a bead gray in coloring, time has softened the hues of all so they blend exquisitely. This bead recalls a happy afternoon on the broad Mississippi with the boys and girls of seventy years ago; the next brings up a picture of a schoolroom where a score of little heads bob over their books and slates, and a third visualizes a wonderful picnic excursion to the woods with a feast of fried chicken and pie and cake.

For Mrs. Frazer is the original of Becky Thatcher, the childhood sweetheart of Tom Sawyer, and the original of Tom Sawyer, of course, was Mark Twain himself.

"Yes, I was the Becky Thatcher of Mr. Clemens's book," Mrs. Frazer said the other day, as she sat in the big second floor front parlor of the old time mansion in Hannibal, which is now the Home for the Friendless.

Mrs. Frazer is the matron of the home.

"Of course I suspected it when I first read the 'Adventures of Tom Sawyer,'" she went on. "There were so many incidents which I recalled as happening to Sam Clemens and myself that I felt he had drawn a picture of his memory of me in the character of Judge Thatcher's little daughter. But I never confided my belief to anyone. I felt that it would be a presumption to take the honor to myself.

"There were other women who had no such scruples--some of them right here in Hannibal--and they attempted to gain a little reflected notoriety by asserting that they were the prototypes of the character. When Albert Bigelow Paine, Mr. Clemens's biographer, gathered the material for his life of the author, he found no fewer than twenty-five women, in Missouri and elsewhere, each of whom declared she was Becky Thatcher, but he settled the controversy for all time on Mr. Clemens's authority when the biography was published. In it you will find that Becky Thatcher was Laura Hawkins, which was my maiden name.

"We were boy and girl sweethearts, Sam Clemens and I," Mrs. Frazer said with a gentle little laugh.

She is elderly, of course, since it was seventy years ago that her friendship with Mark Twain began, and her hair is gray. But her heart is young, and she finds in her work of mothering the twenty-five boys and girls in her charge the secret of defying age. On this particular afternoon she wore black and white striped silk, the effect of which was a soft gray to match her hair, and her placid face was lighted with smiles of reminiscence.

"Children are wholly unartificial, you know," she explained. "They do not learn to conceal their feelings until they begin to grow up. The courtship of childhood, therefore, is a matter of preference and of comradeship. I liked Sam better than the other boys, and he liked me better than the other girls, and that was all there was to it."

If you had seen this lady of Old Missouri as she told of her childhood romance you would have recalled instinctively Mark Twain's description:

> A lovely little blue eyed creature with yellow hair plaited into two long tails, white summer frock and embroidered pantalettes. * * * He worshipped this new angel with furtive eye until he saw that she had discovered him; then he pretended he did not know she was present, and began to "show off" in all sorts of absurd boyish ways, in order to win her admiration.

And you would have found it easy to conceive that this refined, gentle countenance once was apple cheeked and rosy, that the serene gray eyes once sparkled as blue as the Father of Waters on a sunny day and that the frosted hair was as golden as the sunshine.

"I must have been 6 or 7 years old when we moved to Hannibal," Mrs. Frazer said. "My father had owned a big mill and a store and a plantation worked by many negro slaves further inland, but he found the task of managing all too heavy for him, and so he bought a home in Hannibal and was preparing to move to it when he died. My mother left the mill and the plantation in the hands of my grown brothers--I was one of ten children, by the way--and came to Hannibal. Our house stood at the corner of Hill and Main streets, and just a few doors west, on Hill Street, lived the Clemens family.

"I think I must have liked Sam Clemens the very first time I saw him. He was different from the other boys. I didn't know then, of course, what it was that made him different, but afterward, when my knowledge of the world and its people grew, I realized that it was his natural refinement. He played hookey from school, he cared nothing at all for his books and he was guilty of all sorts of mischievous pranks, just as Tom Sawyer is in the book, but I never heard a coarse word from him in all our childhood acquaintance.

"Hannibal was a little town which hugged the steamboat landing in those days. If you will go down through the old part of the city now you will find it much as it was when I was a child, for the quaint old weatherbeaten buildings still stand, proving how thoroughly the pioneers did their work. We went to school, we had picnics, we explored the big cave--they call it the Mark Twain Cave now, you know."

"Were you lost in the cave, as Tom Sawyer and Becky Thatcher were?" Mrs. Frazer was asked.

"No; that is a part of the fiction of the book," she answered. "As a matter of fact, some older persons always went with us. Usually my older sister and Sam Clemens's older sister, who were great friends, were along to see that we didn't get lost among the winding passages where our candles lighted up the great stalagmites and stalactites, and where water was dripping from the stone roof overhead, just as Mr. Clemens has described it."

And then she proceeded to divorce the memory of Mark Twain from "the little red schoolhouse" forever.

"In those days we had only private schools," Mrs. Frazer said. "If there were public schools I never heard of them. The first school I went to was taught by Mr. Cross, who had canvassed the town and obtained perhaps twenty-five private pupils at a stated price for the tuition of each. I do not know how much Mr. Cross charged, but when I was older I remember that a young woman teacher opened a school after getting twenty-five pupils at $25 each for the year's tuition. I shall never forget that Mr. Cross did not belie his name, however, or that Sam Clemens wrote a bit of doggerel about him."

She quoted it this way:

  Cross by name and Cross by nature,
  Cross hopped out of an Irish potato.

"The schoolhouse was a 2-story frame building with a gallery across the entire front," she resumed. "After a year together in that school Sam and I went to the school taught by Mrs. Horr. It was then he used to write notes to me and bring apples to school and put them on my desk. And once, as a punishment for some prank, he had to sit with the girls and occupied a vacant seat by me. He didn't seem to mind the penalty at all," Mrs. Frazer added with another laugh, "so I don't know whether it was effective as a punishment or not.

"We hadn't reached the dancing age then, but we went to many 'play parties' together and romped through 'Going to Jerusalem,' 'King William was King George's Son' and 'Green Grow the Rushes--O.'

"Judge Clemens, Sam's father, died and left the family in straitened circumstances, and Sam's schooling ended there. He began work in the printing office to help out, and when he was 17 or 18 he left Hannibal to go to work in St. Louis. He never returned to live, but he visited here often in the years that followed."

Mrs. Frazer's own story formed the next chapter of her narrative. A young physician, Doctor Frazer of Madisonville, which was a little inland village in Ralls County, adjoining, came often to Hannibal and courted pretty Laura Hawkins. When she was 20 they were married and went to live in the new house Doctor Frazer had built for his bride at Madisonville. There they reared two sons until they required better school facilities, when they went to Rensselaer, also in Ralls County, but nearer Hannibal. They lived in Rensselaer until Doctor Frazer's death, when the mother and younger son moved to the General Canby farm. This son's marriage led to Mrs. Frazer's return to Hannibal twenty-two years ago. She was offered the position of matron at the Home for the Friendless, and for twenty-two years she has managed it. The boys and girls who have gone out from it in nearly every case have become useful men and women as a result of her guidance at the critical period of their life, for the girls remain in the home until they are 14 and the boys until they are 12. The old mansion which houses the score or more of children always there is to be abandoned in the spring for a new and modern building, a gift from a wealthy citizen to the private charity which has conducted the institution so long without aid from city, county or state.

It was given to Mrs. Frazer and Mark Twain to renew their youthful friendship after a lapse of half a century. In 1908 Mrs. Frazer made a trip East, accepting an invitation to visit Albert Bigelow Paine at Redding, Conn. Mr. Paine had visited Hannibal two years before in a search for material for his biography of Mark Twain and had made Mrs. Frazer's acquaintance then. He mentioned the approaching visit to the great humorist and Mark Twain promptly sat down and wrote Mrs. Frazer that she must be a guest also at Stormfield, his Redding estate. So it came about that the one-time little Laura Hawkins found herself lifting the knocker at the beautiful country home of Mark Twain in the Connecticut hills.

"The door was opened by Clara Clemens, Mr. Clemens's daughter," Mrs. Frazer said, "and she threw her arms about me and cried:

'I know you, for I've seen your picture, and father has told me about you. You are Becky Thatcher, and I'm happy to see you.'

"And that," Mrs. Frazer said, "was the first time I really knew I was the original of the character, although I had suspected it for thirty years. Clara Clemens, you know, even then was a famous contralto, and Ossip Gabrilowitsch, whose wife she is now, was 'waiting' on her at the time.

"It was a wonderful visit," she went on. "Mr. Clemens took me over

Stormfield. It must have been a tract of three hundred acres. We went through the fields, which were not fields at all, since they were not cultivated, and across a rustic bridge over a little rushing brook which boiled and bubbled among the rocks in the bed of a great ravine, and we sat down under a rustic arbor and talked of the old days in Hannibal when he was a little boy and I a little girl, before he went out into the world to win fame and before I lived my own happy married life. Mr. Clemens had that rare faculty of loyalty to his friends which made the lapse of fifty years merely an interim. It was as if the half century had rolled away and we were there looking on the boy and girl we had been.

"Mr. Clemens had won worldwide fame; he had been a welcome guest in the palaces of Old World rulers and lionized in the great cities of his own country. He had been made a Doctor of Literature by the University of Oxford, the highest honor of the greatest university in the world, and yet there at Stormfield to me he seemed to be Sam Clemens of old Hannibal, rather than the foremost man in the American world of letters.

"That, I believe, is my most treasured memory of Sam Clemens," Mrs. Frazer ended. "I love to think of him as the curly-headed, rollicking, clean minded little boy I played with as a child, but I like better still to think of him as he was in his last days, when all that fame and fortune had showered on him did not, even momentarily, make him waver in his loyalty to the friends of his youth."

In Hannibal stands the quaint little 2-story house flush with the sidewalk which Samuel Langhorne Clemens's father built in 1844, after he had moved to the old river town from Florida, Mo., where the great story teller was born. Restored, it houses many reminders of the author and is maintained as a memorial to Mark Twain. There, November 30, the eighty-second anniversary of the birth of Clemens, the people of Hannibal and persons from many cities widely scattered over America will go to pay tribute to his memory.

And there they will see Becky Thatcher in the flesh, silkengowned, gray-haired and grown old, but Becky Thatcher just the same, seated in a chair which once was Mark Twain's and pouring tea at a table on which the author once wrote. And if the aroma of the cup she hands out to each visitor doesn't waft before his mind a vision of a curly-headed boy and a little girl with golden long-tails at play on the wharf of old Hannibal while the ancient packets ply up and down the rolling blue Mississippi, there is nothing whatever in the white magic of association.

        *   *   *   *   *

(_Milwaukee Journal_)

FOUR MEN OF HUMBLE BIRTH HOLD WORLD DESTINY IN THEIR HANDS

BY WILLIAM G. SHEPHERD

WASHINGTON--Out of a dingy law office in Virginia, out of a cobbler's shop in Wales, out of a village doctor's office in France and from a farm on the island of Sicily came the four men who, in the grand old palace at Versailles, will soon put the quietus on the divine right of kings.

In 1856, three days after Christmas, a boy named Thomas was born in the plain home of a Presbyterian parson in Staunton, Va. When this boy was 4 years old, there was born in Palermo, on the island of Sicily, 4,000 miles away, a black-eyed Sicilian boy. Into the town of Palermo, on that July day, came Garibaldi, in triumph, and the farmer-folk parents of the boy, in honor of the occasion, named their son Victor, after the new Italian king, whom Garibaldi had helped to seat.

Three years later still, when Thomas was playing the games of 7-year-old boys down in Virginia, and when Victor, at 3, spent most of his time romping on the little farm in Sicily, there was born in the heart of the foggy, grimy town of Manchester, in England, a boy named David. His home was the ugliest of the homes of all the three. It was of red brick, two stories high, with small windows, facing a busy stone sidewalk. Its rooms were small and little adorned, and not much hope of greatness could ever have sprung from that dingy place.

There was one other boy to make up the quartet. His name was George. He was a young medical student in Paris twenty-two years old when David was born in England. He thought all governments ought to be republics, and, by the time he was 25, he came over to the United States to study the American republic, and, if possible, to make a living over here as a doctor. He had been born in a little village in France, in a doctor's household.

While George was in New York, almost starving for lack of patients, and later, while he taught French in a girls' school in Stamford, Conn., little Thomas, down in Virginia, at the age of 10 years, had buckled down to his studies, with the hope of being a lawyer; Victor, at 6, was studying in a school in far-away Palermo, and David, at 3, fatherless by this time, was getting ready for life in the home of his uncle, a village shoemaker, in a little town of Wales. The only city-born boy of the four, he was taken by fate, when his father died, to the simplicity of village life and saved, perhaps, from the sidewalks.

The years whirled on. George married an American girl and went back to France, to write and teach and doctor. Thomas went to a university to study law. David, seven years younger, spent his evenings and spare time in his uncle's shoe shop or in the village blacksmith shop, listening to his elders talk over the affairs of the world.

Victor, with law as his vision, crossed the famous old straits of Messina from his island home and went to Naples to study in the law school there.

In the '80s things began to happen. Down in Virginia, Thomas was admitted to the bar. In old Wales, David, who, by this time, had learned to speak English, was admitted to practice law in 1884, and, in 1885, the black-eyed, hot-blooded Sicilian Victor received the documents that entitled him to practice at the Italian bar.

George, in France, by this time had dropped medicine. Bolshevism had arisen there in the form of the Commune, and he had fought it so desperately that he had been sentenced to death. He hated kings, and he also hated the autocracy of the mob. He fled from Paris.

Soon they will sit at a peace table together, the first peace table in all human history from which divine-right kings are barred. The future and the welfare of the world lie in their four pairs of hands. Their full names are: Georges Clemenceau, premier of France; David Lloyd George, prime minister of England; Victor Emanuel Orlando, premier of Italy, and Thomas Woodrow Wilson, president of the United States.

        *   *   *   *   *

(Saturday Evening Post)

Three half-tone reproductions of wash-drawings by a staff artist.

THE CONFESSIONS OF A COLLEGE PROFESSOR'S WIFE

A college professor--as may be proved by any number of novels and plays--is a quaint, pedantic person, with spectacles and a beard, but without any passions--except for books. He takes delight in large fat words, but is utterly indifferent to such things as clothes and women--except the dowdy one he married when too young to know better.... It is always so interesting to see ourselves as authors see us.

Even more entertaining to us, however, is the shockingly inconsistent attitude toward academic life maintained by practical people who know all about real life--meaning the making and spending of money.

One evening soon after I became a college professor's wife I enjoyed the inestimable privilege of sitting next to one of America's safest and sanest business men at a dinner party given in his honor by one of the trustees of the university.

When he began to inform me, with that interesting air of originality which often accompanies the platitudes of our best citizens, that college professors were "mere visionary idealists--all academic theories; no practical knowledge of the world"--and so on, as usual--I made bold to interrupt:

"Why, in the name of common sense, then, do you send your own sons to them to be prepared for it! Is such a policy safe? Is it sane? Is it practical?" And I am afraid I laughed in the great man's face.

He only blinked and said "Humph!" in a thoroughly businesslike manner; but throughout the rest of the evening he viewed me askance, as though I had become a dangerous theorist too--by marriage. So I turned my back on him and wondered why such a large and brilliant dinner was given for such a dull and uninteresting Philistine!

This shows, by the way, how young and ignorant I was. The mystery was explained next day, when it was intimated to me that I had made what is sometimes called, even in refined college circles, a break. Young professors' wives were not expected to trifle with visitors of such eminent solvency; but I had frequently heard the materialistic tendencies of the age condemned in public, and had not been warned in private that we were all supposed to do our best to work this materialist for a million, with which to keep up the fight against materialism.

In the cloistered seclusion of our universities, dedicated to high ideals, more deference is shown to the masters of high finance than to the masters of other arts--let me add not because Mammon is worshiped, but because he is needed for building cloisters.

The search for truth would be far more congenial than the search for wealth; but, so long as our old-fashioned institutions remain, like old-fashioned females, dependent for their very existence on the bounty of personal favor, devious methods must be employed for coaxing and wheedling money out of those who control it--and therefore the truth.

I was a slender bride and had a fresh, becoming trousseau. He was a heavy-jowled banker and had many millions. I was supposed to ply what feminine arts I could command for the highly moral purpose of obtaining his dollars, to be used in destroying his ideals.

Well, that was the first and last time I was ever so employed. Despite the conscientious flattery of the others he gruntingly refused to give a penny. And--who knows--perhaps I was in part responsible for the loss of a million! A dreadful preface to my career as a college professor's wife.

However, before pursuing my personal confessions, I must not overlook the most common and comic characteristic of the college professor we all know and love in fiction. I refer to his picturesque absent-mindedness. I had almost forgotten that; possibly I have become absent-minded by marriage too! Is not the dear old fellow always absent-minded on the stage? Invariably and most deliriously! Just how he manages to remain on the Faculty when absent-minded is never explained on the program; and it often perplexes us who are behind the scenes.

I tell my husband that, in our case, I, as the dowdy and devoted wife, am supposed to interrupt his dreams--they always have dreams--remove his untidy dressing gown--they always wear dressing gowns--and dispatch him to the classroom with a kiss and a coat; but how about that great and growing proportion of his colleagues who, for reasons to be stated, are wifeless and presumably helpless?

Being only a woman, I cannot explain how bachelors retain their positions; but I shall venture to assert that no business in the world--not even the army and navy--is conducted on a more ruthless and inexorable schedule than the business of teaching.

My two brothers drift into their office at any time between nine and ten in the morning and yet control a fairly successful commercial enterprise; whereas, if my husband arrived at his eight-o'clock classroom only one minute late there would be no class there to teach. For it is an unwritten law among our engaging young friends the undergraduates that when the "prof" is not on hand before the bell stops ringing they can "cut"--thus avoiding what they were sent to college for and achieving one of the pleasantest triumphs of a university course.

My confessions! Dear me! What have I, a college professor's wife, to confess? At least three things:

    1--That I love my husband so well that I wish I had never married him.

2--That I have been such a good wife that he does not know he ought
never to have had one.

3--That if I had to do it all over again I would do the same thing
all over again! This is indeed a confession, though whether it be of
weakness of will or strength of faith you may decide if you read the
rest.

The first time I saw the man who became my husband was at the Casino in
Newport. And what was a poor professor doing at Newport? He was not a
professor--he was a prince; a proud prince of the most royal realm of
sport. Carl, as some of you might recall if that were his real name, had
been the intercollegiate tennis champion a few years before, and now,
with the kings of the court, had come to try his luck in the annual
national tournament. He lasted until the finals this time and then was
put out. That was as high as he ever got in the game.

Alas for the romance of love at first sight! He paid not the slightest
attention to me, though he sat beside me for ten minutes; for, despite
his defeat, he was as enthusiastically absorbed in the runner-up and the
dashing defender of the title as--well, as the splendid sportsman I have
since found him to be in disappointments far more grim.

As for me, I fear I hardly noticed him either, except to remark that he
was very good-looking; for this was my first visit to Newport--the last
too--and the pageantry of wealth and fashion was bewilderingly
interesting to me. I was quite young then. I am older now. But such
unintellectual exhibitions might, I fancy, still interest me--a
shocking confession for a college professor's wife!

I did not see Carl again for two years, and then it was in another kind
of pageant, amid pomp and circumstance of such a different sort; and,
instead of white flannel trousers, he now wore a black silk gown. It had
large flowing sleeves and a hood of loud colors hanging down behind; and
he was blandly marching along in the academic procession at the
inaugural ceremonies of the new president of the university.

I wonder why it is that when the stronger sex wishes to appear
particularly dignified and impressive, as on the bench or in the pulpit,
it likes to don female attire! No matter whether suffragists or
antis--they all do it. Now some of these paraders seemed as embarrassed
by their skirts as the weaker sex would be without them; but the way
Carl wore his new honors and his new doctor's hood attracted my
attention and held it. He seemed quite aware of the ridiculous aspect of
an awkward squad of pedagogues paraded like chorus girls before an
audience invited to watch the display; but, also, he actually enjoyed
the comedy of it--and that is a distinction when you are an actor in the
comedy! His quietly derisive strut altogether fascinated me. "Hurrah!
Aren't we fine!" he seemed to say.

As the long, self-conscious procession passed where I sat, smiling and
unnoticed, he suddenly looked up. His veiled twinkle happened to meet my
gaze. It passed over me, instantly returned and rested on ray eyes for
almost a second. Such a wonderful second for little me!... Not a gleam
of recollection. He had quite forgotten that our names had once been

pronounced to each other; but in that flashing instant he recognized, as I did, that we two knew each other better than anyone else in the whole assemblage.

The nicest smile in the world said as plainly as words, and all for me alone: "Hurrah! You see it too!" Then, with that deliciously derisive strut, he passed on, while something within me said: "There he is!--at last! He is the one for you!" And I glowed and was glad.

Carl informed me afterward that he had a similar sensation, and that all through the long platitudinous exercises my face was a great solace to him.

"Whenever they became particularly tiresome," he said, "I looked at you--and bore up."

I was not unaware that he was observing me; nor was I surprised when, at the end of the exhausting ordeal, he broke through the crowd--with oh, such dear impetuosity!--and asked my uncle to present him, while I, trembling at his approach, looked in the other direction, for I felt the crimson in my cheeks--I who had been out three seasons! Then I turned and raised my eyes to his, and he, too, colored deeply as he took my hand.

We saw no comedy in what followed.

There was plenty of comedy, only we were too romantic to see it. At the time it seemed entirely tragic to me that my people, though of the sort classified as cultured and refined, deploring the materialistic tendency of the age, violently objected to my caring for this wonderful being, who brilliantly embodied all they admired in baccalaureate sermons and extolled in Sunday-school.

It was not despite but because of that very thing that they opposed the match! If only he had not so ably curbed his materialistic tendencies they would have been delighted with this well-bred young man, for his was an even older family than ours, meaning one having money long enough to breed contempt for making it. Instead of a fortune, however, merely a tradition of _noblesse oblige_ had come down to him, like an unwieldy heirloom. He had waved aside a promising opening in his cousin's bond-house on leaving college and invested five important years, as well as his small patrimony, in hard work at the leading universities abroad in order to secure a thorough working capital for the worst-paid profession in the world.

"If there were only some future in the teaching business!" as one of my elder brothers said; "but I've looked into the proposition. Why, even a full professor seldom gets more than four thousand--in most cases less. And it will be years before your young man is a full professor."

"I can wait," I said.

"But a girl like you could never stand that kind of life. You aren't fitted for it. You weren't brought up to be a poor man's wife."

"Plenty of tune to learn while waiting," I returned gayly enough, but heartsick at the thought of the long wait.

Carl, however, quite agreed with my brothers and wanted impetuously to start afresh in pursuit of the career in Wall Street he had forsworn, willing and eager--the darling!--to throw away ambition, change his inherited tastes, abandon his cultivated talents, and forget the five years he had "squandered in riotous learning," as he put it!

However, I was not willing--for his sake. He would regret it later. They always do. Besides, like Carl, I had certain unuttered ideals about serving the world in those days. We still have. Only now we better understand the world. Make no mistake about this. Men are just as noble as they used to be. Plenty of them are willing to sacrifice themselves--but not us. That is why so few of the sort most needed go in for teaching and preaching in these so-called materialistic days.

What was the actual, material result of my lover's having taken seriously the advice ladled out to him by college presidents and other evil companions of his innocent youth, who had besought him not to seek material gain?

At the time we found each other he was twenty-seven years of age and had just begun his career--an instructor in the economics department, with a thousand-dollar salary. That is not why he was called an economist; but can you blame my brothers for doing their best to break the engagement?... I do not--now. It was not their fault if Carl actually practiced what they merely preached. Should Carl be blamed? No; for he seriously intended never to marry at all--until he met me. Should I be blamed? Possibly; but I did my best to break the engagement too--and incidentally both our hearts--by going abroad and staying abroad until Carl--bless him!--came over after me.

I am not blaming anybody. I am merely telling why so few men in university work, or, for that matter, in most of the professions nowadays, can support wives until after the natural mating time is past. By that time their true mates have usually wed other men--men who can support them--not the men they really love, but the men they tell themselves they love! For, if marriage is woman's only true career, it is hardly true to one's family or oneself not to follow it before it is too late--especially when denied training for any other--even though she may be equally lacking in practical training for the only career open to her.

This sounds like a confession of personal failure due to the typical unpreparedness for marriage of the modern American girl. I do not think anyone could call our marriage a personal failure, though socially it may be. During the long period of our engagement I became almost as well prepared for my lifework as Carl was for his. Instead of just waiting in sweet, sighing idleness I took courses in domestic science, studied dietetics, mastered double-entry and learned to sew. I also began reading up on economics. The latter amused the family, for they thought the higher education of women quite unwomanly and had refused to let me go to college.

It amused Carl too, until I convinced him that I was really interested in the subject, not just in him; then he began sending me boxes of books instead of boxes of candy, which made the family laugh and call me strong-minded. I did not care what they called me. I was too busy making up for the time and money wasted on my disadvantageous advantages, which may have made me more attractive to men, but had not fitted me to be the wife of any man, rich or poor.

All that my accomplishments and those of my sisters actually accomplished, as I see it now, was to kill my dear father; for, though he made a large income as a lawyer, he had an even larger family and died a poor man, like so many prominent members of the bar.

I shall not dwell on the ordeal of a long engagement. It is often made to sound romantic in fiction, but in realistic life such an unnatural relationship is a refined atrocity--often an injurious one--except to pseudo-human beings so unreal and unromantic that they should never be married or engaged at all. I nearly died; and as for Carl--well, unrequited affection may be good for some men, but requited affection in such circumstances cannot be good for any man--if you grant that marriage is!

A high-strung, ambitious fellow like Carl needed no incentive to make him work hard or to keep him out of mischief, any more than he needed a prize to make him do his best at tennis or keep him from cheating in the score. What an ignoble view of these matters most good people accept! In point of fact he had been able to do more work and to play better tennis before receiving this long handicap--in short, would have been in a position to marry sooner if he had not been engaged to marry! This may sound strange, but that is merely because the truth is so seldom told about anything that concerns the most important relationship in life.

Nevertheless, despite what he was pleased to call his inspiration, he won his assistant professorship at an earlier age than the average, and we were married on fifteen hundred a year.

Oh, what a happy year! I am bound to say the family were very nice about it. Everyone was nice about it. And when we came back from our wedding journey the other professors' wives overwhelmed me with kindness and with calls--and with teas and dinners and receptions in our honor. Carl had been a very popular bachelor and his friends were pleased to treat me quite as if I were worthy of him. This was generous, but disquieting. I was afraid they would soon see through me and pity poor Carl.

I had supposed, like most outsiders, that the women of a university town would be dreadfully intellectual and modern--and I was rather in awe of them at first, being aware of my own magnificent limitations; but, for the most part, these charming new friends of mine, especially the wealthier members of the set I was thrown with, seemed guilelessly ignorant in respect of the interesting period of civilization in which they happened to live--almost as ignorant as I was and as most "nice people" are everywhere.

Books sufficiently old, art sufficiently classic, views sufficiently venerable to be respectable--these interested them, as did foreign travel and modern languages; but ideas that were modern could not be nice because they were new, though they might be nice in time--after they became stale. College culture, I soon discovered, does not care about what is happening to the world, but what used to happen to it.

"You see, my dear," Carl explained, with that quiet, casual manner so

puzzling to pious devotees of "cultureine"--and even to me at first,
though I adored and soon adopted it! "--universities don't lead
thought--they follow it. In Europe institutions of learning may
be--indeed, they frequently are--hotbeds of radicalism; in America our
colleges are merely featherbeds for conservatism to die in respectably."
Then he added: "But what could you expect? You see, we are still
intellectually _nouveaux_ over here, and therefore self-consciously
correct and imitative, like the _nouveaux riches_. So long as you have a
broad _a_ you need never worry about a narrow mind."

As for the men, I had pictured the privilege of sitting at their feet
and learning many interesting things about the universe. Perhaps they
were too tired to have their feet encumbered by ignorant young women;
for when I ventured to ask questions about their subject their answer
was--not always--but in so many cases a solemn owllike "yes-and-no" that
I soon learned my place. They did not expect or want a woman to know
anything and preferred light banter and persiflage. I like that, too,
when it is well done; but I was accustomed to men who did it better.

I preferred the society of their wives. I do not expect any member of
the complacent sex to believe this statement--unless I add that the men
did not fancy my society, which would not be strictly true; but, even if
not so intellectual as I had feared, the women of our town were far more
charming than I had hoped, and when you cannot have both cleverness and
kindness the latter makes a more agreeable atmosphere for a permanent
home. I still consider them the loveliest women in the world.

In short my only regret about being married was that we had wasted so
much of the glory of youth apart. Youth is the time for love, but not
for marriage! Some of our friends among the instructors marry on a
thousand a year, even in these days of the high cost of living; and I
should have been so willing to live as certain of them do--renting
lodgings from a respectable artisan's wife and doing my own cooking on
her stove after she had done hers.

Carl gave me no encouragement, however! Perhaps it was just as well; for
when first engaged I did not know how to cook, though I was a good
dancer and could play Liszt's Polonaise in E flat with but few mistakes.

As it turned out we began our wedded life quite luxuriously. We had a
whole house to ourselves--and sometimes even a maid! In those days there
were no flats in our town and certain small but shrewd local capitalists
had built rows of tiny frame dwellings which they leased to assistant
professors, assistant plumbers, and other respectable people of the same
financial status, at rates which enabled them--the owners, not the
tenants--to support charity and religion.

They were all alike--I refer to the houses now, not to all landlords
necessarily--with a steep stoop in front and a drying yard for Monday
mornings in the rear, the kind you see on the factory edges of great
cities--except that ours were cleaner and were occupied by nicer people.

One of our next-door neighbors was a rising young butcher with his bride
and the house on the other side of us was occupied by a postman, his
progeny, and the piercing notes of his whistle--presumably a cast-off
one--on which all of his numerous children, irrespective of sex or age,
were ambitiously learning their father's calling, as was made clear

through the thin dividing wall, which supplied visual privacy but did not prevent our knowing when they took their baths or in what terms they objected to doing so. It became a matter of interesting speculation to us what Willie would say the next Saturday night; and if we had quarreled they, in turn, could have--and would have--told what it was all about.

"Not every economist," Carl remarked whimsically, "can learn at first hand how the proletariat lives."

I, too, was learning at first hand much about my own profession. My original research in domestic science was sound in theory, but I soon discovered that my dietetic program was too expensive in practice. Instead of good cuts of beef I had to select second or third quality from the rising young butcher, who, by the way, has since risen to the dignity of a touring car. Instead of poultry we had pork, for this was before pork also rose.

My courses in bookkeeping, however, proved quite practical; and I may say that I was a good purchasing agent and general manager from the beginning of our partnership, instead of becoming one later through bitter experience, like so many young wives brought up to be ladies, not general houseworkers.

Frequently I had a maid, commonly called along our row the "gurrul"--and quite frequently I had none; for we could afford only young beginners, who, as soon as I had trained them well, left me for other mistresses who could afford to pay them well.

"Oh, we should not accuse the poor creatures of ingratitude," I told Carl one day. "Not every economist can learn at first hand the law of supply and demand."

If, however, as my fashionable aunt in town remarked, we were picturesquely impecunious--which, to that soft lady, probably meant that, we had to worry along without motor cars--we were just as desperately happy as we were poor; for we had each other at least. Every other deprivation seemed comparatively easy or amusing.

Nor were we the only ones who had each other--and therefore poverty. Scholarship meant sacrifice, but all agreed that it was the ideal life.

To be sure, some members of the Faculty--or their wives--had independent means and could better afford the ideal life. They were considered noble for choosing it. Some of the alumni who attended the great games and the graduating exercises were enormously wealthy, and gave the interest of their incomes--sometimes a whole handful of bonds at a time--to the support of the ideal life.

Was there any law compelling them to give their money to their Alma Mater? No--just as there was none compelling men like Carl to give their lives and sacrifice their wives. These men of wealth made even greater sacrifices. They could have kept in comfort a dozen wives apiece--modest ones--on what they voluntarily preferred to turn over to the dear old college. Professors, being impractical and visionary, cannot always see these things in their true proportions.

We, moreover, in return for our interest in education, did we not shamelessly accept monthly checks from the university treasurer's office? It was quite materialistic in us. Whereas these disinterested donors, instead of receiving checks, gave them, which is more blessed. And were they not checks of a denomination far larger than those we selfishly cashed for ourselves? Invariably. Therefore our princely benefactors were regarded not only as nobler but as the Nobility.

Indeed, the social stratification of my new home, where the excellent principles of high thinking and plain living were highly recommended for all who could not reverse the precept, struck me, a neophyte, as for all the world like that of a cathedral town in England, except that these visiting patrons of religion and learning were treated with a reverence and respect found only in America. Surely it must have amused them, had they not been so used to it; for they were quite the simplest, kindest, sweetest overrich people I had ever met in my own country--and they often took pains to tell us broad-mindedly that there were better things than money. Their tactful attempts to hide their awful affluence were quite appealing--occasionally rather comic. Like similarly conscious efforts to cover evident indigence, it was so palpable and so unnecessary.

"There, there!" I always wanted to say--until I, too, became accustomed to it. "It's all right. You can't help it."

It was dear of them all the same, however, and I would not seem ungrateful for their kind consideration. After all, how different from the purse-proud arrogance of wealth seen in our best--selling--fiction, though seldom elsewhere.

For the most part they were true gentlefolk, with the low voices and simple manners of several generations of breeding; and I liked them, for the most part, very much--especially certain old friends of our parents, who, I learned later, were willing to show their true friendship in more ways than Carl and I could permit.

One is frequently informed that the great compensation for underpaying the college professor is in the leisure to live--_otium cum dignitate_ as returning old grads call it when they can remember their Latin, though as most of them cannot they call it a snap.

Carl, by the way, happened to be the secretary of his class, and his popularity with dear old classmates became a nuisance in our tiny home. I remember one well-known bachelor of arts who answered to the name of Spud, a rather vulgar little man. Comfortably seated in Carl's study one morning, with a cigar in his mouth, Spud began:

"My, what a snap! A couple of hours' work a day and three solid months' vacation! Why, just see, here you are loafing early in the morning! You ought to come up to the city! Humph! I'd show you what real work means."

Now my husband had been writing until two o'clock the night before, so that he had not yet made preparation for his next hour. It was so early indeed that I had not yet made the beds. Besides, I had heard all about our snap before and it was getting on my nerves.

"Carl would enjoy nothing better than seeing you work," I put in when

the dear classmate finished; "but unfortunately he cannot spare the
time."

Spud saw the point and left; but Carl, instead of giving me the thanks I
deserved, gave me the first scolding of our married life! Now isn't that
just like a husband?

Of course it can be proved by the annual catalogue that the average
member of the Faculty has only about twelve or fourteen hours of
classroom work a week--the worst-paid instructor more; the highest-paid
professor less. What a university teacher gives to his students in the
classroom, however, is or ought to be but a rendering of what he
acquires outside, as when my distinguished father tried one of his
well-prepared cases in court. Every new class, moreover, is a different
proposition, as I once heard my brother say of his customers.

That is where the art of teaching comes in and where Carl excelled. He
could make even the "dismal science," as Carlyle called economics,
interesting, as was proved by the large numbers of men who elected his
courses, despite the fact that he made them work hard to pass. Nor does
this take into account original research and the writing of books like
Carl's scholarly work on The History of Property, on which he had been
slaving for three solid summers and hundreds of nights during termtime;
not to speak of attending committee meetings constantly, and the furnace
even more constantly. The latter, like making beds, is not mentioned in
the official catalogue. I suppose such details would not become one's
dignity.

As in every other occupation, some members of the Faculty do as little
work as the law requires; but most of them are an extremely busy lot,
even though they may, when it suits their schedule better, take exercise
in the morning instead of the afternoon--an astonishing state of affairs
that always scandalizes the so-called tired business man.

As for Carl, I was seeing so little of him except at mealtimes that I
became rather piqued at first, being a bride. I felt sure he did not
love me any more!

"Do you really think you have a right to devote so much time to outside
work?" I asked one evening when I was washing the dishes and he was
starting off for the university library to write on his great book.--It
was the indirect womanly method of saying: "Oh, please devote just a
little more time to me!"--"You ought to rest and be fresh for your
classroom work," I added.

Being a man he did not see it.

"The way to advance in the teaching profession," he answered, with his
veiled twinkle, "is to neglect it. It doesn't matter how poorly you
teach, so long as you write dull books for other professors to read.
That's why it is called scholarship--because you slight your scholars."

"Oh, I'm sick of all this talk about scholarship!" I cried. "What does
it mean anyway?"

"Scholarship, my dear," said Carl, "means finding out all there is to
know about something nobody else cares about, and then telling it in

such a way that nobody else can find out. If you are understood you are popular; if you are popular you are no scholar. And if you're no scholar, how can you become a full professor? Now, my child, it is all clear to you."

And, dismissing me and the subject with a good-night kiss, he brushed his last year's hat and hurried off, taking the latchkey.

So much for _otium_.

"But where does the dignity come in?" I asked Carl one day when he was sharpening his lawnmower and thus neglecting his lawn tennis; for, like a Freshman, I still had much to learn about quaint old college customs.

"Why, in being called p'fessor by the tradesmen," said Carl. "Also in renting a doctor's hood for academic pee-rades at three dollars a pee-rade, instead of buying a new hat for the rest of the year. Great thing--dignity!"

He chuckled and began to cut the grass furiously, reminding me of a thoroughbred hunter I once saw harnessed to a plow.

"P'fessors of pugilism and dancing," he went on gravely, "haven't a bit more dignity than we have. They merely have more money. Just think! There isn't a butcher or grocer in this town who doesn't doff his hat to me when he whizzes by in his motor--even those whose bills I haven't paid. It's great to have dignity. I don't believe there's another place in the world where he who rides makes obeisance to him who walks. Much better than getting as high wages as a trustee's chauffeur! A salary is so much more dignified than wages."

He stopped to mop his brow, looking perfectly dignified.

"And yet," he added, egged on by my laughter, for I always loved his quiet irony--it was never directed at individuals, but at the ideas and traditions they blandly and blindly followed--

"And yet carping critics of the greatest nation on earth try to make out that art and intellectuality are not properly recognized in the States. Pessimists! Look at our picture galleries, filled with old masters from abroad! Think how that helps American artists! Look at our colleges, crowded with buildings more costly than Oxford's! Think how that encourages American teachers! Simply because an occasional foreign professor gets higher pay--bah! There are better things than money. For example, this!"

And he bent to his mower again, with much the same derisively dignified strut as on that memorable day long ago when I came and saw and was conquered by it--only then he wore black silk sleeves and now white shirtsleeves.

And so much for dignity.

I soon saw that if I were to be a help and not a hindrance to the man I loved I should have to depart from what I had been carefully trained to regard as woman's only true sphere. Do not be alarmed! I had no thought of leaving home or husband. It is simply that the home, in the industrial sense, is leaving the house--seventy-five per cent of it social scientists say, has gone already--so that nowadays a wife must go out after it or else find some new-fashioned productive substitute if she really intends to be an old-fashioned helpmate to her husband.

It was not a feminist theory but a financial condition that confronted us. My done-over trousseau would not last forever, nor would Carl's present intellectual wardrobe, which was becoming threadbare. Travel abroad and foreign study are just as necessary for an American scholar as foreign buying is for an American dealer in trousseaus.

I thought of many plans; but in a college town a woman's opportunities are so limited. We are not paid enough to be ladies, though we are required to dress and act like them--do not forget that point. And yet, when willing to stop being a lady, what could one do?

Finally I thought of dropping entirely out of the social, religious and charitable activities of the town, investing in a typewriter and subscribing to a correspondence-school course in stenography. I could at least help Carl prepare his lectures and relieve him of the burden of letter writing, thus giving him more time for book reviewing and other potboiling jobs, which were not only delaying his own book but making him burn the candle at both ends in the strenuous effort to make both ends meet.

I knew Carl would object, but I had not expected such an outburst of profane rage as followed my announcement. The poor boy was dreadfully tired, and for months, like the thoroughbred he was, he had repressed his true feelings under a quiet, quizzical smile.

"My heavens! What next?" he cried, jumping up and pacing the floor. "Haven't you already given up everything you were accustomed to--every innocent pleasure you deserve--every wholesome diversion you actually need in this God-forsaken, monotonous hole? Haven't I already dragged you down--you, a lovely, fine-grained, highly evolved woman--down to the position of a servant in my house? And now, on top of all this--No, by God! I won't have it! I tell you I won't have it!"

It may be a shocking confession, but I loved him for that wicked oath. He looked so splendid--all fire and furious determination, as when he used to rush up to the net in the deciding game of a tennis match, cool and quick as lightning.

"You are right, Carl dear," I said, kissing his profane lips; for I had learned long since never to argue with him. "I am too good to be a mere household drudge. It's an economic waste of superior ability. That's why I am going to be your secretary and save you time and money enough to get and keep a competent maid."

"But I tell you--"

"I know, dear; but what are we going to do about it? We can't go on this way. They've got us down--are we going to let them keep us down? Look into the future! Look at poor old Professor Culberson. Look at half of the older members of the Faculty! They have ceased to grow; their usefulness is over; they are all gone to seed--because they hadn't the courage or the cash to develop anything but their characters!"

Carl looked thoughtful. He had gained an idea for his book and, like a true scholar, forgot for the moment our personal situation.

"Really, you know," he mused, "does it pay Society to reward its individuals in inverse ratio to their usefulness?" He took out his pocket notebook and wrote: "Society itself suffers for rewarding that low order of cunning called business sense with the ultimate control of all other useful talents." He closed his notebook and smiled.

"And yet they call the present economic order safe and sane! And all of us who throw the searchlight of truth on it--dangerous theorists! Can you beat it?"

"Well," I rejoined, not being a scholar, "there's nothing dangerous about my theory. Instead of your stenographer becoming your wife, your wife becomes your stenographer--far safer and saner than the usual order. Men are much more apt to fall in love with lively little typewriters than with fat, flabby wives."

Though it was merely to make a poor joke out of a not objectionable necessity, my plan, as it turned out, was far wiser than I realized.

First, I surreptitiously card-catalogued the notes and references for Carl's "epoch-making book," as one of the sweet, vague wives of the Faculty always called her husband's volumes, which she never read. Then I learned to take down his lectures, to look up data in the library, to verify quotations, and even lent a hand in the book reviewing.

Soon I began to feel more than a mere consumer's interest--a producer's interest--in Carl's work. And then a wonderful thing happened: My husband began to see--just in time, I believe--that a wife could be more than a passive and more or less desirable appendage to a man's life--an active and intelligent partner in it. And he looked at me with a new and wondering respect, which was rather amusing, but very dear.

He had made the astonishing discovery that his wife had a mind!

Years of piano practice had helped to make my fingers nimble for the typewriter, and for this advantage I was duly grateful to the family's old-fashioned ideals, though I fear they did not appreciate my gratitude. Once, when visiting them during the holidays, I was laughingly boasting, before some guests invited to meet me at luncheon, about my part in the writing of Carl's History of Property, which had been dedicated to me and was now making a sensation in the economic world, though our guests in the social world had never heard of it.

Suddenly I saw a curious, uncomfortable look come over the faces of the family. Then I stopped and remembered that nowadays wives--nice wives, that is--are not supposed to be helpmates to their husbands except in name; quite as spinsters no longer spin. They can help him spend. At that they are truly better halves, but to help him earn is not nice. To our guests it could mean only one thing--namely, that my husband could not afford a secretary. Well, he could not. What of it?

For a moment I had the disquieting sensation of having paraded my poverty--a form of vulgarity that Carl and I detest as heartily as a display of wealth.

The family considerately informed me afterward, however, that they thought me brave to sacrifice myself so cheerfully. Dear me! I was not being brave. I was not being cheerful. I was being happy. There is no sacrifice in working for the man you love. And if you can do it with him--why, I conceitedly thought it quite a distinction. Few women have the ability or enterprise to attain it!

One of my sisters who, like me, had failed to "marry well" valeted for her husband; but somehow that seemed to be all right. For my part I never could see why it is more womanly to do menial work for a man than intellectual work with him. I have done both and ought to know.... Can it be merely because the one is done strictly in the home or because no one can see you do it? Or is it merely because it is unskilled labor?

It is all right for the superior sex to do skilled labor, but a true womanly woman must do only unskilled labor, and a fine lady none at all--so clothed as to prevent it and so displayed as to prove it, thus advertising to the world that the man who pays for her can also pay for secretaries and all sorts of expensive things. Is that the old idea?

If so I am afraid most college professors' wives should give up the old-fashioned expensive pose of ladyhood and join the new womanhood!

Well, as it turned out, we were enabled to spend our sabbatical year abroad--just in time to give Carl a new lease of life mentally and me physically; for both of us were on the verge of breaking down before we left.

Such a wonderful year! Revisiting his old haunts; attending lectures together in the German and French universities; working side by side in the great libraries; and meeting the great men of his profession at dinner! Then, between whiles, we had the best art and music thrown in! Ah, those are the only real luxuries we miss and long for! Indeed, to us, they are not really luxuries. Beauty is a necessity to some persons, like exercise; though others can get along perfectly well without it and, therefore, wonder why we cannot too.

Carl's book had already been discovered over there--that is perhaps the only reason it was discovered later over here--and every one was so kind about it. We felt quite important and used to wink at each other across the table. "Our" book, Carl always called it, like a dear. His work was my work now--his ambitions, my ambitions; not just emotionally or inspirationally, but intellectually, collaboratively. And that made our emotional interest in each other the keener and more satisfying. We had fallen completely in love with each other. For the first time we two were really one. Previously we had been merely pronounced so by a clergyman who read it out of a book.

Oh, the glory of loving some one more than oneself! And oh, the blessedness of toiling together for something greater and more important than either! That is what makes it possible for the other thing to endure--not merely for a few mad, glad years, followed by drab duty and dull regret, but for a happy lifetime of useful vigor. That, and not leisure or dignity, is the great compensation for the professorial life.

What a joy it was to me during that rosy-sweet early period of our union to watch Carl, like a proud mother, as he grew and exfoliated--like a plant that has been kept in a cellar and now in congenial soil and sunshine is showing at last its full potentialities. Through me my boy was attaining the full stature of a man; and I, his proud mate, was jealously glad that even his dear dead mother could not have brought that to pass.

His wit became less caustic; his manner more genial. People who once irritated now interested him. Some who used to fear him now liked him. And as for the undergraduates who had hero-worshiped this former tennis champion, they now shyly turned to him for counsel and advice. He was more of a man of the world than most of his colleagues and treated the boys as though they were men of the world too--for instance, he never referred to them as boys.

"I wouldn't be a damned fool if I were you," I once overheard him say to a certain young man who was suffering from an attack of what Carl called misdirected energy.

More than one he took in hand this way; and, though I used to call it--to tease him--his man-to-man manner, I saw that it was effective. I, too, grew fond of these frank, ingenuous youths. We used to have them at our house when we could spare an evening--often when we could not.

None of this work, it may be mentioned, is referred to in the annual catalogue or provided for in the annual budget; and yet it is often the most vital and lasting service a teacher renders his students--especially when their silly parents provide them with more pocket money than the professor's entire income for the support of himself, his family, his scholarship and his dignity.

"Your husband is not a professor," one of them confided shyly to me--"he's a human being!"

After the success of our book we were called to another college--a full professorship at three thousand a year! Carl loved his Alma Mater with a passion I sometimes failed to understand; but he could not afford to remain faithful to her forever on vague promises of future favor. He went to the president and said so plainly, hating the indignity of it and loathing the whole system that made such methods necessary.

The president would gladly have raised all the salaries if he had had the means. He could not meet the competitor's price, but he begged Carl to stay, offering the full title--meaning empty--of professor and a minimum wage of twenty-five hundred dollars, with the promise of full pay when the funds could be raised.

Now we had demonstrated that, even on the Faculty of an Eastern college, two persons could live on fifteen hundred. Therefore, with twenty-five hundred, we could not only exist but work efficiently. So we did not have to go.

            *   *   *   *   *

I look back on those days as the happiest period of our life together. That is why I have lingered over them. Congenial work, bright prospects,

perfect health, the affection of friends, the respect of rivals--what
more could any woman want for her husband or herself?

Only one thing. And now that, too, was to be ours! However, with
children came trouble, for which--bless their little hearts!--they are
not responsible. Were we? I wonder! Had we a right to have children? Had
we a right not to have children? It has been estimated by a member of
the mathematical department that, at the present salary rate, each of
the college professors of America is entitled to just two-fifths of a
child.

Does this pay? Should only the financially fit be allowed to survive--to
reproduce their species? Should or should not those who may be fittest
physically, intellectually and morally also be entitled to the privilege
and responsibility of taking their natural part in determining the
character of America's future generations, for the evolution of the race
and the glory of God?

I wonder!

                *   *   *   *   *

(_Boston Transcript_)

A PARADISE FOR A PENNY

MADDENED BY THE CATALOGUES OF PEACE-TIME, ONE LOVER OF GARDENS YET
MANAGED TO BUILD A LITTLE EDEN, AND TELLS HOW HE DID IT FOR A SONG

By WALTER PRICHARD EATON

War-time economy (which is a much pleasanter and doubtless a more
patriotically approved phrase than war-time poverty) is not without its
compensations, even to the gardener. At first I did not think so.
Confronted by a vast array of new and empty borders and rock steps and
natural-laid stone, flanking a wall fountain, and other features of a
new garden ambitiously planned before the President was so inconsiderate
as to declare war without consulting me, and confronted, too, by an
empty purse--pardon me, I mean by the voluntarily imposed necessity for
economy--I sat me down amid my catalogues, like Niobe amid her children,
and wept. (Maybe it wasn't amid her children Niobe wept, but for them;
anyhow I remember her as a symbol of lachrymosity.) Dear, alluring,
immoral catalogues, sweet sirens for a man's undoing! How you sang to me
of sedums, and whispered of peonies and irises--yea, even of German
irises! How you spoke in soft, seductive accents of wonderful lilacs,
and exquisite spireas, and sweet syringas, murmurous with bees! How you
told of tulips and narcissuses, and a thousand lovely things for beds
and borders and rock work--at so much a dozen, so very much a dozen,
and a dozen so very few! I did not resort to cotton in my ears, but to
tears and profanity.

Then two things happened. I got a letter from a Boston architect who had
passed by and seen my unfinished place; and I took a walk up a back road
where the Massachusetts Highway Commissioners hadn't sent a gang of
workmen through to "improve" it. The architect said, "Keep your place
simple. It cries for it. That's always the hardest thing to do--but the
best." And the back-country roadside said, "Look at me; I didn't come

from any catalogue; no nursery grew me; I'm really and truly 'perfectly hardy'; I didn't cost a cent--and can you beat me at any price? I'm a hundred per cent American, too."

I looked, and I admitted, with a blush of shame for ever doubting, that I certainly could not beat it. But, I suddenly realized, I could steal it!

I have been stealing it ever since, and having an enormously enjoyable time in the bargain.

Of course, stealing is a relative term, like anything else connected with morality. What would be stealing in the immediate neighborhood of a city is not even what the old South County oyster fisherman once described as "jest pilferin' 'round," out here on the edges of the wilderness. I go out with the trailer hitched to the back of my Ford, half a mile in any direction, and I pass roadsides where, if there are any farmer owners of the fields on the other side of the fence, these owners are only too glad to have a few of the massed, invading plants or bushes thinned out. But far more often there is not even a fence, or if there is, it has heavy woods or a swamp or a wild pasture beyond it. I could go after plants every day for six months and nobody would ever detect where I took them. My only rule--self-imposed--is never to take a single specimen, or even one of a small group, and always to take where thinning is useful, and where the land or the roadside is wild and neglected, and no human being can possibly be injured. Most often, indeed, I simply go up the mountain along, or into, my own woods.

I am not going to attempt any botanical or cultural description of what I am now attempting. That will have to wait, anyhow, till I know a little more about it myself! But I want to indicate, in a general way, some of the effects which are perfectly possible, I believe, here in a Massachusetts garden, without importing a single plant, or even sowing a seed or purchasing any stock from a nursery.

Take the matter of asters, for instance. Hitherto my garden, up here in the mountains where the frosts come early and we cannot have anemone, japonica, or chrysanthemums, has generally been a melancholy spectacle after the middle of September. Yet it is just at this time that our roadsides and woodland borders are the most beautiful. The answer isn't alone asters, but very largely. And nothing, I have discovered, is much easier to transplant than a New England aster, the showiest of the family. Within the confines of my own farm or its bordering woods are at least seven varieties of asters, and there are more within half a mile. They range in color from the deepest purple and lilac, through shades of blue, to white, and vary in height from the six feet my New Englands have attained in rich garden soil, to one foot. Moreover, by a little care, they can be so massed and alternated in a long border (such a border I have), as to pass in under heavy shade and out again into full sun, from a damp place to a dry place, and yet all be blooming at their best. With what other flower can you do that? And what other flower, at whatever price per dozen, will give you such abundance of beauty without a fear of frosts? I recently dug up a load of asters in bud, on a rainy day, and already they are in full bloom in their new garden places, without so much as a wilted leaf.

Adjoining my farm is an abandoned marble quarry. In that quarry, or, rather, in the rank grass bordering it, grow thousands of Solidago rigida, the big, flat-topped goldenrod. This is the only station for it in Berkshire County. As the ledges from this quarry come over into my pastures, and doubtless the goldenrod would have come too, had it not been for the sheep, what could be more fitting than for me to make this glorious yellow flower a part of my garden scheme? Surely if anything belongs in my peculiar soil and landscape it does. It transplants easily, and under cultivation reaches a large size and holds its bloom a long time. Massed with the asters it is superb, and I get it by going through the bars with a shovel and a wheelbarrow.

But a garden of goldenrod and asters would be somewhat dull from May to mid-August, and somewhat monotonous thereafter. I have no intention, of course, of barring out from my garden the stock perennials, and, indeed, I have already salvaged from my old place or grown from seed the indispensable phloxes, foxgloves, larkspur, hollyhocks, sweet william, climbing roses, platycodons and the like. But let me merely mention a few of the wild things I have brought in from the immediate neighborhood, and see if they do not promise, when naturally planted where the borders wind under trees, or grouped to the grass in front of asters, ferns, goldenrod and the shrubs I shall mention later, a kind of beauty and interest not to be secured by the usual garden methods.

There are painted trilliums, yellow and pink lady's slippers, Orchis spectabilis, hepaticas, bloodroot, violets, jack-in-the-pulpit, masses of baneberries, solomon's seal, true and false; smooth false foxglove, five-flowered and closed gentians, meadow lilies (Canadensis) and wood lilies (Philadelphicum), the former especially being here so common that I can go out and dig up the bulbs by the score, taking only one or two from any one spot. These are but a few of the flowers, blooming from early spring to late fall, in the borders, and I have forgotten to mention the little bunch berries from my own woods as an edging plant.

Let me turn now for a moment to the hedge and shrubbery screen which must intervene between my west border and the highway, and which is the crux of the garden. The hedge is already started with hemlocks from the mountain side, put in last spring. I must admit nursery in-grown evergreens are easier to handle, and make a better and quicker growth. But I am out now to see how far I can get with absolutely native material. Between the hedge and the border, where at first I dreamed of lilacs and the like, I now visualize as filling up with the kind of growth which lines our roads, and which is no less beautiful and much more fitting. From my own woods will come in spring (the only safe time to move them) masses of mountain laurel and azalea. From my own pasture fence-line will come red osier, dogwood, with its white blooms, its blue berries, its winter stem-coloring, and elderberry. From my own woods have already come several four-foot maple-leaved vibernums, which, though moved in June, throve and have made a fine new growth. There will be, also, a shadbush or two and certainly some hobble bushes, with here and there a young pine and small, slender canoe birch. Here and there will be a clump of flowering raspberry. I shall not scorn spireas, and I must have at least one big white syringa to scent the twilight; but the great mass of my screen will be exactly what nature would plant there if she were left alone--minus the choke cherries. You always have to exercise a little supervision over nature!

A feature of my garden is to be rock work and a little, thin stream of a brooklet flowing away from a wall fountain. I read in my catalogues of marvellous Alpine plants, and I dreamed of irises by my brook. I shall have some of both too. Why not? The war has got to end one of these days. But meanwhile, why be too down-hearted? On the cliffs above my pasture are masses of moss, holding, as a pincushion holds a breastpin, little early saxifrage plants. From the crannies frail hair bells dangle forth. There are clumps of purple cliffbrase and other tiny, exquisite ferns. On a gravel bank beside the State road are thousands of viper's bugloss plants; on a ledge nearby is an entire nursery of Sedum acre (the small yellow stone crop). Columbines grow like a weed in my mowing, and so do Quaker ladies, which, in England, are highly esteemed in the rock garden. The Greens Committee at the nearby golf club will certainly let me dig up some of the gay pinks which are a pest in one of the high, gravelly bunkers. And these are only a fraction of the native material available for my rock work and bank. Many of them are already in and thriving.

As for the little brook, any pond edge or brookside nearby has arrowheads, forget-me-nots, cardinal flowers, blue flag, clumps of beautiful grasses, monkey flowers, jewel-weed and the like. There are cowslips, too, and blue vervain, and white violets. If I want a clump of something tall, Joe-pye-weed is not to be disdained. No, I do not anticipate any trouble about my brookside. It will not look at all as I thought a year ago it was going to look. It will not look like an illustration in some "garden beautiful" magazine. It will look like--like a brook! I am tremendously excited now at the prospect of seeing it look like a brook, a little, lazy, trickling Yankee brook. If I ever let it look like anything else, I believe I shall deserve to have my spring dry up.

Probably I shall have moments of, for me, comparative affluence in the years to come, when I shall once more listen to the siren song of catalogues, and order Japanese irises, Darwin tulips, hybrid lilacs, and so on. But by that time, I feel sure, my native plants and shrubs will have got such a start, and made such a luxuriant, natural tangle, that they will assimilate the aliens and teach them their proper place in a New England garden. At any rate, till the war is over, I am 100 per cent Berkshire County!

             *   *   *   *   *

WANTED: A HOME ASSISTANT

(_Pictorial Review_)

One illustration made by a staff artist, with the caption, "The New Home Assistant is Trained for Her Work."

WANTED: A HOME ASSISTANT

BUSINESS HOURS AND WAGES ARE HELPING WOMEN TO SOLVE THE SERVANT PROBLEM

BY LOUISE F. NELLIS

WANTED: A HOME ASSISTANT--Eight hours a day; six days a week. Sleep and eat at home. Pay, twelve dollars a week.

Whenever this notice appears in the Help Wanted column of a city newspaper, fifty to one hundred answers are received in the first twenty-four hours!

"Why," we hear some one say, "that seems impossible! When I advertised for a maid at forty dollars a month with board and lodging provided, not a soul answered. Why are so many responses received to the other advertisement?"

Let us look more closely at the first notice.

Wanted: A Home Assistant! How pleasant and dignified it sounds; nothing about a general houseworker or maid or servant, just Home Assistant! We can almost draw a picture of the kind of young woman who might be called by such a title. She comes, quiet, dignified, and interested in our home and its problems. She may have been in an office but has never really liked office work and has always longed for home surroundings and home duties.

I remember one case I was told of--a little stenographer. She had gladly assumed her new duties as Home Assistant, and had wept on the first Christmas Day with the family because it was the only Christmas she had spent in years in a home atmosphere. Or perhaps the applicant for the new kind of work in the home may have been employed in a department store and found the continuous standing on her feet too wearing. She welcomes the frequent change of occupation in her new position. Or she may be married with a little home of her own, but with the desire to add to the family income. We call these Home Assistants, Miss Smith or Mrs. Jones, and they preserve their own individuality and self-respect.

"Well, I would call my housemaid anything if I could only get one," says one young married woman. "There must be more to this new plan than calling them Home Assistants and addressing them as Miss."

Let us read further in the advertisement: "Eight hours a day; six days a week." One full day and one half day off each week, making a total of forty-four hours weekly which is the standard working week in most industrial occupations. At least two free Sundays a month should be given and a convenient week-day substituted for the other two Sundays. If Saturday is not the best half day to give, another afternoon may be arranged with the Home Assistant.

"Impossible," I can hear Mrs. Reader say, "I couldn't get along with eight hours' work a day, forty-four hours a week." No! Well, possibly you have had to get along without any maid at all, or you may have had some one in your kitchen who is incompetent and slovenly, whom you dare not discharge for fear you can not replace her. Would you rather not have a good interested worker for eight hours a day than none at all? During that time the Home Assistant works steadily and specialization is done away with. She is there to do your work and she does whatever may be called for. If she is asked to take care of the baby for a few hours, she does it willingly, as part of her duties; or if she is called upon to do some ironing left in the basket, she assumes that it is part of her work, and doesn't say, "No, Madam, I wasn't hired to do that," at the same time putting on her hat and leaving as under the old system.

The new plan seems expensive? "Twelve dollars a week is more than I have

paid my domestic helper," Mrs. Reader says. But consider this more
carefully. You pay from thirty-five to fifty dollars a month with all
the worker's food and lodging provided. This is at the rate of eight to
eleven dollars a week for wages. Food and room cost at least five
dollars a week, and most estimates are higher. The old type of
houseworker has cost us more than we have realized. The new system
compares favorably in expense with the old.

"I am perfectly certain it wouldn't be practical not to feed my helper,"
Mrs. Reader says. Under the old system of a twelve to fourteen-hour
working day, it would not be feasible, but if she is on the eight-hour
basis, the worker can bring a box-luncheon with her, or she can go
outside to a restaurant just as she would if she were in an office or
factory. The time spent in eating is not included in her day's work.
Think of the relief to the house-keeper who can order what her family
likes to eat without having to say, "Oh, I can't have that; Mary
wouldn't eat it you know."

"I can't afford a Home Assistant or a maid at the present wages," some
one says. "But I do wish I had some one who could get and serve dinner
every night. I am so tired by evening that cooking is the last straw."

Try looking for a Home Assistant for four hours a day to relieve you of
just this work. You would have to pay about a dollar a day or six
dollars a week for such service and it would be worth it.

How does the Home Assistant plan work in households where two or more
helpers are kept? The more complicated homes run several shifts of
workers, coming in at different hours and covering every need of the
day. One woman I talked to told me that she studied out her problem in
this way! She did every bit of the work in her house for a while in
order to find out how long each job took. She found, for instance, that
it took twenty-five minutes to clean one bathroom, ten minutes to brush
down and dust a flight of stairs, thirty minutes to do the dinner
dishes, and so on through all the work. She made out a time-card which
showed that twenty-two hours of work a day was needed for her home. She
knew how much money she could spend and she proceeded to divide the work
and money among several assistants coming in on different shifts. Her
household now runs like clockwork. One of the splendid things about this
new system is its great flexibility and the fact that it can be adapted
to any household.

Thoughtful and intelligent planning such as this woman gave to her
problems is necessary for the greatest success of the plan. The old
haphazard methods must go. The housekeeper who has been in the habit of
coming into her kitchen about half past five and saying, "Oh, Mary, what
can we have for dinner? I have just come back from down-town; I did
expect to be home sooner," will not get the most out of her Home
Assistant. Work must be scheduled and planned ahead, the home must be
run on business methods if the system is to succeed. I heard this
explained to a group of women not long ago. After the talk, one of them
said, "Well, in business houses and factories there is a foreman who
runs the shop and oversees the workers. It wouldn't work in homes
because we haven't any foreman." She had entirely overlooked her job as
forewoman of her own establishment!

"Suppose I have company for dinner and the Home Assistant isn't through her work when her eight hours are up, what happens?" some one asks. All overtime work is paid for at the rate of one and one-half times the hourly rate. If you are paying your assistant twelve dollars for a forty-four-hour week, you are giving her twenty-eight cents an hour. One and one half times this amounts to forty-two cents an hour, which she receives for extra work just as she would in the business world.

"Will these girls from offices and stores do their work well? They have had no training for housework unless they have happened to do some in their own homes," some one wisely remarks. The lack of systematic preparation has always been one of the troubles with our domestic helpers. It is true that the new type of girl trained in business to be punctual and alert, and to use her mind, adapts herself very quickly to her work, but the trained worker in any field has an advantage. With this in mind the Central Branch of the Young Women's Christian Association in New York City has started a training-school for Home Assistants. The course provides demonstrations on the preparation of breakfasts, lunches, and dinners, and talks on the following: House-cleaning, Laundry, Care of Children, Shopping, Planning work, Deportment, Efficiency, and Duty to Employer. This course gives a girl a general knowledge of her duties and what is even more important she acquires the right mental attitude toward her work. The girls are given an examination and those who successfully pass it are given a certificate and placed as Trained Home Assistants at fifteen dollars a week.

The National Association would like to see these training-schools turning out this type of worker for the homes all over the country. This is a constructive piece of work for women to undertake. Housewives' Leagues have interested themselves in this in various centers, and the Y.W.C.A. will help wherever it can. There are always home economics graduates in every town who could help give the course, and there are excellent housekeepers who excel in some branch who could give a talk or two.

The course would be worth a great deal in results to any community. The United States Employment Bureaus are also taking a hand in this, and, with the coöperation of the High Schools, are placing girls as trained assistants on the new basis. I have talked with many women who are not only using this plan to-day but have been for several years.

It has been more than six years ago since Mrs. Helene Barker's book "Wanted a Young Woman to Do Housework" was published.

This gave the working plan to the idea. Women in Boston, Providence, New York, Cleveland, and in many other cities have become so enthusiastic over their success in running their homes with the Home Assistants that a number are giving their time to lecturing and talking to groups of women about it.

Let me give two concrete illustrations of the practical application of housework on a business basis.

Mrs. A. lives in a small city in the Middle West. Her household consists of herself, her husband, and her twelve year old son. She had had the usual string of impossible maids or none at all until she tried the new system. Through a girls' club in a factory in the city, she secured a

young woman to work for her at factory hours and wages. Her assistant
came at seven-thirty in the morning. By having the breakfast cereal
prepared the night before, breakfast could be served promptly at eight,
a plan which was necessary in order that the boy get to school on time.
Each morning's work was written out and hung up in the kitchen so that
the assistant wasted no time in waiting to know what she had to do.
Lunch was at twelve-fifteen, and at one o'clock the Home Assistant went
home.

She came back on regular duty at five-thirty to prepare and serve the
dinner. Except for times when there were guests for dinner she was
through her work by eight. When she worked overtime, there was the extra
pay to compensate. Mrs. A. paid her thirteen dollars a week and felt
that she saved money by the new plan. The assistant was off duty every
other Sunday, and on alternate weeks was given all day Tuesday off
instead of Sunday. Tuesday was the day the heavy washing was done and
the laundress was there to help with any work which Mrs. A. did not feel
equal to doing. Even though there are times in the day when she is
alone, Mrs. A. says she would not go back to the old system for
anything.

Mrs. B. lives in a city apartment. There are four grown people in the
family. She formerly kept two maids, a cook-laundress, and a
waitress-chambermaid. She often had a great deal of trouble finding a
cook who would do the washing. As her apartment had only one maid's
room, she had to give one of the guestrooms to the second maid. She paid
these girls forty dollars apiece and provided them with room and board.
Her apartment cost her one hundred and fifteen dollars a month for seven
rooms, two of which were occupied by maids.

Mrs. B. decided to put her household on the new business basis last
Fall. She moved into a five-room apartment which cost her ninety
dollars, but she had larger rooms and a newer building with more
up-to-date improvements than she had had before. She saved twenty-five
dollars a month on rent plus eighty dollars wages and about thirty
dollars on her former maids' food. All together she had one hundred and
thirty-five dollars which could be used for Home Assistants. This is the
way the money was spent:

    A laundress once a week................................ $2.60
    Home Assistant, on duty from 7.30 A.M. to 2 P.M....... 10.00
    Home Assistant, on duty from 12 M. to 9 P.M........... 15.00
                                                          _____
        Week..$27.60

On this schedule the work was done better than ever before. There was no
longer any grievance about the washing. Mrs. B. had some one
continuously on duty. The morning assistant was allowed a half hour at
noon to eat her luncheon which she brought with her. As Mrs. B.
entertained a great deal, especially at luncheon, she arranged to have
the schedule of the two assistants overlap at this time of day. The
morning worker, it will be noted, was employed for only six hours. The
afternoon worker was a trained assistant and, therefore, received
fifteen dollars a week. She had an hour off, between three-thirty and
four-thirty and was on duty again in time to serve tea or afternoon
refreshments. If there were a number of extra people for dinner, the
assistant was expected to stay until nine and there was never any

complaining about too much company. Mrs. B. has a better apartment and saves money every month besides!

                *   *   *   *   *

(_New York Sun_)

SIX YEARS OF TEA ROOMS

BUSINESS CAREER OF A WOMAN COLLEGE GRADUATE

"For the last three years I have cleared $5,000 a year on my tea rooms," declared a young woman who six years ago was graduated with distinction at one of the leading colleges of the country.

"I attained my twenty-third birthday a month after I received my diploma. On that day I took stock of the capital with which I was to step into the world and earn my own living. My stock taking showed perfect health, my college education and $300, my share of my father's estate after the expenses of my college course had been paid.

"In spite of the protests of many of my friends I decided to become a business woman instead of entering one of the professions. I believed that a well conducted tea room in a college town where there was nothing of the kind would pay well, and I proceeded to open a place.

"After renting a suitable room I invested $100 in furnishings. Besides having a paid announcement in the college and town papers I had a thousand leaflets printed and distributed.

"Though I couldn't afford music I did have my rooms decorated profusely with flowers on the afternoon of my opening. As it was early in the autumn the flowers were inexpensive and made a brave show. My only assistant was a young Irish woman whom I had engaged for one month as waitress, with the understanding that if my venture succeeded I would engage her permanently.

"We paid expenses that first afternoon, and by the end of the week the business had increased to such an extent that I might have engaged a second waitress had not so many of my friends persisted in shaking their heads and saying the novelty would soon wear off. During the second week my little Irish girl and I had so much to do that on several occasions our college boy patrons felt themselves constrained to offer their services as waiters, while more than one of the young professors after a long wait left the room with the remark that they would go elsewhere.

"Of course it was well enough to laugh as we all knew there was no 'elsewhere,' but when I recalled how ready people are to crowd into a field that has proved successful, I determined no longer to heed the shaking heads of my friends. The third week found me not only with a second assistant but with a card posted in a conspicuous place announcing that at the beginning of the next week I would enlarge my quarters in such a way as to accommodate more than twice as many guests.

"Having proved to my own satisfaction that my venture was and would be successful, I didn't hesitate to go into debt to the extent of $150. This was not only to repair and freshen up the new room but also to equip it with more expensive furnishing than I had felt myself justified in buying for the first.

"Knowing how every little thing that happens is talked about in a college town, I was sure the difference in the furnishings of the rooms would prove a good advertisement. I counted on it to draw custom, but not just in the way it did.

"Before I realized just what was happening I was receiving letters from college boys who, after proclaiming themselves among my very first customers, demanded to know why they were discriminated against. I had noticed that everybody appeared to prefer the new room and that on several occasions when persons telephoning for reservations had been unable to get the promise of a table in there, they had said they would wait and come at another time. What I had not noticed was that only men coming alone or with other men, and girls coming with other girls, would accept seats in the first room.

"I learned from the letters of 'my very first patrons' that no gentleman would take a girl to have tea in a second class tea room. They were not only hitting at the cheaper furnishings of my first room but also at the waiter whom I had employed, because I felt the need of a man's help in doing heavy work. The girl in her fresh apron and cap was more attractive than the man, and because he happened to serve in the first room he also was second class.

"No, I couldn't afford to buy new furniture for that room, so I did the only thing I could think of. I mixed the furniture in such a way as to make the two rooms look practically alike. I hired another girl and relegated the man to the kitchen except in case of emergency.

"Although my custom fell off in summer to a bare sprinkling of guests afternoons and evenings and to almost no one at lunch, I kept the same number of employees and had them put up preserves, jams, syrups, and pickles for use the coming season. I knew it would not only be an economical plan but also a great drawing card, especially with certain of the professors, to be able to say that everything served was made on the place and under my own supervision.

"My second winter proved so successful that I determined to buy a home for my business so that I might have things exactly as I wished. I was able to pay the first instalment, $2,500, on the purchase price and still have enough in bank to make alterations and buy the necessary furnishings.

"The move was made during the summer, and when I opened up in the autumn I had such crowds afternoons and evenings that I had to put extra tables in the halls until I could get a room on the second floor ready. At present I have two entire floors and often have so many waiting that it is next to impossible to pass through the entrance hall.

"Three summers ago I opened a second tea room at a seashore resort on the New England coast. I heard of the place through a classmate whose family owned a cottage down there. She described it as deadly dull, because there was nothing to do but bathe and boat unless you were the happy possessor of an automobile or a horse.

"I was so much interested in her description of the place that I went down one warm day in April and looked things over. I found a stretch of about three miles of beach lined with well appearing and handsome cottages and not a single place of amusement. The village behind the beach is a lovely old place, with twenty or more handsome old homes surrounded by grand trees. There are two or three small stores, a post office, two liveries and the railroad station half a mile away.

"Before I left that afternoon I had paid the first month's rent on the best of the only two cottages to be rented on the beach. Of course it needed considerable fixing up and that had to be done at my own expense, but as I was getting it at a rental of $200 for the season I was not worried at the outlay. The cottages told me enough of the character of the people who summered on that beach to make me sure that I would get good interest on all the money spent.

"Immediately after commencement I shut up my college tea rooms, leaving only the kitchen and storeroom open and in charge of an experienced woman with instructions to get more help when putting up preserves and pickles made it necessary. Then I moved.

"The two first days on the beach my tea room didn't have a visitor. People strolled by and stared at the sign, but nobody came in to try my tea. The third day I had a call from my landlord, who informed me that he had been misled into letting me have his cottage, and offering to return the amount paid for the first month's rent, he very politely requested me to move out.

"After considerable talking I discovered that the cottagers didn't like the way my waitresses dressed. They were too stylish and my rooms appeared from the outside to be so brilliantly lighted that they thought I intended to sell liquor.

"I didn't accept the offered rent, neither did I agree to move out, but I did assure my landlord that I would go the very day anything really objectionable happened on my premises. I told him of my success in the college town and then invited him to bring his family the following afternoon to try my tea.

"Well, they came, they saw, and I conquered. That evening all the tables on my piazza were filled and there was a slight sprinkling indoors. A few days later the classmate who had told me of the place came down for the summer and my troubles were at an end.

"The secret of my success is hard work and catering to the taste of my patrons. Had I opened either a cheap or a showy place in the college town, I would not have gained the good will of the faculty or the patronage of the best class of students. If my prices had been too high or the refreshments served not up to the notch, the result would not have been so satisfactory.

"Knowing one college town pretty well, I knew just about what was needed in the student's life; that is, an attractive looking place, eminently respectable, where you can take your best girl and get good things to eat well served at a reasonable cost.

"The needs of the beach were pretty much the same. People can't stay in the water all the time, neither can they spin around the country or go to an unlighted village at night in their carriages and automobiles. My tea room offers a recreation, without being a dissipation.

"Another point about which many people question me is the effect of my being a business woman on my social standing. I haven't noticed any slights. I receive many more invitations than it is possible for me to accept. I go with the same set of girls that I did while I was in college.

"Two of my classmates are lawyers, more than one is a doctor, and three have gone on the stage. I know that my earnings are far more than any of theirs, and I am sure they do not enjoy their business any more than I do. If I had to begin again I would do exactly as I have done, with one exception--I would lay out the whole of my $300 in furnishing that first tea room instead of keeping $75 as a nest egg in bank."

*   *   *   *   *

(_Country Gentleman_)

Two illustrations:
   1. Half-tone reproducing photograph of dressed chickens with
      the caption, "There is this rule you must observe: Pick your
      chickens clean."
   2. Reproduction in type of shipping label.

BY PARCEL POST

ONE MAN'S WAY OF SERVING THE DIRECT-TO-CONSUMER MARKET

By A. L. SARRAN

If you live within a hundred and fifty miles of a city, if you possess ordinary common sense and have the ability to write a readable and understandable letter, you may, from September to April of each year, when other farmers and their wives are consuming instead of producing, earn from fifty to a hundred and fifty dollars net profit each month. You may do this by fattening and dressing chickens for city folks, and by supplying regularly fresh country sausage, hams, lard and eggs.

This is not an idle theory. Last September I began with one customer; today--this was written the end of March--I have nearly 500 customers to whom I am supplying farm products by parcel post.

Instead of selling my chickens to the huckster or to the local poultry house for twelve cents a pound, I am selling them to the consumer in the city for twenty cents a pound, live weight, plus the cost of boxing and postage. Not only that, I am buying chickens from my neighbors at a premium of one to two cents over the huckster's prices, "milk feeding" them, and selling them to my city customers at a profit of six to seven cents a pound.

I buy young hogs from my neighbors at market prices and make them into extra good country sausage that nets me twenty-five cents a pound in the city, and into hams for which I get twenty-five cents a pound, delivered. The only pork product on which I do not make an excellent profit is lard. I get fifteen cents a pound for it, delivered to the city customer, and it costs me almost that much to render and pack it.

At this writing storekeepers and egg buyers in my county are paying the farmer seventeen cents for his eggs. I am getting twenty-five cents a dozen for eggs in thirty-dozen eases and twenty-nine cents a dozen in two-dozen boxes. My prices to the city man are based upon the Water Street, Chicago, quotation for "firsts," which, at this writing, is nineteen cents. If this price goes up I go up; if it goes down I go down.

I got my customers by newspaper advertising--almost exclusively. It is a comforting belief that one satisfied customer will get you another, and that that customer will get you another, and so on, but it has not so worked out in my experience. Out of all my customers less than twelve have become customers through the influence of friends.

My experience has taught me another thing: That direct advertising does not pay. By direct advertising I mean the mailing of letters and circulars to a list of names in the hope of selling something to persons whose names are on that list.

I tried it three times--once to a list of names I bought from a dealer in such lists; once to a list that I myself compiled from the society columns of two Chicago dailies; and once to a classified list that I secured from a directory.

The results in these cases were about the same. The net cost of each new customer that I secured by circulars and letters was $2.19. The net cost of each new customer that I secured by newspaper advertising was fifty-four cents.

Not every city newspaper will get such results. In my case I selected that paper in Chicago which in my judgment went into the greatest number of prosperous homes, and whose pages were kept clean of quack and swindling advertisements. I used only the Sunday issues, because I believe the Sunday issues are most thoroughly read.

The farmer will want to use, and properly so, the classified columns of the paper for his advertising. But he should patronize only that paper whose columns provide a classification especially for farm and food products.

I spent twelve dollars for advertising in one clean Chicago daily with a good circulation, and got three orders. The trouble was that my advertisement went into a column headed "Business Personals," along with a lot of manicure and massage advertising.

He on the farm who proposes to compete with the shipper, commission man and retailer for the city man's trade should devote his efforts to producing food of a better quality than the city man is accustomed to get via the shipper-commission-man-retailer route. Wherefore I proposed to give the city man the fattest, tenderest, juiciest, cleanest, freshest chicken he could get--and charge him a profitable price in so doing.

When I wrote my advertisements I did not stint myself for space. An advertisement that tells no reason why the reader should buy from the advertiser is, in my opinion, a poor advertisement. Therefore, I told my story in full to the readers of the Sunday paper, although it cost me six cents a word to do it. Here is a sample of my advertising:

> I send young, milk-fed chickens, ready for the cook, direct to you from the farm. These chickens are fattened in wire-bottomed, sanitary coops, thus insuring absolute cleanliness, on a ration of meal, middlings and milk. The chicken you get from me is fresh; it is killed AFTER your order is received; is dressed, drawn, cooled out for 24 hours in dry air, wrapped in waxed paper and delivered to you on the morning of the third day after your order is mailed; it is fat, tender and sweet. The ordinary chicken that is fattened on unspeakable filth in the farmer's barnyard, and finds its way to your table via the huckster-shipper-commission-man-retailer route cannot compare with one of mine. Send me your check--no stamps--for $1.15 and I will send you a five-pound--live-weight--roasting chicken for a sample. If it does not please you I'll give your money back. Add 62 cents to that check and I'll mail you in a separate box a two-pound package of the most delicious fresh-ground sausage meat you ever ate. Made from the selected meats of young hogs only; not highly seasoned. These sausage cakes make a breakfast fit for a President. Money back if you don't like them.
>
> A. L. SARRAN.

Notice that I told why the reader should buy one of my chickens rather than a chicken of whose antecedents he knew nothing. That it paid to spend six cents a word to tell him so is proved by the fact that this particular advertisement brought me, in four days, twenty-three orders, each accompanied by a check. I repeated my advertisements in Sunday issues, stopping only when I had as many customers as I could take care of.

Getting a customer and keeping him are two different propositions. A customer's first order is sent because of the representation made in the advertisement that he read. His second and his subsequent orders depend upon how you satisfy him and continue to satisfy him.

My rule is to select, weigh, dress, draw, handle, wrap and box the chicken with the same scrupulous care that I would exercise if the customer were actually present and watching me.

I have another rule: The customer is always right. If he complains I satisfy him, immediately and cheerfully. It is better to lose a chicken than to lose a customer.

I am now about to make a statement with which many of my readers will not agree. It is more than true; it is so important that the success of a mail-order business in dressed chickens depends upon a realization of it. It is this: _A majority of farmers and their wives do not know what constitutes a fat chicken._

I make this statement because of the experience I have had with country folks in buying their chickens for my feeding coops. If they really consider to be fat the chickens which they have assured me were fat, then they do not know fat chickens. A chicken can be fat to a degree without being so fat as he can or should be made for the purpose of marketing.

There is a flavor about a well-fattened, milk-fed chicken that no other chicken has. Every interstice of his flesh is juicy and oily. No part of him is tough, stringy muscle, as is the case if he is "farm-fattened" while being allowed to range where he will.

If you think your chicken is a fat one, pick it up and rub the ball of your thumb across its backbone about an inch behind the base of the wings. If the backbone is felt clearly and distinctly the chicken is not fat.

I fatten my chickens in coops the floors of which are made of heavy wire having one-inch mesh; underneath the wire is a droppings pan, which is emptied every day. My coops are built in tiers and long sections. I have ninety of them, each one accommodating nine chickens. I have enough portable feeding coops with wire bottoms and droppings pans underneath to enable me to feed, in all, about one thousand chickens at one time.

Chickens should be fed from ten to fourteen days in the coops. I give no feed whatever to the chicken the first day he is in the coop, but I keep a supply of sour milk in the trough for him. I feed my chickens three times a day.

At seven A.M. I give them a fairly thick batter of meal, middlings or oat flour, about half and half, and sour milk. I feed them only what they will clean up in the course of half an hour. At noon I feed them again only what they will clean up in half an hour. This feed is the same as the morning feed except that it is thinner. About four o'clock I give them a trough full of the same feed, but so thick it will barely pour out from the bucket into the trough.

The next morning the troughs are emptied--if anything remains in them--into the big kettle where the feed is mixed for the morning feeding. The idea is this: More fat and flesh are made at night than in the daytime; therefore see that no chicken goes to bed with an empty crop.

About the eighth to tenth day force the feeding--see to it that the chicken gets all it will eat three times a day.

By keeping an accurate account of the costs of meal, milk, and so on, I find that I can put a pound of fat on a coop-fed chicken for seven cents. When one considers that this same pound brings twenty cents, and that milk feeding in coops raises the per pound value of the chicken from twelve to twenty cents, one must admit that feeding chickens is more profitable than feeding cattle.

Do not feed your chicken anything for twenty-four hours before killing it. Do not worry about loss in weight. The only weight it will lose will be the weight of the feed in its crop and gizzard, and the offal in its intestines--and you are going to lose that anyway when you dress and draw it. If you will keep the bird off feed for twenty-four hours you will find that it will draw much more easily and cleanly.

Hang the chicken up by the feet and kill it by bleeding it away back in the mouth. Let it bleed to death. Grasp the chicken's head in your left hand, the back of its head against the palm of your hand. Do not hold it by the neck, but grasp it by the bony part of its head and jaws. Reach into the throat with a three-inch, narrow, sharp knife and cut toward the top and front of the head.

You will sever the big cross vein that connects the two "jugular" veins in the neck, and the blood will pour out of the mouth. If you know how to dry-pick you will not need to be told anything by me; if you do not know it will do you no good to have me tell you, because I do not believe a person can learn to dry pick chickens by following printed instructions. At any rate, I could not. I never learned until I hired a professional picker to come out from town to teach me.

So far as I can judge, it makes no difference to the consumer in the city whether the chicken is scalded or dry-picked. There is this to be said for the scalded chicken--that it is a more cleanly picked chicken than the dry-picked one. The pin feathers are more easily removed when the chicken is scalded.

On the other hand, there are those feed-specializing, accurate-to-the-ten-thousandth-part-of-an-inch experts, who say that the dry-picked chicken keeps better than the scalded one. If the weather is warmer than, say, seventy-five degrees, it might; under that, there is no difference.

I do the most of my selling in Chicago, and my place is a hundred and fifty miles south of that city; if a scalded chicken will keep when I am selling it that far away it will keep for almost anyone, because none of you is going to sell many chickens at any point more than a hundred and fifty miles from your place.

There is this caution to be observed in scalding a chicken: Do not have the water too hot. I had trouble on this score, and as a result my chickens were dark and did not present an appetizing appearance. Finally I bought a candy thermometer--one that registered up to 400 degrees. By experimenting I found that 180 degrees was the point at which a chicken scalded to pick the easiest, but that a chicken scalded at 165 degrees presented a better appearance after being picked and cooled. Whichever method you use, observe this rule: Pick your chicken clean.

After my chicken has cooled out enough so the flesh will cut easily, I draw it. I chop off the head close up, draw back the skin of the neck a couple of inches, and then cut off the neck. The flap of skin thus left serves to cover the bloody and unsightly stub of the neck. Next I open up the chicken from behind and below the vent and pull out the gizzard--if the chicken has been kept off feed for twenty-four hours the empty crop will come with it--intestines and liver. I remove the gall bladder from the liver, open and clean the gizzard, and replace it and the liver in the chicken.

Then I cut a slit across the chicken just back of the keel of the breast bone. I cut the feet off at the knee joint and slip the drumstick through this slit. Then I lay the chicken up to cool out overnight. The next morning it may be wrapped and boxed, and is then ready for mailing.

Wrapping and boxing must not be slighted. The clean, sanitary appearance of the chicken when it is unpacked in the kitchen of your customer goes a long way toward prejudicing that customer in your favor. I buy thirty pounds of waxed paper, twenty-four by thirty-six inches, and have the paper house cut it in two. This gives me 1000 sheets, each eighteen by twenty-four inches, for the price of a ream of the full size--at this time about five dollars, or a half cent a sheet.

Each chicken is wrapped in one sheet of this waxed paper, and is then packed in a corrugated paper box made especially for sending chickens by parcel post.

I buy three sizes of these boxes. One size, which costs me four cents each, will hold one four-pound chicken when dressed and drawn. The next size, costing five cents each, will hold two very small chickens, or one large chicken. The third size, costing six cents each, will hold two large chickens, three medium-sized ones, or four small ones.

Do not use makeshifts, such as old shoe boxes. In the first place, your shipment is not properly protected by such a box; in the second place, your postmaster is likely to refuse to accept it for mailing, as he would be justified in doing; and in the third place, your customer receives his chicken in a box that has been used for he wonders what, and has been in he wonders what places.

It is for this reason that I never ask a customer to return a box to me. I do not want to use a box a second time. If I were a city man, getting my chickens by mail, I should want them sent to me in a brand-new box, made for the special purpose of sending chickens by mail--and I'd want them in no other box. Then I'd feel sure of them.

The cost of shipping by parcel post is low. I live ten miles from my county seat, and the postage required to send a five-pound, live-weight chicken, dressed and boxed, from my place to town is eight cents. The postage required to send that same five-pound chicken from here to Chicago, one hundred and fifty miles, is eight cents. The express company charges twenty-six cents for the same service, and does not deliver so quickly.

But parcel-post delivery was not always so admirably done in Chicago. When I began shipping up there last September it was no uncommon thing for my packages to be so delayed that many chickens would spoil.

I recall the "straw that broke the camel's back." I mailed twenty-six chickens one day--and in due course I received thirteen letters, each advising me of the same mournful event. The chicken had spoiled because of delay in delivery. My wife wanted to quit. I didn't. I made good the losses to the customers and prepared a label, a copy of which I forwarded to the Third Assistant Postmaster General at Washington, asking his permission to use it, and telling him of the vexatious and expensive delays in delivering my packages in Chicago.

In due time I received the desired permission, and ordered the labels printed. The scheme worked. Every time a package was not delivered on schedule time the customer notified me, and I made complaint to the postmaster at Chicago.

Gradually the service improved until now I have no trouble at all. If I were to ship two packages today to the same address in Chicago, sending one by parcel post and the other by express, I believe the parcel-post package would be delivered first. At any rate, it has been done for me.

The weakness in the parcel-post delivery lies in the fact that perishable products--such as dressed chickens--cannot be handled in warm weather. I think that if the Post Office Department would cut some of its red tape and permit the shipment of air-tight packages in air-tight conveyors this particular problem could be solved.

You will, of course, have more or less correspondence with your customers. By all means use your own letterheads, but do not let your printer embellish them with cuts of roosters, chickens, pigs, or the like. Not that we are ashamed of them; far be it from such. You do not, however, need to have a sheet of paper littered up with pictures of imaginary animals in order to convince your customer that you are selling the meats of that animal. I like a plainly printed letterhead that carries my name, my address and my business. That's all.

By all means keep books on your farm-to-table venture, if you undertake it. Set down on one side of the page what you pay for boxes, labels, postage, and so on, including what you pay yourself for chickens at your huckster's prices. On the other side of the page set down what your city customer pays you. Add up the pages, do a simple sum in subtraction, and you will know just how much you have made.

If I kept only twenty-five hens I should sell my eggs and my chickens direct to the city consumer. When the farmer learns to sell direct instead of letting the huckster, the poultry house, the commission man, the dresser and the retailer stand between him and the consumer, then poultry raising will become really profitable.

There are too many folks who sell their eggs and "take it out in trade."

        *   *   *   *

(Saturday Evening Post)

One large illustration, a wash drawing, made by a staff artist.

SALES WITHOUT SALESMANSHIP

BY JAMES H. COLLINS

"Say, you're a funny salesman!" exclaimed the business man. "Here I make up my own mind that I need two motor trucks and decide to buy 'em from your company. Then I send for a salesman. You come down and spend a week looking into my horse delivery, and now you tell me to keep my horses. What kind of a salesman do you call yourself anyway?"

"What made you think you needed motor trucks?" was the counterquestion of the serious, thick-spectacled young chap.

"Everyone else seems to be turning to gasoline delivery. I want to be up to date."

"Your delivery problem lies outside the gasoline field," said the salesman. "Your drivers make an average of ninety stops each trip. They climb stairs and wait for receipts. Their rigs are standing at the curb more than half the time. Nothing in gasoline equipment can compete with the horse and wagon under such conditions. If you had loads of several tons to be kept moving steadily I'd be glad to sell you two trucks."

"Suppose I wanted to buy them anyway?"

"We could not accept your order."

"But you'd make your commission and the company its profit."

"Yes; but you'd make a loss, and within a year your experience would react unfavorably upon us."

So no sale was effected. Facts learned during his investigation of this business man's delivery problem led the salesman to make suggestions that eliminated waste and increased the effectiveness of his horse rigs.

About a year later, however, this business man sent for the salesman again. He contemplated motorized hauling for another company of which he was the president. After two days' study the salesman reported that motor trucks were practicable and that he needed about five of them.

"All right--fill out the contract," directed the business man.

"Don't you want to know how these trucks are going to make you money?" asked the salesman.

"No; if you say I need five trucks, then I know that's just what I need!"

A new kind of salesmanship is being developed in many lines of business--and particularly in the rebuilding of sales organizations made necessary by the ending of the war and return to peace production. "Study your goods," was the salesman's axiom yesterday. "Study your customer's problem," is the viewpoint to-day; and it is transforming the salesman and sales methods.

Indeed, the word salesman tends to disappear under this new viewpoint, for the organization which was once charged largely with disposing of goods may now be so intimately involved in technical studies of the customers' problems that selling is a secondary part of its work. The Sales Department is being renamed, and known as the Advisory Department or the Research Staff; while the salesman himself becomes a Technical Counsel or Engineering Adviser.

Camouflage? No; simply better expression of broader functions.

As a salesman, probably he gave much attention to the approach and argument with which he gained his customer's attention and confidence. But, with his new viewpoint and method of attack, perhaps the first step is asking permission to study the customer's transportation needs, or accounting routine, or power plant--or whatever section of the latter's business is involved.

The experience of the thick-spectacled motor-truck salesman was typical.

Originally he sold passenger cars. Then came the war, with factory facilities centered on munitions and motor trucks. There being no more passenger cars to sell, they switched him over into the motor-truck section. There he floundered for a while, trying to develop sales arguments along the old lines. But the old arguments did not seem to fit, somehow.

It might have been possible to demonstrate the superior construction of his motor truck; but competitors would meet point with point, and customers were not interested in technicalities anyway. He tried service as an argument, but that was largely a promise of what motor trucks would do for people after they bought them, and competitors could always promise just as much, and a little more.

Company reputation? His company had a fine one--but motor-truck purchasers wanted to know the cost of moving freight. Price? No argument at all, because only one other concern made motor trucks calling for so great an initial investment.

So Thick-Specs, being naturally serious and solid, began to dig into motor trucks from the standpoint of the customer. He got permission to investigate delivery outfits in many lines. Selling a five-ton motor truck to many a business man was often equivalent to letting Johnny play with a loaded machine gun. Such a vehicle combined the potentiality of moving from fifty to seventy-five tons of freight daily, according to routing and the number of hours employed; but it involved a daily expense of twenty-five dollars.

The purchaser could lose money in two ways at swift ratios, and perhaps unsuspectingly: He might not use his full hauling capacity each day or would use it only half the year, during his busy season. Or he might underestimate costs by overlooking such items as interest and depreciation.

Thick-Specs' first actual sale was not a motor truck at all, but a motorcycle, made by another company. Within three months, however, this motorcycle added two big trucks to a fleet of one dozen operated by a wholesale firm. That concern had good trucks, and kept them in a well-equipped garage, where maintenance was good. But at least once daily there would be a road breakdown. Usually this is a minor matter, but it ties up the truck while its puzzled driver tries to locate the trouble.

When a motorcycle was bought for the garage, drivers were forbidden to tamper with machinery on the road--they telephoned in to the superintendent. By answering each call on his own motorcycle--about an hour daily--the repairman kept equipment in such good shape that valuable extra service was secured from the fleet each day.

The salesman-adviser did not originate this scheme himself, but discovered it in another concern's motor-truck organization; in fact, this is the advantage the salesman-adviser enjoys--acquaintance with a wide range of methods and the knack of carrying a good wrinkle from one business to another. He brings the outside point of view; and, because modern business runs toward narrow specialization, the outside point of view is pretty nearly always welcome, provided it is honest and sensible.

In another case he had to dig and invent to meet a peculiar situation.

There was a coal company working under a handicap in household deliveries. Where a residence stood back from the sidewalk coal had often to be carried from the motor truck in baskets. This kept the truck waiting nearly an hour. A motor truck's time is worth several dollars hourly. If the coal could have been dumped on the sidewalk and carried in later, releasing the truck, that would have saved expense and made more deliveries possible.

A city ordinance prohibited dumping coal on the sidewalk except by permit. Coal men had never tried to have that ordinance changed. But the salesman-adviser went straight to the city authorities and, by figures showing the expense and waste involved, secured a modification, so that his customer, the coal company, got a blanket permit for dumping coal and gave bonds as an assurance against abuse of the privilege. Then a little old last year's runabout was bought and followed the coal trucks with a crew to carry the coal indoors, clearing sidewalks quickly.

This salesman-adviser's philosophy was as simple as it was sound. Confidence is the big factor in selling, he reasoned. Your customer will have confidence in you if he feels that you are square and also knows what you are talking about. By diligent study of gasoline hauling problems in various lines of business he gained practical knowledge and after that had only to apply his knowledge from the customer's side of the problem.

"Put it another way," he said: "Suppose you had a factory and expected to run it only one year. There would not be time to get returns on a costly machine showing economies over a five-year period; but if you intended to run your factory on a five-year basis, then that machine might be highly profitable.

"In sales work it was just the same; if you were selling for this year's profit alone, you'd close every sale regardless of your customer's welfare. Let the purchaser beware! But if you meant to sell on the five-year basis, then confidence is the big investment, and the most profitable sale very often one you refuse to make for immediate results."

He had a fine following when the draft reached him; and during the eight months he spent in an Army uniform he utilized his knowledge of gasoline transportation as an expert in Uncle Sam's motor service. Upon being discharged he returned to his job and his customers, and to-day the concern with which he is connected is taking steps to put all its motor-truck salesmen on this advisory basis.

War shot its sales force to pieces--the Army and the Navy reached out for men and tied up production facilities; so there was nothing to sell. But war also gave a clean slate for planning a new sales force.

As old salesmen return and new men are taken on for sales instruction, this concern trains them--not with the old sales manual, by standard approach and systematic sales argument, but by sending them out into the field to study gasoline hauling problems. They secure permission to investigate trucking methods of contractors, department stores, wholesale merchants, coal dealers, truck owners hauling interstate freight, mills, factories and other lines of business. They investigate the kinds and quantities of stuff to be moved, the territory and roads covered, the drivers, the garage facilities. They ride behind typical loads and check up running time, delays, breakdowns, gasoline and oil consumption.

Engineering teaches people to think in curves. This youngster had to make a curve of the grocer's trucking before he could visualize it himself. His curve included factors like increase in stuff that had been hauled during the past three years and additions to the motor equipment. When you have a healthy curve showing any business activity, the logical thing to do, after bringing it right down to date, is to let it run out into the future at its own angle. This was done with the grocery curve, and its future extension indicated that not more than three months later the grocery house would need about four more five-ton motor trucks.

Closer investigation of facts behind the curve revealed an unusual growth in sugar hauling, due to the increase in supply and removal of consumer war restrictions. And that grocery concern bought additional trucks for sugar within two months. With the insight made possible by such a curve a salesman might safely have ordered the trucks without his customer's knowledge and driven them up to his door the day the curve showed they were needed.

"Here are the trucks you wanted to haul that sugar."

"Good work! Drive 'em in!"

What has been found to be sound sales policy in the motor truck business applies to many other lines. Yesterday the salesman of technical apparatus sought the customer with a catalogue and a smile--and a large ignorance of the technical problems. To-day that kind of selling is under suspicion, because purchasers of technical equipment have been led to buy on superficial selling points and left to work out for themselves complex technicalities that belong to the manufacturer of the equipment.

In the West during recent years a large number of pumps of a certain type have been sold for irrigating purposes. Purchasers bought from the catalogue-and-smile type of salesman, hooked their pumps up to a power plant--and found that they lifted only about half the number of gallons a minute promised in the catalogue. Manufacturers honestly believed those pumps would do the work indicated in their ratings. They had not allowed for variations in capacity where pumps were installed under many different conditions and run by different men. The situation called for investigation at the customer's end; when it was discovered that these pumps ought to be rated with an allowance for loss of capacity a half to two-thirds of the power, due to friction and lost power.

It might have been dangerous for the salesman to show up again in an irrigation district where a lot of his pumps were "acting up," armed only with his catalogue and smile. But when an engineer appeared from the pump company to help customers out of their difficulties, he won confidence immediately and made additional sales because people felt that he knew what he was talking about.

The superintendent of a big machinery concern found that his expense for cutting oils was constantly rising. Salesmen had followed salesmen, recommending magic brands of the stuff; yet each new barrel of oil seemed to do less work than the last--and cost more in dollars.

One day a new kind of visitor showed up and sent in the card of a large oil company. He was not a salesman, but an investigator of oil problems. The superintendent took him through the plant. He studied the work being done by screw-cutting machines, lathes and other equipment operated with cutting oil. Where salesmen had recommended brands without technical knowledge of either the work to be done or the composition of the oil, this stranger wrote specifications that cut down the percentage of costly lard oil used on some work; and he eliminated it altogether on others.

Moreover, he pointed out sheer losses of oil by picking up a handful of metal cuttings from a box, letting them drip, measuring the oil that accumulated and recommending a simple device for reclaiming that oil before the waste metal was sold.

This new viewpoint in selling is developing in so many lines that to enumerate them would be to make a national directory of business concerns manufacturing milling machinery, office devices, manufacturing and structural materials, equipment for the farm and the mine.

People who purchase such products have been accustomed to meeting two different representatives of manufacturers: First, the salesman skilled in selling, but deficient in technical knowledge.

"This chap is here to see how much he can get out of me," said the prospective consumer to himself; and he was on his guard to see that the visitor got as little as possible, either in the way of orders or information.

The other representative came from the mechanical department to see how present equipment was running, or perhaps to "shoot trouble." He was long on technical knowledge, but probably dumb when it came to salesmanship.

"This fellow is here to help me out of my troubles," said the customer. "I'll see how much I can get out of him."

Presently manufacturers of equipment woke up to the fact that their mechanical men--inspectors and trouble shooters--had a basis of confidence which the salesman pure and simple was rapidly losing. Moreover, the technical man gained a knowledge of the customer's requirements that furnished the best foundation for selling new equipment.

The salesman discovered the technical man and went to him for tips on new equipment needed by customers whose plants he had visited. The technical man also discovered the salesman, for it was plain enough that equipment well sold--skillfully adjusted to the customer's needs--gave the least margin for trouble shooting.

So there has been a meeting of minds; and to-day the salesman studies the technicalities, and the technical man is learning salesmanship, and their boss is standing behind them both with a new policy. This is the

policy of performance, not promises--service before sales. Under that
policy the very terms salesmanship and sales department are beginning to
disappear, to be replaced by new nomenclature, which more accurately
indicates what a manufacturer's representative can do for the customer,
and gives him access to the latter on the basis of confidence and good
will.

                *   *   *   *   *

(Munsey's Magazine)

THE ACCIDENT THAT GAVE US WOOD-PULP PAPER

HOW A MIGHTY MODERN INDUSTRY OWED ITS BEGINNING TO GOTTFRIED KELLER AND
A WASP

BY PARKE F. HANLEY

On the day when President Wilson was inaugurated to his second term,
this country had its fiftieth anniversary of the introduction of
wood-pulp. Were it not for a series of lucky chances that developed into
opportunity, this wood-pulp anniversary might have remained for our
children's children.

Have you ever given thought to the accidentalism of many great
discoveries? The element of haphazard is generally combined with a
series of coincidences. Looking back over the developments that led to
gigantic contributions to our civilization, one cannot fail to be struck
by the coordination of events. Apparently there always has been a
conspiracy of natural forces to compel men of thought and
resourcefulness to add another asset to progress.

Your earliest school readers have been full of these--for instance, Watt
and his steam-kettle, Franklin and his kite. Now the youngsters are
reading that the Wrights derived a fundamental principle of
aviation--the warping-tip--from the flight of crows. With the awe comes
a disquieting thought. How far back should we be were it not for these
fortuitous circumstances?

Among all the great things that have been given to the world in the last
three-quarters of a century, few measure beside the wood-pulp industry.
With its related trades and sciences, it is comprised within the ten
great activities of mankind. In manufacture and distribution, it employs
an army matching in size the Russian battle hordes. Its figures of
investment and production are comparable to the debts of the great war.

Yet it remained for a wasp and Gottfried Keller to bring us out of the
era of rag paper. Together, they saved us from a retardation of
universal thought. Therefore, let us consider the agents.

First, the wasp. She was one of a family of several hundreds, born in
the Hartz Mountains in the year 1839. When death claimed most of her
relatives at the end of the season allotted as the life of a wasp, this
survivor, a queen wasp, became the foundress of a family of her own.
She built her nest of selected wood-fibers, softened them to a pulp with
her saliva, and kneaded them into cells for her larvæ. Her family came
forth in due course, and their young wings bore them out into the world.

The nest, having served its purpose, was abandoned to the sun and the rain.

Maeterlinck, who attributes emotions to plants and souls to bees, might wrap a drama of destiny about this insect. She would command a leading place in a cast which included the butterfly that gave silk to the world, the mosquito that helped to prove the germ theory of disease, and the caterpillar that loosed the apple which revealed the law of gravitation to Sir Isaac Newton.

As to Keller, he was a simple German, by trade a paper-maker and by avocation a scientist of sorts. One day in 1840--and this marks the beginning of the accidents--returning home from his mill, he trod upon the abandoned nest. Had not the tiny dwelling been deserted, he probably would have cherished nothing but bitter reflections about the irascibility of wasps. As it was, he stooped to see the ruin he had wrought.

The crushed nest lay soft in his hand, soft and pliable, and yet tough in texture. It was as soft as his own rag-made paper. It was not paper, and yet it was very much like paper. Crumbling It in his fingers, he decided that its material was wood-pulp.

Keller was puzzled to know how so minute a creature had welded wood into a paperlike nest. His state of mind passed to interest, thence to speculation, and finally to investigation. He carried his problem and its possibilities to his friend, Heinrich Voelter, a master mechanic. Together they began experiments. They decided to emulate the wasp. They would have to granulate the wood as she had done. The insect had apparently used spruce; they used spruce under an ordinary grindstone. Hot water served as a substitute for the wasp's salivary juices.

Their first attempts gave them a pulp astonishingly similar to that resulting from the choicest rags. They carried the pulp through to manufacture, with a small proportion of rags added--and they had paper. It was good paper, paper that had strength. They found that it possessed an unlooked-for advantage in its quick absorption of printing-ink.

Have you followed the chain of accidents, coincidences, and fortunate circumstances? Suppose the wasp had not left her nest in Keller's path. What if he had been in haste, or had been driven off by the queen's yellow-jacketed soldiers? What if he had no curiosity, if he had not been a paper-maker, if he had not enjoyed acquaintance with Voelter? Wood-pulp might never have been found.

Leaving Gottfried Keller and Voelter in their hour of success, we find, sixteen years afterward, two other Germans, Albrecht and Rudolf Pagenstecher, brothers, in the export trade in New York. They were pioneering in another field. They were shipping petroleum to Europe for those rising young business men, John D. and William Rockefeller. They were seeking commodities for import when their cousin, Alberto Pagenstecher, arrived from the fatherland with an interesting bit of news.

"A few weeks ago, in a paper-mill in the Hartz, I found them using a new process," he said. "They are making paper out of wood. It serves. Germany is printing its newspapers on wood-pulp paper."

To his cousins it seemed preposterous that wood could be so converted, but Alberto was convincing. He showed them Voelter's patent grants and pictures of the grinders. The Pagenstechers went to Germany, and when they returned they brought two of the grinders--crude affairs devised for the simple purpose of pressing wood upon a stone. They also brought with them several German mechanics.

A printer in New York, named Strang, had already secured the United States rights of the new process. He was engaged in the manufacture of calendered paper, and, therefore, had no occasion to use wood pulp; so he was willing to surrender the patents in exchange for a small interest.

The Pagenstechers wanted water-power for their grinders, and they located their first mill beside Stockbridge Bowl, in Curtisville, now Interlaken, Massachusetts. On an outlay of eleven thousand dollars their mill was built and their machinery installed. Two or three trials, with cotton waste added to the ground wood, gave them their paper. Their first product was completed on the 5th of March, 1867.

It was a matter of greater difficulty to dispose of the stock. The trade fought against the innovation. Finally Wellington Smith, of the near-by town of Lee, Massachusetts, was persuaded to try it. Rag-paper had been selling at twenty-four cents a pound. Smith's mill still exhibits the first invoice with the Pagenstechers, which shows the purchase of wood-paper at eleven cents.

The paper was hauled to Lee in the dead of night, for Smith's subordinates wished to spare him from the laughter of his fellow millmen. It was sold, and proved successful, and the Pagenstechers were rushed with orders. They built a second mill in Luzeme, New York, but abandoned it soon afterward for the greater water-power to be obtained at Palmer's Falls, where now stands the second largest mill in the United States.

Manufacturers tumbled over themselves to get the benefit of the new process. The originators in this country held the patent rights until 1884, letting them out on royalties until that time. With each new plant the price of paper fell, until at one period it sold at one and a half cents a pound.

Trial had proved that spruce was the only suitable wood for the pulp. Until 1891 rags were combined in about one-quarter proportion. Then it was found that other coniferous woods might be used to replace the rags, after being submitted to what is called the sulfite process. In this treatment small cubes of wood, placed in a vat, have their resinous properties extracted, and the wood is disintegrated. A combination of ground and sulfite wood makes the paper now used for news-print.

As has been told, the primary advantage of the wood-pulp paper was its immediate absorption of ink. This made possible much greater speed in printing, and led in turn to the development of the great modern newspaper and magazine presses, fed by huge rolls of paper, which they print on both sides simultaneously. These wonderful machines have now reached the double-octuple stage--monsters capable of turning out no less than five thousand eight-page newspapers in a single minute, or three hundred thousand in an hour.

With the evolution from the flat-bed to the web or rotary presses there
came further development in typesetting-machines--the linotype, the
monotype, and others. With paper and presses brought to such
simplification, newspapers have sprouted in every town, almost every
village, and the total number of American periodicals is counted by tens
of thousands. There are magazines that have a circulation of more than a
million copies weekly. The leading daily newspapers in New York print
anywhere from one hundred thousand copies to four times as many, and
they can put extra editions on the streets at fifteen-minute intervals.

The aggregate circulation of daily newspapers in the United States is
close to forty million copies. Weekly newspapers and periodicals reach
fifty millions, and monthly publications mount almost to one hundred
millions; and all this would be impossible without wood-pulp paper.

The annual production of wood-pulp in the United States and Canada is
estimated by Albrecht Pagenstecher, the survivor of the innovators, to
be worth nearly five hundred millions of dollars. Take into
consideration the hundreds of thousands employed in the mills, the men
who cut and bring in the raw product, the countless number in the
printing, publishing, and distributing trades. Then hark back to the
accident that put the wasp's nest under the toe of Gottfried Keller!

              *   *   *   *   *

(_Providence Journal_)

One zinc-etching illustration reproducing an old wood-cut of the ship,
with the caption, "The Savannah, First Steamship That Crossed the
Ocean."

CENTENNIAL OF THE FIRST STEAMSHIP TO CROSS THE ATLANTIC

(7-column head)

One hundred years ago this week there was launched at New York the ship
Savannah, which may be called the father of the scores of steamers that
are now carrying our soldiers and supplies from the New World to the Old
World.

The Savannah was the first ship equipped with steam power to cross the
Atlantic ocean. It made the trip in 25 days, using both sails and
engine, and the arrival of the strange craft at Liverpool was the cause
of unusual stir among our English cousins. Like every step from the
beaten path the idea of steam travel between the New World and the Old
World was looked upon with much scepticism and it was not until about 20
years later that regular, or nearly regular, steamer service was
established.

The launching of the Savannah took place on Aug. 22, 1818. It was not
accompanied by the ceremony that is accorded many of the boats upon
similar occasions to-day. As a matter of fact, it is probable that only
a few persons knew that the craft was intended for a transatlantic trip.
The keel of the boat was laid with the idea of building a sailing ship,
and the craft was practically completed before Capt. Moses Rogers, the

originator of the venture, induced Scarborough & Isaacs, ship merchants of Savannah, to buy her and fit her with a steam engine for service between Savannah and Liverpool.

The ship, which was built by Francis Fickett, was 100 feet long, 28 feet broad and 14 feet deep. It had three masts which, of course, were of far greater importance in making progress toward its destination than was the steam engine.

Capt. Rogers had gained a reputation for great courage and skill in sailing. He had already had the honor of navigating the sea with a steamer, taking the New Jersey from New York to the Chesapeake in 1816, a voyage which was then thought to be one of great danger for such a vessel.

It was natural, then, that he was especially ambitious to go down in history as the first master of a steam ship to cross the ocean. As soon as the vessel had been purchased by the Savannah ship merchants, the work of installing the engine was begun. This was built by Stephen Vail of Speedwell, N.J., and the boiler by David Dod of Elizabeth, N. J.

The paddle-wheels were made of iron and were "detachable," so that the sections could be removed and laid on the deck. This was done when it was desired to proceed under canvas exclusively and was also a precaution in rough weather.

In short, the Savannah was an auxiliary steamer, a combination of steam and sail that later became well known in shipping. This is much like the early development of the gasoline marine engine, which was an auxiliary to the sail, a combination that is still used.

Capt. Rogers took the boat from New York to Savannah in eight days and 15 hours, using steam on this trip for 41½ hours. On May 26, 1819, under Capt. Rogers, the Savannah set sail from her home port for Liverpool and made the trip in 25 days.

As long as the trip took, the voyage was considerably shorter than the average for the sailing ship in 1819, and this reduction in time was accomplished in spite of the fact that the Savannah ran into much unfavorable weather. Capt. Rogers used steam on 18 of the 25 days and doubtless would have resorted to engine power more of the time except for the fact that at one stage of the voyage the fuel was exhausted.

It was natural that the arrival of the steamer in English waters should not have been looked upon with any great favor by the Englishmen. In addition to the jeers of the sceptical, the presence of vessels was accompanied by suspicion on the part of the naval authorities, and the merchants were not favorably impressed.

When the Savannah approached the English coast with her single stack giving forth volumes of dense black smoke, it was thought by those on shore that she was a ship on fire, and British men-of-war and revenue cutters set out to aid her. When the truth was known, consternation reigned among the English officers. They were astonished at the way the craft steamed away from them after they had rushed to assist what they thought was a ship in distress.

The reception of the Savannah at Liverpool was not particularly cordial. Some of the newspapers even suggested that "this steam operation may, in some manner, be connected with the ambitious views of the United States."

A close watch was kept on the boat while she lay in British waters, and her departure was welcome. In the second volume of "Memoranda of a Residence at the Court of St. James," Richard Rush, then American Minister in London, includes a complete log of the Savannah. Dispatch No. 76 from Minister Rush reports the arrival of the ship and the comment that was caused by its presence as follows:

London, July 3,1819.

Sir--On the 20th of last month arrived at Liverpool from the United States the steamship Savannah, Capt. Rogers, being the first vessel of that description that ever crossed the sea, and having excited equal admiration and astonishment as she entered port under the power of her steam.

She is a fine ship of 320 tons burden and exhibits in her construction, no less than she has done in her navigation across the Atlantic, a signal trophy of American enterprise and skill upon the ocean.

I learn from Capt. Rogers, who has come to London and been with me, that she worked with great ease and safety on the voyage, and used her steam full 18 days.

Her engine acts horizontally and is equal to a 72 horsepower. Her wheels, which are of iron, are on the sides, and removable at pleasure. The fuel laid in was 1500 bushels of coal, which got exhausted on her entrance into the Irish Channel.

The captain assures me that the weather in general was extremely unfavorable, or he would have made a much shorter passage; besides that, he was five days delayed in the channel for want of coal. I have the honor to be, etc., RICHARD RUSH.

To have made the first voyage across the Atlantic Ocean under steam was a great accomplishment and brought no little credit to Capt. Rogers and the United States. Pioneers in many ventures, the American people had added another honor to their record. And this was even more of a credit because in those early days skilled workmen were comparatively few on these shores and the machine shops had not reached a stage of efficiency that came a short time later.

There were, of course, in 1819 men who had developed into mechanics and there were shops of some account, as the steamboat for short trips had been in existence for some years. But the whole enterprise of planning a steam voyage in which the boat should be headed due east was characteristic of the boldness and bravery of the Americans.

The Savannah did not return to the States directly from England. It steamed from Liverpool to St. Petersburg and brought forth further comment from the Old World. She proved that the marine steam engine and side-wheels were practicable for deep-sea navigation. The idea of transatlantic travel under steam had been born and it was only necessary to develop the idea to "shorten the distance" between the two continents.

This pioneer voyage, however, was then looked upon more as a novelty than as the inception of a new method of long-distance travel. The trip had failed to demonstrate that steam was an entirely adequate substitute for the mast and sail in regular service.

Since the Savannah was primarily a sailing vessel, the loss of steam power by the crippling of the engine would not be serious, as she could continue on her way with paddle-wheels removed and under full sail.

It was 19 years later that the idea of employing vessels propelled by steam in trade between the United States and England came under the serious consideration of merchants and ship builders. In the interval the marine boiler and the engines had been improved until they had passed the stage of experiment, and coasting voyages had become common on both sides of the Atlantic.

The beginning of real transatlantic steam voyages was made by the Sirius and the Great Western. The latter boat had been built especially for trips across the ocean and the former was taken from the Cork and London line. The Sirius started from Liverpool on April 4, 1838, and the Great Western four days later. They arrived in New York within 24 hours of each other, the Sirius at 10 p.m. on April 22 and the Great Western at 3 o'clock the following afternoon. Neither of the vessels carried much sail.

These boats gave more or less irregular service until withdrawn because of their failure to pay expenses. In 1839 the Cunard Company was formed and the paddle steamers Britannia, Arcadia, Columbia, and Caledonia were put into service.

From that time on the steamer developed with great rapidity, the value of which was never more demonstrated than at the present time. It will always be remembered, however, that this Capt. Rogers with his crude little Savannah was the man whose bold enterprise gave birth to the idea of transatlantic travel under steam.

        *   *   *   *   *

(A syndicate Sunday magazine section of the _Harrisburg Patriot_)

SEARCHING FOR THE LOST ATLANTIS

By GROSVENOR A. PARKER

Not so long ago a stubby tramp steamer nosed its way down the English Channel and out into the Atlantic. Her rusty black bow sturdily shouldered the seas aside or shoved through them with an insistence that brought an angry hail of spray on deck. The tramp cared little for this protest of the sea or for the threats of more hostile resistance. Through the rainbow kicked up by her forefoot there glimmered and beckoned a mirage of wealthy cities sunk fathoms deep and tenanted only by strange sea creatures. For the tramp and her crew there was a stranger goal than was ever sought by an argosy of legend. The lost cities of Atlantis and all the wealth that they contain was the port awaiting the searchers under the rim of the western ocean.

It's no wild-goose chase that had started thus unromantically. The men who hope to gain fame and fortune by this search are sure of their ground and they have all the most modern mechanical and electrical aids for their quest. On the decks of their ship two submarine boats are cradled in heavy timbers. One of them is of the usual type, but the other looks like a strange fantasy of another Jules Verne. A great electric eye peers cyclops-wise over the bow and reaching ahead of the blunt nose are huge crab-like claws delicate enough to pick up a gold piece and strong enough to tear a wall apart.

These under-water craft are only a part of the equipment that Bernard Meeker, a young Englishman, has provided to help him in his search for the lost city. There are divers' uniforms specially strengthened to resist the great pressure under which the men must work. Huge electric lamps like searchlights to be lowered into the ocean depths and give light to the workers are stacked close beside powerful generators in the ship's hold. In the chart room there are rolls of strange maps plotting out the ocean floor, and on a shelf by itself rests the tangible evidence that this search means gold. It is a little bowl of strange design which was brought up by a diver from the bottom of the Caribbean. When this bowl first came to light it was supposed to be part of loot from a sunken Spanish galleon, but antiquarians could find nothing in the art of the Orient, or Africa, or of Peru and Mexico to bear out this theory. Even the gold of which it was made was an alloy of a different type from anything on record.

It was this that gave Meeker his first idea that there was a city under the sea. He found out the exact spot from which the divers had recovered the bowl, and compared the reckonings with all the ancient charts which spoke of the location of fabled Atlantis. In one old book he located the lost city as being close to the spot where the divers had been, and with this as a foundation for his theories he asked other questions of the men who had explored that hidden country. Their tale only confirmed his belief.

"The floor of the sea is covered with unusual coral formation," one of them told him, "but it was the queerest coral I ever saw. It looked more like stone walls and there was a pointed sort of arch which was different from any coral arch I had ever seen."

That was enough to take Meeker to the Caribbean to see for himself. He won't tell what he found, beyond the fact that he satisfied himself that the "coral" was really stone walls pierced by arched doors and windows.

Meeker kept all his plans secret and might have sailed away on his treasure hunt without making any stir if he had not been careless enough to name one of his submarines "Atlantis." He had given out that he was sailing for Yucatan to search for evidence of prehistoric civilization. It is true that the shores of Yucatan are covered with the remnants of great cities but the word "Atlantis" awoke suspicion. Questions followed and Meeker had to admit the bare facts of his secret.

"Only half a dozen men know the supposed location of Atlantis," he said, just before sailing, "and we don't intend to let any others into the secret. Those who have furnished the money for the expedition have done so in the hope of solving the mystery of the lost continent, and without thought for the profit. The divers and the other men of the crew have the wildest dreams of finding hoarded wealth. It is not at all impossible that their dreams will come true, and that they will be richly rewarded. At any rate they deserve it, for the work will be dangerous.

"Our plans are simple enough. With the submarine of the usual type we will first explore that part of the sea bottom which our charts cover. This vessel has in its conning tower a powerful searchlight which will reveal at least the upper portions of any buildings that may be there. For work in greater depths we will have to depend on the 'Atlantis' with its special equipment of ballast tanks and its hatch-ways for the divers.

"You see, we do not plan to lower the divers from the steamer or from a raft. Instead they will step directly out on the sea floor from a door in the submarine which opens out of an air chamber. In this the diver can be closed and the air pressure increased until it is high enough to keep out the water. All that he has to do then is to open the door and step out, trailing behind him a much shorter air hose and life line than would hamper him if he worked from the surface. The air hose is armored with steel links so that there will be no danger of an inquisitive shark chopping it in two."

Previous to the diver's exploration the claws of the "Atlantis" will search out the more promising places in the ruins. These claws work on a joint operated electrically, and on the tip of each is a sensitive electrical apparatus which sets off a signal in the conning tower of the submarine. Crawling over the bottom like a strange monster, the claws will also help to avoid collisions with walls when the depths of the water veils the power of the searchlight.

There is, in addition, a small electric crane on the nose of the submarine so that heavy objects can be borne to the surface. Meeker does not expect to gain much in the way of heavy relics of the lost city, for certain parts of the sea bottom are so covered with ooze that he believes it only possible to clear it away through suction hose long enough to make quick observation possible. The subaqueous lights which will help this work are powerful Tungsten lamps enclosed in a steel shell with a heavy prismatic lens at the bottom. These lamps are connected to the power plant on the steamer by armored cables and will develop 5,000 candle power each.

The generating station on the parent ship of the expedition, as the rusty tramp is known, is as extensive as those on a first class liner or a dreadnought. Little of the power will go for the benefit of the steamer though. Its purpose is to furnish the light for the swinging Tungstens and to charge the great storage batteries of the submarines. These batteries run the many motors on which depends the success of the work. If it were not for electricity, the searchers would be handicapped. As it is they call to their aid all the strong magic of modern days.

INDEX

"Accident that Gave Us Wood-Pulp Paper, The," 356

Adventure as a source of interest, 41.

Agricultural journals, 11, 20, 23;
  articles in, 29, 30, 31, 32, 33, 34, 78;
  examples of articles in, 81, 248, 341;
  excerpts from, 127,128, 156

Aims in feature writing, 46

Alliteration in titles, 179

Amateur writers, opportunities for, 7, 12

American Magazine, articles from, 76, 87;
  excerpt from, 158

Amusements as a source of interest, 42

Analysis of articles on factory school, 107, 116

Analysis of special articles, 22;
  outline for, 201

Animals as a source of interest, 41

Appeals, kinds of, 39;
  combinations of, 45

"Arbor Day Advice," 57

Arrangement of material, 101

Balance in titles, 179

"Bedroom in Burlap, A," 68

Beginnings, 131;
  structure of, 131;
  types of, 132

Boston Herald, article from, 204

Boston Transcript, articles from, 209, 326;
  excerpt from, 145

"Boys in Search of Jobs," 209

"Brennan Mono-Rail Car," 274

Browning, John M., personality sketch of, 89

"By Parcel Post," 341

Camera, use of, for illustrations, 194

Captions for illustrations, 196

"Centennial of First Steamship to Cross the Atlantic," 360

Chicago Tribune, excerpt from, 159

Children as a source of interest, 41

Christian Science Monitor, article from, 206

Clark, Thomas Arkle, personality sketch of, 87

Class publications, 11, 20, 23

College training for writing, 16

Collier's Weekly, excerpt from, 139

Collins, James H., article by, 349

Confession articles, 32, 70;
  examples of, 71

"Confessions of a College Professor's Wife," 307

Contests for supremacy as a source of interest, 41

Correspondents as feature writers, 6

Cosgrove, John O'Hara, on Sunday magazine sections, 9

"County Service Station, A," 248

Country Gentleman, articles from, 248, 341;
  excerpt from, 156

Cover page for manuscripts, 183;
  form for, 184

Crime, presentation of, 47

Curiosity as a qualification for writers, 15

Definition of special feature article, 4

Delineator, article from, 293;
  excerpt from, 152

Descriptive beginnings, 138

Designer, article from, 68

Detroit News, article from, 260;
  excerpt from, 125

Diction, 161

Direct address beginnings, 157

Direct address titles, 178

Drawings for illustrations, 197;
  mailing of, 197

Eaton, Walter Prichard, article by; 326

Editorial readers, 187

Editors, point of view of, 19

Entertainment as purpose of articles, 47;
  wholesome, 47

Ethics of feature writing, 23, 47

Everybody's Magazine, article from, 281

Every Week, article from, 72

Examples, methods of presenting, 118

Exposition by narration and description, 52

Factory school, articles on, 102, 107, 115

Familiar things as a source of interest, 42

Farm and Fireside, article from, 81

Farm journals, 11, 20, 23, 78;
  articles in, 29, 30, 31, 32, 33, 34;
  examples of articles in, 81, 248, 341;
  excerpts from, 127, 128, 156

Figures of speech, as element of style, 163;
  in beginnings, 144;
  in titles, 176

Filing material, 38

"Forty Years Bartered for What?" 76

"Four Men of Humble Birth Hold World Destiny," 305

Free-Lance writers, 6

Gardiner, A.G., personality sketch of former kaiser by, 166, 167

"Gentle Art of Blowing Bottles, The," 233

Gibbon, Perceval, article by, 274

"Girls and a Camp," 213

Good Housekeeping, excerpts from, 141, 151

Greeley Smith, Nixola, article by, 115

"Guarding a City's Water Supply," 260

Harper's Monthly, excerpt from, 150

Harper's Weekly, excerpt from, 146

Hartswick, F. Gregory, article by, 233

Headlines, 170;
  types of, 173;
  methods of framing, 180

Hendrick, Burton J., article by, 53

How-to-do-something articles, 49, 78;
  examples of, 68, 79

How-to-do-something units, 127

Hungerford, Edward, article by, 218

Ideals in feature writing, 23, 47

Illustrated World, excerpt from, 144

Illustrations, value of, 193;
  photographs for, 194;
  requirements for, 195;
  captions for, 196;
  mailing of, 197

Imperative beginnings, 157

Imperative titles, 178

Incidents, methods of presenting, 122

Independent, article from, 233;
  excerpt from, 140

Indian princess, interview with, 59

Information, trivial _vs._ significant, 49

Informative articles, 49

Instances, methods of presenting, 118

Interest, sources of, 39

Interview type of article, 56;
  examples of, 57

Interview on Arbor Day, 57;
  with Indian princess, 59

"Job Lady, The," 293

Journalism, college courses in, 17

"Just Like Pocahontas of 300 Years Ago," 59

Kaempffert, Waldemar, on scientific subjects, 27

Kansas City Star, article from, 299;
  excerpts from, 133, 145, 147, 154

Label titles, 173

Length of articles, 100

Leslie's Weekly, excerpts from, 135, 148, 157

London _Daily News_, excerpt from, 166, 167

Magazines, as field for articles, 11;
  contributors to, 11;
  study of, 21

Manuscripts, form for, 182, 184;
  mailing, 186;
  in editorial offices, 187;
  rejected, 188;
  accepted, 189

Manuscript record, 190

McClure's Magazine, article from, 274;
  excerpts from, 53, 151

McClure Newspaper Syndicate, 192

"Mark Twain's First Sweetheart," 299

Milwaukee Journal, article from, 305

Munsey's Magazine, article from, 356;
  excerpts from, 136, 139

Mysteries as a source of interest, 40

Narrative article in third person, 91;
  examples of, 92

Narrative beginnings, 134

"Neighborhood Playhouse, The," 240

"New Political Wedge, A," 281

Newspaper Enterprise Association, 192;
  articles from, 89, 115;
  excerpt from, 152

Newspaper Feature Service, 192;
  excerpt from, 155

Newspaper work as training for magazine writing, 17

Newspapers, as field for articles, 5;
  characteristics of, 8;
  Sunday magazine sections of, 9;
  study of, 21;
  as source of subjects, 33

New York Evening Post, articles from, 213, 242;
  excerpt from, 150

New York Evening Sun, excerpt from, 154

New York Sun, article from, 336

New York Times, excerpts from, 119, 137, 145, 155, 158

New York Tribune, excerpts from, 129, 141

New York World, articles from, 92, 240;
  excerpt from, 133

Nose for news in feature writing, 14

Notebook, value of, 37

"Now the Public Kitchen," 92

Observation, personal, as a source of subjects and material, 28

"Occupation and Exercise Cure, The," 264

Official documents as a source of material, 34

Ohio State Journal, article from, 59

Origin of special feature articles, 3

Outline for analysis of feature articles, 201

Outline of articles on factory schools, 105-07

Outlining articles, value of, 99;
  method of, 105

Outlook, articles from, 95, 264;
  excerpts from, 126, 133, 135, 146, 156

Overline for illustrations, 197

"Paradise for a Penny, A," 326

Paradoxical beginnings, 144

Paradoxical titles, 175

Paragraphs, length and structure of, 168

Payment, rate of, 7;
  time of, 190

Personality sketches, 85;
  examples of, 87

Personal experience articles, 62;
  examples of, 63

Personal experience as a source of subjects, 30

Personal observation as a source of subjects, 28

Personal success as a source of interest, 43

Philadelphia Public Ledger, excerpt from, 130

Photographs, value of, 193;
  securing, 194;
  requirements for, 195;
  sizes of, 195;
  captions for, 196;
  mailing of, 197

Pictorial Review, article from, 331

Planning an article, 99, 102

Popular Science Monthly, excerpt from, 147

Practical guidance articles, 49, 78;

examples of, 79

Practical guidance units, 127

Processes, methods of presenting, 125

Prominence as a source of interest, 42

Providence Journal, article from, 360;
  excerpt from, 142

Purpose, definiteness of, 45;
  statement of, 50

Qualifications for feature writing, 14

Question beginnings, 153

Question titles, 177

Quiller-Couch, Sir Arthur, on jargon, 163

Quotation beginnings, 149

Quotation titles, 176

Railroad Man's Magazine, excerpt from, 148

Readers, editorial, 187

Readers, point of view of, 19, 20

Recipes, methods of presenting, 127

Reporters as feature writers, 6, 17

Revision of articles, 168

Rhyme in titles, 179

Romance as a source of interest, 41

"Sales without Salesmanship," 349

San Francisco Call, excerpt from, 155

Saturday Evening Post, articles from, 218, 307, 349

Scandal, presentation of, 47

Scientific publications as a source of subjects and material, 27, 35

"Searching for the Lost Atlantis," 364

Sentences, structure of, 165;
  length of, 166

Shepherd, William G., article by, 305

Siddall, John M., on curiosity, 15;
  on readers' point of view, 21;
  on making articles personal, 45

"Singular Story of the Mosquito Man, The," 242

"Six Years of Tea Rooms," 336

Slosson, Edwin E., on scientific and technical subjects, 27

Sources of subjects and material, 25

Space rates for feature articles, 7

Staff system on magazines, 11

Statistics, methods of presenting, 122

Stevenson, Frederick Boyd, on Sunday magazine sections, 10

Stovaine, beginning of article on, 53

Striking statement beginnings, 143

Striking statement titles, 175

Study of newspapers and magazines, 21

Style, 160

Subjects for feature articles, 25

Successful Farming, excerpts from, 127, 128

Summary beginnings, 132

Sunday magazine sections, 9

Syndicates, 6, 192

Syndicating articles, 191

System, article from, 79;
  excerpt from, 137

"Taking the School to the Factory," 107

"Teach Children Love of Art Through Story-Telling," 204

Technical publications as a source of subjects and material, 27, 35

"Ten Acres and a Living," 81

"They Call Me the 'Hen Editor,'" 63

"Things We Learned to Do Without," 72

Time of payment for articles, 190

Timeliness in feature articles, 39

Titles, 170;
  types of, 173;
  methods of framing, 180

"Tommy--Who Enjoys Straightening Out Things," 87

Tractor and Gas Engine Review, excerpt from, 153

Trade journals, 11, 23;
  articles in, 30;
  article from, 79;
  excerpts from, 137, 153

Training for feature writing, 16

Types of beginnings, 131

Types of special articles, 55

Types of titles, 170

Typographical style, 183

Units in articles, 117

"Wanted: A Home Assistant," 331

Weed, Inis H., article by, 281

Welfare of other persons as a source of interest, 43

Wheeler, Howard, on newspaper men as magazine writers, 18

"Where Girls Learn to Wield Spade and Hoe," 206

White, Frank Marshall, article by, 264

"Who'll Do John's Work?" 79

Woman's Home Companion, article from, 63

Women as feature writers, 13

"Wonderful America! Thinks Little Austrian," 116

Words, choice of, 161

Writers, opportunities for amateur, 7, 12

"Your Porter," 218

ENGLISH FOR COLLEGE COURSES

EXPOSITORY WRITING
By MERVIN J. CURL.
Gives freshmen and sophomores something to write about, and helps them
in their writing.

SENTENCES AND THINKING
By NORMAN FOERSTER, University of North Carolina, and J.M.
  STEDMAN, Jr., Emory University.
A practice book in sentence-making for college freshmen.

A HANDBOOK OF ORAL READING
By LEE EMERSON BASSETT, Leland Stanford Junior University.
Especial emphasis is placed on the relation of thought and speech,
technical vocal exercises being subordinated to a study of the
principles underlying the expression of ideas. Illustrative selections
of both poetry and prose are freely employed.

ARGUMENTATION AND DEBATING (_Revised Edition_)
By WILLIAM T. FOSTER, Reed College.
The point of view throughout is that of the student rather than that of
the teacher.

THE RHETORICAL PRINCIPLES OF NARRATION
By CARROLL LEWIS MAXCY, Williams College.
A clear and thorough analysis of the three elements of narrative
writing, viz.: setting, character, and plot.

REPRESENTATIVE NARRATIVES
Edited by CARROLL LEWIS MAXCY.
This compilation contains twenty-two complete selections of various
types of narrative composition.

THE STUDY AND PRACTICE OF WRITING ENGLISH
By GERHARD R. LOMER, Ph.D., and MARGARET ASHMUN.
A textbook for use in college Freshman courses.

HOW TO WRITE SPECIAL FEATURE ARTICLES
By WILLARD G. BLEYER, University of Wisconsin.
A textbook for classes in Journalism and in advanced English
Composition.

NEWSPAPER WRITING AND EDITING
By WILLARD G. BLEYER.
This fully meets the requirements of courses in Journalism as given in
our colleges and universities, and at the same time appeals to practical

newspaper men.

TYPES OF NEWS WRITING
By WILLARD G. BLEYER.
Over two hundred typical stories taken from representative American
newspapers are here presented in a form convenient for college classes
in Journalism.

HOUGHTON MIFFLIN COMPANY
1421

FOR COLLEGE LITERATURE COURSES

HISTORY AND CRITICISM

BOTTA--Handbook of Universal Literature.

GRUMBINE -- Stories from Browning.

HINCHMAN AND GUMMERE -- Lives of Great English Writers from Chaucer to
Browning.

MATTHEWS -- A Study of Versification.

MAYNADIER -- The Arthur of the English Poets.

PERRY -- A Study of Prose Fiction.

PERRY -- A Study of Poetry.

ROOT -- The Poetry of Chaucer.

SIMONDS --A Student's History of English Literature.

SIMONDS -- A Student's History of American Literature.

BAKER -- Dramatic Technique.

BROOKE -- The Tudor Drama.

MATTHEWS -- A Study of the Drama.

SCHELLING -- A History of the Elizabethan Drama.   2 vols.

ANTHOLOGIES

POETRY

HOLT -- Leading English Poets from Chaucer to Browning.

NEILSON AND WEBSTER -- The Chief British Poets of the Fourteenth and
Fifteenth Centuries.

PAGE -- The Chief American Poets.

WESTON -- The Chief Middle English Poets.

PROSE

ALDEN -- Readings in English Prose of the Eighteenth Century.

ALDEN -- Readings in English Prose of the Nineteenth Century.
Part I; Part II; Complete.

FOERSTER -- The Chief American Prose Writers.

THE DRAMA

DICKINSON -- Chief Contemporary Dramatists, First Series.

DICKINSON -- Chief Contemporary Dramatists, Second Series.

MATTHEWS -- Chief European Dramatists.

NEILSON -- The Chief Elizabethan Dramatists (except Shakespeare) to the
Close of the Theatres.

HOUGHTON MIFFLIN COMPANY

1825

25711255R00158

Printed in Great Britain
by Amazon